A Brief History of Economic Thought

A Brief History of Economic Thought

From the Mercantilists to the
Post-Keynesians

Edited by

Hassan Bougrine

Full Professor, Laurentian University, Canada

Louis-Philippe Rochon

Full Professor, Laurentian University, Canada, Editor-in-Chief, Review of Political Economy, *and Founding Editor Emeritus,* Review of Keynesian Economics

Edward Elgar PUBLISHING

Cheltenham, UK • Northampton, MA, USA

Published by
Edward Elgar Publishing Limited
The Lypiatts
15 Lansdown Road
Cheltenham
Glos GL50 2JA
UK

Edward Elgar Publishing, Inc.
William Pratt House
9 Dewey Court
Northampton
Massachusetts 01060
USA

Paperback edition 2023

A catalogue record for this book
is available from the British Library

Library of Congress Control Number: 2022937621

This book is available electronically in the **Elgar**online
Economics subject collection
http://dx.doi.org/10.4337/9781786433848

ISBN 978 1 78643 383 1 (Hardback)
ISBN 978 1 78643 384 8 (eBook)
ISBN 978 1 03532 202 2 (Paperback)

Typeset by Cheshire Typesetting Ltd, Cuddington, Cheshire
Printed and bound by CPI Group (UK) Ltd, Croydon, CR0 4YY

Contents

PART III   THE HISTORY OF ECONOMICS AFTER KEYNES

Figures

Contributors

THE EDITORS

Hassan Bougrine holds a PhD in Economics from the University of Ottawa and is Full Professor of Economics at Laurentian University (Canada). He has been a Visiting Professor to many universities in Latin America, Europe and Africa. During the 1990s, he acted as consultant to the Canadian International Development Agency and the International Development Research Centre. He is a member of the editorial boards of the *International Journal of Political Economy* and the *Review of Political Economy*. He has published widely on issues of money, finance, public policy and the economics of development. His book *The Creation of Wealth and Poverty: Means and Ways* (Routledge, 2017) has been translated into several languages. His most recent works include *Credit, Money and Crises in Post-Keynesian Economics* (Edward Elgar Publishing, 2020, with Louis-Philippe Rochon), *Economic Growth and Macroeconomic Stabilization Policies in Post-Keynesian Economics* (Edward Elgar Publishing, 2020, with Louis-Philippe Rochon), and *Aggregate Demand and Employment* (Edward Elgar Publishing, 2020, with Brian MacLean and Louis-Philippe Rochon).

Louis-Philippe Rochon has been Full Professor of Economics at Laurentian University (Canada) since 2004. Before that, he taught at Kalamazoo College, in Michigan. He obtained his doctorate from the New School for Social Research in 1998, earning him the 'Frieda Wunderlich Award for Outstanding Dissertation', for his dissertation on endogenous money and post-Keynesian economics. Since January 2019, he has been Editor-in-Chief of the *Review of Political Economy*. He is also the founder and past editor (now emeritus) of the *Review of Keynesian Economics*. He has been guest editor for the *Journal of Post Keynesian Economics*, the *International Journal of Pluralism and Economics Education*, the *European Journal of Economic and Social Systems*, the *International Journal of Political Economy*, and the *Journal of Banking, Finance and Sustainable Development*. He has published on monetary theory and policy, post-Keynesian economics, and fiscal policy. He is on the editorial board of

Ola Financiera, International Journal of Political Economy, the *European Journal of Economics and Economic Policies: Intervention, Problemas del Desarrollo, Cuestiones Económicas* (Central Bank of Ecuador), and *Credit and Money* (Central Bank of Poland). He is the Editor of the following book series: the *Elgar Series in Central Banking and Monetary Policy, Heterodox Undergraduate Introductions Series*, and *New Directions in Post-Keynesian Economics*. His forthcoming books include *The Future of Central Banking* (Edward Elgar Publishing, 2022), *Aggregate Demand and Employment: International Perspectives* (Edward Elgar Publishing, 2020), as well as two volumes honouring the work of Marc Lavoie and Mario Seccareccia. He has been a Visiting Professor or Visiting Scholar in Australia, Brazil, France, Italy, Mexico, Poland, South Africa, and the United States, and further has lectured in China, Colombia, Ecuador, Italy, Japan, Kyrgyzstan, and Peru. He is the author of some 150 articles in peer-reviewed journals and books, and has written or edited close to 30 books. He has received grants from the Social Sciences and Humanities Research Council in Canada (SSHRC), the Ford Foundation, and the Mott Foundation, among other places.

THE CONTRIBUTORS

Scott Carter is Professor of Economics at the University of Tulsa in Oklahoma, USA. His research interests include capital theory, income distribution theory, and Marxian and Sraffian political economy. He is co-editor with Riccardo Bellofiore of *Towards a New Understanding of Sraffa: Insights from Archival Research* (Palgrave Macmillan, 2014) as well as "Symposium on New Direction in Sraffa Scholarship" published in *Research in the History of Economic Theory and Methodology* (Emerald Publishing, 2020). He specifically focuses on the intellectual and archival legacy of the Italian Cambridge economist Piero Sraffa including the online project *Digital Sraffa*, which endeavors to provide a cogent conceptual arrangement of the archival material rendering it conducive for scientific study. Most recently he has explored the political economy of racism specifically as regards the history and proliferation of white supremacy in the ideology of the American confederacy in an article written for a special issue to appear in *The Review of Black Political Economy*. His publications have appeared in the *Journal of Post Keynesian Economics, American Journal of Economics and Sociology, Journal of the History of Economic Thought, Review of Political Economy, Research in Political Economy*, and the online peer reviewed journal *American Review of Political Economy*. His recent work includes arranging and transcribing the archival material of Piero Sraffa including development of the Trinity 2.0 Arrangement which prototypes the archival architecture necessary to render conceptual cogency to the material; this latter can be found at https://sraffaarchive.org.

Guglielmo Forges Davanzati is Associate Professor of Economics at the University of Salento (Italy), where he teaches Political Economy and Labour Economics. He is the author of numerous papers on the monetary theory of production and on topics in the history of economic analysis. Among his publications, he published the book *Ethical Codes and Income Distribution: A Study of John Bates Clark and Thorstein Veblen* (Routledge, 2006).

Nicola De Liso has been Professor of Economics at the University of Salento, in Lecce, Italy since 2002 in the Faculty of Law, of which he was Dean from 2002 to 2008. From 1989 to 2000, he carried out his research activity at the National Research Council in Milan as a tenured Researcher, and joined in late 2000 the (then) University of Lecce, as Associate Professor. He collaborated with the University of Manchester, UK (where he was awarded his Master's and PhD) and the University of Bologna (Italy). He teaches Economics, Economics of the European Integration and Economics of Innovation, while having also taught in the past International Trade Theory. He has participated in international and national research networks since 1989.

His research activity focuses on the economics of innovation on which he has published many contributions in international journals; he is co-editor of three books and has contributed chapters to a few volumes. Other research topics include the knowledge economy, economic methodology and econophysics.

Amitava Dutt is Professor of Economics and Political Science, Department of Political Science, University of Notre Dame, IN, USA, and Distinguished Professor, FLACSO, Ecuador. After studying at Presidency College and the University of Calcutta, he did his graduate studies and received his PhD in economics from MIT. He is the author of several books, including *Growth, Distribution and Uneven Development* (Cambridge University Press, 1990), *Pathways to Economic Development* (Oxford University Press, 2014), and *Happiness: A Quick Immersion* (coauthored, Tibidabo Publishing, 2019), and is the author of many papers published in edited volumes and journals, including *American Economic Review, Cambridge Journal of Economics, History of Political Economy, International Review of Applied Economics, Journal of Development Economics, Journal of Post Keynesian Economics, Metroeconomica, Oxford Economic Papers, Review* *of Keynesian Economics*, *Review of Political Economy*, *Review of Radical Political Economy* and *World Development*. He is co-editor of *Review of Social Economy* and *Metroeconomica*. He is now working on power, uncertainty and institutions, especially on their relation with inequality, within and between countries, and on consumption, happiness and wellbeing.

John E. King is Emeritus Professor at La Trobe University and Honorary Professor at Federation University Australia. His principal research interests are in the history of heterodox economic thought, especially Marxian political economy and Post Keynesian economics. Recent publications include *The Distribution of Wealth* (Edward Elgar Publishing, 2016; with Michael Schneider and Mike Pottenger), *A History of American Economic Thought* (Routledge, 2018; with Samuel Barbour and James Cicarelli) and *The Alternative Austrian Economics* (Edward Elgar Publishing, 2019), dealing with socialist economic thought in Austria between 1900 and the present day.

William McColloch is Associate Professor of Economics at Keene State College in New Hampshire, US, where he teaches courses in the history of economic thought, macroeconomics, and monetary economics. He received his PhD and MSc degrees in economics from the University of Utah, and holds a BA in economics from Bard College. His work has appeared in the *Journal of Economic Issues*, the *Review of Radical Political Economics*, and the *Review of Keynesian Economics*. His current research concerns the rise to dominance of marginalist analysis, and its relationship to early American Institutionalism.

Suranjana Nabar-Bhaduri is an Assistant Professor of Economics at Frostburg State University, MD, USA. Her areas of specialization include macroeconomics, development economics, international economics and the history of economic thought. Her research areas have included the effects of economic liberalization on productivity and employment in the Indian economy, factors driving the reduction of the balance of payments constraint in developing countries, the financial fragility of persistent external imbalances, evaluating alternative growth trajectories and their implications for development and comparative analyses of the growth trajectories of China and India in the context of the global economy. Her more recent research has focused on the problem of informal employment in the Indian economy and possible policies to address it and on the economic implications of the COVID-19 economic crisis for economic policy and the role of the Fed in the US economy. Her research has been published in the *International Journal of Political Economy*,

Review of Keynesian Economics, and *Development and Change*. Her most recent article, co-authored with Matías Vernengo titled 'The Economic Consequences of COVID-19: The Great Shutdown and the Rethinking of Economic Policy', was published in the *International Journal of Political Economy*, Winter 2020.

Steven Pressman is Affiliate Professor of Economics at Colorado State University, in Fort Collins, Colorado and Emeritus Professor of Economics and Finance at Monmouth University in West Long Branch, New Jersey. In addition, he serves as Associate Editor of the *Review of Political Economy*. His main research areas are poverty and income distribution, post-Keynesian macroeconomics, and the history of economic thought. Over his career, Pressman has published more than 190 articles in refereed journals and as book chapters, and has authored or edited 18 books, including *Understanding Piketty's Capital in the Twenty-First Century* (Routledge, 2015), *A New Guide to Post Keynesian Economics* (Routledge, 2001), *Alternative Theories of the State* (Palgrave Macmillan, 2006), and *Fifty Major Economists* (Routledge, 2013), which has been translated into five languages. He is a frequent contributor to newspapers, such as the *Chicago Tribune*, *Denver Post*, *Los Angeles Times* and *San Francisco Chronicle*, and to popular periodicals such as *Challenge Magazine*, *The Washington Spectator* and *Dollars and Sense*.

Sergio Rossi is Full Professor of Economics at the University of Fribourg, Switzerland, where he has held the Chair of Macroeconomics and Monetary Economics since 2005. He has a PhD in Economics from the University of Fribourg (1996) and a PhD degree in Economics from the University College London (2000). His research interests are in macro-economic analysis, particularly as regards national as well as international monetary and financial issues. He has authored or edited approximately 25 books including an encyclopaedia of central banking and an encyclopaedia of post-Keynesian economics, has widely published in academic journals, and is frequently invited to TV talk-shows discussing contemporary macroeconomic issues both at national and international level. He is a member of the editorial boards of *Cogent Economics and Finance*, *International Journal of Monetary Economics and Finance*, and *Review of Political Economy*. Since 2015, he has been featuring in the list of the most prominent economists in Switzerland published by the *Neue Zürcher Zeitung* yearly.

Malcolm Sawyer is Emeritus Professor of Economics, University of Leeds, UK. He was the lead co-ordinator for the EU-funded, 8-million euro, 15-partner, five-year project on Financialisation Economy Society and Sustainable Development (www.fessud.eu). He was managing editor of *International Review of Applied Economics* for over 30 years, and has served on a range of editorial boards. He is the editor of the book series *New Directions in Modern Economics* (Edward Elgar Publishing) and co-edits (with Philip Arestis) the annual *International Papers in Political Economy* (Palgrave Macmillan). He is the author of 12 books including *The Economics of Michał Kalecki* (Macmillan, 1985); most recently *Can the Euro Be Saved?* (Polity Press, 2017), and is currently working on *The Power of Finance: Financialization and the Real Economy* to be published by Agenda. He has edited or co-edited over 30 books. He has published over 140 papers in refereed journals and contributed over 160 book chapters on a wide range of topics including on financialisation, the eurozone, fiscal policies and alternatives to austerity, money, public–private partnerships, and on Kalecki and Kaleckian economics.

Claus Thomasberger is a sociologist and economist, and until 2017 Professor of Economics and International Politics at the University of Applied Sciences, Berlin, Germany. He is a member of the Executive Committee of the Karl Polanyi Institute of Political Economy (Montreal, Canada), and of the Board of the International Karl Polanyi Society (IKPS) (Vienna, Austria). His main research areas include European integration, international political economy, economic history, history of economic thought, and political philosophy. He is an author and editor of numerous books, including: *Chronik der großen Transformation* (with Michele Cangiani and Kari Polanyi Levitt; 3 volumes, Metropolis, 2002–2005); *Der neoliberale Markt-Diskurs* (with Walter Ötsch; Metropolis, 2009); *Das neoliberale Credo* (Metropolis, 2012); *Auf der Suche nach dem Ökonomischen – Karl Marx zum 200, Geburtstag* (with Rainer Lucas and Reinhard Pfriem; Metropolis, 2018); *Karl Polanyi's Vision of a Socialist Transformation* (with Michael Brie; Black Rose Books, 2018); and *Karl Polanyi: Economy and Society, Selected Writings* (with Michele Cangiani; Polity Press, 2018).

Matías Vernengo is Full Professor at Bucknell University. He was formerly Senior Research Manager at the Central Bank of Argentina (BCRA), Associate Professor of Economics at the University of Utah, and Assistant Professor at Kalamazoo College and the Federal University of Rio de Janeiro (UFRJ). He has been an external consultant to several United Nations organizations like the Economic Commission for Latin America and the Caribbean (ECLAC), the International Labour Organization (ILO), the United Nations Conference on Trade and Development (UNCTAD), and the United Nations Development Programme (UNDP), and has six edited books, two books and more than one hundred articles published in scientific peer-reviewed journals or book chapters. He specializes in macroeconomic issues for developing countries, in particular Latin America, international political economy and the history of economic ideas. He is also the co-editor of the *Review of Keynesian Economics* (ROKE) and co-editor in chief of the *New Palgrave Dictionary of Economics*.

Acknowledgments

The editors would like to thank all the contributors to this book for their collaboration in preparing this volume to enhance the understanding of economic analysis in a pluralistic perspective. They also wish to express their gratitude to the staff at Edward Elgar Publishing for their enthusiastic and continued professional support during the development of the book.

Hassan Bougrine and Louis-Philippe Rochon

Introduction to *A Brief History of Economic Thought*

Economics, like other social sciences, is interested in the analysis and understanding of how societies organize their systems of production, distribution and consumption of resources. In his influential book, *The Great Transformation*, Karl Polanyi (1944) noted that any economic order is necessarily determined within its social context, which gives it its particular shape and structure in conformity with the prevailing set of cultural values – hence the diversity of economic and social forms of organization. This is a general observation that applies to modern as well as to primitive societies. To understand how diverse economic and social organizations are formed, how they function, how they evolve and how they are reproduced, we must recognize that economic relations are only one aspect of human life and whether they pertain to the production of goods and services, redistribution and exchange, or consumption, they reflect – and necessarily are the product of – the prevailing historical conditions, which include the level of (social, technological) development with its modes of thinking, beliefs, religion and culture in general.

This book strives to present a somewhat succinct account of these modes of thinking about the functioning of economic systems that prevailed and prevail today in what is commonly referred to as the 'West' – that is, Western Europe and North America since the 1500s. That makes this book *A Brief History of Economic Thought* because it is confined to a specific civilization and a specific period and does not attempt to deal with economic ideas, whether current or ancient, from other civilizations such as the Chinese, Indian, or Arabo-Islamic. There are indeed some valuable and very rich contributions from scholars from these civilizations but these have been unfairly consigned to history and neglected due to the Eurocentric view of the world, which has prevailed since colonial times.

Given these limitations, the guiding principle for our presentation is to evoke the major contributions which have had a lasting impact on economic thinking, starting with the evolution of economic ideas preceding the birth of classical economics. These major contributions have sometimes been referred to as 'revolutions' in economic thought, such as the classical revolution, the Marxist revolution or the Keynesian revolution. However, just as in exact sciences, economic ideas do not come fully developed all at once. Ideas are socially constructed, continuously redefined, and only mature after a long period of time. None of the great economists known to us today has conjured great explanations of the economic system independently of, and in isolation from, previous contributions. Like Isaac Newton, they all 'stood on the shoulders of giants'.

John Maynard Keynes, for instance, has benefited from the writings of Thorstein Veblen, Karl Marx, David Ricardo and certainly from the physiocrats and the mercantilists. Similarly, Karl Marx's ideas have been influenced by those who preceded him. Contemporaries of Keynes and those who came after him developed their ideas while debating Keynes – whether to prove him wrong or in order to improve upon his teachings. As a result, this book is divided into three parts: (1) economic ideas before Keynes, (2) Keynes and his contemporaries, and (3) economic thought after Keynes. While we have made every effort to include the different schools of thought, we do recognize that some influential scholars were left out. For example, we could have added chapters on Friedrich von Hayek, Joan Robinson and many others but that would have made the textbook too long and not possible to cover in a term of 12 weeks.

We invited a number of heterodox authors to write chapters on key periods or figures in economic thought.

Hassan Bougrine and Louis-Philippe Rochon
Sudbury and Toronto
11 November 2021

PART I

The history of economics before Keynes

1. The Mercantilists and Physiocrats

Hassan Bougrine

KEY FEATURES

- Mercantilists believed that wealth was monetary.
- Mercantilists lobbied for government intervention to regulate trade and legislate monopolies.
- Mercantilists favoured protectionist policies to ensure a positive trade balance.
- Mercantilists supported policies to encourage domestic production of industrial and agricultural commodities destined for export.
- Physiocrats argued that land was the only source of wealth and that agriculture was the activity that can increase it.
- Physiocrats developed the concept of 'net product'.
- Physiocrats presented society as composed of three social classes: productive, proprietary and sterile and developed the notion of a circular flow through which the 'net product' travels to ensure the continuity of the economic cycle.
- Consequently, the physiocrats encouraged spending and discouraged saving.

1. INTRODUCTION

During the 16th and 17th centuries, European economies were still largely based on agriculture. Land was the exclusive ownership of landlords and agricultural production was carried out by serfs, or peasants. Industrial production was not significant and was carried out by independent artisans and craftsmen who still owned their tools and other means of production (Hunt and Lautzenheiser, 2011). Commerce was probably the most lucrative activity, which flourished even more with the growth of overseas trade. Colonial powers during this period (Italy, Spain, Portugal, Holland, France and the United Kingdom) rivaled each other by engaging in bloody conquests, pillage and slavery of the inhabitants of Africa, Asia and the Americas. Colonial trade was so profitable not only because it

4

permitted the import of cheap raw materials and exotic goods, and the export of commodities made in Europe, but also because it brought back precious metals, namely gold and silver. Since these two metals have long been appreciated and sought by most people, they quickly became the only internationally acceptable means of cash settlements. Amassing large quantities of gold meant more purchasing power, and thus more wealth. This notion of wealth was particularly defended by a new social class that became rich because of commerce and finance: they were the rising wealthy merchants – the mercantilists.

2. MERCANTILISTS

In Western Europe, the period that spans the 16th and 17th centuries was a period of great upheaval. In the political sphere, this coincided with the decline of the authority of local landlords and the formation of nation-states. It was also a period of religious reformation and cultural enlightenment that contributed to important transformations in the economic system, which paved the way to the transition from feudalism to capitalism. The first phase of the emerging capitalist system was dominated by the rich merchants who derived their profits from trade, and who progressively took over the production process and became the new merchant-capitalist class.

Many of the mercantilist writers were merchants and financiers or government officials who were confronted with practical economic problems and tried to solve them to their own benefit (Thomas Gresham, 1519–1579; Thomas Mun, 1571–1641; Luis Ortiz, 1588–1649; Jean-Baptiste Colbert, 1619–1683). For instance, given that their income was the profit gained from the difference between the selling price and the purchasing price of commodities, they focused primarily on the exchange sphere and particularly international trade. Commerce was the source of their wealth, and for this reason they devoted most of their attention to finding ways and developing means by which to increase their wealth and secure their social position. This obviously included attempts to increase domestic production of commodities that would be destined for export. They even lobbied government officials for public interventions to protect their businesses and to enact laws granting them special advantages such as monopolies in trade and finance. This is how mercantilists began generalizing their practical solutions into economic 'theories'.

Concerning wealth, there was not much theorizing to do since gold and silver had been socially accepted as a form of wealth for centuries, if not millennia (see Bougrine, 2007). What the mercantilists did was to reinforce the association between wealth and these precious metals, both for individuals and for countries. Wealth and money had become synonymous and the accumulation of gold and silver became an objective in itself. Moreover, since profit is the difference between two prices, it can only be monetary. Prices were obviously expressed in terms of monetary units, which took the form of metal coins but primarily gold and silver coins. The scarcity of these precious metals in Europe only consecrated the obsession with gold and silver and intensified the search for these metals. Consequently, the European expeditions during the 'age of exploration' had the clear goal of expanding trade and bringing in, among other things, large quantities of these precious metals.[1] On that account, colonization was a great success. However, for the aboriginals of Africa, Asia and America it was a great tragedy.

Most of the gold and silver that was brought back by the conquistadors ended up in the coffers of the royalties and served to finance stronger and better-equipped navies. There remained, therefore, a pressing need for more coins to satisfy the desire of the merchants and financiers to accumulate 'wealth'. Hence, the mercantilists turned to foreign trade as a potential source of wealth since it can bring in gold and silver. They argued that gold quantities in the country could be increased if the value of exports is greater than the value of imports – that is, if the country has a surplus in its balance of trade. Similarly, a deficit in the balance of trade would lead to an outflow of precious metals and, therefore, to a 'drain of treasure'. Consequently, British mercantilists pleaded for two complementary measures: (a) a monopoly over the maritime transport network; and (b) free trade to increase the volume of trade transiting through their ports. On the other hand, the French mercantilists, particularly under the leadership of Jean-Baptiste Colbert, sought to increase exports by encouraging domestic industry through the implementation of a wide-ranging interventionist policy.

During this 'mercantile system' as Adam Smith called it, the 'wealth of nations' was measured by money and there was an obvious desire to maximize the stock of gold and silver within a country. Mercantilists, then, proposed two types of policies: (1) a strict prohibition of any outflow of silver and gold bullion; and (2) protectionist trade policies to ensure a favourable trade balance. Both policies required the presence of a strong *state* with wide-sweeping powers – a role fulfilled by the nation-state as represented by the king or the prince. This is why mercantilists supported the absolute powers of the monarchs in Spain, France, the United Kingdom and other European countries, including the power to mint coins in their own image. Such coins were meant for the needs of local trade, and their smuggling out of the country was punishable by death. However, the powerful merchants still found ways to circumvent the restrictions.

Indeed, such exceptions or exemptions were necessary in order for the merchants to continue realizing their large profits through the import of cheap foreign commodities. In a clever way, the mercantilists argued that a country is rich only if its merchants get rich. It was, then, in the king's interest to grant privileges and monopolies to the merchants and financiers since it had become widely accepted that the best way to achieve a surplus in the trade balance was by implementing protectionist trade policies based on the general rule requiring 'raw products not to leave the country and finished goods not to enter it': (a) exports of finished and manufactured products should be *encouraged* while imports of the same should be *discouraged* or even prohibited; and (b) imports of basic goods and raw materials should be *encouraged* while exports of the same should be *discouraged*. These policies remained in place in most countries, in one form or another, throughout the centuries until today – even though the World Trade Organization (WTO) had called for their dismantling back in 1994 (see Bougrine, 2004; Hettne, 1993).

The mercantilists' focus on commerce as a source of wealth led many to believe that mercantilists had no regard for production and considered that profit was generated solely from exchange. However, Perrotta (1993) argued that:

> The followers of the classical school interpreted mercantilist thought in a seriously distorted way. They reduced the mercantilists' favorable-balance-of-trade theory to a pursuit of wealth quite separate from and owing nothing to production ... Historians of mercantilism, in fact, have shown that: (1) the mercantilists were obsessed by the strengthening of domestic production; (2) they closely linked a balance-of-trade surplus with increased production, which would be stimulated by increased exports and restrictions on the importing of finished consumer goods; (3) consequently, they were anything but advocates of chrysohedonism.

Similarly, Robinson and Eatwell (1973: 5) remarked that 'Adam Smith mocked them, saying that they mistook gold for wealth, but they were not really so foolish'.[2] Indeed, mercantilists understood that a surplus of exports amounts to earning incomes that would be spent domestically, which would encourage local production in both manufacturing and agriculture and would, therefore, encourage exports and have positive effects on the entire economy. This mercantilist reasoning was later praised by John Maynard Keynes in the 1930s (see Keynes, 1936: Chapter 23).

3.   PHYSIOCRATS

The political influence of the mercantilists helped create a complex web of tariffs, subsidies, monopolies and other privileges that greatly benefited the financiers and the merchants' class. Indeed, the mercantilist era was dominated by an alliance between the absolutist monarchs, the trading companies and the financial trusts. However, the first half of the 18th century ushered in the beginning of industrial capitalism, during which small manufacturers and capitalist farmers represented the new rising class – the bourgeoisie. In this context, the physiocrats advocated the idea of social harmony and argued that it was based on the 'natural order' that governs society – an ideological phrase that tries to manage the contradictions and conflicts between the various social classes. In her book, *The Origins of Physiocracy*, historian Fox-Genovese (1976: 9, 30) wrote, 'Physiocracy means rule of nature. The term, coined in 1767 by Pierre-Samuel du Pont de Nemours to describe the doctrine of François Quesnay ... captures the complex ideological character of the first French and indeed the first modern school of economics' and that 'Historians of physiocracy have agreed almost unanimously on the bourgeois or capitalist character of the doctrine'.

It is quite common in the literature on the history of economic thought to present the physiocrats as anti-mercantilists, but this is not always true. For instance, although the physiocrats maintained that everyone, including the monarch, must submit to the *natural economic order* and accept the role assigned to them, they never rejected the absolute power of the monarchy. Similarly, it is often argued that, in opposition to the mercantilists who emphasized the importance of exchange, the physiocrats focused only on production. Concerning money, it is also often stated that 'The physiocrats are rightly said to have looked behind money to goods and deemed them true wealth' (Johnson, 1966: 616). However, François Quesnay himself agreed that commercial transactions had to be measured in monetary units and that wealth is realized only when products (of agriculture) are sold in markets. As Fox-Genovese (1976: 272–273) argued:

> He [François Quesnay] opposed merchant and finance capital in practice, as well as the value of monetary stocks in theory; he did not oppose commercial transactions in general. On the contrary, he believed that commercial transactions create the economy or are identical with it. Without a market there can be no economy, only subsistence. But he wanted a complete circular flow: the money realized through the sale of commodities must immediately return to the production of commodities in order to maintain the level of economic performance. Exchange occupies a central position in physiocratic economics. If Quesnay repudiated the mercantilist notion that exchange contributes to the increase of wealth, he believed ... that there would be no wealth at all without it.

The *complete circular flow* of the economy was summarized by Quesnay (1758) in his famous *Tableau économique*. The Tableau contained a somewhat advanced micro- and macroeconomic analysis, which earned Quesnay the title of 'first economist' – although this is not correct since others, like the legendary Ibn Khaldun (1377), some 400 years earlier, had done similar, and perhaps even more sophisticated, work.[3] Quesnay used annual aggregates (in monetary terms) to study the production, distribution and reproduction of commodities within the (French) economy – thus establishing a circular flow – by focusing on the interrelationships between the three main activities: agriculture, manufacturing and trade. Quesnay's motivation, and that of the physiocrats in general, was gaining more knowledge about the *production of wealth* and finding means of increasing it. Their starting point was to declare agriculture (as well as fishing and mining) as the only productive activity – that is, an activity which is capable of producing a *net product* or a surplus over and above costs and allowances for replacement of 'working capital'. Consequently, trade and manufacturing are considered as sterile, in the sense that they cannot produce a net product.

By this categorization, the physiocratic theory marks a clear departure from the previous mercantilists' conceptions, which considered commerce as the source of wealth. The physiocrats literally grounded their analysis in the land when they insisted that land is the only source of all wealth. In his *Maxims*, Quesnay (1768: 331) asserted that 'land is the only source of wealth, and it is agriculture that multiplies it'. Their theory is further detailed in the *Tableau économique* within a social context. The *Tableau* distinguishes three social classes according to their contribution towards the creation of wealth, or net product: (1) the *productive class*, which includes those employed in agriculture, fishing and mining; (2) the *class of proprietors*, which includes the owners of the land who receive the rent from the productive class and those directly supported by the proprietors' income (the monarch, the military and other administrative personnel); and (3) the *sterile class*, which includes merchants, manufacturers, artisans, artists, and members of the liberal professions (see Spengler, 1945a; Gleicher, 1982). The productive class pays the surplus, in the form of rent, to the proprietors who, in turn, buy agricultural products from the farmers and spend the rest on manufactured products and other services provided by the sterile class. The income received by the productive class is used to 'finance' future production (to ensure reproduction) and the rest is spent on manufactured products and other services. The cycle repeats itself when the net product is generated anew.

While there is some justification for considering agriculture as an activity capable of producing a net product, discounting manufacturing as a purely

transformative activity that adds nothing to wealth is obviously problematic. The physiocratic theory is further weakened by the notion of 'sterility
of trade'. In fact, these assertions reveal some internal inconsistencies in
the physiocratic approach. For example, both agriculture and industry
need labour and capital (machines and tools) for cultivating the land and
transforming raw materials to get final products; and it seems arbitrary,
if not odd, to single out the output of agriculture as the only source of
wealth. In addition, while arguing that trade is sterile, physiocrats at the
same time recognize that wealth is only realized when agricultural products
are sold in markets. However, here they consider only *first-hand sales* – that
is, 'a market in which exchange takes place between the farmer who has
produced the good and the merchant who first buys it' (Vaggi, 1987: 40).
Subsequent sales, though not superfluous, add nothing of value and, therefore, nothing to wealth. This last point proves the contradictory nature of
the arguments within the physiocratic theory.

Physiocrats understand and agree that subsequent sales (i.e. generalized
trade) are indeed necessary in order to bring the products to consumers
located in different parts of the country. These sales are even considered
essential to the health and prosperity of the economy because they ensure
the continuity of the circulation of commodities until their final destination: individual consumers. Consumption in the physiocratic theory is
absolutely essential because without it, they argued, production would be
reduced to the creation of commodities without use or value. Spending
ensures the closure or the *completion of the circular flow* and allows
reproduction of wealth to continue.[4] 'The proprietor who receives the
revenue must spend it so that this wealth is distributed throughout the
nation' (Fox-Genovese, 1976: 131). This is why Quesnay (1768: 332–333),
for instance, insisted that the totality of revenues must go back into circulation and that no hoarding – or 'pecuniary fortunes', as he called it – should
take place because such pecuniary fortunes would disrupt the circular flow
and jeopardize the entire economy. Mirabeau (1763: 74) warned that 'it
is always the cessation of spending that ruins nations' and that 'frugality
breeds poverty...' (ibid: 310). Therefore, physiocrats opposed hoarding and
sought to encourage spending – thus anticipating John Maynard Keynes,
who made effective demand the cornerstone of his analysis (see Chapter 5
of this book).

In line with their concern to keep effective demand high, physiocrats also
examined the impact of 'fiscal policy' on the economy and thus developed
a theory of public finance – a contribution that is often ignored in the
history books dealing with economic thought. In this regard, concerning
taxation, Quesnay (1768: 332) recommended 'Let the tax not be destruc-
tive or disproportionate to the mass of the nation's income; let its increase

follow the increase in income; let it be established immediately on the net product ... and not on men's wages, nor on commodities, where it would multiply the costs of collection, harm commerce, and destroy part of the nation's annual wealth'. Regarding government spending, Quesnay (1768: 336–337) recommended that 'The government should be less concerned with saving than with the necessary operations to increase the wealth of the kingdom, because these large expenditures will prove to be less excessive when they increase the wealth' and 'That the administration of [public] finance, either in the collection of taxes or in the expenditure of government, shall not result in pecuniary fortunes [surpluses], which rob part of the revenue from circulation, distribution and reproduction'. These recommendations are widely defended today by Post-Keynesians (see Chapter 14 of this book) who insist on the importance of public spending, particularly through public deficits, in creating wealth in the private sector of the economy.

4. CONCLUSION

The mercantilists were very much interested in understanding the sources of wealth, and given the historical context and perhaps because of their social position, they argued that wealth originates in trade and can only be monetary. Since money at the time was mainly in the form of gold and silver coins, wealth became synonymous to accumulated stocks of gold. To achieve higher wealth meant the expansion of trade overseas and the implementation of protectionist trade policies to ensure a favourable trade balance. However, this did not mean that mercantilists neglected domestic production; on the contrary, they sought to encourage industrial and agricultural production of 'competitive' products to boost exports and bring in more gold.

The physiocrats argued that agriculture is the only activity capable of generating a net product that can support the whole economy. Accordingly, they divided society into three classes: the productive class, employed in agriculture, generates the surplus and pays an income to the proprietors, and through uninterrupted spending and circulation of money, this income reaches also the sterile class. They argued that the production of a surplus from agriculture was the basic requirement for the development of industry and agriculture itself. By condemning saving and encouraging spending, the physiocrats succeeded in developing an interesting, albeit incomplete, theory of consumption.

NOTES

1. Eduardo Galeano, author of *Open Veins of Latin America: Five Centuries of the Pillage of a Continent*, Monthly Review Press (1997), counted that Christopher Columbus wrote in his diary/journal the word 'gold' 139 times and the words 'god'/ 'our Lord' only 51 times. See https://www.arcoiris.com.co/2014/10/el-descubrimiento-de-america-p or-eduardo-galeano/.
2. Adam Smith (1976: 429) wrote, 'A rich country, in the same manner as a rich man, is supposed to be a country abounding in money; and to heap up gold and silver in any country is supposed to be the readiest way to enrich it. For some time after the discovery of America, the first inquiry of the Spaniards, when they arrived upon any unknown coast, used to be, if there was any gold or silver to be found in the neighbourhood? By the information which they received, they judged whether it was worth while to make a settlement there, or if the country was worth the conquering. Plano Carpino, a monk sent ambassador from the king of France to one of the sons of the famous Gengis Khan, says, that the Tartars used frequently to ask him, if there was plenty of sheep and oxen in the kingdom of France? Their inquiry had the same object with that of the Spaniards. They wanted to know if the country was rich enough to be worth the conquering. Among the Tartars, as among all other nations of shepherds, who are generally ignorant of the use of money, cattle are the instruments of commerce and the measures of value. Wealth, there-fore, according to them, consisted in cattle, as, according to the Spaniards, it consisted in gold and silver. Of the two, the Tartar notion, perhaps, was the nearest to the truth.'
3. For an excellent account of Ibn Khaldun's contribution to economics, see Spengler (1964). There are obviously other contributions from other civilizations (India, China, etc.), of which the Western economic thought remains ignorant, and it is beyond the scope of this chapter to deal with them.
4. Several historians agree that the concept of a *circular flow* was a major contribution to economic analysis, which was praised by Karl Marx and John Maynard Keynes (see Gleicher, 1982; Spengler, 1945a and 1945b).

REFERENCES

Bougrine, H., 2004, 'WTO, Free Trade Areas and Regional Integration' in Philip O'Hara (ed.), *Global Political Economy and the Wealth of Nations: Performance, Institutions, Problems and Policies*, London: Routledge, pp. 241–276.

Bougrine, H., 2007, 'Wealth' in the *International Encyclopedia of the Social Sciences*, 2nd edn, Macmillan Reference, Editor in Chief: William A. Darity.

Fox-Genovese, E., 1976, *The Origins of Physiocracy: Economic Revolution and Social Order in Eighteenth-Century France*, Ithaca, NY: Cornell University Press.

Gleicher, D., 1982, 'The Historical Bases of Physiocracy: An Analysis of the "Tableau Économique"' in *Science & Society*, Vol. 46, No. 3, pp. 328–360.

Hettne, B., 1993, 'The Concept of Neomercantilism' in L. Magnusson (ed.), *Mercantilist Economics*, New York: Springer Science, pp. 235–255.

Hunt, E.K. and M. Lautzenheiser, 2011, *History of Economic Thought: A Critical Perspective*, Armonk, New York: M.E. Sharpe.

Ibn Khaldun, 1377, *The Muqaddimah: An Introduction to History*, translated by Franz Rosenthal, London: Routledge and Kegan Paul, 1967.

Johnson, J., 1966, 'The Role of Spending in Physiocratic Theory' in *The Quarterly Journal of Economics*, Vol. 80, No. 4, pp. 616–632.

Keynes, J.M., 1936, *The General Theory of Employment, Interest and Money*, London: Macmillan.

Mirabeau, V.R.M., 1763, *Philosophie rurale, ou économie générale et politique de l'agriculture*, Amsterdam: Les libraires associés <https://archive.org/details/philosophierural00mira/page/n21/mode/2up>.

Perrotta, C., 1993, 'Early Spanish Mercantilism: The First Analysis of Underdevelopment' in L. Magnusson (ed.), *Mercantilist Economics*, New York: Springer Science, pp. 17–58.

Quesnay, F., 1758, 'Analyse du tableau économique', in *Œuvres économiques et philosophiques*, edited by Auguste Oncken, Frankfort: M.J. Baer, 1888 <https://archive.org/details/oeuvresconomiq00ques/page/n5/mode/2up>.

Quesnay, F., 1768, 'Maximes générales du gouvernement économique' in *Œuvres économiques et philosophiques*, edited by Auguste Oncken, Frankfort: M.J. Baer, 1888 <https://archive.org/details/oeuvresconomiq00ques/page/n5/mode/2up>.

Robinson, J. and J. Eatwell, 1973, *An Introduction to Modern Economics*, London: McGraw-Hill.

Smith, A., 1976 [1776], *An Inquiry into the Nature and Causes of the Wealth of Nations*, Oxford University Press.

Spengler, J.J., 1945a, 'The Physiocrats and Say's Law of Markets. I' in *Journal of Political Economy*, Vol. 53, No. 3, pp. 193–211.

Spengler, J.J., 1945b, 'The Physiocrats and Say's Law of Markets. II' in *Journal of Political Economy*, Vol. 53, No. 4, pp. 317–347.

Spengler, J.J., 1964, 'Economic Thought of Islam: Ibn Khaldun' in *Comparative Studies in Society and History*, Vol. 6, No. 3, pp. 268–306.

Vaggi, G., 1987, *The Economics of François Quesnay*, London: Macmillan Press.

2. The Classical School

Suranjana Nabar-Bhaduri and Matías Vernengo[1]

KEY FEATURES

- Classical economists were concerned with the social reproduction of the economic system, rather than exchange. Their main concern was with accumulation and the wealth of nations and not the efficient allocation of resources.
- Some version of the Labor Theory of Value (LTV) was the unifier of the Classical School. The LTV put an emphasis on the objective material needs for the reproduction of society, and emphasized that distribution was conflictive. Class conflict was central to the analytical structure of their theory. On other issues, like the theory of crisis, the theory of accumulation and monetary theory, there was less consensus.
- Say's Law suggesting that supply created its own demand was accepted by some, but not all classical authors. Even classical economists who accepted Say's Law recognized that unemployment was possible in the long-run equilibrium.
- The possibility of economic crises was central to some classical authors. In capitalist societies characterized by unequal income distribution and where capitalists produced to accumulate, crises of realization were possible.
- Classical economists saw distribution, specifically the normal rate of profit, as crucial in determining the rate of accumulation and growth of the economy. Forces that affected the normal rate of profit limited the possibility of growth, and some authors did believe in a tendency of the rate of profit to fall leading to stagnation. Most classical authors did not think that a stationary state was possible in their time.
- While Bullionists and the Currency School thought that inflation resulted from excessive money creation, most classical authors upheld a view according to which money was endogenously created

by the real needs of the economy. This was known as the Real Bills Doctrine. They also believed that banks and financial markets were central institutions for accumulation.

1. INTRODUCTION

Classical political economy authors – basically from William Petty in the 18th century to Karl Marx in the 19th century, including François Quesnay, Adam Smith and David Ricardo – tend to be misunderstood in modern economics. In particular, they are often seen as precursors of modern mainstream neoclassical economics. In reality, classical political economy was markedly different from the neoclassical school, which was developed after the so-called Marginalist Revolution in the 1870s, and which remains the dominant view in economics today.[2] The crucial difference between the two schools revolves around the theory of value and distribution.[3]

Classical authors believed that economics should deal with objective, quantifiable data, and that would be instrumental in the understanding of the material conditions for the reproduction of society. Although it was fairly clear that people demanded goods and services for the satisfaction of their needs, and that a certain degree of subjectivity is inexorable once preferences are taken into consideration, classical authors tended to assume that social tastes were given, at least for short periods of time. They also assumed that the historical and institutional factors that determined social preferences were not directly relevant for the determination of prices. Prices were determined by costs of production, and for the most part the level of output was also taken as given in their analysis. The theory was concerned with the determination of the rate of profit, which was seen as central for the process of capital accumulation and growth. Competition, the process by which a uniform rate of profit was achieved, was seen as a central mechanism of the rising mercantile societies.

In that context, classical authors assumed that real wages were determined by the social and physiological conditions for the reproduction of the labor force. Real wages were close to the subsistence level that prevailed during the period of transition toward modern industrial capitalist societies. By assuming that real wages were determined, not simply by supply and demand in the labor market, but by all kinds of social forces, including the history of the organization of labor and its bargaining power, classical authors were suggesting that income distribution was not simply determined by market forces. Labor was not remunerated in accordance with its contribution to the productive process in general, and capital was not paid for its role in production. Profits resulted from ownership, and were the result of the exploitation of the labor force.[4]

The three main topics that classical authors dealt with that have direct implication for modern macroeconomics are: (1) the possibilities of economic crises, (2) accumulation and growth, and (3) monetary theory. All of these build upon their understanding of value and distribution. On these three issues there was not overwhelming consensus, contrary to the more or less established views on the determination of value and distribution. In these areas, strong debates for and against the possibility of crises, about the role of supply and demand factors in the process of accumulation, and about the causes of inflation took place. Classical political economy authors believed that the policy issues associated with crises, and long-run accumulation, as well as the problems of monetary management, were closer to reality than the issues of the determination of long-term relative prices, and that historical and institutional analysis was necessary to understand crises, economic development and money. In contrast, neoclassical economists relegated this preoccupation with the historical and institutional foundations of policy analysis to a secondary plane.

The rest of this chapter is organized as follows. Section 2 discusses the classical labor theory of value and reproduction, which views labor as the source of value, including the surplus value needed for social reproduction and accumulation. It also discusses the conflicting nature of distribution. Section 3 examines the views of the classical authors on economic crises and shows that contrary to what is often argued, not all classical economists accepted the validity of Say's Law – the proposition that supply creates its own demand and there is no problem of overproduction in the long-run. Section 4 discusses the classical views on accumulation and economic growth. Section 5 focuses on the classical writings on money and inflation, showing that not all classical authors accepted that money supply was exogenously set by the central bank and that the value of money was determined by its relative scarcity. A brief conclusion follows.

2.   LABOR THEORY OF VALUE AND REPRODUCTION

Classical political economy thinkers viewed the technical conditions of production, the level of outputs and exogenous wages as being the main factors that determine prices. The technical conditions refer to the available technological knowledge, skills, and the types of tools, machinery and equipment used in the production process. Wages were exogenously determined by subsistence requirements in terms of the minimum levels of food, clothing, shelter and other necessities vital to sustaining human beings, historically and institutionally determined. In other words, the determinants of distribution, the real wages, were too complex to be viewed as determined merely by the forces of supply and demand.

Garegnani (1984) captured the core of the classical approach in a simple diagram which is shown in Figure 2.1.

Technology and real wages are provided by social and institutional factors. Given the level of output, the labor needed in production is then determined. The real wages make it possible to determine the necessary consumption, or the amount of output needed to reproduce the labor force. Subtracting the output associated with necessary consumption from total output gives the surplus output, which can be used for expanded reproduction or accumulation. Note that the emphasis here is on the material conditions for the reproduction of the economic system. The surplus over the resources advanced for production would determine the normal or natural rate of profit which was seen by some classical authors as essential for economic growth.

Note that in order to determine the surplus, it was necessary to know in advance the prices of the means of production needed to produce output, and the real wage needed to reproduce the labor force. It was also necessary that in the production of the means of production, capitalists earned a normal profit on the capital advanced. Thus, prices were required to obtain the surplus, and, hence, the profit rate, but the profit rate had to be determined beforehand, in order to obtain the equilibrium prices of the goods used in the production process. In other words, it was necessary to determine prices independently from distribution, separately from the rate of profit. The Labor Theory of Value (LTV), a theory of relative prices, provided a solution for that theoretical problem.

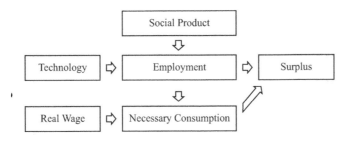

Source: Garegnani, P. (1984), "Value and Distribution in the Classical Economists and Marx", *Oxford Economic Papers*, 36: 291–325.

Figure 2.1   Social reproduction

Notwithstanding differences in their individual theory of prices, there was one unifying theme in the writings of classical economic thinkers: the objective cost of production, in particular. Given that tools and other means of production were themselves the product of labor, their contribution to production of other goods merely reflects the contribution of the labor that originally produced those tools. In the classical LTV, the exchange value of a commodity in a simple and rudimentary economy with no means of production was determined by the amount of labor embodied in the commodity. To quote Adam Smith:

> Labor was the first price, the original purchase-money that was paid for all things. It was not by gold or by silver, but by labor, that all the wealth of the world was originally purchased; and its value, to those who possess it and who want to exchange it for some new productions, is precisely equal to the quantity of labor which it can enable them to purchase or command. (WN: 48)[5]

In more sophisticated economies, with means of production, the prices would have to reflect not only the labor used to produce the commodities, but also the amounts of labor used to produce the means of production. This includes indirect labor (the labor embodied in the means of production used to produce the commodity) and direct labor (the labor which uses the means of production to produce the commodity).

Smith believed that in more advanced economies with significant accumulation of capital, in which goods and services were produced with a large amount of produced means of production, determining the labor incorporated in the commodity was problematic. For Smith, in advanced capitalist societies that had three distinct classes, namely workers, capitalists and landlords, the price of a commodity would reflect the sum of three components: wages, profits and rents. Smith's theory is therefore sometimes referred to as an adding up theory of prices. In other words, in more advanced societies, prices should include the profits of capitalists and the rents of landlords. In Smith's words:

> When the price of any commodity is neither more nor less than what is sufficient to pay the rent of the land, the wages of the labor, and the profits of the stock employed in raising, preparing, and bringing it to market, according to their natural rates, the commodity is then sold for what may be called its natural price. (WN: 72)

Note that market prices, determined by supply and demand, gravitated around the long-run natural prices. The process of competition guaranteed that this would be the case. By competition Smith and other classical authors meant free entry. In other words, if the profits in a sector were high, because of excess demand for the products of that sector, new producers would enter, expand supply, and the market price would fall, eliminating the higher profit rate in that particular sector. A uniform rate of profit in all sectors would be established. Competition guaranteed that market prices gravitated around the long-term natural prices. Smith explicitly followed the Newtonian mechanics analogy in his discussion of natural prices. Under these conditions Smith argued that the amount of labor that could be bought with a commodity or commanded with the production of a commodity at the given real wage was the measure of value. This was later referred to as the labor commanded theory of value.

However, Smith's adding up theory implied that profits and wages had an independent determination. If profits went up, real wages might not decrease and prices would go up. As a result, one could not determine profits independently of prices. That created a problem for the theory of value. Ricardo saw the limitations of the adding up theory. In his early writings he solved the problem by presuming that the economy produced only corn, with corn and labor, and the surplus was a physical amount of corn, so the rate of profit could be measured as the ratio of the surplus amount of corn to the amount of corn used as a means of production.[6] Corn was the term used for grains like wheat, and presumably a proxy for the subsistence needs of workers. Ricardo used the LTV, even though the LTV was valid in simple societies with no capital or that produced essentially one commodity (corn), as an approximation to the solution in his *Principles of Political Economy and Taxation*, first published in 1817, knowing that prices were not exactly proportional to the amounts of labor directly and indirectly used in production. That was, also, essentially the role of the LTV in Karl Marx's volume I of his masterpiece *Capital*, and the reason why some authors see Marx as a Ricardian author.

The price of corn, besides its theoretical relevance, was crucial for political reasons in the England of the time. The Napoleonic Wars meant that an embargo on the importation of corn was imposed, and the English had to use more land, of lower quality and fertility, to feed the population. As a result of the higher demand for land, the rents of landlords went up. Since workers' pay was given at subsistence levels, for the given natural prices, profits would have to go down. Since both rents and profits were part of the surplus, the LTV, contrary to the adding up theory, implied that distribution was conflictive. For Ricardo the main conflict was between the rising bourgeoisie and the landed aristocracy. His debates with Thomas Robert Malthus essentially revolved around the conflicts between rentiers and profit-making capitalists.[7]

Malthus objected to Ricardo's critique of Smith's theory of value, and argued that the LTV encountered problems when there was more than one good produced. The problems with the LTV implied that by the 1830s it was abandoned for the most part. Even John Stuart Mill, a protégé and student of Ricardo, partially abandoned the LTV. Later neoclassical authors developed a theory in which supply and demand determined all prices, including Smith's long-term natural prices, and the price of labor, and capital. That theory also had the advantage, for some neoclassical authors, that it did not emphasize class conflict in distribution.

However, even though the LTV was abandoned, an analytical solution to the LTV was provided by Piero Sraffa, a colleague of John Maynard Keynes at Cambridge, and the editor of Ricardo's *Works*. Sraffa's (1960: 94) solution uses a Ricardian idea, and finds a solution that is very similar to Smith's notion of labor commanded. In other words, the long-term equilibrium price, or what Smith and Ricardo called the natural price, and which Karl Marx referred to as production prices, was determined by the amount of labor that the commodity in question could command or purchase. Sraffa, instead of using the corn model, suggested that the same results as in the LTV could be obtained if one conceived a corn-like commodity. Sraffa called it the standard commodity, a composite commodity that would be produced in such a way that it would have the same proportion of labor to means of production as the means of production used in its production. If the proportion of labor to means of production in the production of the surplus and in the production of the means of production could be measured in terms of the standard commodity, then, as in Ricardo's corn model, the rate of profit could be measured as a physical ratio independently from prices.

The standard commodity implies that the rate of profit is determined by the material conditions of production and the need of reproducing the system, including the labor force, and is a residual. Not only is distribution determined by conflict, and the remuneration of capital is not dependent on the services rendered by capital or the means of production in the productive process, but also exploitation is possible and likely, since it is a common way of extracting surplus from subordinated classes in society.

3.   SAY'S LAW AND ECONOMIC CRISES

Classical political economy authors were concerned with capital accumulation. In other words, classical authors were interested in the causes of economic development or, in Smith's terminology, the wealth of nations. The preoccupation with growth made sense, since the economies of Western Europe, in particular England, were being transformed by what would later be referred to as the Industrial Revolution and the rise of capitalism, even though the term is not widely used until Marx and his followers.

Classical authors did discuss economic crises. Economic growth and the accumulation of capital were, for most classical authors, driven by the rate of profit, and many classical authors were concerned with the falling rate of profit in the long run. Ricardo, for example, was concerned that tariffs on the importation of corn would lead to the use of lands of lower quality, and reduce the rate of profit.[8] A tendency to a declining rate of profit would set the limits to the economic system. In somewhat different, and more problematic fashion, Marx thought that the increasing proportion of machinery, fixed capital, with respect to circulating capital, essentially labor, would reduce the basis for extracting surplus from workers, and lead to a fall in the rate of profit, and eventually a collapse of the capitalist mode of production.

Ricardo and Malthus famously debated the possibility of a general glut, with the former denying its possibility according to what became known as Say's Law. The Law was named after Jean Baptiste Say, a French economist that could be seen more as precursor of neoclassical economics than a member of the Classical School. Say's Law famously implies that supply creates its own demand. In other words, the economic system was supply determined. In the classical view of Say's Law, the notion was that anything that was not consumed was automatically used for accumulation or invested. In other words, savings, the part of the surplus that was not consumed, was identical to investment. There was no mechanism to adjust investment to savings. Also, there was no guarantee that the labor force was fully employed by that level of savings. Causality went from savings to investment. Ricardo incorporated the law, in part as a result of the influence of James Mill, because it provided a simple explanation for the given level of output in the scheme of social reproduction (Figure 2.1), and was instrumental in simplifying his explanation of the LTV.

Ricardo says that:

> M. Say has, however, most satisfactorily shewn, that there is no amount of capital which may not be employed in a country, because demand is only limited by production. No man produces, but with a view to consume or sell, and he never sells, but with an intention to purchase some other commodity, which may be immediately useful to him, or which may contribute to future production. By producing, then, he necessarily becomes either the consumer of his own goods, or the purchaser and consumer of the goods of some other person. (*Works*, Vol. I.: 290)

The Ricardian view was that in the long run a generalized overproduction crisis could not occur, since supply created its own demand. For Ricardo, this meant basically that in general, production resulted from the desire to consume, in other words, supply by definition was the result of an equal desire to demand. Hence, for him, while crises could occur in the short run, since some products would not find demand, in the long run, producers would learn from their mistakes and supply only goods which were socially useful, and that would provide them with purchasing power to fulfill their consumption desires. Ricardo suggested that nobody would continue to produce something for which there was no demand over the long run. Note that while in Ricardo's view, capitalists reinvested all their savings, and capital was fully utilized, the same was not true for labor, so that unemployment was possible in the long-run equilibrium. The level of output was fixed, in the Ricardian model, by the decisions to produce, which contained the seeds of demand. Supply creates its own demand was essentially implied in the notion that all savings were invested.[9]

There was no discussion of business cycles, at least not in the modern sense that the term acquired after the Great Depression of the 1930s, which is more or less what we still think when we talk about economic cycles. Note that in agrarian societies any periodical fluctuation of economic activity would be essentially connected to the alternation of good and bad crops, and, as a result, cycles, if one could talk about them, would be essentially exogenous shocks related to climatic events, pandemics or technological changes in agricultural techniques.

In spite of the dominance of Ricardian economics, some classical authors were critical of Say's Law. In particular, Malthus suggested that the economy could have crises associated to lack of demand. Malthus, it is worth noticing, was also for the Corn Laws, the tariffs on the importation of grain, which were imposed in 1815 after the defeat of Napoleon and the end of the continental embargo. This law favoured landlords, since it led to increased use of land and additional domestic production of wheat, and higher rents, which, in Malthus' view, allowed for the expansion of luxury consumption, creating demand. In the absence of protection, lower demand, presumably, could lead to a crisis. Ricardo objected, by arguing that both agreed that savings detracted from demand, but also that everything that was saved would be invested, which was also an increase in demand. Hence there could be no general lack of demand in the long run.

The two classical economists that made a more relevant and enduring critique of Say's Law were Simonde de Sismondi and Marx.[10] Sismondi noted that in more complex societies there was a divergence between wants of consumers and the exchange value of commodities. In other words, not necessarily all the commodities, even if desired, would be purchased due to a lack of demand associated with insufficient income. In societies in which production and consumption decisions were separated, and income was unevenly distributed, a lack of demand crisis was possible. Marx, following in the steps of Sismondi, noted that the monetary nature of capitalism implied the possibility of crises. In advanced capitalist societies accumulation, and not consumption, was the basis of material production. In other words, capitalists produced to accumulate profits in monetary terms, and they could face realization crises, unable to sell their products. While Say's Law would be valid in a simple reproduction system, where the consumption and production decisions were tied, and monetary transactions were not relevant, it would be invalid in a capitalist economy.

A capitalist economy was prone to crisis, exactly because Say's Law did not hold. And this view of recurrent crises was built into an incipient notion of economic cycles. In this context it is important to understand that, by the mid-19th century, the Industrial Revolution was well under way in England, and the more common business cycles of the modern economy were already visible. Marx, an author who was critical of the bourgeois ethos of classical economics, who saw linear progress in economic history, and praised capitalism, but who built on Ricardian economics, in particular the LTV, was a pioneer in discussing economic cycles. In his words:

> The life of modern industry becomes a series of periods of moderate activity, prosperity, over-production, crisis and stagnation. The uncertainty and instability to which machinery subjects the employment, and consequently the conditions of existence, of the operatives become normal, owing to these periodic changes of the industrial cycle. (Marx, 1867: 495)[11]

In other words, Marx was clearly aware that periodical fluctuations took place, and referred to those as industrial cycles. Marx was also among the first to discuss the role of banking, the stock exchange and finance in what he referred to as monetary crises, which "occurs only where the ever-lengthening chain of payments, and an artificial system of settling them, has been fully developed" (ibid.: 155). However, theories of the business cycles proper would only be developed later. Also, while Marx refuted the validity of Say's Law he did not develop a theory in which demand is central for the determination of the level of output, and that would have to wait for the work of Keynes and Michal Kalecki in the 20th century.

4. ACCUMULATION AND INCOME DISTRIBUTION

Classical economists recognized that the processes of accumulation and income distribution were interconnected. Thus, economic growth was studied in relation to issues of distribution, class relations and at a lower level of abstraction, taking into consideration historical and institutional factors. In particular, since distribution was discussed with regards to actual social classes, and those differed according to the ways of organizing society, there was a preoccupation with the historical stages of economic development. These views coalesced in what has been called the four-stage theory of economic development, originally developed by Anne Robert Jacques Turgot, a follower of Quesnay, and a Finance Minister in France. The idea of a the four-stages – hunting, pastoral, agricultural and commercial societies – was also developed, most likely independently, by Smith (Meek, 1971). Smith talked about modern, developed societies, like the England of his time, as commercial societies. This historical and institutional discussion of modes of organizing production provides a clear materialist conception of economic development, which would lead to Marx's concept of modes of production, an explicit economic conception of history, in general, and an understanding of capitalism as the current stage of the process of development.

In a capitalist society that has three distinct social classes – workers, landlords and capitalists – accumulation depends on the distribution of the social output produced between wages, rent and profits. As discussed, for classical authors wages were set at the subsistence level to meet the basic needs of workers with respect to food, clothing, shelter and other necessities essential for human sustenance. The subsistence level was historically and institutionally determined, meaning that it was not set simply by the physiological needs for survival, but also by what was considered the barely needed under certain specific circumstances. Once the share of the subsistence wages in social output had been determined, the surplus output was divided between the landlords and the capitalists in the form of rent and profits respectively. In the classical view, landlords essentially engaged in non-productive activities or luxurious consumption. Capitalists utilized their profits for investments in the means of production, i.e. capital goods, thereby enabling the accumulation of wealth through increased production, and setting in motion, the process of economic growth. The share of the capitalists in the surplus, closely related to the rate of profit, was therefore crucial in determining the rate of accumulation and growth in an economy.

François Quesnay, the leader of the Physiocrats, the first group to refer to themselves as economists, argued that the surplus could only be obtained in the agricultural sector, since nature provided for an output bigger than the inputs utilized in production. Adam Smith, who met Quesnay during a sojourn in France, extended Physiocratic ideas to deal with the manufacturing sector. In his writings, Adam Smith emphasized that capital accumulation enabled economic growth and, hence, further accumulation by allowing for the division of labor. The division of labor enabled specialization in production processes, thus increasing worker productivity by allowing workers to master specific tasks, become better at performing these tasks over time and by saving on time that would otherwise be lost in moving from one part of the production process to another. However, Smith recognized that the size of the market would impose limits on the division of labor. This implicitly indicates that he was aware of the constraint that a lack of demand could place on the process of growth, unlike other classical authors and later the neoclassical school, which regards to growth as being fundamentally constrained by supply-side factors with respect to resource endowments and technology.

Myint (1977) noted that the Smithian vent for surplus theory provided a demand-led theory of cumulative causation, in which success led to further success, and failure also was self-reinforcing.[12] Given that opportunities for the division of labor and, hence, accumulation and growth, were constrained by the size of the market, Smith viewed international trade as providing a vent, an outlet for surplus output to complement demand in the domestic market. By increasing the size of the market, international trade could provide additional opportunities for the division of labor, and hence for accumulation and economic growth in countries. In his words:

> By means of it, the narrowness of the home market does not hinder the division of labor... from being carried out to the highest perfection. By opening a more extensive market for whatever part of the produce of their labor may exceed the home consumption, it encourages them to improve its productive power, and to augment its annual produce to the utmost, and thereby to increase the real revenue and wealth of the society. (WN: 446–447)

In other words, by increasing demand – the extent of the market – trade increases productivity. It follows that the increase in productivity would make the country more competitive, and it would allow for further expansion of the market, in a process that would be cumulative or path-dependent. Note that this was not developed into a model of economic growth.

It is also not clear that most classical authors, or even Smith himself, saw economic growth as a demand driven process. In fact, Smith explicitly argues that accumulation depended on the increase of productive labor activities, as opposed to unproductive ones, and that this is enhanced by

frugality, and the reduction of unproductive consumption.[13] Activities
that expanded the surplus and the rate of profit, hence, were conducive
to greater improvements in the wealth of nations. Since classical economists viewed the rate of profit as central to accumulation and economic
growth, there was a focus in their writings on movements in the rate of
profit and their implications for accumulation. That corresponded to the
movement of the normal long-run profit rate, associated with natural
prices and the process of competition. In other words, in this case capital
accumulation does not respond directly to higher short term or actual rate
of profit (Garegnani, 1992). David Ricardo argued that with a growing
population, meeting the food requirements of society would require the
cultivation of less fertile grades of land, which would both increase rents
and the subsistence wage. This would reduce the long-term normal rate
of profit and this would lead to stagnation.[14] The economy would move
to a stationary state in which wages would be at the subsistence level and
economic growth would be greatly reduced. However, technical progress
would reduce and check the tendency towards falling profits and stagnation. In his words:

> The natural tendency of profits then is to fall; for, in the progress of society
> and wealth, the additional quantity of food required is obtained by the sacrifice
> of more and more labor. This tendency, this gravitation as it were of profits,
> is happily checked at repeated intervals by the improvements in machinery,
> connected with the production of necessaries, as well as by discoveries in the
> science of agriculture which enable us to relinquish a portion of labor before
> required, and therefore to lower the price of the prime necessary of the laborer.
> (*Works*, vol. I.: 120)

Most classical discussions of accumulation, given the centrality of the
surplus for the amplified reproduction of the economic system, suggested
that it was through the reinvestment of a part of the surplus, mainly
profits, back into the production process that economic growth took place.
Further there was no mechanism by which the saved profits were invested,
reinvigorating Say's Law in the context of the theory of accumulation. This
structure implied, in particular after Ricardo established the inverse relationship between wages and profits, that growth was profit-led. Further,
technical progress was for the most part seen as exogenous. Technical
progress was also seen as the main cause of accumulation and economic
growth, and consequently of employment generation.[15]

It is noteworthy that the insistence on the importance of productivity as
a central factor in the process of accumulation and in promoting the opu-
lence of the population, meaning higher levels of living standards, and the
wealth of nations, differentiated classical authors from the Mercantilists,

which emphasized the accumulation of bullion and the need for trade surpluses for economic growth. In this view, it was the ability to produce goods and services beyond the needs for the reproduction of the system that mattered for growth.

5. MONETARY THEORY AND INFLATION

Classical authors, contrary to what is often believed, did not accept the Quantity Theory of Money (QTM). In other words, classical authors did not think that the value of money was associated with its relative abundance or scarcity, since they did not think that supply and demand determined the long run or natural prices of any reproducible goods and services. The dominant view among all classical authors was based on some version of the LTV, and in that sense the relative price of money with respect to other goods and services, or the general price level, was determined by the amount of labor commanded by a unit of gold, since gold or some metallic standard was often assumed to be the dominant form of monetary arrangement. In other words, the price level depended on the technical conditions for the production of gold when compared to other commodities, and the amount of money or gold in circulation was seen as a result of the needs of trade, meaning the amounts demanded by economic agents for productive or real activities. This view was referred to as the Real Bills Doctrine (RBD).

The idea was based on the notion that banks discounted only real bills, that is, banks would only lend money backed by real assets. In this sense, the amount of money in the economy was endogenously determined and causation ran from prices to money, and not in reverse as in David Hume's QTM.[16] An endogenous variable is one that is explained by the economic model, while the exogenous variable is determined outside the model. In the QTM money is determined by the behavior of the monetary authority, the central bank, while in the RBD it is the functioning of the economy that creates a requirement for a certain amount of money.

Even though monetary systems were fundamentally metallic, classical authors, in general, held positive views about the role of banks and paper money. Adam Smith, an ardent critic of monopolies in general, was very keen about the Bank of England, a quasi-monopoly after all, arguing that it was "the greatest bank of circulation in Europe" and that it acted "not only as an ordinary bank, but as a great engine of the state" (WN: 318–320). In this view, at least, Smith was in accordance with several Mercantilist authors, which, otherwise, he criticized harshly.[17] Smith was apparently concerned that competition, meaning free entry, in the banking sector would lead to a multitude of undercapitalized "beggarly bankers" that would, in turn, lead to a heightened risk of "frequent bankruptcies" (ibid.: 323).

In a sense, classical authors, that as we suggested were concerned with the historical processes of capital accumulation, and understood that certain institutional frameworks were more conducive to a greater wealth for the nation, extended their interest to the role of financial institutions. The Bank of England was central in the process of expansion of public debt during the 18th century, and the maintenance of relatively low levels of interest on government borrowing. Smith, while praising the importance of public debt to promote and expand credit, particularly important during periods of war, was skeptical about its effects on long-term accumulation (Winch, 1998: 15–16). Smith and also Ricardo were concerned with the accumulation of debt, and its impact on accumulation. Although they recognized that public debt, as much as the expansion of credit by banks, could put to work capital that would otherwise remain idle, they noted that it could increase the proportion of labor utilized in unproductive activities (ibid.).[18]

Classical political economy views on inflation were also open to alternative views. An important event for the understanding of classical political economists' views on monetary issues was the suspension of gold payments by the Bank of England during the 1797–1821 period. Under these circumstances, the paper notes of the Bank of England became fiat money, and were not backed by gold. The LTV view according to which prices in gold depended upon the conditions in the gold producing sector were of little use, and a debate ensued. There were essentially two camps, known as the Bullionist and the Anti-Bullionist, and the affair became known as the Bullionist Controversy. For Bullionists, higher prices were the result of excessive money printing by the Bank of England, a view often associated with Ricardo.[19] For anti-Bullionists, the increase in prices was often seen as a result of higher costs, higher price of corn associated with bad crops, or barriers to trade as a result of the continental blockade. In this view, the Bank of England increased money supply in accordance with the higher demand for money caused by higher prices. In fact, that was the defense, based on the RBD that the directors of the Bank presented to Parliament. This anti-Bullionist view was also defended by Thomas Tooke, and later become central for heterodox explanations for inflation.

This controversy continued into the 19th century with the debate between the Banking and Currency Schools. Tooke was the leader of the Banking School, following essentially the anti-Bullionist views he held previously. Robert Torrens was the main opponent, and leader of the Currency School, which exposed the QTM as a rule for monetary management. Torrens was a Ricardian economist who, like Stuart Mill, had abandoned to some extent the LTV. The Currency versus Banking School debate is the direct forerunner of the Monetarist versus Keynesian debates of the 1950s to 1970s. The Currency School was behind the policy of separating the issuing role of the Bank of England from the banking side, to preclude overissuing of money, which was seen as the basis of inflation. For the Banking School authors, inflation was caused by real variables, rather than monetary causes, essentially connected to the costs of production.

According to Tooke:

> the prices of commodities do not depend upon the quantity of money indicated by the amount of bank notes, nor upon the amount of the whole of the circulating medium; but ... on the contrary, the amount of the circulating medium is the consequence of prices. (1844: 123)

Prices increased, still according to Tooke, as a result of bad harvests, the depreciation of the external value of the currency that increased the price of imported goods, and higher interest rates, which led to higher financial costs. Reversal of these trends in the post-Napoleonic War period, hence, explains the deflationary forces in action, and the end of the inflationary pressures after the war. Tooke argued that increasing the money supply would not lead to inflation.[20] Since the amount of money in circulation responded to the needs of trade, there could not be excessive supply of money. If the central bank tried to print money beyond what the system needed, then economic agents would use it to cancel debts, and its effect on the economy would be nil. This was named the Law of Reflux, by Tooke, and essentially was the same idea implicit in the RBD.

The victory of the Ricardian views, as expressed in the Bullionist Report, and later made explicit in 1844 with Sir Robert Peel's Bank Act, implied a complete victory of that camp in the policy debates. Together with the notion of Say's Law they form the basis for Keynes' argument according to which "Ricardo conquered England as completely as the Holy Inquisition conquered Spain" (Keynes, 1936: 32). Note, however, that the classical political economy version of Say's Law did not require full employment, and, hence could be abandoned, without jeopardizing other parts of the theory, and that the notion of endogenous money could also be incorporated with classical economics. Neither Say's Law, nor the QTM that Keynes wanted to displace, was central to classical political economy.

6.   CONCLUDING REMARKS

Classical economics differs from the currently dominant neoclassical paradigm in economics. Classical economists assumed that real wages were determined exogenously by social factors beyond market forces. In that sense, income distribution was seen as a conflictive arena. The relative bargaining power of workers was central for the determination of income distribution. The labour theory of value, which argued that labor was the source of all value, is central to the classical theory of prices.

In the classical view of Say's Law, supply creates its own demand and anything that is not consumed is automatically invested. Consequently, in the long run, savings equal investment and overproduction would not occur. However, even classical economists who accepted Say's Law recognized that unemployment was possible in the long-run as there was no guarantee that the labor force would be fully employed in the long-run equilibrium. Not all classical economists agreed that Say's Law would hold. The possibility of economic crises was central to the writings of many classical authors. In capitalist societies where production and consumption decisions were separated, and income was unevenly distributed, economic crises could arise. Classical economists regarded the normal rate of profit as being crucial in determining the pace of accumulation and growth. Most classical authors, including Smith and Ricardo, assumed that savings were invested. Marx was critical of this view and emphasized the role of economic crisis, and even understood the regularity of what we now refer to as business cycles. A theory of effective demand was not developed, however, until the 20th century.

Smith suggested that the division of labor and the growth in labor productivity were crucially limited by the size of the market, but also failed to develop a theory of how supply adapted to larger demand, to a bigger market. Technological change was in his theory endogenous, since the necessities of competition, when markets were large, would require further division of labor. Ricardo and Marx were, to some extent, more pessimistic about the possibilities of technical change subverting the tendency to a lower profit rate and reduced growth.

Finally, and contrary to what is often believed, classical authors did not accept the QTM or the view that the value of money was determined by its relative abundance or scarcity. The classical view was based on the labor theory of value. The relative price of money or the general price level was regarded as being determined by the amount of labour commanded by one unit of gold. Additionally, contrary to the QTM, in which money supply was determined independently by the central bank, the classical RBD argued that money supply was determined by the amount of money demanded for productive or real activities. While classical economists in the Bullionists and Currency schools viewed inflation as being the result of excessive money printing in line with the QTM, classical economists in the anti-Bullionists and Banking schools saw inflation as being the result of higher production costs.

NOTES

1. The authors thank Hassan Bougrine for extensive comments to a preliminary version.
2. The main founding fathers of marginalist or neoclassical economics were William Jevons, Karl Menger, Léon Walras and Alfred Marshall, and there were some important precursors like Augustin Cournot, Hermann Heinrich Gossen, and Johann Heinrich von Thünen. John Stuart Mill can be seen as a transition author somewhere in between both schools of thought.
3. Classical authors believed in different versions of what has been called the labor theory of value. Piero Sraffa in his *The Production of Commodities by Means of Commodities* developed the modern version of the classical views on value and distribution. On the labour theory of value, see Vianello (1987).
4. Piketty (2014) has recently brought back the attention of the profession to the issue of inequality of income distribution. Even though he admits that supply and demand are not the only forces behind the determination of wages and profits, his theory is based exactly on neoclassical principles.
5. In this regard, Smith rejects the notion upheld by Mercantilist authors, a somewhat loose school of thought that preceded classical political economy, that emphasized the role of metals in their definition of wealth. On Smith definition of wealth as something equivalent to the flow of production of goods and services, see Aspromourgos (2009: 30–35). Note also that in Smith, and the classical framework in general, profits were a residual of the productive process, a surplus, while for Mercantilist authors it was fundamentally the result of buying goods cheap and selling dear, in the process of exchange. On Mercantilism, see LaHaye (2008).
6. This is known as Ricardo's corn model. See Sraffa (1951).
7. Later, Ricardian Socialists and Marx would emphasize the conflict between labor and capital.
8. Classical political economy differs from neoclassical economics, as noted above, in that, for the former authors, real wages were given by social conditions including class conflict, and were often seen to be at subsistence level, while, for latter authors, real wages are seen as being determined by supply and demand. Also, classical authors did not necessarily believe that the economic system would produce optimal utilization of resources, including labor, while the opposite is true of neoclassical authors, as we will see in the next chapter. On the differences between classical and neoclassical theories of employment, see Stirati (2012).
9. This notion is also part of Adam Smith theory (Aspromourgos, 2009: 193). Note that Smith also assumed a natural tendency to save which dominated the desires for present consumption (ibid.: 167).
10. While it is true that Marx was critical of bourgeois classical economists, like Smith and Ricardo, he did not consider them vulgar economists, that is, mere ideologues defending capitalism, and he did use the same analytical framework of the surplus approach (Figure 2.1) and the LTV. Marx praises Ricardo for: "the scientific impartiality and love of truth characteristic of him" (1867: 478, n. 2). We should also note that several other authors had criticized Say's Law, beyond Malthus, Sismondi and Marx. The most famous of the underconsumptionist theories pioneered by Malthus was that of John Hobson, an anti-imperialist British economist, who argued that as the process

of accumulation went further and profits concentrated in fewer hands, the opportunities for profitable investment were reduced, and the lack of demand would make it impossible to increase production on an even larger scale. Later Marxist and Keynesian authors picked up on the critiques of Say's Law, which is still prominent in neoclassical economics.

11. Marx, in fact, suggests that the length of the cycle is approximately a decade, and that it involves fluctuations in the level of employment. He says: "The course characteristic of modern industry, viz., a decennial cycle (interrupted by smaller oscillations), of periods of average activity, production at high pressure, crisis and stagnation, depends on the constant formation, the greater or less absorption, and the re-formation of the industrial reserve army or surplus population" (1867: 694). There is no reason to assume that only external technological or climatic shocks would have this kind of periodicity, and in addition the industrial changes seemed to have transformed the economy, and generated more frequent business fluctuations.

12. However, there is no demand theory of economic growth in Smith, since he did not develop a theory of how supply adjusted to demand. Eltis (1984) and Kurz (2010) echo the notion that Smith's theory implies that growth is endogenous, or that there is a process of cumulative causation.

13. Smith utilizes the Physiocratic distinction between productive and unproductive labor. Productive labor essentially implies the labor employed in activities that are necessary to the production of means of production. For simplicity one can think of luxury consumption as being an example of an unproductive activity. For a precise discussion of the distinction between productive and unproductive labor in Smith's work, see Aspromourgos (2009: 164–172). This distinction has been reintroduced by Barba and DeVivo (2012) and, with some significant analytical differences, by Mazzucato (2018). The notion is that the increase in the financial sector in more recent times has been unproductive and detrimental for development.

14. This idea of a falling rate of profit was present in Adam Smith, and was criticized in that form by Ricardo, and was developed, in somewhat different and less consistent fashion than in Ricardo, by Marx. But it is important to note that it was not a Marxist feature, but a relatively entrenched view among classical economists. Contrary to what is often thought, it is not this pessimism, often associated with the Malthusian notion that the growth of population would outstrip food production, and the Ricardian doubts about the possibilities of growth and diminishing returns in agriculture, that explains the epithet of Dismal Science that accompanies classical economics. On this subject, see Dixon (2006). Also, it is worth noticing that a stationary state with no significant accumulation was seen as a distant possibility by Ricardo (Milgate and Stimson, 2009: 198; Kurz, 2010: 1195).

15. Smith's theory of the division of labor is the exception, providing an endogenous explanation for technical progress, since he explicitly assumed that the extent of the market, meaning the amounts demanded, were central for the utilization of new technologies. Also, Ricardo, in the third edition of his *Principles*, in the famous chapter 'On Machinery' changed his views an argued that Luddites, the workers displaced by machinery in the cotton mills of Lancashire, were correct in assuming that technological change could generate unemployment. For a discussion of Smith, Ricardo and Marx's views on technical change, see Kurz (2010).

16. It is important to note that some neoclassical authors, like Knut Wicksell, have used the idea of endogenous money too, and is now fairly accepted within the mainstream of the profession, as well by many heterodox schools of thought, even though the classical origins of the idea have been forgotten.

17. William Petty was the first author of the surplus approach that actually defended the need of an issuing bank in the 17th century.

18. Note that even though they had an overall negative view of excessive public debt, and its possible burden on accumulation, the theoretical framework is somewhat open to a more favorable stance, if public borrowing is utilized for furthering productive

activities. Malthus had built an argument that, although not always logically consistent, suggested that debt could promote higher accumulation and employment (Milgate and Stimson, 2009). Presumably that was also the reason that Alexander Hamilton suggested that public debt, under certain circumstances, would be a blessing. Hamilton is often characterized as a Mercantilist author for his defense of tariffs and some degree of protection, but a close look at his writings suggests the significant influence of Adam Smith. In fact, the first argument for manufacturing activities being good for the country is that they would further the division of labor (Hamilton, 1791: 87).

19. Ricardo accepted the notion that under inconvertibility, prices went up as a result of excessive circulation of paper money (Green, 1992). The role of the depreciation of the pound on the price of imported goods played a role in his views about inflation according to Marcuzzo and Rosselli (1986).

20. Modern views on the Bullionist debate suggest that inflation was caused by cost-push factors, meaning the embargo and bad crops, as argued by Tooke, rather than excessive demand caused by monetary expansion. See Officer (2008).

REFERENCES

Aspromourgos, T. (2009), *The Science of Wealth. Adam Smith and the Framing of Political Economy*, London and New York: Routledge.

Barba, A. and DeVivo, G. (2012), "An 'Unproductive Labour' View of Finance", *Cambridge Journal of Economics*, 36(6): 1479–1496.

Dixon, R. (2006), "Carlyle, Malthus and Sismondi: The Origins of Carlyle's Dismal View of Political Economy", *History of Economics Review*, 44(1): 32–38.

Eltis, W. (1984), *The Classical Theory of Economic Growth*, London: Macmillan.

Garegnani, P. (1984), "Value and Distribution in the Classical Economists and Marx", *Oxford Economic Papers*, 36: 291–325.

Garegnani, P. (1992), "Some Notes for an Analysis of Accumulation", in Halevi, J., Laibman, D. and Nell, E.J. (eds), *Beyond the Steady State: A Revival of Growth Theory*, London: Palgrave Macmillan.

Green, R. (1992), *Classical Theories of Money, Output and Inflation*, London: Macmillan.

Hamilton, A. (1791), "Manufactures", *The Works of Alexander Hamilton*, Vol. IV, Cabot Lodge, H., (ed.), New York: G.P. Putnam and Sons, 1904.

Keynes, J.M. (1936), *The General Theory of Employment, Interest and Money*, London: Macmillan.

Kurz, H. (2010), "Technical Progress, Capital Accumulation, and Income Distribution in Classical Economics: Adam Smith, David Ricardo and Karl Marx", *European Journal of the History of Economic Thought*, 17(5): 1183–1222.

LaHaye, L. (2008), "Mercantilism", in *The New Palgrave Dictionary of Economics*, 3rd edn, New York: Palgrave-Macmillan.

Marx, K. (1867), *Capital: A Critique of Political Economy*, Chicago: Charles H. Kerr, 1909.

Marcuzzo, M.C. and Rosselli, A. (1986), *Ricardo and the Gold Standard: The Foundations of the International Monetary Order*, New York: St Martin's Press, 1990.

Mazzucato, M. (2018), *The Value of Everything: Making and Taking in the Global Economy*, New York: Public Affairs.

Meek, R.L. (1971), "Smith, Turgot, and the 'Four Stages' Theory", *History of Political Economy* 3(1): 9–27.

Milgate, M. and Stimson, S. (2009), *After Adam Smith: A Century of Transformation in Politics and Political Economy*, Princeton: Princeton University Press.

Myint, H. (1977), "Adam Smith's Theory of International Trade in the Perspective of Economic Development", *Economica*, 44: 231–248.

Officer, L. (2008), "Bullionist Controversies (Empirical Evidence)", in *The New Palgrave Dictionary of Economics*, 3rd edn, New York: Palgrave-Macmillan.

Piketty, T. (2014), *Capital in the Twenty-First Century*, Cambridge: Belknap Press.

Ricardo, D. (1817), "The Principles of Political Economy and Taxation", in Sraffa, P. and Dobb, M. (eds), *The Works and Correspondence of David Ricardo*, Vol. I, Cambridge: Cambridge University Press.

Smith, A. (1776), "An Inquiry into the Nature and Causes of the Wealth of Nations", in Campbell, R.H. and Skinner, A.S. (eds), *The Glasgow Edition of the Works and Correspondence of Adam Smith*, Vol. I, Oxford: Oxford University Press.

Sraffa, P. (1951), "Introduction", in Sraffa P. and Dobb, M. (eds), *The Works and Correspondence of David Ricardo*, Cambridge: Cambridge University Press.

Sraffa, P. (1960), *Production of Commodities by Means of Commodities: Prelude to a Critique of Economic Theory*, Cambridge: Cambridge University Press.

Stirati, A. (2012), "Employment Theory in the History of Economic Thought", Università Degli Studi Roma Tre, Working Paper No 148.

Tooke, T. (1844), *An Inquiry into the Currency Principle; The Connection of the Currency with Prices; and the Expediency of the Separation of Issue from Banking*, London: Longman, Brown, Green and Longmans.

Vianello, F. (1987), "Labor Theory of Value", in *The New Palgrave Dictionary of Economics*, 3rd edn, New York: Palgrave-Macmillan.

Winch, D. (1998), "The Political Economy of Public Finance in the 'Long' Eighteenth Century", in Maloney, J. (ed.), *Debt and Deficits*, Cheltenham: Edward Elgar Publishing.

3. Karl Marx and the Marxist School

Scott Carter

KEY FEATURES

- Marx was a working-class revolutionary thinker whose economic theories were designed for a mass working class audience.
- Marx's economic thought developed as a sustained critique of Classical Political Economy and addressed many of the shortcomings in the labor theory of value of that approach.
- Marx's method of historical materialism considers social formations as evolving and developing from earlier forms often through revolutionary struggle.
- Marx's contribution to the Classical labor theory of value includes the notion of the value of labor power and theory of surplus value defined as the exploitation of the unpaid labor of workers.
- Marx's theory of surplus value expresses itself in an understanding of the division of the working-day into necessary and surplus labor time which serves as the foundation upon which his economic theories are built.
- Marx's economic theories are rich and include among other things theories of accumulation, circuits of revenue and capital, schemes of social reproduction, crisis theory and the falling rate of profit, the reserve army of labor, and the transformation of values into prices of production.

1. INTRODUCTION

Few figures in the history of economic thought have been the source of more controversy, ranging from complete scorn and vilification to sanctification and adulation, than Karl Heinrich Marx (1818–1883). Marx was a philosopher, profoundly deep social thinker, political economist, and working-class intellectual and revolutionary. Marx was a mighty thinker with a very fertile mind of immense prowess and intellectual stature upon whose work the Marxist School is founded. But Marx's impact is not limited to the School that bears his name, as many Schools of thought – friend and foe alike – owe a tremendous debt of gratitude to the Old Moor, as Marx was affectionately called by his friends, ostensibly due to his dark complexion and coarse hair.

Marx envisioned his approach as advancing Political Economy beyond what he called the "bourgeois horizon" that had confounded the Classical Political Economy of his predecessors, namely Adam Smith (1723–1790), David Ricardo (1772–1823), Thomas Robert Malthus (1766–1834), and John Stuart Mill (1806–1873) to name some of the most important figures in that approach (*MECW*, Vol. 35, p. 14; Fowkes, p. 96).[1] It is important also to understand that although Marx is most associated with theories of socialism and communism, in fact the overwhelming majority of his inquiries concerned only capitalism.

One of Marx's impacts on economic science concerns the theory of value and price. Whereas Marx initially accepted the basic tenets of labor theory of value propagated by Smith, Ricardo, Malthus, and the Classical School, he subsequently took it further into the revolutionary direction forged by the Ricardian socialist school that had begun to arise after Ricardo's death in 1823 and which located the source of profit as the exploitation of the labor of workers. The Classical School was correct, argued the Ricardian Socialists and later Marx, that value comes from the labor time necessary to produce a commodity. Where it failed was in the explanation of the *source* of profit. The quagmire became this: if the law of value holds that the prices of commodities comport to the bestowed labor time necessary to produce commodities, how is it that when considered as "capital" a quantity of value has a price that includes a profit over and above the initial cost? Where did this "extra" come from?

The solution to all this would fall to Marx's *theory of surplus value*. Marx agreed with the Classical School that the substance of value was labor time in production; he took it further by arguing that the substance of profit is in the *unpaid labor time* expended in the production process by workers who are paid less than their productivity. Here emerges the theory of extraction of unpaid labor that is the cornerstone of Marx's exploitation theory of profits and indeed his entire theoretical framework.

Marx and the modern Marxian school of thought he inspired approaches the study of capitalism through the lens of historic-specificity, by which is meant that capitalism as a *mode of production* has a lifespan of its own: it was born at a specific historical juncture, has matured since that time in ways that have often been remarkably transformative, and eventually it will die and give way to post-capitalist socio-economic formations. This is a unique feature of the Marxist School that, as discussed below, relies heavily on the Marxian method of *historical materialism*.

2. MARX'S METHOD OF HISTORICAL MATERIALISM

Consider the overall methodology Marx and Engels developed that informed and guided their thought. This is called *historical materialism*, which together with the theory of surplus value constitutes the most important theoretical discoveries and original contributions made by Marx (*MECW*, Vol. 24, pp. 467–468).[2]

Historical materialism conceives of systems of human socio-economic reproduction using two analytical criteria: the *forces of production* and the *relations of production*, the combination of which comprises the concept of the *mode of production*. *Forces of production* consist of the material production processes and include among other things the state of the art and scope of technology, and the level of knowledge of the society. Forces of production representing the material technical conditions of production correspond to the *relations of production*, the latter fundamentally relating to the social form of the labor process, the social relations among people, and the social relation between people and things. Relations of production essentially concern conditions of property ownership in society. Combining the two yields Marx's concept of the *mode of production*, which is the (dialectical and hence conflictual) unity of a society's forces and relations of production that forms the *economic base* of society.

A society's economic base is closely related to the *ideological superstructure*. This comprises the legal, social, political, and other societal mores and relations that emanate from the economic base. The ideological superstructure continually interacts with and reflects upon the economic base causing tension, antagonisms, and eventually social revolutions; Marx refers to this as "fetters" or obstacles articulated by the relations of production onto the forces (see Larrain 1983).

Figure 3.1 illustrates these complex relations. Depicted are the broad stages of modes of production of human society that Marx and Engels outlined in the *Communist Manifesto* of 1848: primitive society and the hunting and gathering mode, the slave mode, the feudal mode, the capitalist mode, and post-capitalist classless society.

Figure 3.1 shows the forward progression of the forces of production as the single-arrowed line on the upward trajectory (the "hypotenuse" of the triangles). The forces correspond with the relations of production, depicted as the double-lined-arrow of the bases of the various smaller triangles

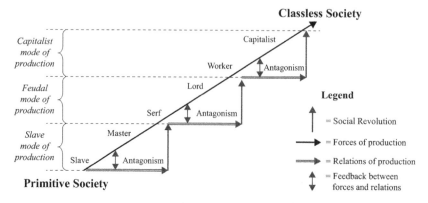

Source: Diagram adapted from P. Kunzmann, F.-P. Burkard and F. Wiedmann (2011)
dtv-Atlas Philosophie; translation from German by S. Bohnen <http://e-ducation.datapeak.
net/marx.htm>

Figure 3.1   Marx's materialist conception of human social history

representing the different modes of production. At the inception of the
productive mode the forces and relations meet at the origin of the angle,
and as time wears on they increasingly deviate causing social revolutions
represented by the height of the triangles where, via social antagonism,
successive modes eventually transform into higher stages of human social
development. The diagram also shows (i) the class character of the intermit-
tent modes: slavery has slave and master, feudalism has serf and lord, and
capitalism has worker and capitalist; and (ii) the classless character of both
the earliest primitive mode as well as the post-capitalist mode of socialism
leading to communism, where the latter is characterized by Marx in *Critique
of the Gotha Program* of 1875 as a society where "only then can the narrow
horizon of bourgeois right be crossed in its entirety and society inscribe on
its banners: From each according to his abilities, to each according to his
needs!" (*MECW*, Vol. 24, p. 87). All this can be summarized in the sentiment that the history of humanity has been the history of class struggle.

3.   MARX'S THEORY OF VALUE

Marx considered his work as uncovering the key to the unresolved contradictions in the Classical tradition of the labor theory of value. The key
for Marx was the *theory of surplus value*, the latter concept defined as the
unpaid labor-time performed by workers in the normal course of the capitalist production process. Marx saw the emergence of profit resultant from

the normal course of developed capitalistic relations, and exploitation of workers as occurring without swindle where the law of value is honored and all commodities exchange at their value. It is on this score that Marx moved beyond the Ricardian Socialists and others Engels would label as Utopian in their socialism, as opposed to the developments by Marx and Engels which were deemed scientific.

It was Marx who first developed the notion that the labor performed by workers is not that which is in fact bought and sold; rather it is the *capacity to labor*, which he termed *labor-power*, that appears as the commodity on the labor market. The difference between labor and labor-power was for Marx huge and, as previously indicated with reference to Engels, together with the method of historical materialism counts among the most important discoveries and contributions Marx considered he made to economic science.

Marx begins his theory of value with the commodity, defined as an article or good produced for sale. Here, two different aspects emerge. The one aspect is the useful character of the article, what Marx calls the *use-value* of the commodity. Here the usefulness of the products of labor is paramount: e.g. pencils are used to write with, paper is used to write on, etc. The use-value character of the commodity is vital, as articles that have no use are ostensibly worthless and have no value in exchange. The other aspect of commodities is their *value*, defined as the socially-necessary labor time for their production. In commodity-producing societies generally, the value of produced goods emerges as the "common third" and therefore the basis from which the relation of exchange manifests.

Marx is clear to indicate that the labor time represents the *socially-necessary labor time* in the production of a commodity given the state of the art and level of technology in society:

> The labour-time socially necessary is that required to produce an article under normal conditions of production, and with the average degree of skill and intensity prevalent at the time. (*MECW*, Vol. 35, p. 49; Fowkes, p. 129).

Inasmuch as the value-creating substance is human labor, Marx reduces the concrete laboring activities of different tasks in the labor process to its essential quality, that being the expenditure of human social laboring capacity generally. Marx refers to this value-creating capacity as labor in the abstract, or *abstract labor*, which stands juxtaposed to *concrete labor* referring to the actual laboring activities performed:

> [W]e put out of sight both the useful character of the various kinds of labour embodied in them, and the concrete forms of that labour; there is nothing left

but what is common to them all; all are reduced to one and the same sort of labour, human labour in the abstract. (*MECW*, Vol. 35, p. 48; Fowkes, p. 128).

Marx meticulously develops the exchange relation between different produced commodities in terms of *exchange-value*, which he sees as the *unity of a commodity's use-value and its value*. He develops the argument sequentially in terms of the *forms of value* which works from the elementary form of biangular 2×2 trade, to the multi-angular expanded form, then the general form, all the way up to the universal money form of value, the latter of which for Marx was commodity-money expressed in ounces of "gold".

"Money" (denoted "$") is introduced into Marx's framework with the assumption of an invariable value of commodity-money ("gold") which we can express in terms of the *mint price of gold*, the latter defined as the exchange ratio between currency notes and ounces of gold. With this convention, the physical quantity of gold produced under the assumption of invariable conditions in the gold-mines can be expressed in terms of currency units, and through conversion of ounces into these notes, prices are now expressed in currency units, and we have money prices. Marx assumes this relation holds for all commodities.[3]

4. MARX'S THEORY OF SURPLUS VALUE

Marx initially develops the labor theory of value in terms of simple commodity production where equivalents exchange and the *circuit of revenue* is assumed to be the rule. Here a quantity of value represented by the socially-necessary labor-time for production appears in its commodity form (C), is exchanged for its money form (M) of equal value, and is again exchanged for another commodity of equal value (C), thereby ending the circuit:

Circuit of revenue:

$$C - M - C$$

Changes occur once Marx introduces the capitalist mode of production, and here Marx's constructive economic-theoretic contributions begin to truly take shape. In the first instance, the circuit of revenue is no longer center stage in the exchange relation, giving way instead to the *circuit of money-capital*, where the purpose of exchange is no longer to secure equivalent values of different commodities, but rather to secure more money-value at the end of the circuit than initially advanced:

Circuit of money-capital:

M – C – M'; where M < M' and ΔM = M' – M

The value form of this "extra" money (ΔM) is referred to by Marx as *surplus value*:

> More money is withdrawn from circulation at the finish than was thrown into it at the start... The exact form of this process is therefore M – C – M', where M' = M + ΔM = the original sum advanced, plus an increment. This increment or excess over the original value I call "surplus value". (*MECW*, Vol. 35, p. 161; Fowkes, p. 251)

Marx next turns to explain where this extra comes from, since the law of value previously defined as the exchange of equivalents is seemingly violated. And here Marx discovers what he calls the "secret of profit making". The key to this is contained in the commodity elements C and C' in the circuit of money-capital as mediated via the production process:

Circuit of money-capital (expanded):

$$M\begin{cases} \text{Labor-power} \\ - C \quad ...P...C' - M' \\ \text{Means of Production} \end{cases}$$

In the expanded circuit of money-capital, the primal role of the production process becomes evident. The initial money advanced (M) purchases on the market two different commodity inputs, means of production and labor-power. These inputs are combined in the production process (P) which results in the new commodity output C' of greater value which is sold on the market for M'. The surplus value come from the fact that the commodity output is of a value greater than the inputs: C < C'. Marx argues that it is within the process of production that value "self-expands". *Capital* is thus defined as a magnitude of self-expanding value; here capital emerges not as a "thing" but rather as a social relation specific to the capitalist mode of production and capitalistic relations of exploitation of labor and private property (Shaikh 1987a).

Given that the process of production results in the creation of more value than that which entered as inputs, Marx concludes that there must therefore be a commodity-input that adds more value to the production process than its cost. That input is *labor-power* where the purchase-price of labor, or wage-rate, is of a magnitude less than the value of the productive consumption of that labor:

> In order to be able to extract value from the consumption of a commodity, [the capitalist] must be so lucky as to find, within the sphere of circulation, in the market, a commodity, whose use-value possesses the peculiar property of being a source of value, whose actual consumption, therefore, is itself an embodiment of labour, and, consequently, a creation of value. The possessor of money does find on the market such a special commodity in capacity for labour or labour-power. (*MECW*, Vol. 35, p. 177; Fowkes, p. 270)

We now arrive at the most important developments of Marx's critique of Classical political economy, namely that in the capitalist production process the quantity of value-added by wage-labor in terms of its productivity is of a greater magnitude than the quantity of value remunerated via the wage-form. This is the foundation for the exploitation theory of profits where the source of surplus value emerges as the *unpaid labor time* conceived as the difference between the value added by labor and the value at which this labor is paid.

Marx makes the strong assumption that the capitalist purchases labor power on the market at its value. This is a marked break with the Ricardian Socialists in that there is no "swindle" involved. For Marx, *surplus value* is defined as the unpaid labor-time performed by the worker in the course of the normal capitalist production process. The use-value expression of this is the surplus product which serves the material foundation from which capitalist consumption and investment expenditures emanate. Formally speaking, surplus value is equal to the value-added by living labor minus the value of labor-power, which can be alternatively expressed as the value of the net product minus the value of the consumption bundle of workers.

Here we arrive at the basic analytical framework of Marx's theory of value in capitalist commodity production. The value of an individual commodity (C) is equal to the value of the means of production which went to produce it (c), plus the value of labor power (v), plus the surplus value (s):

$$C = c + v + s \tag{1}$$

This three-part breakdown of the value of an individual commodity is the hallmark of Marx's approach to which he invented his own nomenclature. He called *c constant capital* in that the value of the means of production is wholly replaced in the value of the gross product; no new value results from the productive consumption of means of production as the value contributed to the gross product involves the wholesale transfer of a constant value. Marx called *v variable capital* in that productive consumption of the commodity labor-power results in a greater value-added than the VLP which the capitalist is assumed to have paid. And *s* is called *surplus value* which is the value created gratis in the normal course of the production process that does not have an equivalent cost. By virtue of the property relations in the capitalist production process, the owner of the produced commodity is the capitalist who advanced the capital and therefore gets the profit; accordingly, surplus value serves as the material and value basis for the profit relation, the latter of course being the lifeblood and heartbeat of the capitalist mode of production.

5. SOME OTHER OF MARX'S ECONOMIC CATEGORIES

The breakdown of the value of an individual commodity given in Equation (1) serves as the basic fundamental building block of a tremendous and rich architecture that is Marxian economic theory. The inclusion from the outset of surplus value (*s*) in the most basic understanding of the value relation adds clarity to the notion of *capital* Marx defined and advanced. As discussed above, for Marx *capital* was a social relation such that a certain magnitude of value was able to draw out of the market a quantity of value greater than itself; Marx is quite clear about this in *Capital*, Volume I:

> Capital, therefore, is not only, as Adam Smith says, the command over labour. It is essentially the command over unpaid labour. All surplus value, whatever particular form (profit, interest, or rent), it may subsequently crystallise into, is in substance the materialisation of unpaid labour. The secret of the self-expansion of capital resolves itself into having the disposal of a definite quantity of other people's unpaid labour. (*MECW*, Vol. 35, p. 534; Fowkes, p. 672)

The transformation of money into capital involves the capitalistically organized labor process. Here the direct producers, defined as the people who actually perform the labor of society, are transformed into wage-laborers, now called *workers*.[4] Capitalist commodity production also involves the tandem process whereby money-owners accrue all of the social wealth and transform themselves into capitalists. And as innocuous as this may sound, in fact historically speaking the actual processes whereby direct producers were transformed into wage-laborers and money-owners transformed into capitalists was often coercive and violent, and the processes whereby this came about in England are described in detail by Marx in the chapters that appear in the seventh and final part of *Capital*, Volume I, dubbed "So-Called Primitive Accumulation".

Once the capitalist mode of production gets hold of the labor process, the *modus operandi* of the endeavor changes. No longer is the matter concerned primarily with the production of use-values but rather with the production of profit, mediated through the production of use-values. Here the labor process is transformed into what Marx calls the *valorization process* and capital as self-expanding value begins to take shape. Marx meticulously analyzes the capitalist working day, where the total value-added by living labor (l) is considered on a per-day basis. By definition the VLP is defined as the labor-value of the "fair" wage-bundle, and under capitalistic relations this value is less than that added by the worker in the course of the working day. This means that over the course of the working day, the worker will perform in a fraction of the day the labor necessary to replace the VLP. Marx calls this the *necessary labor-time* (NLT) as it represents the portion of the working day that is spent reproducing the value of what workers are being paid, i.e. *paid labor*. The remainder of the working day, that over and above the VLP, Marx calls the *surplus labor-time* (SLT) as it represents the portion of the working-day that is unremunerated and hence not paid, i.e. *unpaid labor* (Figure 3.2).

Here Marx is able to clearly identify an important original contribution of the analysis presented in *Capital*, Volume I, namely the ratio of unpaid to paid labor, which he calls the *rate of surplus-value* or *rate of exploitation* (e), defined as the ratio between the SLT and NLT portions of the working day $\left(e = \dfrac{SLT}{NLT} = \dfrac{unpaid\ labor}{paid\ labor} = \dfrac{s}{v} \right)$. Indeed, all of Volume I of *Capital* can be characterized as an effort to explicate and expound on the form exploitation assumes in capitalistically-organized social formations.

Marx proceeds by describing the (logico-historical) process whereby the society's production becomes increasingly subsumed under the law of capital as self-expanding value. Emerging capitalistic social relations of production first confront the technical forces of production (or level of technology) already in existence. Marx refers to this as the *formal subsumption of labor to capital*, where relatively crude production techniques

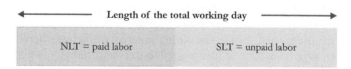

Figure 3.2   Breakdown of working day

already in existence are given capitalistic social expression as direct producers become wage-workers and money-owners become capitalists. Since self-expansion is the prime motive of capital, the way in which surplus-value is expanded given the relatively unsophisticated older production techniques involves the lengthening of the working day, what Marx calls the creation of *absolute surplus value* (ASV) (Figure 3.3).

Marx recognized that the capitalist mode of production in fact eventually transforms and revolutionizes the production techniques themselves resulting in a labor process of much greater efficiency. Marx calls this the *real subsumption of labor to capital* as greater efficiency in techniques of production result in the technical improvements in the production of all commodities included in the wage-bundle. Here the length of the working day remains constant, and *relative surplus-value* results from the cheapening of the wage bundle in the form of a reduction in the labor-time necessary to produce the wage-goods that comprise the VLP (Figure 3.4).

Relative surplus value creation begins to take hold once the technical conditions of the labor process are turned in the conduit from which

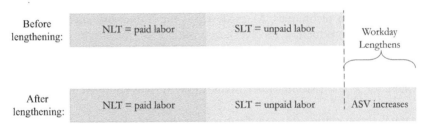

Figure 3.3   Absolute surplus value

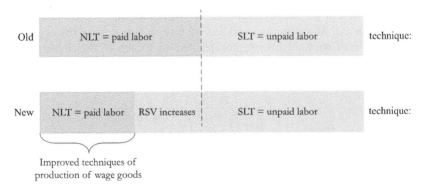

Figure 3.4   Relative surplus value

capital self-expands and the valorization process begins in full force. This
for Marx becomes the fundamental driver of the phenomenal technical
changes that are the hallmark of the capitalist mode of production.
So important is this that all of Part 4 of *Capital*, Volume I, is devoted to
the creation of relative surplus value; it is here that some of Marx's most
riveting chapters are written exploring the history and development of
the modern manufacturing system and the conditions underlying these
processes. Key here is productivity of labor increasing at a pace never
before seen in human history, coupled with the cheapening of commodities
that workers consume as part of their "fair wage" as expressed in the VLP.
Once launched on a world scale, the real subsumption of labor to capital
generates massive quantities of surplus value which serves as the material
foundation for the profit form to flourish, revolutionizing the production
process and ushering in technical changes that have been groundbreaking
in their depth and scope and ongoing in their breadth and intensity.

It is here that the analysis of the *accumulation of capital* expressed in
the growth of the capital stock begins to take root. This accumulation
has effects both on the revolutionized techniques of production as well
as on the labor force these new techniques employ. Regarding effects
on production techniques, Marx develops the framework such that new
methods of production involve heavy outlays of machinery and other
forms of constant capital that causes a rise in the ratio of constant to variable capital, which Marx calls the organic composition of capital (OCK),

where $OCK = \frac{c}{v}$ (Mohun 1983; Shaikh 1987b). This rising OCK aspect of

capital accumulation has ramifications for the rate of profit (r), the latter
defined as the ratio of profit to capital advanced conceived as what Marx
calls *cost-price*, which is constant plus variable capital (c + v).[5] Writing the
profit rate in this manner allows for it to be alternatively expressed as a
direct function of the rate of exploitation (Morishima 1973, p. 53 calls this
the *fundamental Marxian theorem*) and an inverse function of the organic
composition of capital (this is accomplished once each of the elements in
both the numerator and denominator of the ratio are divided by *v*):

$$r = \frac{s}{(c+v)} \rightarrow r = \frac{\dfrac{s}{v}}{\left(\dfrac{c}{v}+1\right)} \tag{2}$$

Equation (2) illustrates the offsetting effects on the profit rate with capital
accumulation. In the numerator is the rate of surplus value which has a
positive or direct effect on the profit rate: with increased exploitation of

labor there is room for the profit rate to rise. However in the denominator the accumulation of capital according to methods of relative surplus value causes the OCK to rise which produces a negative effect on profit causing the tendency for the entire rate to fall. And here we have Marx's theory of the falling rate of profit (FROP) which he characterized as the overarching tendency of long-run capital accumulation (Shaikh 1983c, pp. 159–160).[6]

For Marx the tendency for FROP led him to the conclusion consistent with method of historical materialism that capitalism is historical in character and thereby transient, and that the conditions for its own demise lay within the very belly of that beast and embedded in its life-blood. Hence capital's insatiable need for self-valorization inherent in the underlying processes of accumulation itself plants seeds of crises which become endogenous to the normal functioning of the capitalist system. Marx notes however that this is only a tendency, which means that there can and often are countervailing forces at work that stave-off the FROP, specifically those that raise the rate of exploitation in the numerator at a pace greater than the OCK in the denominator. This speaks to the rich debates within Marxian crisis theories over the possibility versus the necessity of crises related to the FROP (Shaikh 1978a, 1983c).

The effects of capital accumulation are also felt by the labor force. Here Marx introduces the tendency for the system to produce persistent and ever-growing redundant population of potential workers, what he calls the *reserve army of labor* (Shaikh 1983d, pp. 422–423). Indeed Marx was among the first theorists to posit the notion that unemployment and underemployment of labor was a normal part of the capital accumulation process, so much so that John Maynard Keynes, despite being rather allergic to Marx, actually mentions Old Moor when developing his (Keynes') theory of employment and effective demand in the *General Theory of Employment, Interest and Money*.[7] Marx's theory of the accumulation of capital entails offsetting effects on the labor force: on the one hand capital accumulation requires more labor as the methods of production expand in scale, but at the same time the technology adopted is often labor-displacing, which means that in terms of intensity, less labor is required to move more means of production. This results in a dynamic process of ebb and flow, with the reserve army of labor serving as a buffer to the often crisis-prone process of capital accumulation.

Crisis theory serves as one of the major platters upon which Marxian economic inquiry is served. For Marx and the Marxist School, economic crises are not aberrations in the otherwise smooth functioning of the capitalist mode of production (Shaikh 1983b, 2016). Rather, such crises are endemic to the anarchy of social production under the auspice of profit-maximization, private enterprise and capitalistic property relations.

Introduced above is the framework for crises borne of capital accumulation where increasing mechanization leads to a tendential fall in the rate of profit and a rise in displaced workers, causing unemployment. This is related to another source of crises, namely the problem of insufficient realization or sale of the output produced, which in modern guise is often couched in terms of a lack of effective demand, referred to as *underconsumption*, defined as a shortfall in the demand of consumption (as opposed to invest-ment) goods (Desai 1979, pp. 494–497; Bleaney 1976). Each of these types of crises is endemic to the capitalist mode of production, and Marx and the Marxist School incorporate this in their approach from the outset.

The theory of accumulation in Marx also considers *the concentration and centralization* of firms and industries, and the role this plays in socio-economic life within capitalistic social formations. Concentration defines the scope and intensity of power that capitalist firms have over wage-labor in the sense that the labor process becomes a "concentrated mass of means of production commanding an army of workers" (Shaikh 1983a, p. 68). Centralization reinforces the concentration of capital through the process of competition which underlies the establishment of mega-capitals such as multi-national global industries and corporations, some of which have more power than sovereign countries within which they often operate. It is significant that the theory of competition derived from Marx takes the opposite tact of so-called "modern" approaches to competition defined in terms of the number of firms, among other criteria. Marx's theory by contrast recognizes that huge mega-capitals are not the result of the absence of competition but rather its manifestation (on different approaches to the theory of competition including recent developments in Marxian theory see the edited book by Moudud, Bina and Mason, 2011).

The role of competition in Marx's price theory is usually expressed in terms of inter-industry competition and the formation of a uniform or general rate of profit on capital advanced, which in the context of many capitals competing with one another causes deviations with labor values.[8] In the literature this price-value deviation is referred to as the *transforma-tion of labor values into prices of production* and is often derided with the moniker of the *transformation problem*, although frankly there is no "problem" inasmuch as the deviations are not arbitrary or capricious and occur in an orderly and systematic fashion in accordance with the organic compositions of the various competing capitals.

An instructive way to conceive of the transformation is to differentiate extraction of surplus value from its distribution: surplus value is extracted as unpaid labor from the worker and then distributed as profit to the capitalist. However, the process of distribution of the profit accords to different mechanisms than that of its extraction. Specifically, distribution requires a uniform rate of profit (r*) explicit in the principle of inter-industrial competition between capitals. Such competition means that each dollar invested in any industry is thought to receive an equal and aliquot portion of the total surplus value produced according to the value of the capital advanced. In a letter to Engels from 30 April 1868, Marx calls this "capitalistic communism":

> Then it turns out that, assuming *the rate of surplus value*, i.e. the exploitation of labour, as *equal*, the production of value and therefore the production of surplus value and therefore the *rate of profit* are *different* in different branches of production. But from these varying rates of profit a mean or general rate of profit is formed by competition. This rate of profit, expressed absolutely, can be nothing but the *surplus value* produced (annually) by the *capitalist class* in relation to the total of *social* capital advanced…What the competition among the various masses of capital – invested in different spheres of production and differently composed – is striving for is *capitalist communism*, namely that the *mass of capital employed in each sphere of production* should get a fractional part of the total surplus value proportionate to the part of the total social capital that it forms. (*MECW*, Vol. 43, p. 23; emphasis in original)

Here, then, Marx states the matter succinctly. The different compositions of capital across the various industries ensure that the money-expression of labor values, referred to as *direct prices*, no longer correspond to the competitive prices, referred to as *prices of production*, which underlies the actual market prices of commodities. At the immediate level this difference has to do with the quantum of a capital's unpaid labor extracted versus the profits distributed. For industries that are relatively labor intensive the amount of unpaid labor extracted from its workers is greater than the profit distributed to its capitalists, and for industries that are relatively capital intensive the reverse happens and the unpaid labor extracted by its workers falls short of what is necessary to distribute to its capitalists. This process is visualized in Figure 3.5.

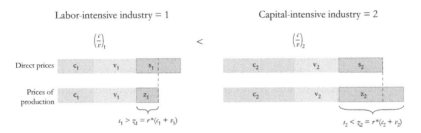

Figure 3.5   Transformation of direct prices into prices of production

Figure 3.5 reflects the matter as Marx characterized it in Volume III, namely under the assumption that the inputs remain of the same magnitude both before and after the transformation (Marx, however, conceives of the matter in his numeric example using five industries rather than two). This leads to the error of not transforming the inputs, an oversight on the part of Marx that became the source of tremendous debate and confusion in the years after the publication of Volume III posthumously by Engels in 1894. However, as Shaikh (1978b) has shown, Marx's own incomplete procedure is only the first of several iterations the end result of which has all inputs transformed and Marx's methodology vindicated.

The literature on the transformation of direct prices to prices of production is enormous and the debates robust.[9] The take-away usually comports with the preconceptions that the various authors bring to the table in the first place. For those sympathetic to Marx and the Marxist School, the transformation is simply another step in the concretization of abstract categories of analysis in moving from value to prices. For those antagonistic, the transformation is evidence of a contradiction between the labor theory of value presented in *Capital*, Volume I and the theory of production prices in *Capital*, Volume III.

6. CONCLUSION

Marxian economic inquiry contains a rich and robust analytical framework developed over a literature vast in content and varied in interpretation from antagonists and sympathizers alike. Written over a period of 150 years in many languages and various local dialects, Marxian economic inquiry comprises oceans of ink penned on forests of paper. This of course means that no single chapter can give proper service to the voluminous material, multiplicity of concepts at varied levels of abstraction, and variety of approaches that characterize Marx and the Marxist School. Readers should view the pages above as written as an effort to arm them with a relatively cogent understanding of the most important foundational notions that comprise the positive content and basis of Marx's theory. Indeed, the reason we study the history of economic thought is not to learn names and dates, etc., of old (mostly) men, but rather gain a keen grasp on the unresolved questions and issues that still plague economic science today. And if looked at with these fresh eyes, Marxian economic inquiry remains very much alive and Marx's theoretical project continues to be robust and relevant for the development of economic science into the 21st century and beyond.

NOTES

1. To facilitate study of the original material, which readers are strongly encouraged to do, quotes by Marx from *Capital* Volume I are cited from two alternative sources: (i) *Marx-Engels Collected Works* (*MECW*) Vol. 35 where Volume I falls; and (ii) citation from the Ben Fowkes' translation originally published in 1976 by Vintage Press and later picked up by Penguin Classics.

2. In his article "Karl Marx's Funeral" written the day after Marx's burial on 17 March 1883 and published just a few days later on 22 March in the newspaper of the Socialist Workers' Party of Germany, *Der Sozialdemokrat*, Engels writes: "Just as Darwin discovered the law of development or organic nature, so Marx discovered the law of development of human history: the simple fact [that] the degree of economic development [is] attained by a given people or during a given epoch, [and] form[s] the foundation upon which the state institutions, the legal conceptions, art, and even the ideas on religion, of the people concerned have been evolved ... . But that is not all. Marx also discovered the special law of motion governing the present-day capitalist mode of production, and the bourgeois society that this mode of production has created. The discovery of surplus value suddenly threw light on the problem, in trying to solve which all previous investigations, of both bourgeois economists and socialist critics, had been groping in the dark" (*MECW*, Vol. 24, pp. 467–468).

3. Of course, the theory of money has developed tremendously since the time Marx wrote his tome, and the question of the role of commodity-money in the analysis is the subject of long and very interesting debate. But as our interest is to develop Marx's own approach we shall continue with the commodity-money assumption. On modern notions of money within the context of Marx's theory, see, among other works, those of de Brunhoff (1976), Bellofiore (1989, 2004, 2005), other entries in the edited work by Moseley (2005), Foley (1983, 1986) and Shaikh (2016, Chapters 5 and 15).

4. The term *direct producer* is the general expression for those who engage in the laboring activities of society. In the slave mode of production, the direct producers are called *slaves*, in feudalism they are called *serfs*, and in capitalism *wage laborers* or *workers*.

5. In Sraffa's (1960) approach the profit rate is assessed on constant capital alone with variable capital not being considered in the formula for r, i.e. $r = \frac{s}{c}$. The reason for this has to do with the specification Sraffa makes for the wage where he chose the wage-share or proportionate wage paid out of productivity rather than the wage-bundle implied in the VLP concept as introduced above.

6. In fact the notion that the rate of profit falls as capitalist production develops is not a Marxian notion exclusively, as one can find, albeit for different reasons, a similar idea in the works of Adam Smith, David Ricardo, John Stuart Mill, and even John Maynard Keynes (Eltis 1987, pp. 276–280).

7. "The great puzzle of effective demand... vanished from the economic literature... It could only live on furtively, below the surface, in the underworlds of [among others] Karl Marx..." (Keynes 1936, p. 32).

8. Formation of the general rate of profit among industries is referred to as *inter-industry competition* or *competition between industries*, which is the methodological point of departure for the transformation problem. However, Marx's theory of competition is very rich and robust and extends to include *intra-competition of firms within an industry*. Regarding value theory, this strictly speaking comes from Marx's theory of rent, in terms of absolute rent (which Ricardo eschewed but Smith did not) as well as differential rent (on which all agreed as relevant) conceived both at the margin of cultivation (so-called *extensive rent*, labelled *differential rent I*) and also at the infra-margin of technical change (so-called *intensive rent* labelled *differential rent II*).

9. For a very useful introduction to the matter, readers can consult Hunt and Glick (1987), and also the two volume *A History of Marxian Economic Theory* by M.C. Howard and J.E. King (1989, 1992).

REFERENCES

Bellofiore, R. (1989). "A monetary labor theory of value", *Review of Radical Political Economics*, **21**(1–2), 1–26.

Bellofiore, R. (2004). "Marx and the macro-foundation of microeconomics" in R. Bellofiore and N. Taylor (eds), *The Constitution of Capital: Essays on Volume I of Marx's Capital*. Basingstoke: Palgrave Macmillan.

Bellofiore, R. (2005). "The monetary aspects of the capitalist process in the Marxian system: an investigation from the point of view of the theory of the monetary circuit" in Fred Moseley (ed.), *Marx' Theory of Money. Modern Appraisals*. Houndmills: Palgrave Macmillan.

Bleaney, M. (1976). *Underconsumption Theories*. New York: International Publishers.

de Brunhoff, S. (1976). *Marx on Money*. New York: Urizen.

Desai, M. (1979). *Marxian Economics*. Totowa, New Jersey: Littlefield, Adams & Co.

Eltis, W. (1987). "Falling rate of profit" in J. Eatwell, M. Milgate and P. Newman (eds), *New Palgrave Dictionary of Economics*. London: Macmillan Press, 276–280.

Foley, D.K. (1983). "Money", in T. Bottomore, L. Harris, V.G. Kiernan and R. Miliband (eds), *A Dictionary of Marxist Thought*. Cambridge, MA: Harvard University Press, 337–340.

Foley, D.K. (1986). *Understanding Capital: Marx's Economic Theory*. Cambridge, MA: Harvard University Press.

Howard, M.C. and King, J.E. (1989). *A History of Marxian Economics*, Volume I. Princeton, NJ: Princeton University Press.

Howard, M.C. and King, J.E. (1992). *A History of Marxian Economics*, Volume II. Princeton, NJ: Princeton University Press.

Hunt, E. and Glick, M (1987). "Transformation problem", in J. Eatwell, M. Milgate and P. Newman (eds), *New Palgrave Dictionary of Economics*. London: Macmillan Press, 688–690.

Keynes, J.M. (1936). *The General Theory of Employment, Interest and Money*. London: Macmillan.

Kunzmann, P., Burkard, F.-P. and Wiedmann F. (2011). *dtv-Atlas Philosophie*. Munich: Deutscher Taschenbuch Verlag GmbH & Co. KG.

Larrain, J. (1983). "Base and superstructure", in T. Bottomore, L. Harris, V.G. Kiernan and R. Miliband (eds), *A Dictionary of Marxist Thought*. Cambridge, MA: Harvard University Press, 42–45.

Marx, K. (1976 [1867]). *Capital: A Critique of Political Economy*, Volume I. Translated by Ben Fowkes. London: Penguin Classics.

Marx, K. and Engels, F. (1989). *Marx-Engels Collected Works (MECW)* Volume 24. London: Lawrence & Wishart.

Marx, K. and Engels, F. (1996). *Marx-Engels Collected Works (MECW)* Volume 35: *Capital: A Critique of Political Economy*, Volume I. London: Lawrence & Wishart.

Mohun, S. (1983). "Organic composition of capital", in T. Bottomore, L. Harris, V.G. Kiernan and R. Miliband (eds), *A Dictionary of Marxist Thought*. Cambridge, MA: Harvard University Press, 356–358.

Morishima, M. (1973). *Marx's Economics: A Dual Theory of Value and Growth*. Cambridge, UK: Cambridge University Press.

Moseley, F. (ed.) (2005). *Marx' Theory of Money. Modern Appraisals*. Houndmills: Palgrave Macmillan.

Moudud, J., Bina, C. and Mason, P. (2011). *Alternative Theories of Competition: Challenges to the Orthodoxy*. New York: Routledge.

Shaikh, A. (1978a). "An Introduction to History of Crisis Theories", *U.S. Capitalism in Crisis*. New York: Union for Radical Political Economics.

Shaikh, A. (1978b). "Marx's theory of value and the 'transformation problem'", in J. Schwartz (ed), *The Subtle Anatomy of Capitalism*. Santa Monica: Goodyear, 108–139.

Shaikh, A. (1983a). "Centralization and concentration of capital", in T. Bottomore, L. Harris, V.G. Kiernan and R. Miliband (eds), *A Dictionary of Marxist Thought*. Cambridge, MA: Harvard University Press, 68–69.

Shaikh, A. (1983b). "Economic crises", in T. Bottomore, L. Harris, V.G. Kiernan and R. Miliband (eds), *A Dictionary of Marxist Thought*. Cambridge, MA: Harvard University Press, 138–143.

Shaikh, A. (1983c). "Falling rate of profit", in T. Bottomore, L. Harris, V.G. Kiernan and R. Miliband (eds). *A Dictionary of Marxist Thought*. Cambridge, MA: Harvard University Press, 159–61.

Shaikh, A. (1983d). "Reserve army of labour", in T. Bottomore, L. Harris, V.G. Kiernan, & R. Miliband (eds), *A Dictionary of Marxist Thought*. Cambridge, MA: Harvard University Press, 422–423.

Shaikh, A. (1987a). "Capital as a Social Relation", in J. Eatwell, M. Milgate and P. Newman (eds), *New Palgrave Dictionary of Economics*. London: Macmillan Press, 333–336.

Shaikh, A. (1987b). "Organic composition of capital", in J. Eatwell, M. Milgate and P. Newman (eds), *New Palgrave Dictionary of Economics*. London: Macmillan Press, 755–757.

Shaikh, A. (2016). *Capitalism: Competition, Conflict, Crises*. Oxford: Oxford University Press.

Sraffa, P. (1960). *Production of Commodities by Means of Commodities: Prelude to a Critique of Economic Theory*. Cambridge, UK: Cambridge University Press.

4.   The Neoclassical School

Hassan Bougrine

KEY FEATURES

- The chapter argues that neoclassical economics came as a reaction to the critical writings that exposed the contradictions of capitalism.
- The utility theory of value was developed as an alternative to the labour theory of value.
- A detailed explanation of the notion of marginal utility and the principle of maximization.
- The neoclassical theory denies the existence of social classes and rejects the theory of income distribution. It argues that factors of production are paid according to their contribution to the value of what is produced.
- The general equilibrium model is an exposition of the general law of exchange in the context of competitive markets while taking the distribution of property rights as given.

1.   INTRODUCTION: THE ECONOMIC AND POLITICAL CONTEXT OF THE RISE OF NEOCLASSICAL ECONOMICS

From an economic perspective, it is safe to say that the most important events in the entire history of humanity have taken place during the last 300 years or so. The Industrial Revolution, which begun in the 18th century, ushered the beginning of some great transformations in human society. As the steam engines became widely used in the late 1780s, a new production system developed. The entrepreneur who owned these machines housed them in factories and hired independent workers and artisans who performed specific tasks on the site in return for a wage, with the implicit and explicit recognition that they had lost any claim over the product of their labour. That product had become the exclusive property of the factory owner, who would then sell it in the market for a price that guaranteed him a profit. This period marked the birth of the factory system – or industrial capitalism, whose development required further mechanization and rationalization of work, expansion of the factory and larger pools of labourers and their concentration in towns and cities. It was during this period that the ideas of 'efficiency' and 'productivity' became key concepts and played an important role in the shift to the system of 'mass production', which allowed the extraction of the maximum effort of the workers and hence the maximum benefit from their labour power.

Chapter 2 showed that income distribution among social classes was a major preoccupation of the classical economists. In their theory of income distribution, classical economists recognized this division of national income among social classes (workers, landowners and capitalists) and attempted to study its implications on accumulation and economic growth. Ricardo (1817), in particular, maintained that there was an inverse relationship between wages and profits, and argued that, since profit is the source of investment, the tendency of wages to increase would lead to a fall in the rate of profit and cause a slowdown in capital accumulation and progress; and thus lead to a stationary state of the economy. Ricardo also considered that there was a conflict between the interests of the capitalists and the landlords. This is why he argued for the abolition of the laws restricting the importation of corn and foodstuffs. He maintained that these laws served to protect the rent of the landlords, and that they would result in higher prices of corn, push the subsistence wage to rise and cause profits to fall. These arguments served as the basis of his support for the capitalist class and his defence of free trade and the principles of laissez-faire.

The socialists of the early nineteenth century, particularly in the 1820s to 1840s, opposed the type of income distribution under capitalism because they considered it to be biased towards property holders. William Thompson, Thomas Hodgskin, Henri de Saint-Simon, Pierre-Joseph Proudhon, Charles Fourier, and many others sought to abolish private property because it allowed idle and unproductive property holders to snatch a share of income to which they were not entitled. They denounced the concentration of wealth in the hands of a minority and fought for social justice and the general welfare of society. To this end, many of them had proposed a cooperative production system and government regulation instead of laissez-faire.

These 'utopian' socialists, as they were later called, opposed capitalism on moral grounds. Their critique was based on humanist concerns for the poor and the working class. In 1848, Karl Marx and Frederick Engels wrote the *Manifesto of the Communist Party* in which they presented a scientific analysis of the capitalist system and its functioning. They argued that antagonism between social classes is a salient feature of all societies. Indeed, the opening statement of the manifesto declared that 'The history of all hitherto existing society is the history of class struggles'. When identifying the social classes in modern capitalism, Marx and Engels paid particular attention to private property, the ownership of the means of production. The dominant class is the bourgeoisie or 'the class of modern capitalists, owners of the means of social production and employers of wage labour'. The proletariat, on the other hand, is 'the class of modern wage labourers who, having no means of production of their own, are reduced to selling their labour power in order to live'.[1]

As shown in Chapter 3, this class division led Marx to investigate further the mechanism of income and wealth distribution under capitalism. The struggle between capitalists and workers is over the length of the working day, the wage rate, and the general working conditions. In his major work *Das Kapital*, Marx came to the conclusion that labour is the source of value creation and that profit is the appropriation by the capitalist of a 'surplus value' through the manipulation of the wage rate either by extending the working day or by increasing the workers' productivity. For Marx, class struggle between the workers and the capitalists is ultimately about 'value' and 'resources', and it concretely takes place where value is created – that is, at the level of the factory or in the 'sphere of production', as he called it. This analysis had a strong influence on the labour movement, which had become more radicalized. The growing inequality and contradictions between wealth and poverty during this period forced social classes into confrontation and accentuated social antagonism.

The birth of neoclassical economics came as an immediate reaction to these growing tensions but also against the critical writings that exposed the contradictions of capitalism. In this context, the most urgent task for the early neoclassical writers was to deflect the workers' attention away from militantism and prevent a deepening of the awareness and consciousness of the masses. They attacked class-consciousness by praising individualism and the pursuit of self-interest. They justified private property of land and capital as a sacred gift of nature. They denied conflict between social classes and argued that workers, landlords and capitalists had mutual interests – and would be living in a 'social harmony' if only they understood the importance of their self-interest. In the neoclassical paradigm, there is no difference between a worker, a capitalist and a landowner. Each one of them provides a service and, through exchange with the others, can increase his own satisfaction. Exchange becomes the crucial means by which people can increase their utility. There is less concern with the creation of value, and focus is now moved away from the 'sphere of production' to the 'sphere of circulation' or exchange. This groundwork has been done by early utilitarians such as Jeremy Bentham (1748–1832), Frédéric Bastiat (1801–1850) and Nassau Senior (1790–1864) who were staunch defenders of the selfish, individualistic, utilitarian approach and strong believers in competition and the superiority of free markets. Later neoclassical economists, who led the so-called marginalist revolution, had mainly refined these arguments using mathematical rigour. The main contributors to the marginalist revolution were William Stanley Jevons (1835–1882), Léon Walras (1834–1910) and Carl Menger (1840–1921). In the next three sections, we will learn more about their ideas and theories on important issues in economics such as (1) value, (2) income distribution, and (3) equilibrium.

2. VALUE, UTILITY AND PRICES: ECONOMIC ARGUMENTS AND IDEOLOGICAL FOUNDATIONS OF THE NEOCLASSICAL SCHOOL

The idea that labour is the source of value creation represented a serious threat to those who acquired a share of income 'without merit or exertion of their own', to use John Stuart Mill's expression. The labour theory of value, as developed by Karl Marx, became an illuminating educational tool and a dangerous weapon in the hands of the workers because it revealed 'the secret of profit making'.[2] It explained that profit was unpaid labour – an extortion of a portion of the value produced by labour. The dominant class in capitalism was badly in need of an alternative explanation to help to defend its position and even justify its existence. As mentioned in the introduction, the alternative was given by the utilitarian economists who chose to focus on the utility gained by making exchanges, thus ignoring the material conditions of production. Therefore, Jevons (1871) began Chapter 1 of his book by directly attacking the labour theory of value. From the outset, on the very first page, he stated: 'Prevailing opinions make labour rather than utility the origin of value; and there are even those who distinctly assert that labour is the cause of value.' He then downplayed these arguments by assuring his readers that 'Repeated reflection and inquiry have led me to the somewhat novel opinion, that *value depends entirely upon utility*' (Jevons, 1871: 1, emphasis in original).

It is interesting to note that in criticizing the labour theory of value, Jevons took issue with Adam Smith and David Ricardo, but never mentioned Karl Marx once. This is an indication that Jevons had deliberately

chosen to attack the weaker, rudimentary formulation of the labour
theory of value rather than the scientific, mathematical formulation given
by Marx. Indeed, Jevons (1871: 161, 168) quoted Ricardo and Smith as
having said that commodities derive their exchangeable value from their
scarcity, and from the quantity of labour required to obtain them, but
avoided any reference to the industrial relations of production under capitalism, which were studied at length by Karl Marx. Jevons (1871: 162–163)
then declared that:

> Economists have not been wanting who put forward labour as the cause of
> value, asserting that all objects derive their value from the fact that labour has
> been expended on them; and it is thus implied, if not stated, that value will be
> proportional to labour. This is a doctrine which cannot stand for a moment,
> being directly opposed to facts.

He added that:

> The mere fact that there are many things, such as rare ancient books, coins,
> antiquities, etc., which have high values, and which are absolutely incapable of
> production now, disperses the notion that value depends on labour. Even those
> things which are producible in any quantity by labour seldom exchange exactly
> at the corresponding values.

The new line of arguments followed by neoclassical economists is that
utility determines value, and that value reflects prices, where in fact value
and prices are presented as synonymous. Labour, now, in the hedonistic
neoclassical theory, is looked at from the perspective of utility. Since
labour means a physical and/or a mental effort, it is treated as pain and
called 'disutility'. As Jevons (1871: 167) put it, 'Labour is the painful exertion which we undergo to ward off pains of greater amount, or to procure
pleasures which leave a balance in our favour'.

Utility becomes the centre of economic analysis. But what is utility?
Jevons has a whole chapter dedicated to 'the theory of utility', and when he
tried to define it, he simply concurred with his intellectual mentor, Jeremy
Bentham, whom he quotes as saying that 'By utility is meant that property
in any object, whereby it tends to produce benefit, advantage, pleasure,
good, or happiness (all this, in the present case, comes to the same thing),
or (what comes again to the same thing) to prevent the happening of mis-
chief, pain, evil, or unhappiness to the party whose interest is considered'
(Jevons, 1871: 38–39).

'Pain and pleasure!', exclaimed Jevons, 'the laws of human enjoyment',
are what determines all human actions: 'They govern us in all we do, in
all we say, in all we think' according to Bentham. For this reason, Jevons

recommends that we must 'transfer our attention as soon as possible to the physical objects or actions which are the source to us of pleasures and pains'. Echoing Bentham, Jevons claimed that 'pleasure and pain are undoubtedly the ultimate objects of the Calculus of Economics. To satisfy our wants to the utmost with the least effort – to procure the greatest amount of what is desirable at the expense of the least that is undesirable – in other words, to *maximise pleasure*, is the problem of Economics' (Jevons, 1871: 37, emphasis in original).

All commodities that can produce pleasure or prevent pain possess 'utility' and therefore have 'value'. This utility, however, is not an intrinsic quality that 'useful' commodities would acquire forever. Utility, and therefore value, of the same commodity for the same person can be high under certain circumstances and may decrease to near zero under other circumstances. In this sense, it is not possible to say absolutely that some commodities are always useful while others are not. Utility, and value, is not an objective characteristic of a commodity but a *subjective* appreciation by the consumer. Moreover, utility depends on the 'circumstantial' feelings of the consumer, in the sense that it varies with the quantities consumed. If you are hungry, a loaf of bread gives you a great satisfaction and is, therefore, highly 'valued'. The utility you would get from a second loaf is not as high and that loaf will have less value for you. A third and a fourth loaf will have even less utility. The addition to a person's happiness, the additional utility, decreases as the quantity consumed increases. But as long as that additional, marginal utility is positive, we would continue to consume because that increases our total utility. The latter is maximized when the additional utility becomes nil. Here, we have two dimensions of utility: one is the quantity of the commodity consumed and the other is the degree of satisfaction, the intensity of the effect it has on the consumer. This is the notion of *decreasing marginal utility*, which is the main innovation of the marginalist school. In mathematical terms, if U(x) is the total utility gained from consuming x units of commodity X, then marginal utility is the first derivative of the total utility function: $MU_x = dU/dx$, and it is positive but decreasing: $MU_x = dU/dx > 0$; $d^2U/d^2x < 0$, as shown in Figure 4.1. Note that total utility is maximized when the marginal utility is zero and X* units are consumed.

Since consumption normally involves more than one commodity, consumers are faced with having to make the rational decision of how much to consume of each commodity in order to find the optimal combination that would maximize their own utility. The basic law is that a consumer would buy additional quantities of a commodity, and pay the price, as long as that increased his/her utility. When the consumer wants to add a second commodity Y to his/her basket, then he/she must compare the marginal

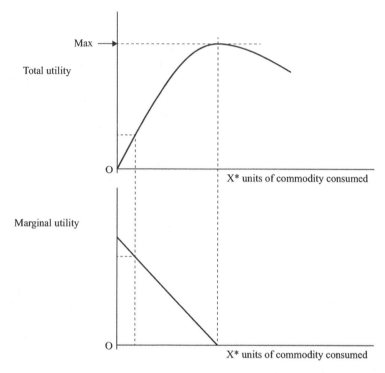

Figure 4.1   Relationship between marginal utility and total utility

utilities as well as the prices of the two commodities. MU_x/p_x is the ratio of the marginal utility of commodity X compared to its cost, the price p_x, which must be compared to the ratio of MU_y/p_y. If MU_x/p_x is higher than MU_y/p_y, then the consumer would benefit from trading, or exchanging, some of Y for more X. By doing so, the marginal utility of X would decrease and the marginal utility of Y would increase due to the law of decreasing marginal utility. The process would continue until the two ratios are equal, and at that point, the total utility is maximized. When $MU_x/p_x = MU_y/p_y$, it also implies that $MU_x/MU_y = p_x/p_y$ and this is the principle or the condition of utility maximization.

Four important implications follow from this psychological law of decreasing marginal utility:

(1) demand for a given commodity is an inverse relationship with the price of that commodity,
(2) relative prices of different commodities are proportional to their respective marginal utilities,

(3) prices are signals and reflect the degree of scarcity of commodities,
(4) prices of commodities are independent of the production cost of said commodities.

However, the important point is that when a consumer was trading with others some of the commodity Y for more of the commodity X, exchange was supposed to be free and voluntary. This ensured that, after exchange, all consumers would have maximized their utilities. Free and voluntary exchange is, therefore, the necessary setting for all transactions and it is proof that people, as 'trading bodies' and calculating maximizers, engage with one another in the pursuit of their self-interest and, by doing so, arrive at a socially optimal outcome in a harmonious – not conflictual – manner. Supply and demand, in a free market, ensure that everyone gets what they need to satisfy their wants at a competitive price – that is equilibrium. As Menger (1871: 191) put it:

> Economizing individuals strive to better their economic positions as much as possible. To this end they engage in economic activity in general. And to this end also, whenever it can be attained by means of trade, they exchange goods. Prices are only incidental manifestations of these activities, symptoms of an economic equilibrium between the economies of individuals.

3. INCOME DISTRIBUTION: 'THERE IS NO SUCH THING AS SOCIETY'[3]

The problem of economics, according to neoclassical thinking, 'is to satisfy our wants to the utmost with the least effort', 'with the least possible sum of labour' (Jevons, 1871: 37, 168). If we want to be cynical and accept this proposition as true, we will certainly have to agree that it only applies to landlords and capitalists, who use the laws of property ownership to collect rents and profits – thus ensuring the means to satisfy their wants without 'merit or exertion of their own'. It certainly does not apply to honest workers who earn their livelihood through toil and sweat. Yet, the existing institutional framework of capitalism since its inception is such that these idle landowners and capitalists are able to amass huge amounts of wealth while the working class often finds itself struggling to secure earnings to satisfy the more pressing wants. This gross inequality in the distribution of incomes and wealth bothered intellectuals, workers and their unions, and large segments of society, who began to question the social position of the landlords and capitalists. Many socialists, such as Pierre-Joseph Proudhon, denounced 'property as theft', while Karl Marx called for its abolition.[4] The laws on private property rights were being challenged and this threatened the very existence of the dominant class.

Again, neoclassical economists came to the defense of the landlords and the capitalists, and the response could only be ideological. Menger (1871: 174), for instance, sought to justify the unequal distribution of income on moral grounds and insisted that workers were paid what they deserve. He wrote:

> It may well appear deplorable to a lover of mankind that possession of capital or a piece of land often provides the owner a higher income for a given period of time than the income received by a laborer for the most strenuous activity during the same period. Yet the cause of this is not immoral, but simply that the satisfaction of more important human needs depends upon the services of the given amount of capital or piece of land than upon the services of the laborer. The agitation of those who would like to see society allot a larger share of the available consumption goods to laborers than at present really constitutes, therefore, a demand for nothing else than paying labor above its value. ... A solution of the problem on this basis, however, would undoubtedly require a complete transformation of our social order.

'A complete transformation of the social order' is what the ruling class and neoclassical economics are trying to avoid. John Bates Clark was even more radical in his opposition to any change to the status quo and claimed that distribution of income in the capitalist system was governed by a *natural law* that should not be challenged. Clark (1899: 3) was well aware of the fact that 'The right of society to exist in its present form, and the probability that it will continue so to exist, are at stake'. Therefore, in the preface to his book, Clark (1899: v) openly stated what his task was about:

> It is the purpose of this work to show that the distribution of the income of society is controlled by a natural law, and that this law, if it worked without friction, would give to every agent of production the amount of wealth which that agent creates. ... At the point in the economic system where titles to property originate, – where labor and capital come into possession of the amounts that the state afterwards treats as their own, – the social procedure is true to the principle on which the right of property rests. So far as it is not obstructed, it assigns to every one what he has specifically produced.

Neoclassical economists never accepted the class division of society, which was the framework used by the classical economists as well as Karl Marx. The philosophical foundation of neoclassical economics was – and still is – the egoistic, utilitarian and competitive individualism. The utility theory was freely applied to labour effort and earnings of factors of production in order to justify the existing type of income distribution. Therefore, labour is reduced to that 'painful exertion which we undergo to ward off pains of greater amount, or to procure pleasures which leave a balance in our favour' (Jevons, 1871: 167). Individuals then, regardless of their social status, are somehow condemned to eternally undergo the painful exertion, which they must minimize, in order to consume – and satisfy their wants. The underlying logic, of course, is that workers, capitalists and landlords – as individuals – have mutual interests and must collaborate with each other by exchanging services for their own benefit. Workers can supply their labour services in exchange for a wage that allows them to acquire the commodities they need to satisfy their wants and maximize their utility. But since labour is a pain and a disutility, workers will need to find a *balance* between the utility they get from consuming and the disutility they suffer by working. That balance is reached when 'the pleasure gained is exactly equal to the labour endured' (Jevons, 1871: 173).

But what painful exertion do absentee landlords and capitalists undergo to justify their rents, interests and profits? The answer given by neoclassical economics is twofold:

(1) Private property of land, machine tools and financial capital is a divine gift. Why is it bestowed only on some but not on others? Well, it is sacred and its distribution cannot be questioned. By the same token, the bequest of private property to heirs – inheritance – is also seen as a law of nature.

(2) When the owner of financial capital lends out his money, he forgoes using it for himself or just keeping it idle and, therefore, suffers the pain of abstinence. He is fully entitled to charging interest (rent on money). Similarly, the owners of land and industrial capital also suffer by letting workers use these means of production; and therefore deserve compensation.

However, the important question that needs to be addressed is what determines the rate at which the worker's pain is paid, that is, what determines the wage rate; and what makes it high or low? And more generally, what determines all incomes, including the profits and rents received by capitalists and landlords? Jevons (1871: 270, 273) does not give a convincing explanation when he states that 'the wages of a working man are ultimately coincident with what he produces', and that 'Every labourer ultimately receives the due value of his produce after paying a proper fraction to the capitalist for the remuneration of abstinence and risk'. Note that several neoclassical economists, including Jevons, do not often talk about profit but instead refer to it as remuneration for risk and abstinence or compensation for the labour of superintendence – the work of the entrepreneur.

Walras (1874), for instance, mentioned the word 'profits' only twice in his book and it was in the context of comparison with 'losses'. Menger (1871: 156), however, rejected the idea of compensation for abstinence and emphasized the importance of exchange: 'Thus the payment of interest must not be regarded as a compensation of the owner of capital for his abstinence, but as the exchange of one economic good (the use of capital) for another (money, for instance).'

In his detailed analysis of income distribution, Jevons (1871: 255) started by claiming that 'the returns to capital and labour are independent of each other', and then proceeded to distinguish between the 'whole yield' (or total product) and the 'final rate of yield' (or marginal product) of each of the factors of production. These ideas represent the core of the neoclassical theory of distribution as developed by Jevons and Menger. The theory was extended subsequently by others such as Alfred Marshall (1890) and John Bates Clark (1899) who were able to apply the principle of diminishing marginal productivity to both capital and labour. The law of decreasing marginal utility in the sphere of consumption now has its equivalent in the sphere of production. In the same way as the marginal utility of a commodity decreases when more of it is available and consumed, so do the marginal productivities of labour and capital decrease as more labour or capital is applied to the production of a given commodity. For a given quantity of capital used in production, increasing the number of workers will result in smaller and smaller additional yields, i.e. the marginal productivity of labour decreases. The same reasoning applies to capital if the quantity of labour is fixed. Now, just as the value of a commodity, and hence its price, was determined by its marginal utility, the prices of both factors of production, or more precisely their earnings, are determined by their marginal contributions to the total product, that is, by their respective marginal productivities.

The relationship between marginal productivity and total product is similar to that between marginal utility and total utility depicted in Figure 4.1. Initially, the marginal product is high when only a few workers are employed, but it starts to decrease as more workers are hired. The capitalist, whose ultimate goal is to maximize profit, must now compare the increment to total output by each additional worker hired (the marginal product of labour) to the cost paid to that worker (the marginal cost of labour). This is shown in Figure 4.2 where it can be seen that as long as the marginal product of labour (MPL) is greater than the marginal cost of labour (MCL), which is the fixed wage (W*), the capitalist finds it profitable to hire more workers. Hiring will continue until MPL is exactly equal to W* where the two curves intersect at point E, which determines the final demand for labour (L*). Therefore, the firm will hire L* number of workers and pay them the ongoing wage W*, which is equal to the value of their marginal product.

Note that in trying to determine the number of workers to be hired, the capitalist moved along the curve MPL until reaching the intersection with the horizontal line W*. Here, the curve MPL becomes identical to the firm's demand for labour. Since all firms behave in the same way, the sum of these individual curves gives the aggregate demand curve for labour in the industry or for the whole economy. The supply of labour is often assumed to be fixed by the available pool of labour, but also allowed to expand and increase if the wage increases. The interaction between the total demand for labour and the total supply of labour determines the ongoing wage, which all firms take as given. Therefore, the wage rate received by the workers at this firm will be the same as that received by all workers of a similar skill who are working in other firms. This result is guaranteed by competition between workers who seek to maximize their wages as well as by competition between firms, which seek to minimize their costs. A closer look at Figure 4.2 shows that the total wages received by the workers will be the wage rate OW* multiplied by the number of workers OL*, or the area OW*EL*, whereas the remainder, represented by the triangle W*EY, is what accrues to the capitalist in the form of compensation for 'superintendence, insurance against risk and interest'. It is important to emphasize here that these payments are compensation for services provided. The workers get their income, which is called the wage, and the capitalists get their income, which is also a compensation for their work. Moreover, the value of the produce is fully distributed among those who contributed to it. There is no left over. There is no such thing as a profit.

In exactly the same way, we could draw a diagram depicting the marginal productivity of capital (MPK) by keeping the number of workers fixed and increasing the units of capital. The ongoing interest rate (R*) would

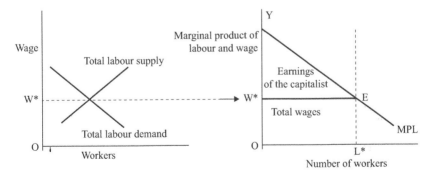

Figure 4.2   Neoclassical theory of distribution

be determined by the interaction between the supply of and demand for capital, which is then taken as given by all firms – in the same manner as the wage rate. When R* is exactly equal to MPK, we get the quantity of capital (K*) used in production. The rectangular area would then represent the earnings of capital and the triangle above it would represent the total wages, and that is the same result as when we focused on the marginal productivity of labour, shown in Figure 4.2. The main driver that ensures these results is unfettered competition – which is a central concept in neoclassical theory. To quote again from Jevons (1871: 271), here is how it works:

> [the capitalists] pay the lowest current rates for the kind of labour required; and if the produce exceeds the average, those who are first in the field make large profits. This soon induces competition on the part of other capitalists, who, in trying to obtain good workmen, will raise the rate of wages. Competition will proceed until the point is reached at which only the market rate of interest is obtained for the capital invested.

In this way, workers and capitalists – the agents of production, as Marshall calls them – would have successfully collaborated in a collective enterprise and generated a 'produce', which is shared among them according to their respective contributions. In the preface to the second edition of his book, Jevons (1871: lxvii) summarized this collaborative effort by stating that:

> It is only when separate owners of the elements of production join their properties, and traffic with each other, that distribution begins, and then it is entirely subject to the principles of value and the laws of supply and demand. Each labourer must be regarded, like each landowner and each capitalist, as bringing into the common stock one part of the component elements, bargaining for the best share of the produce which the conditions of the market allow him to claim successfully.

Therefore, according to neoclassical economics, the price of labour and the price of capital are determined within the ordinary conditions of exchange in the same manner as all other questions of price. And so, as Clark (1899: 82) put it, 'demand and supply ... put a price on men, as they do on commodities'. This brings us to the question of price determination on all markets, and thus to the study of general equilibrium.

4. GENERAL EQUILIBRIUM: SUPPLY AND DEMAND, AUCTION, TÂTONNEMENT

The notion of market equilibrium had been discussed by economists at least since Adam Smith's idea of the 'invisible hand', which implied that competition would equalize rates of profits, wages, and all other prices. Several neoclassical economists such as Jevons and Menger, among others, devoted a great deal of their work to the study of equilibrium, but their analysis remained focused on separate markets and thus dealt with what became known as 'partial equilibrium'. It was Léon Walras (1874) who argued that all markets are interdependent and that they form a general system – i.e., the total economy – whose equilibrium requires that each market be in equilibrium. This is the idea of a general equilibrium. However, Walras' analysis did not differ fundamentally from that of Jevons and Menger since he also relied on the argument of competitive equilibrium in each market via supply and demand. His main point, though, was that if we had n markets and if $n-1$ markets were in equilibrium, then necessarily the nth market had to be also in equilibrium.

The interdependence of the different markets composing the economy was in fact discussed by Menger (1871: 150), who distinguished between what he called 'goods of higher order' (i.e., inputs or factors of production) and 'goods of lower order' or consumer goods. He then argued that 'the value of goods of higher order is always and without exception determined by the prospective value of the goods of lower order in whose production they serve'. This is the basic argument behind the idea that the value or price of a factor of production, such as labour or capital, depended on its marginal product – that is, the neoclassical theory of income distribution. It is clear from this statement that Menger recognized the interrelationship between the labour market, the capital market and the market for consumption goods. This idea was simply generalized by Walras, who posited that the price of one good – whether of a higher or of a lower order – in any market was fundamentally dependent on the prices of all other goods in all other markets.

The reasoning is based on pure mathematical logic. Walras distinguishes between what he calls '*consumable* services' or consumption goods and '*productive* services' or inputs – which is similar to Menger's classification. Assuming there are n consumer goods and m productive services, the maximization of utility requires exchanging one good for another until the ratio of marginal utilities is equal to the ratio of the two prices, as explained in Section 2 above. This establishes a series of relative prices between the n consumer goods and the m productive services. But if we choose one good as a *numeraire* – for which all other (consumable and productive) services can be exchanged – then we have only $m + n-1$ prices. Therefore, there are $m + n$ quantities of productive services and consumer goods that are exchanged at $m + n-1$ prices. This gives us a total of $2m + 2n-1$ unknowns to be determined simultaneously. Walras used his talent as a mathematician to set up a system of dependent and independent equations to solve for the unknown prices and quantities. The results, he claimed, will not only indicate that all markets are in equilibrium but also that this equilibrium is stable.

Next, Walras sought to study the price determination of 'the three *productive* services', namely labour services, land services and capital goods services – that is, the determination of wages, rent and interest. Here, Walras found himself confronted with the difficult problem of income distribution. In the beginning of his chapter dealing with this issue, he was forced to agree with the classical economists that the price of commodities was equal to their *cost of production*. Walras (1874: 192) even claimed that he had *found* 'the two great laws of economics', and named them as 'the law of supply and demand', which determined the prices of commodities and 'the law of the cost of production', which determined the prices of productive services. Had he followed this approach, Walras would have reached some contradictory conclusions, which would have all but destroyed his claims, as well as those by Jevons and Menger, on the role played by subjective utility in determining the price of a commodity, and thus in determining value. But Walras was able to get out of this trap by performing some sort of a pirouette when he resorted to the notion of interdependence of markets and asked whether it was the prices of inputs that determined the prices of commodities or the other way around. He then stated that 'It remains to determine ... if it is, as has been maintained, the prices of productive services that determine the prices of products, or if it is not rather the prices of products, determined, as we have seen, by virtue of the law of supply and demand, that determine the prices of productive services by virtue of the law of costs of production' (Walras, 1874: 192).

In the end, Walras chose to give primacy to the law of supply and demand; and tried to incorporate the approach of the cost of production into – and make it compatible with – the general law of exchange. In this context, it became straightforward for Walras (1874: 152) to claim that the prices of commodities are determined 'by virtue of the law of supply and demand' – the end result of which is that 'in a state of general equilibrium, each commodity has only one exchange value with respect to all other commodities in the market'. After this, Walras began to explain how equilibrium is established in the markets for 'productive services'. Walras described these markets in a manner similar to auction markets where a 'crieur' (crier) had the responsibility of calling out loud the prices announced by buyers and sellers, so that all the participants would know them. If the asking price is higher than the offered price, adjustments will be made until the supply and demand are equal.

Given the multiplicity of exchanges, prices in the first instance are cried at random, and then raised or lowered in accordance with circumstances – in a process that Walras called 'tâtonnement', that is, a process of successive attempts to find the right price by trial and error. This is how Walras (1874: 207) described the process:

> These productive services are exchanged in accordance with the mechanism of free competition with the intervention of a numeraire. For each of them a price is cried in terms of the numeraire; if, at the price cried in that way, the effective demand exceeds the effective supply, the entrepreneurs bid against one another and the price rises; if the effective supply exceeds the effective demand, the landowners, workers, and capitalists underbid one another, and the price falls. The current price is the one for which effective supply and demand are equal.

Walras then concluded that the current price for land is rent; the current price for labour is wages; and the current price for capital goods is interest. In this way, Walras was able to justify the current distribution of income among the different social classes but indirectly through market equilibrium, and after reducing classes to individuals who are simple suppliers of 'productive services'.

Walras' (1874: 43) model of general equilibrium may seem neat and complete because the setting is assumed to be 'a market perfectly organized under the regime of competition, just as in pure mechanics we initially assume that machines are frictionless'. But, in fact, it suffers several deficiencies. The first difficulty is the setting itself or the market structure of perfect competition, which assumes that all firms are price takers. This assumption rules out monopoly and market power enjoyed by big corporations, which had been a dominant feature of capitalism already at the time Walras developed his idea of competitive equilibrium. As it turned out, Walras tried to avoid dealing with the reality that firms actually make their prices in a mark-up fashion where the price includes a profit margin above the cost of production.

A second major problem is that the general equilibrium model has no money in it. It has relative prices but all of them are in terms of a numeraire, which is one of the commodities. Money is integrated into the model only after price determination is resolved and equilibrium is established – in which case money remains neutral and serves only as a medium of exchange to replace the numeraire. Again, this was an attempt to avoid dealing with money as an asset that commanded so much power in the capitalist system, as Marx had shown.

A third problem concerns the internal consistency of the model. Walras' main point about the interdependence of markets is that price changes in one market necessarily affect prices in all other markets, which will induce changes in supply and demand until equilibrium is established. However, consider what will happen if, let us say, two markets are in disequilibrium, one characterized with excess supply and the other with excess demand. Following Walras' logic, as prices in these two markets begin to move in opposite directions, prices in all other markets that were initially in equilibrium will be affected and, consequently, supply and demand in those markets also change, which disturbs the existing equilibria – thus causing a general disequilibrium. Therefore, general equilibrium is not an automatic result that follows from the successive adjustments to prices, as suggested by the 'crier' – nor will it necessarily be stable if there is ever a shock to it. Disequilibrium is as probable as is equilibrium.

A fourth problem has to do with the fact that exchanges (between suppliers and demanders) are intermediated through the 'crier'. As Walras (1874: 42) said:

> The markets that are best organized in regard to competition are those in which purchases and sales are made by the crying out of prices, through the intermediation of agents such as floor traders, commercial agents, criers, who *centralize* transactions in such a way that no transaction takes place without the conditions being announced and known and without the sellers being able to lower their prices and buyers to raise them.

This clearly indicates that the good functioning of the market depends on the presence of a central institution akin to a central planning agency in a socialist economy. However, this is in flagrant contradiction with Walras' description of a market economy, which is supposed to be decentralized and in which individuals are the main players. Still, later contributions by Paul Samuelson, Gérard Debreu and Kenneth Arrow have made the general equilibrium model the core of modern neoclassical microeconomics.

Finally, it is worth noting that the neoclassical theory based on the general equilibrium model – even in its newest form known as the dynamic stochastic general equilibrium (DSGE) – has failed miserably to give even an approximate account of economic reality. To give only two examples: the analysis in terms of general equilibrium provided no explanation to the Great Depression of 1929, except repeating its mantra of long-term convergence. The more sophisticated DSGE modeling had no relevance to the global financial crisis of 2008. While the crisis was wreaking havoc on most industrialized economies, proponents of this approach continued to claim that their theory and policies had succeeded in preventing the recurrence of economic depressions (see Lucas, 2003). No wonder John Maynard Keynes (1938) had warned that 'Good economists are scarce because the gift for using "vigilant observation" to choose good models, although it does not require a highly specialised intellectual technique, appears to be a very rare one'.

5. CONCLUSION

The neoclassical theory did not start with the so-called 'marginalist revolution'. Its philosophical foundation goes back to the early utilitarian theorists of the eighteenth century such as Jeremy Bentham and Nassau Senior, who were advocates of competitive individualism in a market economy. Marginalism is simply a continuation of that individualistic, utilitarian perspective. The difference is that the marginalist writers used mathematics to demonstrate what others had only stated. Marginalists had hoped that mathematical rigour would give a scientific character to their theories and thus make them more convincing. However, a closer look at these theories shows that they were more ideologically driven, with the purpose of deflecting workers and intellectuals from socialist and communist ideas. Indeed, the bulk of the arguments are specifically tailored to defend private property, inequality in the distribution of wealth and income, and the superiority of free markets. The chapter examined three major ideas, which are considered to be the pillars of neoclassical economics, namely the utility theory of value, the determination of incomes, and the notion of general equilibrium – all of which serve as ideological justifications of free market capitalism.

NOTES

1. See the full text of the manifesto at <https://www.marxists.org/archive/marx/works/download/pdf/Manifesto.pdf>.
2. See Karl Marx, *Capital*, Vol. 1, Chapter 6, 'The Buying and Selling of Labour Power' <https://www.marxists.org/archive/marx/works/1867-c1/ch06.htm>.
3. This is a statement by Margaret Thatcher, the ultra-right neoconservative British prime minister, who declared in an interview (23 September 1987) that 'there is no such thing as society. There are individual men and women, and there are families' <https://www.margaretthatcher.org/document/106689>.
4. See Karl Marx, *The German Ideology* (1845) <https://www.marxists.org/archive/marx/works/1845/german-ideology/ch01a.htm>.

REFERENCES

Clark, John Bates, 1899 [reprint], *The Distribution of Wealth: A Theory of Wages, Interest and Profits*, London: Macmillan & Co.

Jevons, W. Stanley, [1871], 2013, *The Theory of Political Economy*, 4th edn, New York: Palgrave Macmillan.

Keynes, John Maynard, 1938, *A letter sent to Harrod Roy* (4 July) <http://economia. unipv.it/harrod/edition/editionstuff/rfh.346.htm>.

Lucas, Robert, Jr, 2003, 'Macroeconomic Priorities', *American Economic Review*, Vol. 93, No. 1.

Marshall, Alfred, [1890], 1920, *Principles of Economics*, London: Macmillan & Co.

Marx, Karl, [1863, 1883], 1972, *Capital*, Volumes 1, 2 and 3, New York: International Publishers Company.

Menger, Carl, [1871], 1976, *Principles of Economics*, Auburn, Ala: Ludwig von Mises Institute.

Ricardo, David, [1817], 1962, *The Principles of Political Economy and Taxation*, London: Dent & Sons.

Walras, Léon, [1874], 2014, *Elements of Theoretical Economics or The Theory of Social Wealth*, Cambridge: Cambridge University Press.

PART II

Keynes and his contemporaries

5. John Maynard Keynes

Amitava Dutt

KEY FEATURES

- Keynes's theory of employment based on aggregate demand and aggregate supply functions and how it differs from neoclassical – what Keynes called classical – theory.
- Keynes's theory of investment, in which investment is affected by expectations, in an environment in which the future is uncertain.
- Keynes's theory of interest in terms of the theory of liquidity preference, the essential properties of money and their relation to unemployment equilibrium.
- Keynes's ideas on the implications for money wage reductions and money wage flexibility.
- Keynes's social philosophy and his views on monetary and fiscal policy, and his method involving the analysis of the economy as a whole, his departure from the constrained optimization approach and the use of mathematics.
- The relation of Keynes's ideas to the similar ones of his predecessors, contemporaries and descendants.

1. INTRODUCTION

While chapter 4 of this book discussed the emergence of the neoclassical school of economic thought, this chapter will examine the theory of John Maynard Keynes, who tried to understand the dramatic economic events of the 1930s by attempting to "escape" from that school's ideas. In the 1930s much of the world was in the throes of what has come to be known as the Great Depression. In the major capitalist countries of the world, the USA and the UK, the unemployment rate rose to 25 per cent in 1933 and above 15 per cent in 1932, respectively. The problem erupted with the New York stock market crash of October 1929, which was followed by widespread bank failures, declining levels of investment spending by firms, sharp reductions in output, income and employment, as well as wage and price deflation, resulting in much human misery. Although depressions and recessions were not unknown, such a deep economic downturn affecting so many people around the globe was unprecedented. It lasted, to varying degrees in different parts of the world, for almost a decade, and it was not until World War II that recovery occurred.[1] Yet, most economists held on to neoclassical economic theories that took the view that the market for labor "clears" in the sense that supply and demand are brought to equality through wage variations, and that unemployment would not persist. To be sure, these theories could explain the existence of unemployment, but only in terms of the rigidity of wages due to, say, the existence of trade unions that prevented wages from falling. Such theories, however, seemed to be incompatible with the persistence of unemployment for a prolonged period, despite declining wages and prices.

In his book *The General Theory of Employment, Interest and Money* (henceforth, the *GT*), written during the Depression and published in 1936, the British economist John Maynard Keynes developed what became the classic analysis of why capitalist economies can experience long bouts of involuntary unemployment and why this unemployment is not necessarily removed by automatic market forces. This analysis has been seen by many as the genesis of modern mainstream macroeconomics, which analyzes the economy as a whole, as a branch of economics separate from microeconomics, which analyzes particular markets and individual actors in the economy, such as firms and households.

Keynes was actually a many-faceted individual, who wrote a number of scholarly treatises in economics, lectured on economics at Cambridge University, wrote about philosophy and statistics, was a trader in financial markets, served as a civil servant working for the British government on economic affairs and policies, including on the Bretton Woods institutions, and a member of the Bloomsbury Group, an influential informal association of English writers, intellectuals, philosophers and artists.[2] Although several of these sides of Keynes – especially his involvement in financial markets, his work as a public servant and his non-economic scholarly writings – are closely related to the ideas on unemployment, this chapter will concentrate on his major book, the *GT*, and on his closely related writings,[3] ignoring his extensive writings on other economic issues, including those on international monetary issues. It will discuss, in turn, his theory of employment and unemployment, his views on uncertainty and expectations, his approach to money and interest, his analysis of the implications of wage flexibility, his views on the role of the state and economic policy, and his method, before concluding with a discussion of his place in the history of economic thought.

2. THE THEORY OF EMPLOYMENT

In chapter 1 of the *GT*, Keynes named his theory the general theory, as opposed to the special theory of the orthodox economists of his time, whom he (somewhat misleadingly) called the classical economists.[4]

The "Classical" Approach

According to these economists, as chapter 2 of the *GT* explains, employment is determined in the labor market with the demand and supply curves of labor, as shown in Figure 5.1, where W denotes the money wage, P the price level, so that W/P is the real wage in terms of goods. The demand for labor by employers is shown as the negatively-sloped curve N^D. This suggests that profit-maximizing, price-taking firms choose to employ workers until the additional benefit they receive from an additional worker, that is, the marginal product of labor, equals the additional cost, that is, the real wage. Assuming that marginal product of labor declines with increases in employment (due to diminishing returns to labor), a reduction in the real wage increases the demand for labor.

As for the supply of labor by workers, it is shown by the positively sloped curve N^S. Utility maximizing workers work up to the point at which their marginal benefit from work, given by the real wage, is equal to the marginal cost of work, that is, their marginal disutility of work, which can be interpreted as the cost of forgoing leisure. Assuming that the marginal disutility of work increases with the amount of work that they do, the curve is positively sloped: a higher real wage induces workers to work more hours even though it results in higher marginal disutility of work, because the higher real wage compensates workers for less leisure.

If the real wage is flexible – so that the real wage falls when there is involuntary unemployment in the sense that workers supply more labor than firms demand – the supply and demand for labor become equalized at the real wage shown by E in Figure 5.1, at which point there is no involuntary unemployment, apart from "frictions" that prevent a worker looking for work not getting employed by an employer seeking workers. In this way, the labor market determines the level of employment in the economy and therefore the output of goods and services produced in it. If the real wage does not decline, but gets stuck, say at U in Figure 5.1, unemployment can persist. Here, two points are important. First, unemployment is explained by a rigid real wage; second, unemployment is explained within the labor market itself.

Given the discussion above, one question remains: what ensures that the output produced by fully employed labor ends up being sold? Since

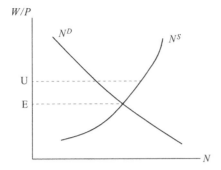

Figure 5.1   The labor market in classical theory

output gives rise to, and is roughly equal to, income, if the income is entirely spent, output and spending on output will be the same, and all goods will be sold. In fact, spending out of income on consumption automatically creates a demand for consumption goods produced; but this is not the same for income that is not spent on consumption, that is, for income that is saved. The answer provided by Keynes's neoclassical contemporaries is that saving (out of full employment income) becomes equal to investment spending (on purchase of new capital goods) through variations in the interest rate. This is shown by the solid lines, *S* and *I*, in Figure 5.2.

The curves show that saving increases with the rate of interest, since an increase in the latter makes people want to reduce current consumption. This is because there is a higher return to reducing consumption and increasing saving. Similarly, investment falls as interest rates increase, since a rise in the interest rate makes firms reluctant to invest in projects that

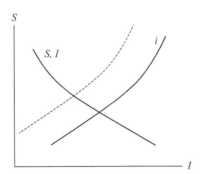

Figure 5.2   The goods market in classical theory

have lower returns than the interest cost. Saving leads to the supply of loans (called the supply of loanable funds), while investment results in the demand for loans (or demand for loanable funds). Assuming that the interest rate increases (decreases) when the demand for loanable funds (which is equal to investment spending) exceeds (is less than) the supply of loanable funds (which is equal to saving), changes in the rate of interest "clear" the loanable funds market, hence making saving equal to planned investment spending, ensuring that all goods produced (at full employment) are sold. This is a version of what is called Say's Law, but in a weaker form (since it requires variations in the interest rate to "clear" the goods market) than the version adopted by the actual classical economists, which states that all output is by definition demanded.[5]

Keynes's Approach

In the *GT*, Keynes found much to object to in the above description of labor and goods markets. First, he argues that employment is not determined in the labor market, but rather in the goods market. While he accepts what he called the first classical postulate, that the real wage is equal to the marginal product of labor (that is, what happens on the demand curve for labor shown by N^D), he does not accept the second classical postulate: that the marginal disutility of work equals the real wage (what happens on the supply curve of labor shown by N^S). Also, he argues that the money wage is rigid in the downward direction. This is because workers in one industry do not normally accept money wage cuts that reduce their wages relative to wages in other industries, since workers consider such relative wage cuts to be unfair. Since wage bargains do not occur simultaneously in all industries this implies downward wage rigidity overall. Moreover, even if the *money* wage (W) falls, it cannot be concluded that the *real* wage (W/P) also falls, as required for clearing the labor market.

To replace this neoclassical theory of wages and employment, Keynes argues instead that the level of employment is determined in the goods (and services, which we will not mention for brevity) market by the demand for and supply of goods, which determines the output of goods. This, then, determines the required level of employment, at which labor supply and labor demand may not be equal.

In chapter 3 of the *GT* Keynes develops his own theory of employment determination. He assumes that the quantity and quality of the stock of capital are given, as are the quantity and quality of the total labor force, available technology, preferences for consumption, saving and leisure, and social and other factors that determine the distribution of income.[6]

He also assumes that the rate of interest is given, although noting that it is capable of further analysis. He then defines two relationships between the level of employment, *N*, and the value of income and production. The first is the *aggregate supply function*, which shows the relationship between *N* and the value of output actually produced (output, *Y*, multiplied by the price level, *P*) and the other is the *aggregate demand function*, which shows the relationship between *N* and the revenue that producers expect to receive. Although Keynes examines the value of output and income, we may simplify by not explicitly examining the role of the price level, and drawing these functions with the real levels of income, output and proceeds on the vertical axis, with *N* on the horizontal axis. In Figure 5.3, the *AS* curve represents the real level of output produced for each level of *N*: as employment increases, the curve shows that the real level of output increases, although at a diminishing rate, given diminishing returns to labor for a given stock of capital. The *AD* curve shows that as *N* rises, the expected receipts of firms in real terms increases, since the increase in *N* implies that output and hence income rises (as already shown by the *AS* curve), which implies that consumption spending increases. This happens according to what Keynes calls a psychological law, which determines the propensity to consume. When income increases, consumption does not rise as much as income, since consumers also save a part of their additional income.[7] The receipts of firms, however, depends not only on consumption spending, but also on investment spending by firms (which adds to their productive capacity in future by increasing the stock of capital over time, the effects of which are not taken into account because capital stock is given). Following Keynes, the level of investment may be assumed to be taken as given exogenously for now. The *AD* curve

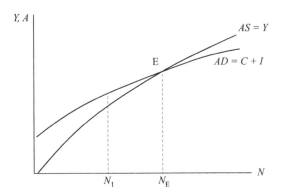

Figure 5.3   Keynes's theory of employment and the goods market

shows the sum of consumption and investment demand by households and firms (ignoring other sources of demand, from the government or from abroad). It is upward sloping because consumption expenditure increases with employment and income, and it has a flatter slope than the *AS* curve since output rises with employment less than aggregate demand, because some of the additional income resulting from employment expansion is saved. Equilibrium employment is determined at N_E, where the *AS* and *AD* curves intersect, and actual output is equal to the firms' expected proceeds or aggregate demand. Keynes calls the point at which the two curves intersect, shown by point E in Figure 5.3, the point of effective demand.[8]

Four features of Keynes's theory of employment are worth emphasizing. First, if employment is at a level different from its equilibrium level, it will tend towards the latter due to variations in output. Thus, suppose that, given what Keynes calls short-term expectations about the price of the product (more on this below), firms employ N_1 workers, the aggregate demand for goods exceeds actual output or aggregate supply. This induces the actual price to increase, which in turn makes firms revise their price expectations upward, thereby increasing their output and employment. When the economy arrives at the point of effective demand, price expectations and actual price coincide and aggregate supply and aggregate demand are equal, so price does not change and nor do firms change their price expectations, output and employment.[9] Second, equilibrium employment is determined in terms of the demand for, and supply of, goods as shown in Figure 5.3, rather than the demand and supply of labor, as in classical theory, shown in Figure 5.1. Third, the equilibrium level of output in Keynes's theory does not necessarily imply that the demand and supply of labor are equal and the economy is at full employment. With (say) investment demand at a low level, equilibrium employment will be less than that shown by the intersection of the two curves in Figure 5.1, so that in general unemployment can exist, and full employment is a special case. Keynes believed that the economy can be seen as usually being in a state of unemployment, except during occasional periods of high demand, which justifies the name he gives his theory, that is, the general theory rather than the special theory according to which full employment prevails. Finally, a change in the level of investment brings about a change in employment and output in the same direction, a change in output which is greater than the change in investment. Aggregate demand and output change through a multiplier, which is greater than unity when investment changes: a change in the latter increases aggregate demand one for one, which then leads to a further change in output and income. This has an induced effect on consumption that changes with income according to the consumption function, which further raises aggregate demand, output and income, and so on. Since consumption increases with income by less than the increase in income, the total change in output due to the change in investment is finite, although the multiplier is greater than unity.[10]

3. INVESTMENT, UNCERTAINTY AND EXPECTATIONS

While initially, as discussed in the previous section, Keynes takes the level of investment as given, in chapters 11 and 12 of the *GT* he examines the factors that determine investment.

In the first of these, he explains how the marginal efficiency of capital and the interest rate determine the level of investment, more or less along the lines discussed by economists before him (such as Fisher, 1930). Keynes defines the marginal efficiency of capital as the return to investment, which depends on the cost of the capital good and the stream of returns from using the capital for production in the future. Firms invest if the marginal efficiency of capital exceeds the interest rate, and will continue to do so until the return to investment is equal to the interest cost, at which point no additional investment is profitable. He states that in fact, lender's risk (due to the possibility that borrowers may not repay their loans) and borrower's risk (which is due to doubts about actually earning the prospective yield that is hoped for) are likely to drive a wedge between the usual market interest rate and the marginal efficiency of capital, which can vary over time.

In the second chapter, he notes that the returns to investment depend on circumstances that will exist in the future, which will affect how much firms will be able to sell in future, which depends on future market prospects, about which they are *uncertain*. To make decisions about investment, therefore, firms depend on their psychological expectation in the longer term when the investment projects will actually yield returns. He calls this the state of long-term expectation, which is different from short-term expectation, which he sees as guiding the production decision of firms. Much of this chapter deals with how firms and people make investment and other decisions under uncertainty. That Keynes laid great emphasis on the importance of uncertainty is shown in a paper published a year after the *GT*. In this paper, which reviews the central ideas of his theory, he states that his two main departures from orthodox (or what he calls classical) theory are: (1) recognizing that knowledge about the future as uncertain; and (2) examining the supply and demand of output as a *whole*, that is what we call macroeconomics today. Commenting on the issue of uncertainty, Keynes (1937: 213–214) writes:

> By "uncertain" knowledge, let me explain, I do not mean merely to distinguish what is known for certain from what is only probable. The game of roulette is not subject, in this sense, to uncertainty ... The sense in which I am using the term is that in which the prospect of a European war is uncertain, or the price of copper and the rate of interest twenty years hence, or the obsolescence of a new invention ... About these matters there is no scientific basis on which to form any calculable probability whatsoever. We simply do not know.

Keynes is saying that uncertainty is different from risk, a distinction also made in a similar way by Frank Knight (1921), where *risk* exists when the expected outcome of a future event is known in terms of an objective probability distribution, either through repeated occurrences of the event under the same (or at least similar) conditions, or through logical reasoning, while uncertainty exists when no such objective probability distributions exist. Keynes argues that the state of long-term expectation depends not just on the most probable forecast of the future, but also on what he calls the *confidence* with which such a forecast is made, that is, "how highly we rate the likelihood of our best forecast turning out to be wrong. If we expect large changes but are very uncertain as to what precise form these changes will take, then our confidence will be weak" (*GT*: 148).[11] Keynes recognizes that not much a priori can be said about the state of confidence, and what we can say about it "must mainly depend on the actual observation of markets and business psychology" (*GT*: 149).

Keynes (1936, 1937) argues from such observation that people have devised a variety of techniques, "in a manner which saves our faces as rational, economic ... [people]" (Keynes, 1937: 214). First, they rely on facts about which they are more confident even though they may not be as relevant to the issue as facts about which people's knowledge is vague and scanty, so that present conditions are a very important guide to future conditions, much more than is suggested by past experience. This means that they largely ignore the prospect of future changes about which nothing is known unless there are clear reasons to expect changes in the future. Second, they assume that opinions embodied in actual prices of goods and financial instruments provide a correct assessment of future prospects. For instance, firms can use the price of stocks to guide their investments by taking it to be the stock market's valuation of their profitability. Third, they fall back on the judgment of the majority or average, that is, a conventional judgment, under the assumption that others are better informed than themselves.

A judgment based on these techniques may at times lead to fairly stable behavior patterns. However, at other times:

> being based on so flimsy a foundation, ... is subject to sudden and violent changes. The practice of calmness and immobility, of certainty and security, suddenly breaks down. New fears and hopes will, without warning, take charge of human conduct. The forces of disillusion may suddenly impose a new conventional basis of valuation. All these pretty, polite techniques, made for a well-panelled Board Room and a nicely regulated market, are liable to collapse. At all times the vague panic fears and equally vague and unreasoned hopes are not really lulled, and lie but a little way below the surface. (Keynes, 1937: 214–215)

It may be supposed that professional investors with expert knowledge beyond what is known by ordinary investors can correct the vagaries dependent on the mass psychology of many ignorant individuals when it comes to determination of the price of financial assets such as stocks. This, however, is not so, since these experts are trying to ascertain how to obtain returns by buying assets, the prices of which are affected by mass psychology. Keynes writes that:

> professional investment may be likened to those newspaper competitions in which the competitors have to pick out the six prettiest faces from a hundred photographs, the prize being awarded to the competitor whose choice most nearly corresponds to the average preferences of the competitors as a whole; so that each competitor has to pick, not those faces which he himself finds prettiest, but those which he thinks likeliest to catch the fancy of the other competitors, all of whom are looking at the problem from the same point of view. It is not a case of choosing those which, to the best of one's judgment, are really the prettiest, nor even those which average opinion genuinely thinks the prettiest. We have reached the third degree where we devote our intelligences to anticipating what average opinion expects the average opinion to be. And there are some, I believe, who practise the fourth, fifth and higher degrees. (*GT*: 156)

Thus:

> our decisions to do something positive, the full consequences of which will be drawn out over many days to come, can only be taken as a result of animal spirits – of a spontaneous urge to action rather than inaction, and not as the outcome of a weighted average of quantitative benefits multiplied by quantitative probabilities ... Thus if the animal spirits are dimmed and the spontaneous optimism falters, leaving us to depend on nothing but a mathematical expectation, enterprise will fade and die; though fears of loss may have a basis no more reasonable than hopes of profit had before. (*GT*: 161–162)

Several implications follow from this analysis, especially about investment behavior. First, animal spirits may be depressed for long periods of time, resulting in low levels of investment and aggregate demand, which can make unemployment persist. Second, small changes in the economy can, at times, lead to large changes in expectations, since the expectations are based on rather flimsy foundations. Third, as Keynes discusses in chapter 22 of the *GT* on the trade cycle, there are likely to be alternating periods in which optimism about the future leads to further optimism, which makes investment and output increase, and in which pessimism leads to further pessimism, reducing aggregate demand and output. Fourth, a reduction in the interest rate may do little to restore investment spending and output when animal spirits are low and investors believe the future to be bleak. But what determines the interest rate or, rather, the different rates of interest in the economy?

4.   MONEY AND INTEREST

According to Keynes's classical economics, the interest rate is determined by the demand for and supply of loans, which in turn is determined by investment and saving, as shown in Figure 5.2. In this figure, the level of saving (and possibly investment) depends, in addition to the interest rate, on the levels of income and production, but this is at the full employment level determined in the labor market at the intersection of the demand and supply curves, as shown in Figure 5.1. According to this theory, the interest rate can be seen as being equal to psychological propensity to trade current consumption for future consumption, as reflected by the saving curve.

For Keynes this is an inadequate theory for understanding interest rate determination, for two main related reasons. First, as seen in section 2, his general theory implies that output and income are not necessarily at the full employment level and that they are determined by the demand and supply of goods, which allows unemployment to exist. Considering the case in which saving depends on income, different levels of income imply different saving curves, and therefore different levels of the rate of interest that equated saving and investment. Thus, the saving-investment diagram cannot determine the equilibrium interest rate without specifying what determines the level of income and output. Keynes's only diagram in the *GT*, in chapter 14, shows this indeterminacy of the interest rate using saving and investment curves with different saving curves for different hypothetical levels of income. Second, Keynes argues in chapter 13 that the interest rate is not determined by saving and investment but by money supply and what he called liquidity preference, or the demand for holding money.

In chapters 13 and 15, Keynes distinguishes between three motives for holding money:

(1)   the transactions motive (from the public and businesses to bridge the gap between their payments and their receipts);
(2)   the precautionary motive (to make payments for unexpected contingencies, including those for unforeseen advantageous purchases and for meeting future liabilities that are fixed in terms of money);
(3)   the speculative motive (to benefit from possible changes in the price of assets through purchases and sales of these assets).

The total demand for money can be expected to increase with real income and production as well as the price level (because more money is needed for transactions and precautionary purposes). Demand for money can also be expected to fall with the interest rate, other things constant, since most forms of money yield no interest payments, so that wealth holders lose more by not lending or buying interest yielding assets by holding money. But why do people hold money despite the fact that it yields no (or little) interest?

Keynes argues that this is because the return to money depends not only on the current rate of interest but also on the future rate of interest, and with active markets for securities, on the future price of these securities. The future rate of interest, however, is uncertain, and issues similar to those discussed in the previous section about investment are relevant in the decision of how much money to hold. A change in the current rate of interest is likely to affect expectations about the future rate of interest, and hence the expected change in the interest rate and the price of assets like bonds. The expected future rate is affected by the convictions of asset holders. Keynes (*GT*: 203) states that "*Any* level of interest which is accepted with sufficient conviction as *likely* to be durable *will* be durable, subject, of course, in a changing society to fluctuations for all kind of reasons round the expected normal" (emphasis in original). Expectations regarding the future policy of the monetary authorities can therefore affect expected future interest rates. Keynes also argues that people hold money in part to have liquidity, or to postpone decisions in the face of uncertainty about the future. Of all the assets people can hold, money holds its value best in terms of itself (by definition), and money is the thing in terms of which the prices of most goods bought and sold are set, and in terms of which most of the debt is held, which makes it have a high degree of liquidity in making payments. Holding other assets exposes people to the chance that they have to sell these assets (at prices that are not known now) to obtain money to buy what they need.

In some cases, when uncertainty is high and people expect the interest rate to increase (so that the price of assets would fall), people may just hold on to money as in a "bottomless sink for purchasing power" (Keynes, *GT*: 231), which does not increase the aggregate demand for goods and employment. This is because of what Keynes calls the two essential properties of money (discussed in chapter 17). First, it has a zero elasticity of production and employment (that is, an increase in money supply when its demand increases does not increase employment, and thereby income and aggregate demand). Second, it has a zero or very low elasticity of substitution (that is, having too much of it does not lead to its substitution towards other goods or assets that can directly or indirectly increase aggregate demand and output). The result is that people can hold more and more money in a bottomless sink without there being a reduction in the interest rate and increase in aggregate demand, and the economy can get stuck in a situation with unemployment.

5.   THE EFFECTS OF WAGE FLEXIBILITY

As mentioned earlier, in presenting his theory of employment Keynes initially assumes that the money wage is given and he notes that unemployment does not lead to a reduction in the (average) money wage because workers resist money wage reductions since they are concerned about their relative wage. But what happens if the money wage is actually flexible and falls when there are unemployed workers? Is it possible, as neoclassical theory states, that a fall in the money wage induces employers to increase employment and thereby bring about a reduction in unemployment?

In chapter 19 of the *GT*, Keynes answers that this depends on how the money wage reduction affects aggregate demand for goods, which works in a number of ways. The wage reduction results in some reduction in the average price level because of the lower costs of production,[12] so the effect of both wage and price reductions has to be examined. First, there is a shift in income from wage earners to other recipients of income (if the money wage falls more than the price level) and from entrepreneurs whose profits depend on the price to rentiers with fixed money incomes. Such redistributions are likely to reduce aggregate demand since wage earners typically have a higher propensity to consume than other income recipients (because their income is lower) and if entrepreneurs have a lower propensity to consume than rich rentiers. Second, if the reduction of the money wage makes firms expect further reductions in the money wage, they may postpone investment spending, thereby reducing aggregate demand (although, if no further wage reductions are expected, the opposite can happen). Third, if it leads to labor unrest and therefore disturbs political confidence and increases uncertainty, the demand for money can increase, reducing aggregate demand. Fourth, it can make heavily indebted entrepreneurs insolvent because of a reduction in their revenues, and this is likely to reduce investment spending. In general, price reductions will increase the real burden of both private and public debt, which is likely to reduce real aggregate spending. Keynes also notes that wage and price reductions can have a positive effect on aggregate demand. First, they can reduce the demand for cash for spending purposes, which can reduce the rate of interest as people lend out their cash, thereby increasing investment; this effect has come to be called the Keynes effect. Second, the reduction in the wage increases profits for individual firms, and, other things constant, may increase business optimism and, therefore, investment. Third, for an economy that is open to foreign trade, a fall in the wage and price has the effect of making domestic goods relatively cheaper than foreign goods, and this is likely to increase aggregate demand by increasing exports and reducing imports. Overall, a reduction in the wage and price is *unlikely* to increase employment since, especially in conditions of unemployment and low levels of aggregate demand, the negative effects are more likely to outweigh the positive effects, especially in economies that are relatively closed.[13] Making wages more flexible, moreover, is likely to lead to more uncertainty about the future, and reduce investment by entrepreneurs. Keynes argues that the chief result of such a policy "would be to cause a great instability of prices, so violent perhaps as to make business calculations futile in an economic society functioning after the manner of that in which we live. To suppose that a flexible wage policy is a right and proper adjunct of a system which on the whole is one of *laissez-faire*, is the opposite of the truth" (*GT*: 269).

6. ECONOMIC POLICY AND THE ROLE OF THE STATE

The policy implications of Keynes's *GT* need to be understood in terms of his overall social philosophy, which he discusses in the final chapter of the *GT*, where he states that "[t]he outstanding faults of the economic society in which we live are its failure to provide for full employment and its arbitrary and inequitable distribution of wealth and incomes" (*GT*: 372). With wage reductions unlikely to reduce unemployment (see section 5), Keynes discusses the possibility of using government policies to directly increase aggregate demand.

An increase in money supply through open market purchases of government securities by the Central Bank can be used to increase aggregate demand by reducing the interest rate and increasing investment. However, Keynes argues that the rate of interest is influenced by many factors, including uncertainty and expectations, which makes it very difficult for monetary policy to influence the interest rate, as discussed in section 4. And even if monetary policy does influence the interest rate, investment is affected by long-term expectations, as discussed in section 3, which the government is unlikely to affect in a way that will keep investment at a high level. As Keynes says, if "we are tempted to assert that money is the drink which stimulates economic activity, we must remind ourselves that there may be several slips between the cup and the lip" (chapter 13), particularly when the interest rate is very low.

For Keynes, fiscal expansion – increasing government spending and reducing taxes – can have an important role in expanding aggregate demand directly and therefore reducing unemployment. Moreover, fiscal policy that leads to a more equal distribution of income can increase consumption demand and reduce unemployment (*GT*: 95). However, Keynes does not argue that fiscal expansion is always expansionary, or that general fiscal expansion is always a good idea. He states (*GT*: 220):

> "To dig holes in the ground", paid for out of savings, will increase, not only employment, but the real national dividend of useful goods and services. It is not reasonable, however, that a sensible community should be content to remain dependent on such fortuitous and often wasteful mitigations when once we understand the influences upon which effective demand depends.

He even recognizes that "[w]ith the confused psychology which often prevails, the government programme may, through its effect on 'confidence', increase liquidity-preference or diminish the marginal efficiency of capital, which, again, may retard other investment unless measures are taken to offset it" (*GT*: 120). In general, he seems to be in favor of maintaining a surplus in the government's "ordinary" budget for current spending, with the capital budget on government investment spending kept at a high level (Skidelsky, 2010: 100). On public investment, Keynes opined that government is in a better position to make investment decisions on the basis of "general social advantage", and take "an ever greater responsibility for directly organising investment" (*GT*: 164). He argued that a "somewhat comprehensive socialisation of investment will prove the only means of securing an approximation to full employment; though this need not exclude all manner of compromises and of devices by which public authority will co-operate with private initiative" (*GT*: 378). While calling for the reduction of inequality and the "socialization" of investment, Keynes favored the decentralized market system because of its efficiency and because of its emphasis on "individualism, [which] if it can be purged of its defects and its abuses, is the best safeguard of personal liberty in the sense that, compared with any other system, it greatly widens the field for the exercise of personal choice" (*GT*: 380).

Keynes also had views on whether or not the kinds of policies and the role of the state he had in mind would in fact be politically feasible. While he expressed no definitive views on the issue, he argued in the concluding pages of the *GT* that:

> [T]he ideas of economists and political philosophers, both when they are right and when they are wrong, are more powerful than is commonly understood. Indeed the world is ruled by little else. Practical men, who believe themselves to be quite exempt from any intellectual influences, are usually the slaves of some defunct economist. Madmen in authority, who hear voices in the air, are distilling their frenzy from some academic scribbler of a few years back. I am sure that the power of vested interests is vastly exaggerated compared with the gradual encroachment of ideas ... [S]oon or late, it is ideas, not vested interests, which are dangerous for good or evil. (*GT*: 383–384)

Whether or not Keynes underestimated the power of vested interests, he seems to be right on the mark in saying that there is great value in developing proper theories to understand the world and to guide policies, if not right away, at least a few decades later.

7. KEYNES'S METHOD

In the preface to the *GT*, Keynes confessed that the writing of the book has been for him:

> a long struggle of escape ... from habitual modes of thought and expression. The ideas which are explained here so laboriously are extremely simple and should be obvious. The difficulty lies, not in the new ideas, but in escaping from the old ones, which ramify, for those brought up as most of us have been, into every corner of our minds. (*GT*: xxiii)

The old ideas from which he was escaping involved not only his views on the economic theory and policy, but also some features of his method of analysis. Three aspects of this method should be mentioned.

First, Keynes's method, as noted earlier, looks at the economy as a whole, in terms of his notions of aggregate demand and aggregate supply, rather than looking at individual actors and markets, which are then brought together. Keynes (1937: 219) states that one of his major differences with "traditional theory concerns its apparent conviction that there is no necessity to work out a theory of the demand and supply of output as a whole", which led that theory to at least implicitly assume Say's Law, or the doctrine that the supply of goods creates its own demand. This holistic approach in the *GT* is explained and anticipated in some of his earlier writings. Keynes (1921: 267–268) discusses the atomic hypothesis, usually adopted for the study of natural phenomena, according to which the material universe consists of "*legal atoms*, such that each of them exercises its own, separate, independent invariable effects, a change of the total state being compounded of a number of separate changes each of which is solely due to a separate portion of the preceding state ... Each atom can, according to this theory, be treated as a separate cause." He distinguishes his approach to the world of social relations where "[w]e are faced at every turn with the problem of Organic Unity, of Discreteness, of Discontinuity ... the whole is not equal to the sum of the parts, comparisons of quantity fail us, small changes produce large effects" (Keynes, 1933: 232–233). In fact, in his theoretical work published before the *GT*, Keynes (1930: Books III and IV) had already developed a framework for examining the theory of the economy as a whole. He used the "fundamental equations" to analyze the determination of the price level in a static model in which the level of aggregate output is given and to analyze the determination of the levels of price, output and employment over a sequence of periods (see Dutt and Amadeo, 1990: 31–36).

Second, although some of the chapters of the *GT* follow the marginalist approach in which firms maximize profits (yielding the condition that the real wage equals the marginal product of labor) and individuals maximize utility, in much of the book, he eschews the maximizing approach, and conducts his discussion in terms of fundamental psychological laws, animal spirits and conventional behavior. The *GT* can thus be interpreted as reflecting a struggle to escape from the method in which all decisions are examined in terms of constrained optimization.

Third, although the *GT* has many symbols, functions, equations and mathematical derivations, much of the book is written in literary prose. Money demand is assumed to be a function of income and the interest rate, but it also depends on uncertainty and expectations, which are subject to sudden changes, so the function is not a stable one. A money wage reduction has complex effects on aggregate demand and employment, which are not analyzed using mathematical relations. Keynes seems to have nothing against the use of mathematics in economics in general, but recognizes its limits and appearance of spurious precision. In fact, he writes that "[t]oo large a proportion of recent 'mathematical' economics are merely concoctions ... which allow the author to lose sight of the complexities and interdependencies of the real world in a maze of pretentious and unhelpful symbols" (*GT*: 298).

8. CONCLUSION

Keynes was not the first economist to understand the importance of aggregate demand and the role of the government in reducing unemployment. In chapter 23 of the *GT* Keynes acknowledges the earlier contributions of the mercantilists who flourished before Adam Smith, especially the views of Bernard Mandeville (who argued that greed and consumption leads to economic prosperity), the arguments made in favor of usury laws, the views of Malthus (who argued, against the doctrines of Smith and Ricardo, that over-saving can lead to a general glut of commodities), and even of his contemporaries, John Hobson and Silvio Gesell. Thus, he was well aware that his theory of employment, interest and money was not completely novel, but had a long tradition, although not a well-developed theory, behind it. Keynes could also have mentioned the writings of Karl Marx on the monetary circuit in which capitalists want to increase their money capital through the production process, rather than producing commodities to buy other commodities, on the hoarding of money and the credit system, and on the realization crisis, in which some of the produced goods cannot be sold due to the insufficient demand for them.

Keynes's analysis has some similarities with those of some of his contemporaries. Proponents of the Stockholm school followed Knut Wicksell, who distinguished between the natural rate of interest (as determined by saving and investment decisions) and examined in terms of the analysis of the income-expenditure process by which output and employment can fall below full employment (see Jonung, 1991). The Polish economist, Michał Kalecki (1971) came even closer to Keynes by developing a theory of profits, output and demand, in which output is determined by consumption and investment demand, and in which income distribution, determined by what he called the degree of monopoly, affected aggregate demand and output. Kalecki also argued that wage-price deflation is unlikely to take the economy to full employment.

For a variety of reasons, however, Keynes's analysis of aggregate demand and unemployment is by far the most well-known and popular. In fact, the subsequent history of macroeconomics can be seen as partly interpreting (and often misinterpreting) what Keynes said using mainstream economic tools, in rescuing what some have seen to be the true message of Keynes and building on it, and in reacting to it by attempting to show how involuntary unemployment does not exist and why activist government policy is unnecessary, ineffective or actually harmful. But whether debunked, misinterpreted or properly interpreted and developed, whether read, talked about without reading it, or rediscovered (especially after the recent global financial crisis), Keynes's *General Theory* remains the most influential work of modern macroeconomics.

NOTES

1. For a classic account of the Great Depression, see Kindleberger (1973).
2. See Skidelsky (2010), which draws on his monumental three-volume life of Keynes, for a short discussion.
3. The book is very much worth reading, although some parts of it are rather opaque, and not only for the uninitiated reader. For an accessible discussion of its chapters and some more recent debates about them, see Chick (1983).
4. Classical theory is now referred to as that based on theory developed by Adam Smith, Thomas Robert Malthus, David Ricardo, and John Stuart Mill, among others (see chapter 1 of this book), to which Karl Marx (in some interpretations) is also seen as a contributor (see chapter 2 for a discussion of Marx). What Keynes meant by classical theory is more accurately called marginalist or neoclassical theory, whose proponents included Alfred Marshall, Francis Y. Edgeworth and A. C. Pigou (see chapter 3). Keynes may have put the two groups together because most of the proponents of both schools ignored the issue of aggregate demand by adopting some version of Say's Law. We will distinguish the two with the names actual classical theory or economists and Keynes's classical theory or economists.
5. Some of the actual classical economists argued that people supply some goods only because they demand other goods (to obtain the income by selling the former to buy the latter), so that on aggregate, the supply and demand for goods are by definition equal. If saving is done by some people and organizations and investment is done by others, and investment is financed by loans, this definitional equality breaks down.
6. This is a partial list of assumptions he makes, as summarized in chapter 18 of the *GT*, entitled "The general theory of employment restated".
7. Keynes focuses on the notion that the main determinant of consumption is income, but notes in chapters 8 and 9 of the *GT* that consumption is also affected by a number of objective conditions (such as capital gains on wealth, fiscal policy, and interest rates) and subjective or psychological propensities (such as habits, financial prudence in the face of an uncertain future).
8 A popular and the simplest presentation of the Keynesian approach is usually shown with real output rather than employment on the horizontal axis, following Samuelson's (1939) presentation, where equilibrium is determined where aggregate demand (consumption plus investment) intersects the 45 degree line. In the presentation shown here the *AD* and *AS* curves are drawn with employment rather than output on the horizontal axis, both because it is closer to Keynes's own analysis (although, as noted earlier, measuring values of income and output rather than real amounts in the version discussed here), and because it shows both the aggregate demand and aggregate supply sides explicitly.
9. Keynes discusses short-term and long-term expectations in chapter 5 of the *GT*. Keynes does not refer to short-term expectations explicitly as price expectations; but, with his usual assumption of pure competition and price taking behavior, it is reasonable to assume that firms have a given price expectation in choosing employment and output, given the money wage.
10. Keynes states that the concept was developed by Richard Kahn (1931), a member of Keynes's inner circle of economists at Cambridge. Keynes did not take the multiplier

to be a given number, since its magnitude depends on expectations about the future (see Skidelsky, 2010: 98).

11. Keynes's theory of uncertainty is related to his earlier work, *A Treatise on Probability* (Keynes, 1921), in which he shifts the discussion of cause and chance from material and physical connections to the study of knowing and believing. For Keynes, probability consists of logical relations between propositions and depends on the amount of knowledge available in a world with limited knowledge. With limited knowledge, additional information regarding something may increase, if not the probability, the "weight" of the argument.

12. In fact, in Keynes's formal theory, for a given level of employment, the fall in the money wage leads to a proportional reduction in the price level, according to the condition that the real wage is equal to the marginal product of labor at that level of employment.

13. Keynes could have added even in open economies for which other countries also face wage and price reductions due to low levels of aggregate demand for them under conditions of global depression.

REFERENCES

Chick, Victoria (1983). *Macroeconomics after Keynes: A Reconsideration of the General Theory*, Cambridge, MA: MIT Press.

Dutt, Amitava Krishna and Amadeo, Edward J. (1990). *Keynes's Third Alternative*, Aldershot, UK: Edward Elgar Publishing.

Fisher, Irving (1930). *The Theory of Interest*, London and New York: Macmillan.

Jonung, Lars (ed.) (1991). *The Stockholm School of Economics Revisited*, Cambridge, UK: Cambridge University Press.

Kahn, Richard F. (1931). "The relation of home investment to unemployment", *Economic Journal*, 41(162), 173–198.

Kalecki, Michał (1971). *Selected Essays on the Dynamics of the Capitalist Economy*, Cambridge, UK: Cambridge University Press.

Keynes, John Maynard (1921). *A Treatise on Probability*, London: Macmillan.

Keynes, John Maynard (1930). *A Treatise on Money: Vol. 1: The Pure Theory of Money*, London: Macmillan, St. Martin's for the Royal Economic Society, 1971.

Keynes, John Maynard (1933). *Essays in Biography*, London: Harcourt, Brace.

Keynes, John Maynard (1936). *The General Theory of Employment, Interest and Money*, London: Macmillan.

Keynes, John Maynard (1937). "The general theory of employment", *Quarterly Journal of Economics*, 51(2), February, 209–223.

Kindleberger, Charles P. (1973). *The World in Depression, 1929–1939*, revised and enlarged edition, 1986, Berkeley, CA: University of California Press.

Knight, Frank (1921). *Risk, Uncertainty and Profit*, Boston and New York: Houghton Mifflin Co.

Samuelson, Paul A. (1939). "Interactions between the multiplier analysis and the principle of acceleration", *Review of Economics and Statistics*, 21(May), 75–78.

Skidelsky, Robert (2010). *Keynes: The Return of the Master*, New York: PublicAffairs.

6. Michał Kalecki

Malcolm Sawyer

KEY FEATURES

- Kalecki's development of the idea that the determination of economic activity is based on aggregate demand.
- Kalecki's analysis of investment, in which investment decisions are based on changes in the level of economic activity and by profitability.
- Kalecki's analysis of money, and how it has to be created to enable expenditure, private and public, to be financed.
- Kalecki's development of the 'degree of monopoly' and its relevance for the determination of the mark-up of price over costs, and the implications for the shares of profits and wages in national income and for the real wage.
- Kalecki's view that the capitalist economies were generally characterised by unemployment of labour and spare capacity, and the roles of budgetary policy and re-distribution of income in the achievement of full employment.
- Kalecki's use of the relationships between sectoral balances.

1. INTRODUCTION

Michał Kalecki was born in 1899 into a Polish-Jewish family in Łodz, Poland, then occupied by Russia. His academic training was in the field of engineering though his formal education, after an interruption for military service, was brought to an end by his father's unemployment. He was self-taught in economics. His employment during the 1920s varied widely, from making credit ratings of firms applying for loans, to undertaking market research and economic and political journalism. In 1929, he obtained his first quasi-academic employment at the Research Institute of Business Cycles and Prices in Warsaw, where his work involved the study of business cycles and the preparation of reports on specific industries. During the first half of the 1930s, Kalecki published a series of papers which form the basis of the claim that he published some of the key ideas developed by Keynes (1936) in *The General Theory of Employment, Interest and Money* before Keynes himself.[1] Kalecki wrote a review of the *General Theory* in which he argued that:

> Mr Keynes's book, *The General Theory of Employment, Interest and Money* is, without any doubt, a turning point in the history of economics. It can be roughly divided into two fundamental parts:
> (1)   The determination of short-period equilibrium with a given productive apparatus, once the level of investment (per unit of time) is given;
> (2)   The determination of the volume of investment. (Kalecki, CWI, p. 223).

In the first part, Kalecki argued that, subject to some caveats, 'the first problem has been satisfactorily solved in Keynes's theory', and he presented his own 'interpretation of this part of Keynes's theory, arriving at his basic conclusions, following a slightly different route'. Kalecki then argued that in respect of determination of volume of investment Keynes's approach had 'serious deficiencies', which are summarised below.

Kalecki was awarded a Rockefeller Foundation Fellowship which enabled him first to travel to Sweden to study the Swedish school of economics. He travelled to England in April 1936 and made contact with Keynes, Joan Robinson and others. He resigned from his post in Poland in late 1936 in protest at limits on freedom of research, and an extension of his scholarship by eight months enabled him to stay in England. He eventually stayed and worked in England, initially on research projects in Cambridge and then in Oxford for most of the next ten years. During the Second World War, Kalecki was employed at the Oxford University Institute of Statistics, undertaking important independent work and contributing to the debates on economic policy. After working for the International Labour Office in Montreal in 1945 and 1946, Kalecki was appointed deputy director of a section of the economics department of the United Nations secretariat in New York at the end of 1946. At the UN, he supervised studies of food shortages and inflationary pressures in the post-war economies, and then contributed chapters on the economic situation in major countries for the *World Economic Report*. He resigned from the UN in 1954 in response to the appointment of a board of directors to exercise control over the *World Economic Report*, which was seen as resulting from American involvement in the work of the UN.

From the beginning of 1955 to his death in 1970, Kalecki's home was in Poland. Kalecki was heavily involved in the debates over the role of decentralisation and of workers' councils, the speed of industrialisation and the relative size of consumption and investment. In the second half of the 1950s, Kalecki was the Chairman of the Commission of Perspective Planning, but his official role was effectively ended in 1960. In the last decade of his life, Kalecki was heavily involved with problems of economic development, including seminars organised at the Academy of Sciences, Warsaw University and the Central School for Planning and Statistics.

Kalecki's writings have all been published in English in the seven volumes of Collected Works edited by Jerzy Osiatyński, and listed in the References. His writings on capitalist economies are largely in volumes I and II, planning and socialism in volumes III and IV and developing countries in volume V. Volumes VI and VII are entitled *Studies in Applied Economics*, and cover the periods 1927 to 1941 and 1940 to 1967 respectively.[2] In this chapter the focus is on Kalecki's main ideas relating to capitalist economies, and Kalecki (1971) provides a selection of the key papers.

2. INVESTMENT AND ECONOMIC ACTIVITY

There are many ideas associated with Kalecki, but I begin with two related ideas which have interesting overlaps with Keynes' *General Theory*. The first concerns the role of the level of aggregate (effective) demand for the determination of the level of economic activity, and the second concerns the central role played by investment in the level of and fluctuations in aggregate demand. However, there are notable differences in the ways in which Kalecki and Keynes analysed investment. While Keynes focused on the relationship between the marginal efficiency of capital and the rate of interest where the state of expectations and animal spirits in a world of fundamental uncertainty are important factors in that relationship, Kalecki's focus was on profitability and (changes in) economic activity. In his reviews of Keynes (1936), Kalecki noted that 'the volume of investment is then determined in Keynes's analysis by the equalization of the expected profitability and the rate of interest' (CWI, p. 230). Kalecki saw this as having two serious deficiencies. 'First, it does not say anything about the sphere of investment *decisions* of the entrepreneurs, who makes his calculations in "disequilibrium" on the basis of *existing* market prices of investment goods' (emphasis in original). The second point was that 'the growth of investment not only generates an increase in the prices of investment goods but also, ... stimulates a general recovery, producing a rise in prices and output in all sectors' leading to expectations becoming more optimistic and that 'a difference between the marginal efficiency of capital and the rate of interest will arise again'.

Kalecki developed a simple relationship between investment and profits of the form:[3]

$$P_t = \frac{C_0 + I_{t-w}}{1 - \lambda} \qquad (1)$$

where P is profits, C_0 constant part of capitalists' consumption, and I gross investment and λ is marginal propensity to consume out of profits. This equation was derived from two simple ideas that workers spend all their income (wages) whereas capitalists spend a proportion of profits according to capitalists' consumption function $C = C_0 + \lambda P$ and profits of capitalists are equal to their spending on consumption plus their spending on accumulation, $P = C + A$. Equation (1) has a 'multiplier' interpretation – an increase in constant component of capitalist consumption or an increase in investment leads to an increase in profits which is $1/(1 - \lambda)$ times the increase in expenditure.

In terms of equation (1), the direction of causation runs from right to left, that is from investment to profits. Kalecki summarised this as 'capitalists as a class gain exactly as much as they invest or consume, and if – in a closed system – they ceased to construct and consume they could not make any money at all' (Kalecki, CWI, p. 79). This was reflected in aphorism that was ascribed by Joan Robinson to Kalecki that 'the workers spend what they get, and capitalists get what they spend' (Robinson, 1966, p. 341), though it cannot actually be found in his writings.

An important feature of this general approach is that 'saving does not determine investment but, on the contrary, it is precisely investment which creates savings ... [as] investment always *forces* savings of the same amount' (Kalecki, CWI, p. 228, emphasis added). The use of the word 'forces' clearly indicates the causal nature of the investment-savings link. This view reverses the neo-classical perspective of the role of savings in respect of growth.

Kalecki undertook most of his analysis of aggregate demand and the level of economic activity within a framework of cyclical movements in economic activity. Steindl (1981) identified three versions of the analysis of the trade cycle made by Kalecki, each of them having a different view of the determinants of investment, and there are differences in the ways through which profits influence investment and the impact of the size of the existing capital stock on investment. The phenomenon of the business cycle was central to Kalecki's economic analysis of capitalism; and his discovery of the importance of aggregate demand for the level of economic activity was undertaken in the context of cyclical fluctuations. The central feature of Kalecki's explanation of the business cycle is the influence of investment on economic activity, and on the determinants of investment decisions. While Kalecki clearly developed mechanisms through which cyclical fluctuations would be generated, he did not succeed in developing a mathematical analysis which led to continuous fluctuations that neither die away nor explode. Kalecki struggled with the technical problem of finding a mathematical formulation which would generate self-perpetuating cycles (see Sawyer, 1996 for elaboration).

In 'Essays on the Business Cycle Theory' first published in Polish in 1933 (and in English in Kalecki, CWI, pp. 65–108) investment orders are an increasing function of gross accumulation and decreasing function of the volume of capital equipment. Profits are linked with accumulation (from consumption out of profits plus accumulation). The volume of fixed assets increases through new investment (minus depreciation), and there is a time lag between orders and deliveries of new equipment.

Kalecki envisaged a number of stages leading to investment occurring. The distinction is drawn between investment orders, production of investment goods and deliveries of finished equipment. There is a simple lag between orders and deliveries, but the recognition of the lag makes it reasonable to assume that the demand for investment (the orders) is fulfilled by supply (the deliveries). Any decision to increase investment expenditure can only come to fruition if finance is available, and the provision of finance through the banking system. Kalecki emphasised that the level of present investment was 'the result not of *present* but of *former* investment decisions, as ... a certain, relatively long, time is needed to complete the investment projects. This fact is of fundamental importance for the dynamics of an economic system' (Kalecki, CWI, p. 534, emphasis in original).

Consider, first, the role of change in economic activity: this leads into cyclical behaviour from the links that changes in economic activity influence investment which in turn influences the level of economic activity. Kalecki viewed 'the determination of investment decisions by, broadly speaking, the level and the rate of change of economic activity' as the pièce de résistance of economics (Kalecki, CWII, p. 435). This has similarities with the well-known multiplier-accelerator approach to cycles, though Kalecki highlighted some differences between his formulation and that of the Samuelson version, notably the role of changes in profits rather than changes in economic activity.

Second, the importance of profits on investment decisions arising from the capitalists striving to enhance profits and to do so through expansion of productive capacity. It is the prospects of future profits which are particularly relevant though the expectations of profits are heavily conditioned by current profits. This forms the basis of the mechanism of the cycle, which runs as follows. An increase in investment orders leads to a rise in production of investment goods (accumulation) which further stimulates investment activity. However, at some stage the capital stock begins to rise, and this initially slows down and then reverses the increase in investment orders.

The second version of Kalecki's approach to the business cycle (Kalecki, 1943b) makes this influence of the availability of finance clearer ('the inflow of new gross savings ... push forward the barriers set to investment plans by the limited accessibility of the capital market and "increasing risk"' (Kalecki, CWII, p. 164)), and also expresses the idea that previous additions to the capital stock have an adverse impact on current investment decisions. In addition, it brings in the demand prospects facing firms into the investment decisions. The firm's financial resources are based on its current savings, though, in Kalecki's terms, there is 'incomplete re-investment': that is, additional savings generate some additional investment but on a less than one-for-one basis. In this formulation, investment decisions on gross investment for the next period of time are here driven by replacement investment, the difference between net investment and rentiers savings as the availability of internal finance, the change in profits and negatively to the net addition to fixed capital equipment, all relating to the present time. In this formulation, Kalecki considered, but largely dismissed, the influence of the rate of interest.

In his final version Kalecki's discussion of investment decisions draws on the idea of looking at the parts of (existing) profits which are 'captured' by new investment. At the aggregate level, there is a rearrangement of profits between firms as well as some change in the level of profits. Kalecki then related the level of investment in a particular year to the rate of profit generated on that investment. Kalecki postulated two aspects of this. The first is that any new investment captures only a small proportion of the total increase in profits in a year, with the old equipment capturing the remainder. The profit accruing to the new equipment is taken as a proportion of the change in profits. The second aspect arises only from technical progress, which leads to new machines that are more productive than old ones, and the real costs of operating old machines rise through the introduction of new machines and the consequent increases in productivity and real wages. The profit on the old machines falls and is in effect transferred to the new machines. The profit yielded by old machines falls each year by a proportion of real labour costs, with the proportion larger, the greater the increase in productivity from technical progress.

There are two-way links between investment and profits: profits – investment at the firm level; and investment – profits at the aggregate level. Profits and the prospects for profits encourage investment at the level of the firm. The aggregate investment expenditure which takes place generates a corresponding amount of savings (in a closed private economy). Using a closed private economy to highlight the relationship, Kalecki argued that savings were undertaken predominantly out of profits, and often assumed as a first approximation that workers did not save, and hence investment expenditure in aggregate determined the volume of profits. If s_p is the propensity to save out of profits, and if there are no savings out of wages, then in a closed economy $s_p P = I$ where P is profits and I is investment with the direction of causation here running from investment to profits. This is an aggregate relationship between profits and investment. There is also a reverse direction of causation at the level of the enterprise, whereby the profitability of the enterprise will influence its investment decisions. Profits provide internal finance for investment, and the present level of profits influences expectation on future profits.

3.   THE DEGREE OF MONOPOLY, PRICES AND WAGES

Kalecki approached the relationships between prices, wages and costs in terms of the 'degree of monopoly'. Kalecki brought in the idea of the 'degree of monopoly' and the idea that the market power of firms in an industry was a strong factor in the determination of the mark-up of prices over costs.

Kalecki's formulation of price decisions evolved over time. The general approach is to view the price set by a firm for its output in terms of a mark-up over costs. The determinants of the mark-up and the nature of the costs to be included in Kalecki's analysis changed. Kriesler (1987, 2011) provides a detailed discussion of Kalecki's analysis of pricing and distribution, and he divided the discussion into three phases – covering the periods 1938–1939, 1939–1942 and 1943–1971. Kalecki's research work at Cambridge in 1938/39 related to prices and costs and his approach brought him into some disputes with Kahn, Keynes and Robinson, as discussed by Toporowski (2013) and Marcuzzo (2020), who writes that 'Keynes, Kahn and Robinson all joined in, criticizing Kalecki's finding in the Research Scheme project. Their main criticism was levelled at the notion of "degree of monopoly".'

At the level of the enterprise, the degree of monopoly is an approach to pricing behaviour. It expresses the simple notion that the market power which an enterprise possesses will strongly influence the mark-up of its price over its (production) costs. The extent of market power, in turn, depends on factors such as the dominance of the enterprise in its market, the barriers to entry into the industry, etc. In a paper which was published posthumously, Kalecki (1971) viewed the strength of trades unions and the organisation of collective bargaining as modifying the degree of monopoly. Essentially, the argument was that upward movement of money wages at the enterprise level may put pressure on the profit margin of the enterprise, if it is unable to fully pass on wage increases as price increases.

The first formulation came in 'The Determinants of Distribution of the National Income' (Kalecki, 1938). This was more in the profit maximising tradition and makes explicit reference to Lerner (1934). Kalecki wrote short-run marginal costs for an enterprise in terms of:

$$m = d_m + s_m + w_m + r_m \tag{2}$$

where subscript indicates marginal and d depreciation, s salaries, w wages and r raw materials.

The price can be written as:

$$p = c_a + d_a + s_a + w_a + r_a \tag{3}$$

where subscript a refers to average, and c is capitalist income (profits plus interest).

It is worth remarking on the separation of labour earnings into wages and salaries. At the time Kalecki was writing in the 1930s, wages were labour payments to manual workers and some non-manual workers paid on a weekly basis, and salaries were paid to non-manual workers on a monthly basis. The first sentence of Kalecki (1938) speaks of the analysis of the relative share of manual labour in the national income. There had been much discussion surrounding the constancy of the wage share (at around 40 per cent in the case of the UK) and often labelled Bowley's Law. In more recent times, it has referred to the constancy of the share of labour income, though the record has undermined the notion of a constancy of labour share. In this paper, Kalecki sought to use his approach to understand the constancy of the wage share.

He followed Lerner (1934) in calling $\mu = (p - m)/p$ the degree of monopoly and noting that for a firm that is profit maximising then μ is the reciprocal of the elasticity of demand for the firm's product.[4]

For a single firm with output x the following can be derived:

$$xp\mu = x.c_a + x.(d_a - d_m) + (s_a - s_m) + (w_a - w_m) + r_a - r_m \tag{4}$$

Summing over all firms gives:

$$\Sigma xp\mu = \Sigma x.c_a + \Sigma x.(d_a - d_m) + \Sigma(s_a - s_m) + \Sigma(w_a - w_m) + \Sigma(r_a - r_m) \quad (5)$$

Kalecki then made a range of approximations that marginal depreciation and salaries are small relative to their averages and that marginal wages are small relative to average wages, with average direct labour costs virtually constant. This leads to:

$$\Sigma xp\mu = (C + D + S) - (D\alpha + S\beta - W\gamma) \quad (6)$$

Dividing through by aggregate turnover (Σxp) would lead to the view that the relative share of gross capitalist income and salaries is 'with great approximation equal to the average degree of monopoly' (Kalecki, CWII, p. 9). Kalecki stated that this approach would not apply in 'free competition' as enterprises under 'free competition' had to close down or maintain a situation where marginal costs of labour and materials are higher than average costs.

In 'Degree of Monopoly and Distribution of Income' (CWII p. 209) Kalecki started from ideas of oligopolistic independence, where 'in fixing prices the firm takes into consideration its average price costs and the prices of other firms producing similar products'. This was expressed as:

$$p = mu + n\bar{p} \quad (7)$$

m, n are positive and $n < 1$ where $\bar{p}$ is the weighted average of all firms.

In this context Kalecki discussed the causes of changes in the degree of monopoly. Foremost amongst those causes are the degree of industrial concentration which facilitates collusion and sales promotion and advertising, with price competition being replaced by competition through advertising.

The distribution of national income is then derived in terms of Overheads + Profits = $(k - 1)(W + M)$ where k is determined by degree of monopoly, noting here that W refers to labour income in general.

The share of labour income w is then given by:

$$w = \frac{1}{1 + (k-1)(j+1)} \quad (8)$$

where j is the ratio of aggregate cost of materials to wage bill.

Kalecki then aggregated across enterprises (in an informal manner) to arrive at a comparable aggregate relationship. Hence, the share of wages is negatively related with k, j, and share of profits positively related. There is what has been termed the 'paradox of costs' that an increase in material costs would lead to an increase in profits and profit share. Kalecki also argued that there was a tendency for concentration to increase over the long term leading to a rise in the degree of monopoly. But it was not possible a priori to say how the relationship between wages and the price of raw materials would develop. Hence, he envisaged the share of profits to rise and that of wages to decline over time.

The degree of monopoly serves to set the real product wage at the level of the enterprise for the price sets the relationship between price and money wages, for given material costs. For example, from $p = (1+m).c$ (c being average direct costs) the following can be derived:

$$\frac{w}{p} = \frac{Q}{L}\left(\frac{1}{1+m} - \frac{f}{p}\right) \qquad (9)$$

where Q is output, L labour input, w an index of wages, and f an index of material costs. This has (at least) two significant implications. First, it suggests that the real product wage depends on the product market rather than the labour market, and that within the product market the degree of monopoly influences the real wage. Second, how real product wages move with the level of employment (and output) depends on the structure of average labour costs. If, for example, average labour costs are constant with respect to output, then real product wages will be constant with respect to employment.

4.   MONEY AND FINANCE

Although Kalecki was not considered a monetary economist, he was always aware of the role that the availability of finance played with regard to expenditure. Plans to spend can only proceed if there is prior possession of money to finance the expenditure. Kalecki used the working assumption that 'the financing of additional investment is effected by the so-called creation of purchasing power. The demand for bank credit increases, and these are granted by the banks' (Kalecki, CWI, p. 190). However, he argued that credit was generally available at the relevant prevailing rate of interest, though noting that banks could respond to an increased demand for loans by raising the corresponding rate of interest:

> [T]he possibility of stimulating the business upswing is based on the assumption that the banking system, especially the central bank, will be able to expand credits without such a considerable increase in the rate of interest. If the banking

system reacted so inflexibly to every increase in the demand for credit, then no boom would be possible on account of a new invention, nor any automatic upswing in the business cycle. ... Investments would cease to be the channel through which additional purchasing power, unquestionably the *primus movens* of the business upswing, flows into the economy. (Kalecki, CWI, p. 489)

In a similar vein, he argued that 'if this rate [of interest] were to increase sufficiently fast for the influence of the increase in gross profitability to be fully offset, an upswing would prove impossible' (Kalecki, CWI, p. 473).

In a similar vein, Kalecki recognised that public expenditure had also to be financed through provision of money. He noted that a fiscal expansion could come from 'the government obtaining large credits from the central bank and spending them on massive public works of one sort or another. In this case the money no doubt would be spent and this would result in increased employment' (Kalecki, CWVI, p. 175). In a similar vein, he spoke of 'starting up major public-investment schemes, such as construction of canals or roads, and financing them with government loans floated on the financial markets, or with special government credits drawn on their bank of issue' (Kalecki, CWI, p. 53). Similarly, 'the government raises credits in the central bank and uses them, e.g. to construct public service units' (Kalecki, CWI, p. 156). In this and similar discussions, Kalecki often emphasised the effects of government spending on profits and also the constraints on the level of economic activity imposed by balance of payments considerations.

Kalecki (like Keynes) viewed the rate of interest as a monetary phenomenon, and specifically not as a mechanism for bringing about the equality between savings and investment. Kalecki argued that the rate of interest cannot be determined by the demand for and supply of capital because 'investment automatically brings into existence an equal amount of savings'; 'Thus, investment "finances itself" whatever the level of the rate of interest' (Kalecki, CWII, p. 262).

A major feature of the lending by financial institutions to entrepreneurs comes from the 'principle of increasing risk'. This principle can be simply stated. The more a company wishes to borrow (relative to its profits and to its own wealth) the greater is the perceived risk (on the part of the potential lender and of the borrower) that the company will not be able to repay the loan (interest and principal). The lender will charge a risk premium to cover the greater risk exposure, and hence the cost of borrowing will rise with the volume of borrowing. But the higher cost would raise the risk of default and at some point the cost of borrowing may become prohibitive. Kalecki, in his paper on the principle of increasing risk, does not explicitly mention banks and their lending but rather is concerned with the cost of finance facing the individual firm where 'the entrepreneur is not cautious enough in his investment activity, it is the creditor who imposes on his calculation the burden of increasing risk, charging the successive portions of credits above a certain amount with a rising rate of interest' (Kalecki, CWI, p. 288). For the individual firm, for a given amount of entrepreneurial capital, the risk increases with the amount invested.

Kalecki viewed the 'principle of increasing risk' and the rising cost of finance as a significant factor limiting the expansion of the individual firm. He dismissed the significance of diseconomies of large scale and the limitations of the size of the market as constraints on the expansion of the firm. He continued by arguing that the amount of capital owned by the firm was a decisive factor in limiting the size of the firm. A firm's ability to borrow was limited by the amount of its own capital. Then the expansion of the firm depends on its savings out of current profits.

Over the course of the business cycle, an enterprise's ability to borrow from banks can be seen to depend on two sets of factors. On the one hand, there is the balance between loan repayment commitments and its flow of profits. The loan repayment commitments would depend, inter alia, on its past borrowing and the extent to which it has been able to repay loans based on borrowing from households in the form of bonds, equity, etc. On the other hand, the banks' willingness to lend may vary as their 'liquidity preference' and general optimism and pessimism varies. It is then a complex matter to say how the volume of borrowing in the form of loans and the relationship between loans and interest rates will vary during the course of the business cycle. There is no general prediction which can be given as to the co-movements of loans, the stock of money and interest rates over the course of the cycle.

5. UNEMPLOYMENT, FULL EMPLOYMENT AND BUDGET DEFICITS

Kalecki's 'working assumption' in respect of capitalist economies was that they operated with spare productive capacity and unemployment of labour. He contrasted capitalist economies, in terms of being demand constrained, with socialist economies, which were viewed as capacity and resource constrained, and developing economies, where employment was constrained by a lack of capital equipment.

Unemployment in capitalist economies was viewed as a result of inadequate demand, which in turn could be related to low investment and recession. Unemployment of labour was viewed as the usual condition of such economies, though the extent of unemployment fluctuates over the business cycle and full employment may be attained at the top of the business cycle. In general, Kalecki treated the quantity of productive capacity as sufficient to enable full employment of labour if there were sufficient aggregate demand. Inflation could well arise from aggregate demand beyond the scale of productive capacity and the full employment of labour.

Kalecki (1944b) argued that there would be the need for permanent budget deficits in the face of intentions to save exceeding intentions to invest. He criticised those who accepted that budget deficits would rise during economic downswings but who did not accept the arguments for the need for permanent budget deficits. He argued that 'there will emerge out of a consistent anti-cyclical policy a certain more or less stable level of private investment which by itself, i.e. without considerable assistance by loan expenditure of the public authorities, may fall short of the level required to "fill the gap" of savings out of a full employment income'. His criticisms were particularly directed against a 1944 White Paper on Employment Policy issued by the UK government which had proposed that, while the budget position should fluctuate over the business cycle, the principle that the budget must be balanced over a longer period was maintained. His arguments remain relevant in light of policies, such as those of the 'fiscal compact' of the EU, for a budget balanced over the business cycle. He argued that even if counter-cyclical measures were successful in stabilising effective demand, it did not follow that full employment would be achieved. The simple reason was that the relatively stable level of private investment may well fall below the level required to match savings out of full employment income.

When a budget deficit was required in order to sustain a high level of aggregate demand, Kalecki clearly set out the argument that the funding of a deficit did not constitute a problem.

In a sub-section headed 'Where does the money come from?', Kalecki (CWI, p. 358) wrote that 'the budget deficit always finances itself – that is to say, its rise always causes such an increase in incomes and changes in their distribution that there accrue just enough savings to finance it'; nevertheless, 'the matter is still frequently misunderstood' (and, of course, it is still).

Kalecki wrote that 'a solid of majority of economists is now [that is 1943] of the opinion that, even in a capitalist economy, full employment may be secured by a government spending programme, provided there is in existence adequate plan to employ all existing labour power, and provided adequate supplies of necessary foreign raw-materials may be obtained in exchange for exports' (Kalecki, CWI, p. 347). This was a view which he clearly supported, and he often placed some emphasis on the possible balance of payments constraints. Kalecki argued that the right balance between capital equipment and available labour, with sufficient capital equipment needs to employ all the available labour and to leave some capacity in reserve, would be needed to enable full employment without inflationary pressures.

Kalecki (1944) evaluated 'three ways to full employment' of which budget deficit was one, with re-distribution of income another one that Kalecki favoured. The stimulation of investment would contribute to aggregate demand, but Kalecki saw that there were severe limits to doing so. He argued that there would need to be continuing and cumulative stimulation of investment, and that the rate of interest, taxes on income and profits would have to be continuously reduced, or subsidies to investment continuously increased. The basis of the argument was that a high level of investment would lead to the capital: output ratio rising and the rate of profit declining, and to maintain a high level of investment would require measures to offset the effects of a declining rate of profit.

Kalecki warned that amongst those opposed to the idea that full employment can be achieved by government spending 'there were (and are) prominent so-called "economic experts" closely connected with banking and industry. This suggests that there is a political background in the opposition to the full employment doctrine, even though the arguments advanced are economic. That is not to say that people who advance them do not believe in their economics, poor though it is. But obstinate ignorance is usually a manifestation of underlying political motives' (Kalecki, CWI, p. 349).

Kalecki argued that in a laissez faire neo-liberal system the level of employment depends on what is termed confidence, for example, confidence is deemed to raise investment. Policy measures have then to be adopted to bolster the state of confidence, and any policy measure which is deemed to undermine confidence avoided: 'Hence budget deficits necessary to carry out government intervention must be regarded as perilous. The social function of the doctrine of "sound finance" is to make the level of employment dependent on the state of confidence' (Kalecki, CWI, p. 350).

Kalecki (CWI, pp. 347–356) foresaw a number of social and political obstacles to the achievement of prolonged full employment in a laissez faire capitalist economy. He argued that under sustained full employment 'the social position of the boss would be undermined, and the self-assurance and class consciousness of the working class would grow. Strikes for wage increases and improvements in conditions of work would create political tensions' (Kalecki, CWI, p. 351). He suggested that 'discipline in the factories' and 'political stability' would also be undermined. Full employment may involve significant wage inflation and a fall in work intensity and labour productivity along with a decline of 'discipline in the factories'. The volume of profits would be higher under full employment (and hence the rate of profit, though perhaps not the share), with money wage rises leading to rising prices (to protect profits) and a squeeze on rentier income. As the threat of dismissal ceases to play its threatening role, work intensity may be lower at full employment, and labour productivity thereby lower than otherwise.

6. SECTORAL BALANCES AND PROFITS

Kalecki made considerable use of the major components of national income (from the income perspective and the expenditure perspective) and of the balances between the sectors of the economy. Kalecki, as many have done subsequently, focused on three sectors – the domestic private sector, the government sector and the foreign sector, with the domestic sector often divided into households who receive labour income which is largely spent and firms (capitalists) who receive profits some of which is spent on consumption and who undertake investment in capital equipment.

In Kalecki's writings, the sectoral relations were often closely linked with the determination of profits. Kalecki (CWII pp. 239–246) started from the relationships for gross national product in terms of investment (I) plus export surplus (XS) plus government expenditure on goods and services plus capitalist consumption (CC) plus workers consumption. From the income side, gross national product is the sum of (post-tax) wages plus profits plus tax revenue. Putting these together yields

$$\text{Gross profits} = I + XS + BD - WS + CC$$

where BD is budget deficit and WS is workers' savings.

It is evident from this approach that a budget deficit has an effect similar to that of an export surplus so far as profits are concerned: 'The counterpart of the export surplus is an increase in the indebtedness of the foreign countries towards the country considered. The counterpart of the budget deficit is an increase in the indebtedness of the government towards the private sector' (Kalecki, CWII, pp. 245–246).

In his work on the role of the budget deficit in influencing the level of demand, and on the funding of the budget deficit by the corresponding net private savings (in a closed economy), Kalecki drew on the sectoral equations, namely that $(I - S) + (G - T) + (X - M) = 0$ where the first term is private investment I minus private savings, the second the budget deficit of government expenditure G minus tax revenues T, and the third term trade surplus of exports X minus imports M. Kalecki also used this framework in considering the possible evolution of industrialised economies following the end of the Second World War.

7. CONCLUDING COMMENTS

In Kalecki's analysis of capitalist economies, the levels of economic activity and thereby employment are determined by the level of aggregate demand. In turn, aggregate demand is heavily reliant on investment decisions. The implementation of investment decisions requires availability of finance, and the implementation generates corresponding volume of savings. The 'degree of monopoly' and market power are strong influences on the mark-up of prices over costs, and in turn on distribution of income between wages and profits and on real wages. The propensity to spend out of wages is substantially higher (and may be unity) than the propensity to spend out of profits, and the distribution of income between wages and profits influences the level of spending.

Joan Robinson (1977) wrote that 'Kalecki was able to weave the analysis of imperfect competition and of effective demand together and it was this that opened up the way for what goes under the name of post-Keynesian economic theory' (p. 14). The price-cost margin linked with the degree of monopoly, effective demand driven by investment, itself related with profits and capacity utilisation and differential savings propensities (out of profits and of wages) have formed the basis of a Kaleckian macroeconomics. Blecker and Setterfield (2019, Chapter 4) set out a broad ranging set of developments within Kaleckian macroeconomics based on these ideas.

NOTES

1. See Sawyer (2019) for further discussion on the relationships between Kalecki and Keynes.
2. Sawyer (1985) on *The Economics of Michał Kalecki* covers ideas on capitalist economies, and also on socialist planning and on development, and makes comparisons between Kalecki and Keynes, and Kalecki and Marx. López and Assous (2010) cover mainly Kalecki's writing on capitalist economies, though with a chapter each on development and socialist economies. Toporowski (2013, 2018) is a two-volume intellectual biography.
3. A first appearance comes in Kalecki (1933) without the lag on investment. The lagged formulation appears in Kalecki (1943b).
4. The paper 'The Supply Curve of an Industry Under Imperfect Competition' (Kalecki, 1940) is more explicitly in the use of a profit maximisation framework.

REFERENCES

References in the text to Kalecki's Collected Works are signified by Kalecki CWI where I is the volume number. The page numbers for quotes from Kalecki in the text refer to the Collected Works rather than the original place of publication.

The Collected Works of Michał Kalecki in seven volumes are:

Osiatyński, J. (1990) (ed) *Collected Works of Michał Kalecki Volume I Capitalism: Business Cycles and Full Employment*, Oxford: The Clarendon Press.
Osiatyński, J. (1991) (ed) *Collected Works of Michał Kalecki Volume II Capitalism: Economics Dynamics*, Oxford: The Clarendon Press.
Osiatyński, J. (1991) (ed) *Collected Works of Michał Kalecki Volume III Socialism: Functioning and Long-run Planning*, Oxford: The Clarendon Press.
Osiatyński, J. (1991) (ed) *Collected Works of Michał Kalecki Volume IV Socialism: Economic Growth and Efficiency of Investment*, Oxford: The Clarendon Press.
Osiatyński, J. (1991) (ed) *Collected Works of Michał Kalecki Volume V Developing Countries*, Oxford: The Clarendon Press.
Osiatyński, J. (1996) (ed) *Collected Works of Michał Kalecki Volume VI Studies in Applied Economics 1927–1941*, Oxford: The Clarendon Press.
Osiatyński, J. (1997) (ed) *Collected Works of Michał Kalecki Volume VII Studies in Applied Economics, 1940–1967*, Oxford: The Clarendon Press.

Blecker, R.A. and Setterfield, M. (2019) *Heterodox Macroeconomics: Models of Demand, Distribution and Growth*, Cheltenham: Edward Elgar Publishing.
Kalecki, M. (1932a) 'Is a "capitalist" overcoming of the crisis possible?' Przeglad Socjalistyczny, English translation in CWI, pp. 48–53.
Kalecki, M. (1932b) 'Inflation and War', reproduced in CWVI, pp. 175–179.
Kalecki, M. (1933) 'Essays on the Business Cycle Theory', first published in Polish, English translation in CWI, pp. 66–106.
Kalecki, M. (1936) 'Some remarks on Keynes's Theory', first published in Polish in *Ekonomista*; translation by B. Kinda-Hass in *Australian Economic Papers*, 21/32, pp. 245–253, reproduced in CWI, pp. 223–232.
Kalecki, M. (1937) 'The principle of increasing risk', *Economica*, 4(16), pp. 440–447.
Kalecki, M. (1938) 'The determinants of distribution of the national income', *Econometrica*, 6(2), pp. 97–112, reproduced in CWII, pp. 3–20.
Kalecki, M. (1940) 'The supply curve of an industry under imperfect competition', *Review of Economic Studies*, 7(2), pp. 91–122, reproduced in CWII, pp. 51–78.
Kalecki, M. (1943a) 'Political aspects of full employment', *Political Quarterly*, 14(4), pp. 322–331, reproduced in CWI, pp. 347–356.
Kalecki, M. (1943b) *Studies in Economic Dynamics*, London: Allen and Unwin, reproduced in CWII, pp. 117–190.
Kalecki, M. (1944a) 'Three ways to full employment' in Oxford University Institute of Statistics, *The Economics of Full Employment*, Oxford: Blackwell, reproduced in CWI, pp. 357–376.
Kalecki, M. (1944b) 'The White Paper on Employment Policy', *Bulletin of the Oxford University Institute of Statistics*, 6/8, pp. 137–144, reproduced in CWVII, pp. 238–244.
Kalecki, M. (1968) 'Trend and the business cycle', *Economic Journal*, 78(2), pp. 263–276, reproduced in CWII, pp. 435–450.

Kalecki, M. (1971) 'Class struggle and distribution of national income', *Kyklos*, 24(1), pp. 1–9, reproduced in CWII, pp. 96–103.

Keynes, J.M. (1936) *The General Theory of Employment, Interest and Money*, London: Macmillan.

Kriesler, P. (1987) *Kalecki's Microanalysis*, Cambridge: Cambridge University Press.

Kriesler, P. (2011) 'Kalecki's pricing theory revisited' in J. Halevi, G.C. Harcourt, P. Kriesler and J.W. Nevile (eds), *Post-Keynesian Essays from Down Under Volume 1: Essays on Keynes, Harrod and Kalecki. Theory and Policy in an Historical Context*, Houndmills: Palgrave Macmillan.

Lerner, A. (1934) 'The concept of monopoly and the measurement of monopoly power', *Review of Economic Studies*, 1, pp. 157–175.

López, J. and Assous, M. (2010) *Michał Kalecki*, Houndmills: Palgrave Macmillan.

Marcuzzo, M.C. (2020) 'Kalecki and Cambridge', *Review of Political Economy*, 32(4), pp. 500–510.

Ministry of Reconstruction (1944) *Employment Policy*, Cmnd 6527, London: HMSO.

Robinson, J. (1966) 'Kalecki and Keynes' in *Economic Dynamics and Planning: Essays in Honour of Michał Kalecki*, Oxford: Pergamon, pp. 335–341.

Robinson, J. (1977) 'Michał Kalecki on the economics of capitalism', *Oxford Bulletin of Economics and Statistics*, 39(1), pp. 7–17.

Sawyer, M. (1985) *The Economics of Michał Kalecki*, Basingstoke: Macmillan.

Sawyer, M. (1996) 'Kalecki on the trade cycle and economic growth' in John King (ed.), *An Alternative Macroeconomic Theory: The Kaleckian Model and Post Keynesian Economics*, New York: Kluwer, pp. 93–114.

Sawyer, M. (2019) 'Michał Kalecki' in Robert W. Dimand and Harald Hagemann (eds), *The Elgar Companion to John Maynard Keynes*, Cheltenham, UK: Edward Elgar Publishing, Chapter 57.

Steindl, J. (1981) 'Some comments on the three versions of Kalecki's theory of the trade cycle' in J. Los et al. (eds), *Studies in Economic Theory and Practice: Essays in Honour of Edward Lipinski*, Amsterdam, North Holland, reprinted in J. Steindl, *Economic Papers 1941–88*, London: Macmillan, 1990.

Toporowski, J. (2013) *Michał Kalecki: An Intellectual Biography, vol 1: Rendezvous in Cambridge 1899–1939*, Houndmills: Palgrave Macmillan.

Toporowski, J. (2018) *Michał Kalecki: An Intellectual Biography, vol 2: By Intellect Alone 1939–1970*, Houndmills: Palgrave Macmillan.

7. Thorstein Bunde Veblen

Guglielmo Forges Davanzati

KEY FEATURES

- This chapter deals with Thorstein Veblen's economic thought, with particular reference to his theory of conspicuous consumption and his theory of the firm.
- Veblen criticised the dominant (neoclassical) view that economic agents are perfectly rational, arguing that economic behaviour is driven by "institutions". He conceived institutions as the prevailing codes of behaviour. In his view, economic behaviour is profoundly affected by social norms, including emulation, instincts, power relations.
- He proposed an original approach to the determinants of consumption, based on the idea that it is based on emulation and that it is ostentative. The so-called Veblen goods are luxury goods and they are subject to the "Veblen effects": the quantity demanded rises when prices rise. Veblen's approach refers to the "leisure class" of the US of his time.
- Veblen also proposed an original theory of the firm. Contrary to the dominant view that the individual firm is a price-taker in perfectly competitive markets, he observed that capitalist firms can fix prices and stay competitive mainly via the acceleration of capital turnover.
- He conceived the firm as a locus of conflict between managers (interested in money profits) and "technicians" (interested in expanding production via innovation). He emphasised the role of the credit sector in selecting the most efficient firms.
- This process leads to the increase of industrial concentration.
- Although not explicitly, some Veblenian ideas are present in Schumpeter's thought. In particular, as shown in Chapter 8, the role of credit and the fundamental role of innovation and technical progress are at the core of Schumpeter's theory of economic growth.

1. INTRODUCTION: BIOGRAPHICAL ASPECTS

The study of Thorstein Veblen's work can be useful also for interpreting it in the light of the subsequent debate between Keynesians (see Chapter 5) and Austrians. Although only implicitly, both Keynesian economists and Austrian economists took from Veblen some important insights, related to Veblen's fundamental critique of the neoclassical view of instrumental rationality. In the *History of Economic Thought*, Veblen's critique is probably one of the first and most effective. As will be shown, Veblen maintains that economic behaviour is driven by institution, i.e. habits of thought, which cannot enter the neoclassical picture of an optimising *homo oeconomicus*. Both Keynesians and Austrians share this fundamental point. Moreover, while the emphasis on innovations will be present in the Austrian school (and relevant in Veblen), Veblen's emphasis on the role of demand – although not conceptualised as the standard Keynesian aggregate demand – will be crucial for the development of Keynesianism. Finally, Veblen's view that contemporary markets are not perfectly competitive will enter current post-Keynesian economics.

Born on 30 July 1857, Veblen was raised in the isolated Norwegian township of Wheeling, Rice County, Minnesota, and entered Carleton College Academy in 1874; he graduated three years later. He continued his studies at Johns Hopkins University, and then at Yale. As an undergraduate, he worked under John Bates Clark. In 1884, he finished his final dissertation for his PhD in philosophy (*The Ethical Grounds of a Doctrine of Retribution*), studying Immanuel Kant with Noah Porter and economics with the Social Darwinist William Graham Sumner. In 1892, after futile attempts to find teaching positions, he moved to Chicago and worked as a teaching fellow at the University of Chicago, mainly thanks to the interest of J. Laurence Laughlin, head of the economics department. In 1906, he became assistant professor of political economy. Because of his inability to keep his courses well organized (or more generally, because of his non-academic attitude), he had a difficult academic career: in December 1906 the Chicago administration forced him out for flagrant marital infidelities. In 1918 he worked for the Food Administration in the US government. He was one of the founders of the New School of Social Research in New York City and, from 1896, managing editor of the *Journal of Political Economy*. On 3 August 1929 he died from heart disease in the Menlo Park area (California).[1]

The work of Thorstein Bunde Veblen is not easy to classify, since it involves economic, sociological, anthropological and psychological reflections. This "eclecticism" may be seen both as the main cause of the long-term devaluation (if not oblivion) of his thought and, by contrast, as the principal reason for the interest that his reflections may hold for many contemporary economists. His profound analysis of the role of social norms in orienting agents' behaviour is of major importance in interpreting the functioning of market economies, where this interpretation is based on the idea that markets do not wok in an institutional *vacuum*.

Institutions are defined by Veblen as "prevalent habits of thought with respect to particular relations and particular functions of the individual and of the community" (Veblen, 1975 [1899], p. 190). They are selected in the process of social evolution, according to the principle of the "selective conservation of favourable variations" (i.e. natural selection), and, in turn, they affect the habits and customs of the community where they are accepted:

> Institutions are not only themselves the result of a selective and adaptive process which shapes the prevailing or dominant types of spiritual attitude and aptitudes; they are at the same time special method of life and of human relations, and are therefore in their turn efficient factors of selection. (ibid., p. 188)

In Veblen's view, the principle of selective conservation of favourable variations is at the basis of the genesis of institutions, according to two opposite forces:

(a)   "The development of [the] institutions is the development of society" (ibid., p. 190), because individuals – and hence society – tend to change their habits of thought as well as their behavioural models in response to the stimuli that external changes provide. This mechanism favours the emergence of new institutions.

(b)   By contrast, social and psychological inertia favours conservatism, therefore generating a twofold effect: (i) slowing the process of institutional change and (ii) amplifying the gap between present institutions and present widespread mental attitudes. In Veblen's words: "Institutions are products of the past process, are adapted to past circumstances, and are therefore never in full accord with the requirements of the present" (ibid., p. 191).

Inertia is seen both as a psychological as well as a social phenomenon. In the first case, Veblen refers to an "instinctive resistance" to change (ibid., p. 203). In the second case, inertia arises from the *non convenience* (on the part of the leisure class) and *non possibility* (on the part of the lower class) to try to modify the present institutional profile. The "leisure class" is a class which "[is] by custom exempt or excluded from industrial occupations, and [is] reserved for certain employments to which a degree of honour attaches" (ibid., p. 1). By contrast, the lower class is employed in industrial occupations. In Veblen's view, the privileges enjoyed by the leisure class act as an obstacle to social change, while the lack of "mental effort" and "nervous energy" does not allow the lower class to promote institutional innovations. Furthermore, the convenience of maintaining the existing institutions for the leisure class favours the widespread view that innovations imply chaos and social disorder (ibid., pp. 202–203).

In this chapter, we will provide a reconstruction of Veblen's economic thought, with particular reference to his theory of consumption and his view of the operation of capitalist firms. This chapter will present the basic Veblenian ideas on the determinants of the patterns of consumption and the operation of the capitalist firm. The chapter is organised as follows. Section 2 approaches Veblen's theory of consumption, section 3 deals with his theory of the firms and section 4 provides some concluding remarks.

2. VEBLEN'S THEORY OF CONSUMPTION

The concepts of conspicuous consumption, invidious comparison and the instinct of workmanship are at the basis of Veblen's theoretical framework. These concepts will be discussed now.

Conspicuous Consumption

Veblen argues that the primary motive for consumption, apart from the consumption devoted to satisfying basic needs, is *ostentation*. This particularly affects the leisure class – whose main aim is to preserve its *reputation*, as well as to keep the gap between its own living standard and that of the lower class[2] almost constant – and, as regards the class of goods, to preserve "the more desiderable things", such as "rare articles of adornment" (Veblen, 1975 [1899], p. 69). These goods (the so-called "Veblen goods") are not desired (only) for their intrinsic utility, insofar as they serve no other purpose apart from ostentation. They are desired because they are scarce, and, in the second place, because they fit the prevailing norms of taste (ibid., ch. VI). Furthermore, a Veblen good is a good for which the quantity demanded rises when its price rises:

> The consumption of expensive goods is meritorious, and the goods which contain an appreciable element of cost in excess of what goes to give them serviceability for their ostensible mechanical purpose are honorific. (ibid., pp. 154–155)

It is worth noting that Veblen goods do not rest on the contemporary idea that a positive price-quantity ratio is likely to occur in cases of asymmetric information problems. They do not presuppose that the quality of the product is unknown to the buyer. Accordingly, Veblen goods are such that a high price is per se a mark of *beauty* (see Edgell, 1999).[3] Moreover, ostentation involves waste (in Veblen's terms, this is "the law of conspicuous waste"). In *The Theory of the Leisure Class*, waste is defined as "usefulness as seen from the point of view of the generically human". As a matter of fact, this definition is rather ambiguous insofar as what "generically human" means is not further clarified by the author.

In reviewing *The Theory of the Leisure Class*, Cummings (1899) criticizes Veblen since "The economist accepts individual wants uncritically, and considers that expenditure economic which is direct to their satisfaction, that wasted which is not directed". Cummings is right if one accepts (as opposed to Veblen's view) the methodological viewpoint of the neoclassical approach (individualism), i.e. preferences are assumed to be exogenous and agents' choices are perfectly rational. Otherwise, by accepting Veblen's holistic methodology, Cummings's critique is nonsensical: *from the point of view of society as a whole*, conspicuous consumption is waste because it prevents some resources from being used in a *more efficient way*, primarily for the increase of real investment. In other words, rents acquired by the "leisure class" subtract resources from productive uses. As Bush (1999, p. 136) remarks, "the notion of the 'generically human' simply has no synonym in the classical/neoclassical lexicon. It is a notion that smacks of some sort of social conception of usefulness, which is beyond the reach of orthodox methodological individualism".

The Invidious Comparison

In *The Theory of the Leisure Class*, Veblen refers to envy as a strong motive to strive for success:

> The term ["invidious"] is used in a technical sense as describing a comparison of persons with a view to rating and grading them in respect of relative worth of value – in an aesthetic or moral sense – and so awarding and defining the relative degrees of complacency with which they may legitimately be contemplated by themselves and by others. *An invidious comparison is a process of valuation of persons in respect of worth.* (Veblen, 1975 [1899], p. 34, emphasis added)

Accordingly, the accumulation of wealth, and its consequent ostentation, is not the result of the purpose of satisfying needs, via consumption, but it is an intermediate goal in order to gain reputation, esteem and respect within a given social group.[4] In other words, consumption is not an end in itself, as in the standard neoclassical view: it is, above all, a *means to excel*.

The Instinct of Workmanship

This is typical of agents who are outside the leisure class, and – particularly – of those who are engaged in generating new knowledge. In Veblen's words (1975 [1899], p. 15): "As a matter of selective necessity, man is an agent [...]. He has a sense of the merit of serviceability or efficiency and of the demerit of futility, waste, or incapacity. This aptitude or propensity may be called the instinct of workmanship", and "idle curiosity" ultimately supports it. The instinct of workmanship involves the pleasure in useful work, the dislike of waste and the adoption of a way of thinking based on mechanical sequences. In this case, esteem is not gained via ostentation of consumption, but "by putting one's efficiency in evidence" (ibid., p. 16).

On the basis of the habits described above, Veblen analyses the functioning of a capitalistic economy by assuming the existence of four macro-agents:

(a)   the leisure class, whose aim is conspicuous consumption;
(b)   "businessmen" (i.e. managers), interested in making profits;
(c)   technicians who are engaged in producing new knowledge;
(d)   workers, whose aim is to obtain a wage level that ensures a desired standard of living, which, in turn, depends on the level of consumption they consider "fair" in given historical contexts. The perception of a *decent* living standard is largely affected by the ruling class: "It is for this class to determine, in general outline, what scheme of life the community shall accept as decent or honorific" (ibid., p. 104).[5,6] A *decent* standard of living is what is permitted by the subsistence wage, which – in Veblen's words (ibid., p. 107) – is "of course not a rigidly determined allowance of goods, definite and invariable in kind and quantity [...]. This minimum, it may be assumed, is ordinarily given up last in case of a progressive retrenchment of expenditure".

3.   THE THEORY OF THE FIRM

To Veblen, the capitalist firm is primarily a locus of conflict between managers and technicians. The conflict between businessmen and technicians is based on the two different and opposed goals they pursue and, as a result, on their different and incompatible habits of thought: i.e. the search for money profits versus the pursuit of knowledge. In other words, a conflict arises between the industrial way of thinking (*to make goods*) and the pecuniary way of thinking (*to make money*).[7] These different habits of thought produce two major economic effects: first, due to the effort of technicians and the support of the banking system, competition leads to the bankruptcy of smaller firms and, hence, to a movement towards a market configuration where monopolistic positions prevail; second, the financial control of firms by businessmen involves a policy of "sabotage", i.e. "a deliberate restriction of the productivity of capital and labor in order to keep prices and profits higher" (Hobson [1937] in Tilman, 2003, vol. II, p. 34). The technicians' aim of increasing productivity, via the use of new knowledge, and thus expanding production is in conflict with the businessmen's purpose of obtaining money profits.

Moreover, to Veblen, the firm appears as a pure bureaucratic structure that is able to produce only because of its exploitation of common "industrial knowledge". Knowledge is a public good that is appropriated by firms via legal rights – what Veblen calls "sabotage". In his own words:

> It appears [...] that the prime creative factor in human industry is the state of the industrial arts; that is to say, the determining fact which enables human work to turn out a useful product is the accumulated knowledge, skill and judgement that goes into work [...]. For the transient time being, therefore, any person who has a legal right to withold any part of the necessary industrial apparatus or materials from current use will be in a position to impose terms and exact obedience, on pain of rendering the community's joint stock of technology inoperative to that extent. (Veblen, 1994 [1923], vol. IX, pp. 62–65)

The notion of "sabotage" is linked to the propensity towards "predatory behaviours". In *The Theory of the Leisure Class*, Veblen writes: "Industry is effort that goes to create a new thing, with a new purpose given it by he fashioning hand of its maker out of passive ('brute') material; while *exploit, so far as it results in an outcome useful to the agent, is the conversion to his own ends of energies previously directed to some other end by another agent*" (1975 [1899], pp. 12–13, emphasis added).

As O'Hara maintains, "An important aspect of Veblen's theory of social wealth is the notion of *institutional exploitation*" (O'Hara, 1999, emphasis added). The idea is that human labour and knowledge (also "incorporated" into labour) are the main inputs for the production of social wealth. Wages are at the subsistence level and the surplus results in profits and rents, and profits derive from "predatory behaviours". The continuous production of surplus – over subsistence wages – and the establishment of the institution of property rights made the economic system class-based and allowed "parasitism" in favour of a "leisure class". Moreover, freed from productive labour, the leisure class became the *ruling class*: "The upper classes" – Veblen (1975 [1899], p. 1) writes – "are by custom exempt or excluded from industrial occupations, and are reserved for certain employment to which a degree of honour attaches. Chief among the honourable employments in any feudal community is warfare; and priestly office is commonly second to warfare." And, in the course of historical evolution, when the exercise of physical power lost importance, politicians became the most important part of the "upper classes".

Of course, the leisure class is interested in preserving its standard of living and privileges, and it is consequently interested in preserving the status quo. In order to achieve this end, two main devices are used:

- *Controlling education.* The ruling class is able to minimise possible worker discontent – and thus possible social conflict – by controlling the education system. In Veblen's view, the management of schooling by the ruling classes is a powerful institutional strategy for the purpose of transmitting habits of thought functional to the preservation of the existing socio-economic order. Hence, "schools [...] are shaped by and rest upon a leisure-class culture", based on humanities and erudition (Veblen, 1975 [1899], p. 391).
- *Controlling income distribution.* The ruling classes are also interested in keeping wages at the lowest level, or – according to Veblen – an unequal distribution of wealth is necessary (ibid., p. 205). The rationale for this thesis can be found in three points. First, for a given output, the greater the surplus available for conspicuous consumption (and for a given level of profits), the lower wages obviously are. Second, the greater the difference between the consumption of the leisure class and that of other classes, the more intense is the effect of ostentation on the aggregate plane. Third, the lower the workers' consumption level,[8] the lower their "available energy" to promote social conflict.

This picture, where ruling classes are able to control workers' possible tendencies to conflict, is a picture of a stationary economy and a stationary society, where conservative interests prevail. Veblen's main interest lies in his explaining institutional change "upon the materialistic framework to such an extent that the role of technology, economic action and institutions are to the forefront of all his major studies" (Edgell [1975] in Tilman, 2003, vol. I, p. 104).

Veblen maintained that it is technical advancement which ultimately promotes economic growth. This is not (only) because technical progress – as in the neoclassical model – determines an increase in productivity without causing unemployment, but mainly because it can modify the prevalent habits of thought with particular regard to workers. The effect of technical progress on the patterns of consumption is double.

First, Veblen maintained that the basic dichotomy with regard to *values* involves *waste versus efficiency*. In the case where workers internalise codes of behaviour oriented to efficiency, waste on the part of the leisure class becomes unacceptable, both on economic and on moral grounds. As a result, social conflict is likely to occur. However, Veblen was sceptical about the possibility that institutional change can be driven by social conflict:

> the institution of a leisure class acts to make the lower class conservative by withdrawing from them as much as it may of the means of sustenance, and so reducing their consumption, and consequently their *available energy*, to such a point as to make them incapable of the effort required for the learning and the adoption of new habits of thought. (Veblen, 1975 [1899], p. 204, emphasis added).

Second, particularly in the work *The Theory of Business Enterprise* of 1904, Veblen observed that, in the course of social evolution, firms tend to become larger and larger. The increase in firm size occurs above all because of the technical advancement, which – insofar as it produces economies of scale – generates the processes of mergers and acquisitions, affecting industrial concentration ratios. The pursuit of money profits – and the growing connections between industry and finance – lead, in Veblen's view and in normal conditions, to a kind of competition based on the acceleration of capital turnover. This strategy allows the individual firm to produce and sell *before* its competitors, gaining extra-profits. This is a case of *time-based competition*.

Furthermore, according to Veblen, advertising acts as a stimulus to increase working hours on the part of workers. This occurs because advertising creates *new needs* and, in order to satisfy them, workers are induced to work more (cf. Bowles and Park, 2002). Importantly, firms need finance from the banking system. They need credit because both innovation (via the acceleration of capital turnover) and advertising are costly. Veblen suggested that banks as a whole can create credit money *ex-nihilo*. Insofar as money is a social construct, the production of money does not face problems of scarcity and, as a consequence, no technical limits to its expansion are in order. In such a context, money supply is endogenous and demand-driven (Wray, 2007).

4.   CONCLUDING REMARKS

Although sometimes implicitly, Veblen's thought affected both the subsequent developments of the so-called radical institutionalism and the evolutionary political economy of the twentieth century. In particular, his idea that economic growth is basically driven by innovations produced by technicians can be considered as a fundamental contribution to the development of Schumpeter's approach to economic dynamics. Schumpeter argued that innovation does not only pertain to the economic sphere, implying that it profoundly affects habits of thought (even in the form of social resistance to innovation) and, more generally, the social and institutional environment. Moreover, the emphasis on the role of credit is a relevant part of Schumpeter's theory of economic growth, as well as the social resistance to institutional change. As will be shown in the Chapter 8, in Schumpeter's view, innovations can be generated only in where the credit sector finances them: which can happen in a context where banks as a whole can create credit-money. Also in this case, this is a Veblenian intuition. More generally, Veblen's view that the dynamics of a capitalist economy is inherently unstable, that a capitalist economy is a monetary theory of production, that its development crucially depends on the functioning of the credit market and the flux of innovation is very similar to that of Schumpeter and, at the same time, it is at the core of "heterodox economics" of today.

NOTES

1. For further biographical information see Bates (1934).
2. One may conceive conspicuous consumption as a device for producing "symbolic boundaries", that is lines that include and define certain people, groups and things while excluding others. These distinctions can be expressed through normative interdictions (taboos), cultural attitudes and practices, and more generally through patterns of likes and dislikes. They play an important role in the creation of inequality and the exercise of power.
3. The Veblen effect (i.e. the possible existence of a positive relation between price and quantity) has been incorporated in many contemporary textbooks as an exceptional case deriving from "snobbery". This approach usually reflects methodological individualism and is based on the dominant microeconomics: Veblen goods are treated as a very peculiar case, where the "law of demand" is not in operation and their consumption is the outcome of the *individual* rational choice.
4. Although ostentation can also involve comparison between individuals belonging to different groups.
5. The spread of these codes is basically guaranteed by schooling: "schools [...] are shaped by and rest upon a leisure-class culture", based on the humanities and erudition (Veblen, 1975 [1899], p. 391).
6. These schemes of life become *habits*.
7. J.A. Hobson ([1937] in Tilman, 2003, vol. II, pp. 34–35) remarks that "Living a generation after Marx and in a country where the sharp distinction of workers and owners, capital and labor, was less applicable than in early nineteenth-century England, [Veblen] saw a different array of economic forces and a different procedure of class conflict". In particular, according to this interpretation, Veblen minimised "the direct conflict between wage-earners and their employers as seen in the opposition of the latter to trade unions and collective bargaining". Veblen did not emphasise so much the conflict between

workers and the capitalist class. On this point he did not accept Marx's view maintaining that the working class is in essence "docile" and that, as a consequence, class struggle is impossibile within a capitalist system. He considered that workers tend to *emulate* capitalists not to conflict with them.

8. In particular, the living standard of what Veblen (1975 [1899], p. 319) calls the "indigent class".

BIBLIOGRAPHY

Adorno, T.W. 1967 [1941]. *Prisms*. London: Neville Spearman.

Argandoña, A. 2002. 'The social dimensions of labour market institutions', in A. Argandoña and J. Gual (eds), *The Social Dimension of Employment. Institutional Reforms in Labour Markets*. Cheltenham: Edward Elgar Publishing.

Argyruos, G. and Sethi, R. 1996. 'The theory of evolution and the evolution of theory: Veblen's methodology in contemporary perspective', *Cambridge Journal of Economics*, pp. 475–495.

Asso, P.F. and Fiorito, L. 2004. 'Human nature and economic institutions: Instinct psychology, behaviorism, and the development of American institutionalism', *Journal of the History of Economic Thought*, 26(4), pp. 445–477.

Axelrod, R. 1984. *The Evolution of Cooperation*. New York: Basic Books.

Ayer, A.J. 1936. *Language, Truth and Logic*. Reprinted New York: Dover, 1952.

Backhouse, R. 1994. *New Directions in Economic Methodology*. London: Routledge.

Bates, E.S. 1934. *Thorstein Veblen: A Biography*, 'Scribner's Magazine', December.

Becker, G.S. 1976. 'Altruism, egoism, and genetic fitness: Economics and Sociobiology', *Journal of Economic Literature*, 14(3) (September), pp. 817–826.

Bentham, J. 1970 [1789]. *An Introduction to the Principles of Morals and Legislation*. London: Athlone Press.

Bergstrom, T.C. and Stark O. 1993. 'How altruism can prevail in a Evolutionary Environment', *The American Economic Review*, 83(2) (May), pp. 149–155.

Bernheim, D.B. and Stark, O. 1988. 'Altruism within the family reconsidered: Do nice guys finish last?', *The American Economic Review*, 78, pp. 1034–1045.

Bicchieri, C. 1993. *Rationality and Coordination*. Cambridge: Cambridge University Press.

Blank, R.M. and McGurn, W. 2004. *Is the Market Moral? A Dialogue on Religion, Economics and Justice*. Washington DC: Brooking Institution Press.

Blaug, M. 1985. *Economic Theory in Retrospect*. Cambridge: Cambridge University Press.

Bowles, S. and Gintis, H. 1976. *Schooling in Capitalist America*. New York: Basic Books.

Bowles, S. and Gintis, H. 2002. *Prosocial emotions*, Santa Fe Institute, working paper n. 02-07-028.

Bowles, S. and Park, Y. 2002. *Emulation, inequality and work hours: Was Thorstein Veblen right?*, Santa Fe Institute working paper, 12 November.

Bowles, S., Gintis, H. and Gustaffson, B. 1993. *Markets and Democracy. Participation, Accountability and Efficiency*. Cambridge: Cambridge University Press.

Brekkle, K.A., Kverndokk, S. and Nyborg, K. 2003. 'An economic model of moral motivation', *Journal of Public Economics*, 87(9) (September), pp. 1967–1983.

Bush, P. 1999. 'Veblen's "Olympian Detachment" reconsidered', *History of Economic Ideas*, VII, 3, pp. 127–151.

Campbell, C. 1996. 'Veblen's theory of conspicuous consumption: A critical appraisal', *Yearbook of Sociology*, 1, 1, pp. 61–82.

Cummings, J. 1899. 'The theory of the leisure class', *The Journal of Political Economy*, 7 (September), pp. 425–455.

Cutrona, S. 2003. 'Cumulative causation in Veblen and Young', *Storia del pensiero economico*, 45, pp. 55–89.

Edgell, S. 1999. 'Veblen's theory of conspicuous consumption after 100 years', *History of Economic Ideas*, VII, 3, pp. 99–125.

Fiorito, L. 2002. 'John Maurice Clark on marginal productivity theory. A note on some unpublished correspondence', *Storia del pensiero economico*, 40, pp. 181–201.

Fisscher, O., Nijhof, A. and Steensma, H., 2003. 'Dynamics in responsible behaviour in search of mechanisms for coping with responsibility', *Journal of Business Ethics*, 44(2–3), pp. 209–224.

Forges Davanzati, G. 2002. 'Wages fund, high wages and social conflict in a classical model of unemployment equilibrium', *Review of Radical Political Economics*, 34, pp. 463–486.

Griffin, R. and Karayiannis, A.D. 2002. 'T. Veblen's theory of entrepreneurship', *History of Economic Ideas*, X, 3, pp. 61–83.

King, J. 2002. *A History of Post Keynesian Economics Since 1936*. Cheltenham and Northampton: Edward Elgar Publishing.

Leathers, C.G. and Evans, J.S. 1973. 'Thorstein Veblen and the new industrial state', *History of Political Economy*, 2, pp. 420–437.

Nayaradou, M. 2004. 'The influence of firm strategy on business cycles in Veblen's economic theory', *Oeconomicus*, VII, pp. 37–56.

Negishi, T. 1989. *History of Economic Theory*. Amsterdam: Elsevier Science Publishers.

Nelson, R.R. and Winter, S.G. 1982. *An Evolutionary Theory of Economic Change*. Cambridge MA: Harvard University Press.

North, D.C. 1990. *Institutions, Institutional Change and Economic Performance*. Cambridge: Cambridge University Press.

O' Hara, P.A. 1999. 'Thorstein Veblen's theory of collective social wealth, instincts and property relations', *History of Economic Ideas*, VII, 3, pp. 153–179.

O' Hara, P.A. 2000. *Marx, Veblen, and Contemporary Institutional Political Economy*. Cheltenham: Edward Elgar Publishing.

Stabile, D. 1997. 'The intellectual antecedents of Thorstein Veblen: A case for John Bates Clark', *Journal of Economic Issues*, 31, 3 (September), pp. 817–825.

Tilman, R. 1992. *Thorstein Veblen and his Critics, 1891–1963*. Princeton: Princeton University Press.

Tilman, R. 2003. *The Legacy of Thorstein Veblen*, 3 vols. Cheltenham: Edward Elgar Publishing.

Veblen, T.B. 1899. 'Mr. Cummings's strictures on the "Theory of the leisure class"' (in Notes), *The Journal of Political Economy*, 8(1) (December), pp. 106–117. Review to: John Cummings, 'The theory of the leisure class', *The Journal of Political Economy*, 7(4) (September 1899), pp. 425–455.

Veblen, T.B. 1904. *The Theory of Business Enterprise*. New York: Scribner's.

Veblen, T.B. 1906. 'The socialist economics of Karl Marx and his followers: 1. The theories of Karl Marx', *Quarterly Journal of Economics*, 20 (April), pp. 575–595.

Veblen, T.B. 1908. 'On the nature of capital. I, The productivity of capital goods',
    Quarterly Journal of Economics, 22(4) (August), pp. 517–542.
Veblen, T.B. 1956 [1904]. *The Theory of Business Enterprise*. New York:
    A.M. Kelley.
Veblen, T.B. 1964 [1914]. *The Instinct of Workmanship and the State of Industrial
    Arts*. New York: A.M. Kelley.
Veblen, T.B. 1964 [1923]. *Absentee Ownership and Business Enterprise in Recent
    Times: The Case of America*. New York: A.M. Kelley.
Veblen, T.B. 1972 [1909]. 'Professor Clark's economics', in E.K. Hunt and
    J.B. Schwartz (eds), *A Critique of Economic Theory*. Baltimore: Penguin Books,
    pp. 172–185.
Veblen, T.B. 1975 [1899]. *The Theory of the Leisure Class*. New York: A.M. Kelley.
Veblen, T.B. 1994 [1923]. 'Absentee ownership and business entreprise in recent
    times: The case of America', in *The Collected Works of Thorstein Veblen*.
    London: Routledge.
Viano, C.A. 1990. *Teorie etiche contemporanee*. Torino: Boringhieri.
Walker, D. 1977. 'Thorstein Veblen's economic system', *Economic Inquiry*, 15,
    pp. 217–222.
Wray, L. (2007). 'Veblen's theory of business enterprise and Keynes's monetary
    theory of production', *Journal of Economics Issues*, XLI, 1, pp. 1–8.

8. Joseph Alois Schumpeter

Nicola De Liso

KEY FEATURES

- The central theme of Schumpeter's economic theory is innovation; as we shall see, what he means by 'innovation' is a broader concept than the usual idea of product and process innovation.
- Innovation is carried out by entrepreneurs – which, in Schumpeter's language, are defined as such only when they innovate; any person running an established firm is not an entrepreneur but a 'simple' manager.
- In capitalist economies profit is the fundamental lever which stimulates entrepreneurs to do things differently; profit is the endogenous force which stimulates innovation and thus economic change.
- Innovation gives rise to business cycles and economic development; however, development occurs through a process of creative destruction, i.e. while in the long run on average the economic system is better off, there will always be winners and losers.
- How important is firms' size for innovation? Are competitive or oligopolistic markets more favourable to innovation? We will refer to 'Schumpeter Mark I' and 'Schumpeter Mark II' ideas which provide two different answers (which can be alternative but also complementary).
- Schumpeter departed from Neoclassical and Classical theory in many respects. Equilibrium and static efficiency are irrelevant, profit rates can differ – and not only across sectors, but also within the same sector.
- During his life Schumpeter – who died in 1950 – did not create a 'Schumpeterian School'. Such a School emerged in the 1980s, under the 'evolutionary' label. How are Schumpeter's ideas connected to evolutionism? Population thinking, variety and selection are the key words.

1. INTRODUCTION

The name and the economic theory of Joseph Alois Schumpeter have been getting more and more attention since the 1980s. However, as many scholars note, he was literally a contemporary of John Maynard Keynes since he was born in the same year, i.e. 1883 – the year that Karl Marx died.

Schumpeter, Keynes and Marx are interconnected through the year 1883, and many observers (e.g. Samuelson, 1983) start from this coincidence to propose their reflections on the three of them.

Often Schumpeter is compared with Keynes, the question being: who is to be acknowledged as the most influential economist of the twentieth century? The juxtaposition between Schumpeter and Marx, instead, concerns the intellectual debt of the former with respect to the latter. Let us shortly elaborate on these two aspects.

While Keynes became widely famous to the public at large during his life, Schumpeter until his death – in 1950 – was known 'only' within the realm of academia. Thus, for a long while, there was little to be debated on whom had to be praised as the most influential. From the 1980s, though, the question is no longer idle. In fact, despite the fact that still today a majority of observers would indicate Keynes as the greatest, in 1983 the US business magazine *Forbes* asked which of the two, Keynes or Schumpeter, made the greater, more endurable contributions to economic theory: to the great surprise of its readers, *Forbes* concluded that Schumpeter was the greatest economist of the 20th century (Viner, 1990, p. ix).

An early acknowledgement of Schumpeter's stature is contained in a 1953 review article of a book entitled *Schumpeter, Social Scientist*. Writes the reviewer:

> Where will Schumpeter stand hundred years hence, in the longer perspective of the growth of economics? I suspect that in retrospect he will prove to be a more commanding figure than he was among his own contemporaries. For it may well turn out (my own view is that it will) that Schumpeter was asking the really important and enduring questions about the causes and conditions of economic development. (Robinson, 1953, p. 126).

We do not need a hundred years to answer Robinson's question. Schumpeter stands undoubtedly high, among the most influential economists of the 20th century, still flying high in the early decades of the 21st century.

With regards to the intellectual debt of Schumpeter towards Marx, Schumpeter himself acknowledges it, in particular by devoting to the Marxian doctrine the first four chapters of his book *Capitalism, Socialism and Democracy* (1950a). As we shall see in this chapter, Schumpeter wanted to build a theoretical model capable of explaining the 'laws of motion' of the capitalistic economy. Schumpeter shared with Marx the idea according to which the incentives structure – and in particular the lever of profit – together with the institutional set up create an environment in which an evolutionary self-transformation process is continuously taking place through a process of creative destruction (Rosenberg, 2011; Elliott, 1980). Both Marx and Schumpeter believed that capitalism would not survive, however for opposite reasons: for Marx, capitalism would be overturned by impoverished masses of proletarians; for Schumpeter, capitalism would fade away through its own success.[1]

We will provide a short résumé of Schumpeter's life in the next section.[2] Let us here anticipate the fact that he had a monumental knowledge of the history of economic thought, while he mastered Classical, Neoclassical and the emerging Austrian theory (as a university student in Vienna he was taught by Friedrich von Wieser and Eugen von Böhm-Bawerk, two co-founders of the Austrian School). Worthy of an immediate comment is also the fact that his first language was German, but he was fluent in English, French and Italian: in this way he could read virtually all the available economic literature.

It is important to explicitly point out that in this chapter we will focus on a *selection* of Schumpeter's economics works and themes – a full discussion would require a whole book.

Schumpeter was a fully-fledged social scientist (Backhaus, 2003; Seymour, 1951), also aware of the methodological issues which economics and the broader social sciences raise (Schumpeter, 1908, 1909, 1949; Kurz, 2017).[3] However, these aspects go beyond the topics that can be covered in a book devoted to economic thought.

We will concentrate on Schumpeter's grand theme, namely his economics of innovation, which is at the core of his three most cited books – *Theory of Economic Development*, *Business Cycles*, and *Capitalism, Socialism and Democracy*. These books cover a time span ranging from 1911 to 1950. In fact, his analysis of innovation constitutes a landmark in economic theory, and its importance can hardly be overestimated: the title of McCraw's 2007 book, which contains the words 'prophet of innovation', fits perfectly Schumpeter's fundamental idea (McCraw, 2007).

As we shall see, the recognition of the importance of Schumpeter's ideas took a long time. During his life Schumpeter was not able to create a 'Schumpeterian School' despite the fact that he was widely known in Europe, America, as well as Japan. No group of 'Schumpeterians' had been created, despite the fact that he had been a professor at Harvard University since 1932. To speak of such a school we have to wait until the 1980s. And yet, his fundamental ideas concerning the role of innovation as the engine of capitalism have gained so much ground that today nobody can ignore Schumpeter's works: the economics of innovation constitutes a central theme of the economic agenda, which always becomes part of the political agenda. In fact, a *technology policy* is a fundamental issue for any government.

This chapter is structured as follows. In section 2 we provide a short résumé of Schumpeter's life. In section 3 we provide a short résumé of the theoretical panorama, which characterised Schumpeter's time. In section 4 we examine the relationships between innovation, entrepreneurship, profit and economic development. In section 5 we further investigate the connection between innovation, profit and capitalist dynamics. In section 6 we make explicit one main departure of Schumpeter's theory from Neoclassical theory: while for the latter equilibrium is a central theme, for the former it becomes irrelevant. Section 7 considers the question concerning the relationship between firm size, market structure and innovation. Section 8 focuses on the emergence of a 'Schumpeterian School' of thought during the 1980s under the label 'evolutionary': we shall see why Schumpeterians can call themselves evolutionists. In section 9, we draw the conclusions, pointing once more at the central theme of capitalism as an economic system which can never be stationary.

2.   A SHORT RÉSUMÉ OF SCHUMPETER'S LIFE

Schumpeter was born in 1883 in the Moravia region, in a small town called Triesch,[4] which at the time belonged to the Austro-Hungarian Empire. He lost his father when he was four years old, and his mother decided to move to Graz, where she re-married in 1893 to an army general belonging to Austrian nobility. The new family then moved to Vienna, where Schumpeter attended the *Theresianum*, one of the best high schools of the empire. Attending the University of Vienna was the obvious follow-up.

At the turn of the 20th century, Vienna provided one of the most stimulating environments in the world. While at university, Schumpeter was taught by Friedrich von Wieser and Eugen von Böhm-Bawerk – as we mentioned above, they are co-founders of the Austrian School and prominent figures in the European economics arena. After graduation he spent time in Germany, France, England and Egypt.

His first university position, when he was 26 years old, was in the small-town of Czernowitz (now part of Ukraine). Afterwards he held positions in Graz (Austria) and Bonn (Germany), before moving to the United States, to Harvard, in 1932, where he stayed until the end of his life in 1950.

Schumpeter had an intense, and sometimes sad, life, particularly before he moved to the United States.

On the personal side, Schumpeter lost his beloved mother in 1926, a woman who was devoted to the young Joseph. Moreover, not only was he married three times, but his second wife, Annie, died in 1926 while giving birth to their son, who also died. These events left a heavy mark on Schumpeter.

Professionally, things were no different when he adventured outside academia. For a few years he held a key position in a small Viennese bank; in the mid-1920s the bank went bankrupt and Schumpeter ended up losing a fortune and in huge debt. In 1919 he was for a few months a rather unsuccessful Austrian Minister of Financial Affairs in a socialist government.

There seems to be also a dark side to Schumpeter's mind and behaviour. At times he would make unpleasant comments aimed at Jewish and Black people. While at Harvard, he made disparaging comments about Roosevelt, and students and colleagues sometimes got the impression that he supported the Nazi movement. Some also perceived his jealousy and rivalry of Keynes, due to the fact that Keynes was more famous than he was. However, while all these aspects have been debated, they were shown as being ill-founded.[5]

A further necessary remark concerns the language(s) and timing of his works. On the original German version of Schumpeter's works, Haberler writes:

> His somewhat involved literary style which can be perhaps best described as 'baroque' gives adequate expression to the complex structure of his mind. It is characterized by long sentences, numerous qualifying phrases, qualifications of qualifications, casuistic distinctions of meanings. These qualities of his style are especially pronounced, as one would expect, in his German writings, because the German language offers more freedom for complicated constructions. (Haberler, 1950, pp. 369–370)[6]

When his works were translated from German into English, Schumpeter usually cooperated with the translator, sometimes introducing changes with respect to the original German.

Worthy of a comment is the history of Schumpeter's famous – and probably most influential – book, *Theorie der wirtschaftlichen Entwicklung*, which was translated in English as *The Theory of Economic Development* in 1934. Some authors refer to the first German edition as 1911, while some others as 1912.[7] The English translation, though, was carried out on the basis of the second German edition, which appeared in 1926. The latter did not contain the long seventh final chapter whose title in English is

'The economy as a whole'.[8] According to Shionoya (1990) this is a big loss because the missing chapter constituted an attempt at providing a research programme for a universal social science.

Many of his works, though – and in particular *Business Cycles* and *Capitalism, Socialism and Democracy* – were written directly in English.

3. ECONOMIC SCIENCE AT THE BEGINNING OF THE 20TH CENTURY

When Schumpeter published his first book in 1908,[9] economics was already dominated by the Neoclassical-Marginalist School (see Chapter 4 of this book), which started with the publication in the early 1870s of the works by William S. Jevons, Carl Menger and Léon Walras – the first written in English, the second in German and the third in French. Neoclassical ideas were further developed and diffused through the works of scholars such as Alfred Marshall, John B. Clark and Vilfredo Pareto.

A central idea of Neoclassical theory is the equilibrium in the markets for products and production factors. This argument must be emphasised because Schumpeter, despite the fact that he was an admirer of Walras in particular – who made general economic equilibrium his grand theme – challenged the importance of such an idea.

Comparative statics was the privileged method of Neoclassical theory. Basically, this means we take as a starting point a position of equilibrium, and, after whatever shock takes place, we simply consider the new equilibrium position, but we overlook the process through which the new equilibrium is reached. In other words, we omit any discussion of how we go from one equilibrium to another.

Schumpeter was very critical of such a method, and was far more interested in the dynamics of that process: he wanted to propose a dynamic theory taking advantage of statistical data, which were being increasingly made available, while also integrating history into his framework. This attempt clearly emerges in his monumental work *Business Cycles*, which carries as a subtitle *A Theoretical, Historical, and Statistical Analysis of the Capitalist Process* (Schumpeter, 1939).[10]

In general, Schumpeter's ambition was to provide a theory capable of explaining the way in which capitalist economies develop through endogenous forces. In fact, by 'development' he means only such changes in economic life as are not forced upon it from outside, but arise by their own initiative, from within (Schumpeter, 1926, Engl. Transl. 1934, p. 63). Put another way, he criticised any economic theory that considered how capitalism administers existing structures, whereas the relevant problem is how it creates and destroys them; as long as this is not recognised, the investigator does a meaningless job (Schumpeter, 1950a, p. 84).

If Neoclassical theory constituted the 'natural' benchmark for any theory, other schools of thought existed and were nevertheless important. For instance, the echoes of the Classical school could still clearly be heard, while Marxian ideas were experiencing renewed waves of interest. Indeed, some Schumpeterian ideas concerning the driving forces of capitalism are not so far from Marxian analysis, and Schumpeter paid a tribute to Marx in his later work *Capitalism, Socialism and Democracy*, devoting to him the first part of the book (Schumpeter, 1950a). Furthermore, the German Historical School was strong, while the Austrian School was also developing.

Being a German native speaker, fluent in English and French, Schumpeter could benefit from the most important bibliographical sources available in his time – Max Weber and Werner Sombart, to name just two.

4. INNOVATION, ENTREPRENEURS, PROFIT AND ECONOMIC DEVELOPMENT

Schumpeter's economic theory revolves around the idea of innovation, which is the driving force of capitalist economies, and it constitutes the fundamental lever of development. Innovation is an endogenous phenomenon, which arises from within the system, the basic mechanism being the search for profit by entrepreneurs – although what Schumpeter specifically means by 'entrepreneur' is discussed below.

Innovation, in turn, engenders development. We are used to thinking of development in a positive way, however development itself does not occur smoothly throughout the system. In fact, capitalistic development takes place through *creative destruction* (Schumpeter, 1950a, p. 83). New firms emerge, but often they displace existing ones. Whole sectors can be reorganised as a consequence of innovation, but along the process there are winners – the innovators – and losers – those who lag behind.

As a whole the system improves, in the sense that more and better goods and services are provided to society at large, but this improvement is not painless. New firms do not simply emerge alongside the old ones: they often destroy them.

In the *Theory* – but he will use basically the same words over and over again[11] – Schumpeter refers to innovation as the 'carrying out of new combinations', and this concept covers five cases:

(1) The introduction of a new good ... or of a new quality of a good. (2) The introduction of a new method of production ... (3) The opening of a new

market ... (4) The conquest of a new source of supply of raw materials or half-manufactured goods ... (5) The carrying out of the new organisation of any industry, like the creation of a monopoly position ... or the breaking up of a monopoly position (Schumpeter, 1926/1934, p. 66).[12]

First, it is important to stress the fact that innovation need not be based on a particular invention. As Schumpeter (1947, p. 152) puts it, the entrepreneur 'gets things done' independently of the fact that innovation contains anything really new. Put another way, often innovation consists in adapting existing knowledge, devices and materials to a different use. Steam-engines were originally conceived of in order to suck water from coalmines, but were adapted to provide motion to textile machinery and to ships: three completely different uses of basically the same technology.[13]

Second, let us stress the fact that Schumpeter considers as 'innovation' not only product and process innovation, but also other aspects such as – repeating what is indicated in the quote above – the opening of a new market, the acquisition of new sources of raw materials or semi-manufactured goods, and the mutation of market conditions.

Another issue emerges immediately: once we have clarified what an innovation is, we then have to consider who the *innovator* is. In everyday language we associate the word 'entrepreneur' with anyone running an enterprise, yet according to Schumpeter's specific language, the entrepreneur is the person whose function is to carry out new combinations. In other words, for Schumpeter, the innovator is the *entrepreneur*, defined as such only when he or she innovates. Once the enterprise runs routinely, the entrepreneur becomes a simple manager.

The entrepreneurial activity consists in the distinct function of carrying out innovations. Therefore, nobody is ever an entrepreneur all the time, and nobody can ever be only an entrepreneur, notes Schumpeter (1939, p. 103).

It is also important to say explicitly what the entrepreneur is *not*. First of all, as already pointed out, the entrepreneur is not necessarily an inventor, i.e. the 'new combinations' can be a 'simple' new and original assemblage of existing devices, materials and ideas. Secondly, the entrepreneur is not the capitalist: these two functions must be kept separate. The capitalist is the institution or person who provides the capital for entrepreneurial activities, but need not be the entrepreneur. It was Marx who conflated the two functions, always referring to capitalists as those who owned the factories. Obviously, there can exist some overlapping between the two functions, but they must conceptually be kept separate. Third, we are used to thinking of the entrepreneur as the agent who bears the risk of innovation. In the Schumpeterian model, as a rule, the banking system is the risk-bearer, as the entrepreneur *qua entrepreneur* looses other people's money, that is, it is the one who gives credit that comes to grief if the undertaking fails.[14]

Obviously, one can think of the entrepreneur as an inventor, who uses his or her personal assets to innovate, thus bearing the risk of failure. However, these aspects, according to Schumpeter, must not be conflated.

Expectation of profit is the prime mover of the capitalist – or, if one prefers, market – economies. We have to stress the fact that it is the *expectation* that drives the actual entrepreneurial action. However, as Shackle reminds us:

> *Expectation of profit* must be provided with a language for expressing its uncertainty and its dual resulting character of threat and promise, and this language must be such that a precise subjective comparison can be made, *ex post facto*, between the system of expectations and the recorded result. (Shackle, 1970, p. 152, emphasis in original)

As many observers point out,[15] most entrepreneurs end up disappointed; however, the reward for the successful ones is the *entrepreneurial profit*.

Profit can be defined as the excess of the value of outputs over that of inputs, or as the difference between receipts and costs. This notion, though, is not as simple or as innocent as it seems according to the definition just provided. Actual profits, in fact, depend on actions undertaken at a time in which the entrepreneur ignored much of those future circumstances whose character determines the actual outcome – and in this sense profit is not a simple idea, but a system of concepts (Shackle, 1970, p. 152).

Considering the example of product innovation, once the successful entrepreneur has innovated, he or she will buy the input needed at market price, and will sell his or her product at a price which takes as a benchmark the prevailing price set by 'old' firms. Being more efficient, the innovative entrepreneur will experience a bigger margin – i.e. entrepreneurial profit – of receipts over costs. Profit is thus the premium put upon successful innovation in capitalist society. Profit, though, is temporary by nature: it will vanish in the subsequent process of competition, imitation and adaptation (Schumpeter, 1939, p. 105).

We now have the basic elements we need to fully appreciate Schumpeter's economics and its explanation of the working of the economy.

5. FROM THE FINANCING OF INNOVATION TO BUSINESS CYCLES

As we have already mentioned, Schumpeter's economic theory revolves around the theme of innovation. Innovations and entrepreneurs shape the evolution of the capitalistic system, changing the landscape continuously through the process of creative destruction – a process that implies a painful form of development.

If innovation – sought by entrepreneurs hunting profits – is the fundamental lever of development of capitalist economies, one question we have to answer concerns the financing of innovation itself. As a rule, Schumpeter's innovators have no means of their own. Instead, they borrow the funds they need in order to carry out innovation.

It is important to stress the fact that those funds are means of payment created ad hoc. Put another way, credit creation is the necessary monetary complement of innovation:

> It is always a question not of transforming purchasing power which already exists in someone's possession, but of the creation of new purchasing power out of nothing ... which is added to the existing circulation. [...] The banker, therefore, is not so much primarily a middleman in the commodity 'purchasing power' as a *producer* of this commodity. ... He is essentially a phenomenon of development. (Schumpeter, 1926/1934, pp. 73–74, emphasis in original)[16]

This quotation gives us the opportunity to refer to Schumpeter's account of 'real' and 'monetary' analysis. In 'real analysis' the essential phenomena of economic life are described in terms of goods and services, and money is a 'veil' which must be drawn aside if we are to analyse the fundamental features of the economic process. 'Monetary analysis' considers the fact that money *does* affect the economic process, so that we have to abandon the idea according to which the essential features of economic life can be represented by a barter-economy model. Money prices, money incomes and other monetary magnitudes acquire their own life so that the capitalist process depends on that 'veil', and there is no face behind the veil itself: capitalism's face would be incomplete without that veil (Schumpeter, 1954, pp. 276–278). The money market and the newly ad hoc created deposits are thus an essential driver of development through innovation (Schumpeter, 1930/2014, p. 316).

One very strong statement of Schumpeter's theory is that entrepreneurial profits and related gains, which arise in the disequilibria caused by innovation, are the *only* source of interest payments and thus the only cause of the existence of positive interest rates in capitalist societies. The interest rate, in turn, is a monetary phenomenon, and what matters is the *nominal* – as distinct from *real* – rate of interest, and occupies a central position in the economic system in that it is a coefficient of tension which expresses the degree of disequilibrium present in the system itself (Schumpeter, 1939, pp. 124–126).

The entrepreneur expects a profit which exceeds the rate of interest, and the successful innovation will actually be characterised by this inequality, that is, indicating profit with π and the nominal rate of interest with i, we must have $\pi > i$. More correctly, we should say that profit is big enough to more than repay the *capital sum plus interest*. The 'marginal entrepreneur' will be the one whose profit is just enough to repay the capital sum plus interest. All the other entrepreneurs will have a higher return, and what is important is the fact that profit rates are neither equal in different sectors, nor within the same sector.

The latter statement must be emphasised as it marks a departure from Classical and Neoclassical economic theory. In fact, in both schools, the profit rate must be the same across sectors and, all the more so, within the same sector:

> [T]here is no reason for speaking about a tendency towards equalisation of profits which does not exist at all in reality: for only the jumbling together of interest and profit explains why many authors contend for such a tendency, although we can observe such extraordinarily different profits in one and the same place, at the same time and in the same industry. (Schumpeter, 1926/1934, p. 153)[17]

The Schumpeterian profit is 'monopolistic' in kind, in the sense that the entrepreneur benefits for a certain period from the exclusive advantage of his or her innovation. In fact, considering once more the example of product innovation, the entrepreneur has no competitors when the new product first appears, so that the determination of its price proceeds wholly, or within certain limits, according to the principle of monopoly price; put another way, there is a monopoly element in profit in a capitalist economy (Schumpeter, 1926/1934, p. 152).

Entrepreneurial profits, however, are temporary by definition, due to the processes of imitation, competition and further creative destruction.

A successful innovation is likely to stimulate further innovations along the same trajectory as well as of tributary innovations. For instance, during the first Industrial Revolution machinery for the textile industry was continuously developed. Better machines gave rise to bigger production, and this made necessary improvements in the treatment of cotton and wool, from bleaching to dyes, that is improvements in the mechanical industry stimulated innovation in the chemical sector.

The process of development, which is based on innovation, is not a smooth one. One observes the existence of waves of innovation, that is – paraphrasing once more Schumpeter's words – innovations are not isolated events and are not uniformly distributed through time and space. They tend to cluster and emerge in a swarm-like manner, largely because once a successful path is opened, many difficulties disappear, and many new entrepreneurs will follow the early pioneers. Along the way opportunities and threats become reality:

> For some of the 'old' firms, new opportunities for expansion open up: the new methods or commodities create New Economic Space. But for others, the emergence of the new methods means economic death; for still others contraction and drifting into the background. Finally, there are firms and industries which are forced to undergo a difficult and painful process of modernization, rationalization and reconstruction. (Schumpeter, 1939, p. 134).

Innovations constitute also the basic mechanism capable of engendering business cycles, that is to give rise to 'recurrent business fluctuations', which means that innovations produce sequences of prosperity and recession. Schumpeter was aware of the fact that business cycles are affected by many factors, however he explicitly stated that innovation is the *dominant* factor (Schumpeter, 1939, p. 139).

Schumpeter's cycle is made up of four phases.[18] The cycle begins (the first phase) with the occurrence of an innovation. A successful innovation is followed by a further wave in which further innovations take place, which means further stimulus to the economy, while also increasing consumers' spending; borrowing will increase, each loan will induce another loan, and each rise in prices will induce another rise. What we observe in the first phase is thus a general expansion of the economy. The upswing contains the seeds of recession (the second phase). In this second phase a painful process of readjustment of prices, quantities and values takes place. Firms, which could survive only because of the expansion of the economy, now have to close down. A process of deflation takes place, thus reinforcing the liquidation of many activities, while many investments will be displaced. A third phase, for which Schumpeter reserves the name *depression*, may occur if abnormal liquidation takes place, defined as a vicious spiral in which a further downward revision of values and a shrinkage of operations occurs, so that we face further bankruptcies, breaks in individual markets and shutdowns. The vicious spiral is bound to decelerate and eventually to stop. Thus, the fourth phase, that of *recovery* (or *revival*), will begin.

It is important to note that in Schumpeter's business cycle model the first phase, i.e. prosperity, is not necessarily synonymous with welfare, while recession does not necessarily mean misery. In fact, recession is a time of harvesting the results of preceding innovation and its positive indirect effects. Furthermore, as Sylos-Labini (1969, p. 166) has pointed out, through the process of deflation typical of the second and third phase, real incomes rise because money incomes fall less than prices.

6. THE IRRELEVANCE OF (NEOCLASSICAL) EQUILIBRIUM AND THE PROBLEM OF KNOWLEDGE

We must now consider a fundamental question, which emphasises once more Schumpeter's departure from Neoclassical theory: the concept of equilibrium. The question is the following: Are cycles to be understood as movements – however turbulent – from one equilibrium to another, maybe economically superior? At first, Schumpeter (1939, p. 138) uses the equilibrium metaphor, that is he expresses himself in terms of moving from one equilibrium to another.

However, whenever and wherever we look at the economy, Schumpeter tells us that we are never, nor can we be, in equilibrium because of the presence of 'undigested elements of previous prosperities and depressions, innovations not yet completely worked out, results of faulty or otherwise imperfect adaptations, and so on' (Schumpeter, 1939, p. 157).

The point is more immediate to understand in *The Theory of Economic Development*.[19] In this book, Schumpeter begins his analysis by assuming that the economy actually *is* in a condition of equilibrium, that is in a Neoclassical circular flow, in which all magnitudes are in equilibrium. Such a condition, even if it existed, would become devoid of real content because of the way the capitalist economy works: entrepreneurs hunting profits would look for new and different ways to do things, and through innovation they would take the economy away from whatever equilibrium. In other words, even if we were in equilibrium, that equilibrium would become irrelevant.

It is important to stress that while in Neoclassical theory the process through which we move from disequilibrium to equilibrium is important, that is the process of convergence towards an equilibrium, in Schumpeter we have a complete theoretical inversion: what matters is the opposite process, from equilibrium to disequilibrium – the fundamental lever being always the role of entrepreneurs and their innovations.

Neoclassical theory at best is thus capable of explaining gradual change, for instance, writes Schumpeter, the gradual enlargement of a small retail shop which becomes a supermarket. However, this is not the typical process of change which characterises capitalism: the mechanisation of the textile industry during the Industrial Revolution represented a discontinuity, as did the widespread use of electricity, the development of chemistry and, more recently, the development of information and communication technologies (ICTs), which have deeply changed our lives. Neoclassical theory does not provide the necessary tools to predict the consequences of discontinuous changes in the traditional way of doing things; it can neither explain the occurrence of such productive revolutions nor the phenomena that accompany them (Schumpeter, 1926/1934, pp. 62–63).

As Metcalfe put it, the concept of equilibrium is lifeless because of its inability to encompass entrepreneurial behaviour: by definition the rewards to entrepreneurship are transient and relate to the operation of markets in a state of *disequilibrium* (Metcalfe, 1998, p. 18).

Moreover, the meaning of 'competition' must be qualified. In fact, Schumpeter distinguishes 'textbook competition' from 'real capitalist competition', where the latter is:

> Competition which commands a decisive cost or quality advantage and which strikes not at the margins of the profits and the outputs of the existing firms but at their foundations and their very lives. This kind of competition is as much more effective than the other as a bombardment is in comparison with forcing a door. (Schumpeter, 1950a, p. 84).

Much of what has been said about innovation, imitation and competition impinges on the problem of *knowledge*. To innovate means to do something new, which diverges from what has been done up to now. Innovation studies have a bias, since they tend to focus on *successful* innovations. However, we should never forget that failures are much more frequent than successes – that is, often to undertake a different route on the basis of a suppositious 'better' knowledge leads to a crash rather than to the Eldorado of profits.

The search and achievement of novelty must in some degree discredit what passed for knowledge, and to hit upon something new that will beat what exists is the only way for a firm to alter its rating in the table of success (Shackle, 1970, p. 155). However, the exploitation of the unknown may reveal itself a dangerous game.

7. 'SCHUMPETER MARK I' AND 'SCHUMPETER MARK II', OR OF MARKET STRUCTURE AND INNOVATION

Another important issue must now be tackled. Up to now, we have neither spoken of (innovative) firms without explicit reference to the size of firms, nor have we referred to the kind of market – competitive, oligopolistic, monopolistic – in which innovation is more likely to occur. Economists have long debated this theme under the heading 'market structure and innovation'. Schumpeter anticipated – and created – this debate, and this is what we study in this section.

At first, Schumpeter, in his *Theory of Economic Development*, empha-sised the role played by new firms. The market would be a competitive one in the sense that there exist low entry barriers; entrepreneurs do not own the means to put into practice their innovative ideas but have access to credit to transform their ideas into practice. As an example, we can think of innovative small-sized start-ups, which was the case of Silicon Valley. This condition, in which firms are not large and the market is fairly competitive, is what has been called the 'Schumpeter Mark I' pattern of creative destruction: innovations, as a rule, are embodied in new firms, which generally do not arise out of the old ones but start producing beside them (Schumpeter, 1926/1934, p. 66).

In his most mature work, *Capitalism, Socialism and Democracy*, the protagonists are large oligopolistic established firms, and barriers to entry are relevant. This is what has been defined the 'Schumpeter Mark II' pat-tern of innovation, which Baumol (2002) synthesises as the routinisation of innovation through oligopolistic rivalry. Large firms are endowed with their own resources to carry out innovation; should they need credit they have as a rule easier access to it than small firms. Moreover, as soon as they can afford it, they establish a research department 'every member of which knows that his bread and butter depends on his success in devising improvements' (Schumpeter, 1950a, p. 96).

While Schumpeter seems to have changed his vision from 'Mark I' to 'Mark II' throughout his work, the prevalence of the former or of the latter pattern of innovativeness may be sector-specific or technology-specific. Stated differently, 'Mark II' does not follow chronologically or logically from 'Mark I', but we can observe the existence of 'Mark I' processes of innovation somewhere in the economy, and 'Mark II' somewhere else *at the same time*.[20]

References to the simultaneous presence of 'Mark I' and 'Mark II' pro-cesses can be found in Schumpeter's 1928 article devoted to the instability of capitalism. Here he refers to two types of capitalism: *competitive* capitalism and *trustified* capitalism. In the former case, innovation is typically embod-ied in the foundation of new firms, and given the comparatively small size of firms, innovation is extremely risky and a difficult thing to embark upon. In the latter case, innovation is no longer typically embodied in new firms and takes place routinely in the existing giant oligopolistic firms. It is important to stress the fact that while the innovative process failure in competitive capitalism leads the would-be firm to bankruptcy, in trustified capitalism giant firms – often using their own reserves and having direct access to capital – can survive innovation failure itself (Schumpeter, 1928, p. 384).

Until now, we have looked at causation as flowing from market structure and firm size to innovation, but according to Nelson and Winter (1982), there is also, under Schumpeterian competition, a reverse flow as well. According to the authors, 'Market structure should be viewed as endogenous to an analysis of Schumpeterian competition, with the connections between innovation and the market structure going both ways' (Nelson and Winter, 1982, p. 281).

Schumpeter alluded to these arguments in *The Theory of Economic Development*, where he considers the carrying out of the new organisation in any industry as an innovation, like the creation of a monopoly position or the reverse process, that is the breaking up of a monopoly position.

At this point, we need to once again point out how this marks a departure with respect to Neoclassical and Classical economic theory, specifically with respect to the evaluation of monopolistic practices. In Classical and Neoclassical theories, large monopolistic firms are invariably looked at with suspicion, as monopolists almost by definition tend to abuse their dominant position, typically restricting output and charging high prices.

However, Schumpeter points out that the latter statement is not necessarily correct. First, 'the position of a single seller can in general be conquered – and retained for decades – only on the condition that he does not behave like a monopolist' (Schumpeter, 1950a, p. 99). Second, when we look at improvements of the standard of life and inquire into the individual items in which progress was most conspicuous,

> the trail leads not to the doors of those firms that work under conditions of comparatively free competition but precisely to the doors of the large concerns ... and a shocking suspicion dawns upon us that big business may have had more to do with creating that standard of life than with keeping it down. (Schumpeter, 1950a, p. 82)

This can happen because there may exist superior methods readily available only to the monopolist, such that in the end output and prices are, respectively, higher and lower – i.e. we are better off – than the ones which we would get in competitive markets. Thus, in general perfect competition is impossible to reach, but should it be possible, it could provide inferior results, and cannot be considered the model of ideal efficiency.[21]

8.   THE EVOLUTIONARY THEORY OF ECONOMIC CHANGE: THE SCHUMPETERIAN SCHOOL

When Schumpeter died in 1950, he was undoubtedly very famous but, as we have already argued, he was unable to create a Schumpeterian School during his lifetime. In order to find such a school, we had to wait until the early 1980s.

A turning point for the creation of such a school was the publication of Nelson and Winter's 1982 book, *An Evolutionary Theory of Economic Change* – which inspired the title of this section (Nelson and Winter, 1982). The authors systematise their own and other early works,[22] while explaining why an evolutionary economic theory was needed, and also explicitly pointing out the relationship between their evolutionary economic theory and Schumpeter's ideas. According to the authors:

> The influence of Joseph Schumpeter is so pervasive in our work that it requires particular mention here. Indeed, the term 'neo-Schumpeterian' would be as appropriate a designation for our entire approach as 'evolutionary'. More precisely, it could reasonably be said that we are evolutionary theorists *for the sake* of being neo-Schumpeterians – that is, because evolutionary ideas provide a workable approach to the problem of elaborating and formalizing the Schumpeterian view of capitalism as an engine of progressive change. (Nelson and Winter, 1982, p. 39, original emphasis).

Schumpeter never defined himself as an evolutionist, and actually wrote that the evolutionary idea was 'discredited' in the economic field and, in general, was sometimes surrounded by 'unscientific and extra-scientific mysticism' (Schumpeter, 1926/1934, pp. 57–58).[23] Nevertheless, throughout his work, expressions such as 'industrial mutation', 'organic process', 'evolutionary process' and 'capitalist organism' are not an exception.[24] Furthermore, he explicitly wrote 'The essential point to grasp is that in dealing with capitalism we are dealing with an evolutionary process' (Schumpeter, 1950a, p. 82).

The emergence and growth of an Evolutionary-Schumpeterian School comes together with the increasing awareness of the need to understand the *economics* of innovation in market economies. Innovation is the prime mover of capitalist development, but the way in which the dominant Neoclassical theory has studied it – basically through the production function and the toolkit developed around it – found it difficult to include technological change within the theoretical framework because the standard competitive assumptions cannot be maintained.[25] Thus, despite the many Neoclassical scholars' efforts starting from the 1950s, a different theoretical basis had to be found, a natural candidate being Schumpeterian theory – fully centred on innovation.

While up until the early 1970s, many economists could still complain at the insufficient attention given to innovation, we witness an upsurge of interest on the topic starting from the 1980s, and an increasing number of contributions began to refer to Schumpeter's work.[26] Noteworthy is the creation of the 'International Joseph A. Schumpeter Society' in 1986, and the *Journal of Evolutionary Economics* in 1991.[27]

It would today be impossible to make an exhaustive list of the themes and scholars that can be labelled as 'Schumpeterian' or 'Neo-Schumpeterian'. The themes range from entrepreneurship to knowledge creation, from agent-based modelling to national and sectoral systems of innovation,[28] from case studies to self-organisation in economic systems, and many more. As for the scholars who belong to the Schumpeterian School, the list is too long even to begin to list them.[29]

Rather, let us briefly summarise – through the masterly book by Metcalfe (1998) on which the following paragraphs are based – why evolutionary economists find so much inspiration in Schumpeter's writing and the meaning of evolutionary theorising. The main point lies in the idea that evolutionary theory is a manner of reasoning, and the fact that it was developed in biology does not mean that it is an inherently biological concept.

Three principles characterise evolutionary processes: variation, heredity and selection. *Variation* means that the members of a 'population' vary with respect to at least one characteristic; *heredity* means there exist copying mechanisms, which ensure continuity over time in the form and behaviour of the entities in the population; *selection* means some entities are better adapted to cope with evolutionary pressure, and consequently increase in relative significance (Metcalfe, 1998, p. 22).

Here 'population' refers to firms, and two firms competing in the same market belong to the same population. Among firms we have a variety of characteristics, i.e. firms are not identical, and they can evolve along different paths. Market forces provide selection.

With respect to the selection mechanism, it is important to emphasise the fact that the growth rates of different firms are determined by the interaction between members of the population; and the fitness of any firm is a function not only of its own characteristics and behaviour, but also of the characteristics and behaviour of all its rivals in that population (Metcalfe, 1998, p. 33).

To sum up, the ingredients of an evolutionary process are the existence of a population, of variety and of a selection mechanism. These ingredients we find in the economy as well as in biology: thus, the evolutionary *logic* can be applied to both.

> It may now be clear why evolutionary economists have found so much inspiration in Schumpeter's writing. For he was describing economic worlds of continual structural change, driven from within by entrepreneurs ... Acts of entrepreneurship meant differential behaviour ... the consequences of which spread throughout the economic system. (Metcalfe, 1998, p. 37)

9. CONCLUSIONS: THE CREATIVE RESPONSE IN ECONOMIC HISTORY

Innovation is a central aspect of capitalist economies, and economics – qua science – must explain, or at least try to explain, the way in which innovation takes place. Schumpeter's works focused on the study of the processes that lead to innovation, which in turn means structural change of the economy and economic development.

Development does not mean that everyone is better off, as the development process itself takes place through *creative destruction*. Innovation sometimes simply adds to what already exists, i.e. new firms provide completely new goods and services, but often displaces existing firms, goods and services and brings about heavy restructuring of whole sectors.

One fundamental lever in a capitalist economy is the search for profit, and this stimulates entrepreneurs to do things differently. Whenever we do something that is outside the range of existing practice we have what Schumpeter calls a *creative response*. This process is usually reinforced by the fact that a successful innovation stimulates further innovation, so that innovations cluster densely together.

The creative response is characterised by three features: first, it can be understood only *ex post*; second, it shapes the whole course of subsequent events and their long-run outcome; third, the frequency of its occurrence depends on the quality of the personnel available and on their decisions, actions and pattern of behaviour (Schumpeter, 1947, p. 150).

When we look at the history of capitalist economies since the first Industrial Revolution we see that innovation has always been a central feature. Mechanisation spread from textile industry to all manufacturing sectors, reliable steam-engines provided motion to the machines but also to ships and trains, electricity brought about a new wave of innovations, as did the invention of the internal combustion engine, not to mention the development of ICTs, biotechnology and nanotechnology.

The words that best synthesise the overall capitalistic process and capture the very idea of capitalism as an evolving system are probably due to Stan Metcalfe (2008), when he speaks of *restless capitalism*. The economy does not, and cannot, converge towards any equilibrium. It moves forward, development takes place, and in the long run the average economic condition improves. However, the search for improvement sometimes generates the expected results, but those expectations can also be falsified, thus creating a completely unexpected condition. It is fundamental to an understanding of restlessness that modern capitalism is a creative system in which new forms of economic behaviour are continually stimulated (Metcalfe, 2008, pp. 173–174).

The fact that we are systematically in an out-of-equilibrium position – should an equilibrium position exist – does not constitute a problem. In fact, a short-run optimal system may yet in the long run be inferior to a system that does so at *no* given point of time, because the latter's failure to do so may be a condition for the speed of long-run performance (Schumpeter, 1950a, p. 83).

The best way to conclude this chapter is to make use, once more, of Schumpeter's words synthesising the evolutionary essence of capitalism:

> Capitalism is essentially a process of (endogenous) economic change. Without that change or, more precisely, that kind of change which we have called evolution, capitalist society cannot exist, because the economic functions and, with the functions, the economic bases of its leading strata ... would crumble if it ceased: without innovations, no entrepreneurs; without entrepreneurial achievement, no capitalist returns and no capitalist propulsion. The atmosphere of industrial revolutions – of 'progress' – is the only one in which capitalism can survive. Hence the capitalist organism cannot ... settle down into a stationary stage without being vitally affected ... In this sense stabilized capitalism is a contradiction in terms. (Schumpeter, 1939, p. 1033)

NOTES

1. On capitalism destroying itself by its virtues, see Schumpeter, 1950a, chapters XII and XIII and, for a concentrated synthesis 1950b, pp. 448–449.
2. One can find many books on Schumpeter, which also give an account of his life, including many 'private' details: see McCraw (2007), Stolper (1994), Swedberg (1991), Allen (1991), März (1991); in relation to the latter book, the Preface by James Tobin should be read carefully. For short introductions see Heertje (2008) and Morgenstern (1951); the latter is interesting in that it provides an image of how Schumpeter's work was perceived immediately after his death.
3. The issues referred to in these works range from 'methodological individualism' to the overlapping between science and ideology, to what Schumpeter called the 'Ricardian vice' – that is theorising through so many simplifying assumptions that the results obtained emerge almost as tautologies.
4. Today the town belongs to the Czech Republic and is called Třešt.
5. For a full account one can refer to the books indicated in note 2 above.
6. Backhaus (2003, p. 1) writes that Schumpeter's German work poses difficulties that go beyond a simple language barrier.
7. The original copy I saw in the Berliner *Staatsbibliothek* had '1912' in the first internal page of the book; however, from a pdf I had access to, it looks like there was '1911' on what seems to be the book's dust jacket.
8. The original chapter in German and an English translation of the chapter itself are provided in the book edited by Backhaus (2003).
9. *Das Wesen und der Hauptinhalt der Theoretischen Notionalökonomie*, translated in English only in 2010 – see references (Schumpeter, 1908). The original German book never became a best seller but made him reasonably well known among the economists' community. The book was reviewed in German, British and American journals.
10. Let us here point out that the mathematical and statistical tools which today make possible dynamic analysis were in their infancy in the early decades of the 20th century.

11. See for instance Schumpeter, 1939, p. 87; 1950a, p. 83; 1947, p. 153.
12. It is here worth recalling that Balabkins speaks of an overlooked influence by the 19th-century economist Albert Schäffle on Schumpeter; in fact, he stresses the 'striking similarity' between Schumpeter's and Albert Schäffle's concept of innovation (Balabkins, 2003, pp. 213–215). Schäffle's book referred to by Balabkins was published in 1867 (in German), and the shortened title is *Die nationalökonomische Theorie der ausschließenden Absatzverhältnisse*, Tübingen: Laupp.
13. Usher (1955, p. 534) criticises Schumpeter, pointing out that the latter underestimates the degree of novelty implied in the creation of new combinations.
14. On this specific point see Schumpeter 1939, p. 104 and 1926/1934, p. 137.
15. E.g. Kahneman, 2011; see in particular Chapter 24 of his book.
16. See also Schumpeter, 1939, pp. 110–111.
17. 'There is no tendency toward equalization of these temporary premia [i.e. profit rates]' (Schumpeter, 1939, p. 105); see also ibid., p. 127, note 3.
18. In the very first pages of chapter IV of his *Business Cycles* Schumpeter presents a simplified skeleton made up of two phases of prosperity and recession: see in particular, Schumpeter, 1939, p. 138.
19. A similar expository scheme is also used in *Business Cycles*, but is not as clear-cut.
20. See also Malerba and Orsenigo (1995).
21. See Schumpeter, 1950a, chapter VIII on 'Monopolistic practices' and in particular pp. 99, 101 and 106.
22. E.g. Alchian (1950).
23. See also the section on 'Evolutionism' in the chapter devoted to the 'Intellectual scenery' of chapter 3 of part III of Schumpeter's *History of Economic Analysis* (1954, pp. 435–446).
24. See Schumpeter, 1950a, p. 83; 1939, pp. 114, 1033.
25. One of the main problems is the emergence of increasing returns to scale when nonrival ideas are considered as factors of production (see Barro and Sala-i-Martin, 2003, p. 18).
26. Freeman (2007) speaks of a Schumpeterian Renaissance; for early bibliographies on Schumpeter see Stevenson (1985) and Augello (1990).
27. Worthy of comment is also the fact that the weekly magazine *The Economist* has had a 'Schumpeter' column since September 2009: a clear, and further, acknowledgement of the importance of Schumpeterian ideas.
28. See De Liso and Metcalfe (1996).
29. Starting points can be the names that one finds on the editorial board of the *Journal of Evolutionary Economics*, the names of the contributors to the same journal and to the book edited by Hanusch and Pyka (2007); see also Hanusch (1999).

REFERENCES

Alchian, A.A. (1950), 'Uncertainty, Evolution and Economic Theory', *Journal of Political Economy*, **58** (3), pp. 211–222.

Allen, R.L. (1991), *Opening Doors: The Life and Work of Joseph Schumpeter – Vol. 1 Europe, Vol. 2 America*, New Brunswick: Transaction Books.

Augello, M.M. (1990), *Joseph Alois Schumpeter. A Reference Guide*, Berlin: Springer.

Backhaus, J. (ed.) (2003), *Joseph Alois Schumpeter. Entrepreneurship, Style and Vision*, Boston: Kluwer Academic Publisher.

Balabkins, N.W. (2003), 'Adaptation Without Attribution? The Genesis of Schumpeter's Innovator', in J. Backhaus (ed), *Joseph Alois Schumpeter. Entrepreneurship, Style and Vision*, Boston: Kluwer Academic Publisher, pp. 203–220.

Barro, R.J. and Sala-i-Martin, X. (2003), *Economic Growth*, 2nd edn, Cambridge, Mass.: MIT Press [1st edn 1995].

Baumol, W.J. (2002), *The Free-Market Innovation Machine: Analyzing the Growth Miracle of Capitalism*, Princeton: Princeton University Press.

De Liso, N. and Metcalfe, J.S. (1996), 'On Technological Systems and Technological Paradigms', in E. Helmstädter and M. Perlman (eds), *Behavioral Norms, Technological Progress and Economic Dynamics*, Ann Arbor: University of Michigan Press, pp. 71–95.

Elliott, J.E. (1980), 'Marx and Schumpeter on Capitalism's Creative Destruction: A Comparative Restatement', *Quarterly Journal of Economics*, **95** (1), pp. 45–68.

Freeman, C. (2007), 'A Schumpeterian Renaissance?', in H. Hanusch and A. Pyka (eds), *Elgar Companion to Neo-Schumpeterian Economics*, Cheltenham: Edward Elgar, pp. 130–141.

Haberler, G. (1950), 'Joseph Alois Schumpeter, 1883–1950', *Quarterly Journal of Economics*, **64** (3), pp. 333–372.

Hanusch, H. (ed) (1999), *The Legacy of Joseph A. Schumpeter*, Cheltenham: Edward Elgar Publishing, two volumes.

Hanusch, H. and Pyka, A. (eds) (2007), *Elgar Companion to Neo-Schumpeterian Economics*, Cheltenham: Edward Elgar Publishing.

Heertje, A. (2008), 'Schumpeter, Joseph Alois (1883–1850)', in S.N. Durlauf and L.E. Blume (eds), *The New Palgrave Dictionary of Economics*, Vol. 7, London: Palgrave Macmillan, pp. 319–324.

Kahneman, D. (2011), *Thinking, Fast and Slow*, New York: Farrar, Straus & Giroux.

Kurz, H.D. (2017), 'Is there a "Ricardian Vice"?', *Journal of Evolutionary Economics*, **27** (1), pp. 91–114.

Malerba, F. and Orsenigo, L. (1995), 'Schumpeterian Patterns of Innovation', *Cambridge Journal of Economics*, **19** (1), pp. 47–66.

Marx, K. (1867, Engl. Tr. 1976), *Capital*, Vol.1, Harmondsworth: Penguin Books.

März, E. (1991), *Joseph Schumpeter: Scholar, Teacher and Politician*, New Haven: Yale University Press [translation-cum-revision of the original German edition 1983 *Joseph Alois Schumpeter: Forscher, Lehrer und Politiker*, München: Oldenbourg].

McCraw, T.K. (2007), *Prophet of Innovation. Joseph Schumpeter and Creative Destruction*, Cambridge, Mass.: The Belknap Press.

Metcalfe, J.S. (1998), *Evolutionary Economics and Creative Destruction*, The Graz Schumpeter Lectures, London: Routledge.

Metcalfe J.S. (2008), 'Restless Capitalism', in F. Amatori and M. Amendola (eds), *Ricerca Avanzata e Alta Divulgazione. Le Momigliano Lectures 1997–2008*, Terni: ICSIM, pp. 171–192.

Morgenstern, O. (1951), 'Obituary. Joseph A. Schumpeter, 1883–1950', *Economic Journal*, **61** (March), pp. 197–202.

Nelson, R. and Winter, S.G. (1982), *An Evolutionary Theory of Economic Change*, Cambridge, Mass.: Harvard University Press.

Robinson, A. (1953), Review article of the book '*Schumpeter, Social Scientist*, edited by Seymour E. Harris', *Economic Journal*, **63** (March), pp. 126–129.

Rosenberg, N. (2011), 'Was Schumpeter a Marxist?', *Industrial and Corporate Change*, **20** (4), pp. 1215–1222.

Samuelson, P.A. (1983), '1983: Marx, Keynes and Schumpeter', *Eastern Economic Journal*, **9** (3), pp. 166–179.

Schumpeter, J.A. (1908, Engl. Transl. 2010), *The Nature and Essence of Economic Theory*, New Brunswick, N.J.: Transactions Publishers [repr. 2017 by Routledge].

Schumpeter, J.A. (1909), 'On the Concept of Social Value', *Quarterly Journal of Economics*, **23** (Feb), pp. 213–232.

Schumpeter, J.A. (1926, Engl. Transl. 1934), *The Theory of Economic Development*, repr. 1961, New York: Oxford University Press, first original German edition 1911 *Theorie der wirtschaftlichen Entwicklung*, Duncker & Humblot [English translation based on the second German edition, 1926].

Schumpeter, J.A. (1928), 'The Instability of Capitalism', *Economic Journal*, **38** (Sept), pp. 361–386.

Schumpeter, J.A. (1930, Engl. Transl. 2014), *Treatise on Money*, Aalten: WordBridge Publishing [NB: 1930 is the date of the original manuscript, published in German in 1970 as *Das Wesen des Geldes*, Göttingen: Vandenhoeck & Ruprecht].

Schumpeter, J.A. (1939), *Business Cycles: A Theoretical, Historical and Statistical Analysis of the Capitalist Process*, New York: McGraw-Hill, repr. 2005, Martino Publications, two volumes.

Schumpeter, J.A. (1946), 'John Maynard Keynes 1883–1946', *American Economic Review*, **36** (4), pp. 495–518.

Schumpeter, J.A. (1947), 'The Creative Response in Economic History', *Journal of Economic History*, **7** (2), 149–159.

Schumpeter, J.A. (1949), 'Science and Ideology', *American Economic Review*, **39** (2), pp. 345–359.

Schumpeter, J.A. (1950a), *Capitalism, Socialism and Democracy* [first American edition 1942, last edition supervised by the author: 1950; edition here used: fifth, repr. 1996, London: Routledge].

Schumpeter, J.A. (1950b), 'The March into Socialism', *American Economic Review*, **40** (2), Papers and Proceedings, pp. 446–456.

Schumpeter, J.A. (1954), *History of Economic Analysis*, London: George Allen & Unwin [repr. 1986].

Seymour, E.H. (ed) (1951), *Schumpeter, Social Scientist*, Cambridge, Mass.: Harvard University Press.

Shackle, G.L.S. (1970), *Expectation, Enterprise and Profit. The Theory of the Firm*, London: Routledge.

Shionoya, Y. (1990), 'The Origin of the Schumpeterian Research Program: A Chapter Omitted from Schumpeter's Theory of Economic Development', *Journal of Institutional and Theoretical Economics*, **146**, pp. 314–327.

Stevenson, M.I. (1985), *Joseph Alois Schumpeter. A Bibliography, 1905–1984*, Westport and London: Greenwood Press.

Stolper, W.F. (1994), *Joseph Alois Schumpeter: The Public Life of a Private Man*, Princeton: Princeton University Press.

Swedberg, R. (1991), *Joseph A. Schumpeter: His Life and Work*, Cambridge: Polity Press.

Sylos-Labini, P. (1969), *Oligopoly and Technical Progress*, 2nd edn, Harvard: Harvard University Press (1st edn 1962) [repr. 1993 by A.M. Kelley].

Tobin, J. (1991), 'Preface', in E. März, *Joseph Schumpeter: Scholar, Teacher & Politician*, New Haven: Yale University Press, pp. vii–xiv.

Usher, A.P. (1955), 'Technical Change and Capital Formation', in National Bureau of Economic Research, *Capital Formation and Economic Growth*, Princeton: Princeton University Press, pp. 523–550.

Viner, J. (1990), 'Foreword', in M.M. Augello, *Joseph Alois Schumpeter. A Reference Guide*, Berlin: Springer, pp. vii–xii.

9. Karl Polanyi: The Place of the Economy in Society

Claus Thomasberger

KEY FEATURES

- The chapter poses the question of the historical origins as well as the limits of the market economy.
- It analyzes key institutional features which distinguish the market economy from other social formations.
- The focus is not on economic laws as such but on the relationship between the economy and society.
- The dynamic of the capitalist market society is explained as a result of a double movement based on the principles of economic liberalism on the one hand and protection on the other hand.
- The market economy is presented as a first, provisional and (in the final analysis) utopian answer to the challenges of an industrial society.
- The market society is compared to other historical formations based on the distinction of three principle forms of integration in the human economy: reciprocity, redistribution, and exchange.

The social struggles of the first half of the 20th century, the two World Wars, the Great Depression and the rise of fascism formed the background of Karl Polanyi's writings. Defending a position on the fringes of Austrian-Marxism he developed his approach in the 1920s in debates with the second and third generation of the Austrian School of Economics (Böhm-Bawerk, Wieser, Mises, Schumpeter). Karl Polanyi appreciated Adam Smith's work but criticized strongly all kinds of economic determinism which gained the upper hand with Malthus, Ricardo, Say and their followers. Even if he rejected the labor theory of value, Marx's philosophy exerted a strong impact on Polanyi's thinking. Polanyi agreed with Keynes on the need for government intervention. But he opposed Keynes's aim of safeguarding the capitalist market society.

1. INTRODUCTION

In the last few decades, the work of Karl Polanyi has become an indispensable point of reference not only for activists and critical minds but also for economists and social scientists who feel uncomfortable with the current trends of economic globalization, commodification, liberalization and privatization. Notions such as 'embeddedness', 'double movement', 'fictitious commodities', 'liberal utopia', 'self-regulating market system', 'transformation', 'patterns of integration' have conquered a crucial place in the critical discourse about globalization and neoliberalism. Polanyi's increasing relevance to popular discourse could already be noted in connection with a World Trade Organization (WTO) meeting in 1999 in Seattle, when environmental, labor and civil rights advocates protested against the commodification of nature, the dominance of the profit motive and economic globalization, i.e. the topics which are at the heart of his writings. Since the financial crisis of 2008, predatory financialization, increasing inequality of income and wealth, the rise of right-wing political movements and the crisis of democracy parallels between the current situation and the conditions in the interwar period that Polanyi analyzed have moved into the focus of scientific debate.

In this chapter, we will begin with a short overview of Polanyi's life, which will be followed by a look at his most famous publication, *The Great Transformation* (Polanyi, 1944 [2001]). Polanyi's approach will be compared with two other approaches which share the vision that the market system, left to itself, produces results which are in conflict with the aims of society: Marx's critique of political economy on the one hand, and Keynes's theory on the other hand. This will then allow for the introduction of the well-known categories 'double movement', 'embeddedness', 'self-regulation' and 'market utopia'. Section 3 will give an overview of his comparative research on primitive, archaic and modern economies. In the final section, we will discuss the relevance of Polanyi's work for the 21st century.

2. POLANYI'S LIFE

Polanyi's life was marked by the upheavals and struggles that characterized the end of 19th-century civilization and the first decades of the 20th century in Europe. For most of his life he worked as a journalist and adult teacher. In the academic field he remained an outsider. Indeed, only in the last years of his life was he appointed to an academic position. Even if his most famous book *The Great Transformation* was written in America and addressed above all an Anglo-Saxon audience, the roots of Polanyi's thinking lay in Central Europe, especially in Hungary and Austria where he lived and worked for the greater part of his life.

Born in 1886 in Vienna, Polanyi spent his youth in Budapest, where he studied law and philosophy, became the founding president of the student movement known as the 'Galilei Circle' (1908–1909) and editor of the periodical *Free Thought* (Szabádgondolat, 1913–1919). The circle, which organized innumerable courses, debates and conferences, allowed him to become acquainted with many intellectuals and artists: among others György Lukács, Karl Mannheim, Werner Sombart, Max Adler, Eduard Bernstein, the psychoanalyst Sándor Ferenczi, the poet Endre Ady and the composer Béla Bartók. At the same time he cooperated with Oszkár Jászi, who was the editor of the journal *Twentieth Century* (Hszadik Század), leader of the Radical Party and a Minister of the first Hungarian Republic in 1918. The early period of his life ended after World War I when health conditions and political reasons (the foreseeable seizure of power by the reactionary government of Miklós Horthy) prompted him to seek exile in Vienna.

In 'Red Vienna', Polanyi was faced with a fundamentally different situation compared to the conditions in Hungary. The Great War and the Russian Revolution had profoundly changed the conditions in at least two ways. First, the war had revealed that economic determinism and the faith in the laws of economic and social development were illusory. As he pointed out in an article written in 1919, 'the outbreak of the world war was the turning point for all capitalist and, with it, Marxist thinking. ... It became plain to see that not the material world but the conception of it is the driving force (however false and erroneous this conception is), that it is therefore the conceptions and not the material itself, which governs the masses' (Polanyi, 1919, p. 461, translation by the author). Secondly, in Vienna a socialist transformation seemed to be achievable within a relatively short period of time. In May 1919, the Social Democratic Workers' Party had won the elections for the city council of Vienna. A whole series of local measures aiming at a fundamental improvement of the working and living conditions and the education of the workers had been tackled, such as limiting rents, the expansion of social housing and the creation of community colleges.

The years from 1919 to 1933, which Polanyi spent in Vienna, were decisive for his further development. The fertile and vibrant intellectual climate in 'Red Vienna' – the discussions with K. Popper, H. Kelsen, J. Schumpeter, the 'Vienna Circle' (including O. Neurath), the engagement with the work of the 'German Historical School', M. Weber and especially the Austrian School of Economics (F. Wieser, L. Mises, F.A.

Hayek) and the protagonists of Austro-Marxism (O. Bauer, M. Adler, R. Hilferding, and K. Renner) formed the background of Polanyi's thinking. As he wrote in a letter to a friend in 1925: 'During these years my ideas on social issues have found passionate expression. The social sciences, activity, but above all the possibility of freedom of thought on social issues' (Polanyi, 1925 [2000], p. 317). In all these years he worked and earned his living as a journalist, first for the newspaper *Bécsi Magyar Ujság* (Hungarian News in Vienna), and from 1924 for the weekly magazine *Der Österreichische Volkswirt*. Holding a position on the fringes of Austro-Marxism, Polanyi (1922 [2016] and 1924 [2018]) also participated in the 'Socialist Calculation Debate' (initiated by L. Mises, 1920 [2008] and 1922 [1951]), organized seminars with students and scholars, gave speeches and wrote numerous articles about theoretical and practical aspects of a socialist reorganization of society. There can be no doubt that the debates in Vienna shaped Polanyi's thought for the rest of his life.

In 1933, Polanyi had to emigrate for the second time for political reasons. Considering the authoritarian course adopted by the Dollfuss government, his anti-fascist and socialist position could have caused serious trouble for *Der Österreichische Volkswirt*. He chose to move to England, which gave him the possibility to continue his activities for the journal as a 'foreign editor' (until 1938 when the publication of the journal was interrupted due to the annexation of Austria by the Third Reich). In England he engaged with the Christian Left and taught for the Workers' Educational Association (WEA) which brought him not only into direct contact with the economic historians H. Tawney and G.D.H. Cole, but also opened a new field of activity: 'I was fifty years old when circumstances in England led me to studies in economic history. I earned my living that way, as a teacher. For I was born to be one' (Polanyi, 1950 [1977]). The main topics of his teaching were international relations and English social and economic history. In addition, several lecture tours in the United States allowed him to establish contacts with American universities.

In 1941–1943, a two-year fellowship granted by the Rockefeller Foundation enabled him to write *The Great Transformation* at Bennington College, Vermont, USA. Later, aged 61 and close to retirement, he won his first academic appointment. In 1947 the Economics Department of Columbia University, New York, invited him as a visiting professor. This allowed him to become acquainted with institutional economists, among them John M. Clark and Carter Goodrich as well as the sociologists Paul Lazarsfeld and Robert Merton. Until 1953 he taught a seminar on General Economic History for graduate students. After retiring from his teaching position he continued to co-direct the so-called Columbia Interdisciplinary

Project resulting in the publication of the book *Trade and Market in the Early Empires* (Polanyi et al., 1957). Due to the fact that his wife Ilona Duczynska, a former member of the Hungarian Communist Party, was banned from the United States, he then took up residence in Pickering, Ontario, where he drew up the manuscripts for the two posthumously published books *Dahomey and the Slave Trade* (Polanyi, 1966) and *The Livelihood of Man* (Polanyi, 1977).

3.   THE THEORETICAL FRAMEWORK OF *THE GREAT TRANSFORMATION*

'Nineteenth-century civilization has collapsed' (Polanyi, 1944 [2001], p. 3), is the first sentence of *The Great Transformation*. Indeed, the interwar period saw the end of the crucial institutions upon which 19th-century civilization was based: the balance-of-power system, the liberal state, the self-regulating market system and the international gold standard. Polanyi's most famous book was published directly after Peter Drucker's *The Future of Industrial Man*, Karl Mannheim's *Diagnosis of Our Time*, Joseph Schumpeter's *Capitalism, Socialism and Democracy* and in the same year as Karl Popper's *The Open Society and its Enemies*, Ludwig Mises' *Omnipotent Government* and Friedrich Hayek's *Road to Serfdom*. It is one of the important 'Austrian contributions' at a crucial moment in the history of the modern Western world. All of these books are written by authors who had spent their youth in the Austrian-Hungarian Empire and decided under the fascist threat to leave central Europe and emigrate to the Anglo-Saxon world. The central question these books try to answer is the same: How can the collapse of the central European civilization of the 19th century be explained? Polanyi's contribution challenges all those interpretations which seek refuge in economistic and deterministic explanations. The disasters of the interwar period occurred, he argues, not because of economic contradictions, or the falling rate of profit, or over-accumulation or under-consumption, but because of a deadlock between the economy and the political realm which in Europe undermined the stability of society. The Great Depression, the rise of fascism and the World Wars are not the results of an economic breakdown, but of a profound crisis of Western civilization.

In *The Great Transformation* Polanyi draws on an analysis which he had developed already a decade earlier in Vienna when he explained: 'A chasm has opened between the economy and politics. These scant words give the diagnosis of the times. The economy and politics, two manifestations of the life of society, have declared their autonomy and wage unceasing war against each other. ... society whose political and economic systems are in conflict is doomed to decline – or to be overthrown' (Polanyi, 1932 [2018], p. 61). The World Wars, the Great Depression and the rise of fascism cannot be understood, Polanyi maintains, if the conflict between the market economy and democracy is ignored.

Focusing on the relative position of the economy in society, Polanyi draws on the *description* of the double movement which had been put forward by 'liberal writers like Spencer and Sumner, Mises and Lippmann' (Polanyi, 1944 [2001], p. 143), but he reverses the *interpretation*. While the protagonists of economic liberalism accused the protective countermovement of having undermined the working of the market system by pursuing unrealistic dreams or sectional interests, Polanyi turns the relationship 'back on its feet'. Not protection, he claims, but the liberal creed itself, the belief in a self-regulation of the market system is the *utopia* which was ultimately responsible for the Great Depression, the rise of fascism and the World Wars. The market system alone, he underlines, 'would have physically destroyed man and transformed his surroundings into a wilderness. Inevitably, society took measures to protect itself' (Polanyi, 1944 [2001], p. 3). Therefore, protection was (and continues to be) not only realistic, but also vital. The groups which function as its protagonists cannot be blamed for defending society against the consequences of a fatal utopia. Economic liberalism itself bears the principal responsibility for the disasters of the 20th century. This is the core of his message: The supporters of economic liberalism confound utopia and social reality. Based on conceited economic theories they design a utopian world in which the laws of the market dominate society. *The Great Transformation* is essentially a defense of common people's *realism* against the utopian vision of the liberal economic elite.

Polanyi characterizes economic liberalism as a 'stark utopia'. What does he mean when he criticizes economic liberalism as a utopian creed? Most misinterpretations identify 'utopian' with 'not achievable'. But this is not what Polanyi has in mind. On the contrary, he contends that the liberal utopia is dangerous exactly because it is much more attainable than one may have expected. Nineteenth-century society is the proof. Even if it was based on a utopian belief, it was real. The liberal creed was *in reality* the driving force behind the transformation of society. So what then does Polanyi refer to when he talks of economic liberalism as a utopian belief?

In order to find an answer to this question we have to go back to the roots of his critique of economic liberalism. Polanyi accredits the protagonists of economic liberalism a fundamental insight: They understood that the *Industrial Revolution* marked the beginning of a new period in the history of the human race. The 19th century gave birth to what he calls 'the machine age'. Polanyi builds on one insight upon which Adam Smith and Ludwig Mises, Robert Owen and Karl Marx, Max Weber and Friedrich Hayek agree: 'The machine created a new civilization' (Polanyi, 1977, p. xlviii). The introduction of specialized machines into an agrarian and commercial society gave rise to totally new and unprecedented 'technological civilization'. Technology, sciences, mass production and mass consumption, the division of labor on a global scale, the interruption of direct human relations, the loss of transparency and overview (Übersicht) present humanity with completely new challenges.

The strength of economic liberalism is that its protagonists were well aware of the challenges. Even before the Industrial Revolution had gathered pace, Adam Smith called attention to the difference between the conditions of 'barbarous societies' in which 'every man is in some measure a statesman, and can form a tolerable judgment concerning the interest of the society' from those 'in a civilized state' in which 'though there is little variety in the occupations of the greater part of individuals, there is an almost infinite variety in those of the whole society', so that the individual actors lose their overview and understanding of the general state of affairs. 'The man whose whole life is spent in performing a few simple operations,' Smith continued, 'generally becomes as stupid and ignorant as it is possible for a human creature to become' (Smith, 1776 [1976], 782). In Polanyi's times the question took again the center stage of the discussion. Max Weber problematized not only bureaucratization but also the differentiation and rationalization which results in a loss of awareness and understanding of the social context by the single actor. 'The rationalization of community action,' Weber stated, 'will most certainly not result in a universalization of the knowledge about its conditionalities and interrelations, but mostly in the exact opposite. The "savage" knows infinitely more about the economic and social conditions of his own existence than "civilized man"' (Weber, 1913 [2012], pp. 300–301). The Austrian School of Economics seized the issue. 'In the narrow confines of a closed household economy', Ludwig Mises wrote in his article which opened the so-called 'socialist accountancy debate', 'it is possible throughout to review the process of production from beginning to end, and to judge all the time whether one or another mode of procedure yields more consumable goods. This, however, is no longer possible in the incomparably more involved circumstances of our own social economy. ... The human mind cannot orientate itself properly among the bewildering mass of intermediate products and potentialities of production' (Mises, 1920 [2008], pp. 12–13).

Polanyi accepts the problem. The new civilization based on the machine 'has come to stay. It is our fate. We must learn to live with it, if we are to live at all' (Polanyi, 1977, p. xlviii). The conditions of a complex technological civilization pose problems which in traditional community-based societies did not exist. But Polanyi rejects the liberal answer which presents the market system as the solution to the challenges of a complex society. It is well known that Adam Smith identified the social division of labor with exchange and market transactions. Since Marx's distinction between the productive forces and the social relations of production, this naïve answer has no longer been sufficient. Mises, Hayek, Friedman and their followers distinguish, in principle, two possible solutions to the challenges of a technological society: central planning or markets. But because central planning necessitates coercion and dictatorship over needs, it is regarded as being incompatible with personal freedom. Their conclusion is obvious: Only the mechanism of supply and demand fulfills the prerequisites of a free and at the same time technological society. If we want to safeguard personal freedom under modern conditions, 'there is no alternative' to the market system, as M. Thatcher summed up the liberal creed.

It is this latter conclusion which Polanyi regards as utopian. Exactly because the market system regulates itself, because it brings about its *own* laws, it negates the needs of society. All various attempts by equilibrium theory to 'humanize the market' obscure the real issue. The self-regulating market system can never be a solution to the challenges of the machine age which is compatible with human freedom. No blind and soulless mechanism can take over responsibility for the destiny of humanity. Only human beings can assume this task which implies nothing less than the subordination of the economy to a democratic society.

In the 1920s Polanyi discusses the issue in great detail in his contributions not only to the socialist accountancy debate but also to the theoretical debate concerning a socialist transformation of society (Polanyi, 1922 [2016], 1925 [2018], 1927 [2018]). After his emigration to England he continued to work on the questions within the context of the Christian Left Study Circle (Polanyi, 1935, 1937a [2018], 1937b [2018]). The self-regulating market system, we may summarize from his conclusion, is no more than an initial adjustment to the conditions of a technological civilization. The disasters of the interwar period demonstrate, Polanyi maintains, that 19th-century civilization was past its best.

3.1 Polanyi and Marx

The theoretical framework which Polanyi develops in order to underpin this statement can perhaps be best understood if it is compared to Marx's critique of political economy on the one hand and Keynes's critique of the classical theory on the other. Let's start with the former. It is well known that Marx also considers the Industrial Revolution as an event which prepared for the birth of a new type of civilization, the bourgeois society. The starting point of Marx's Critique of Political Economy is the inhuman character of the new society which originates in the domination of economic system over a truly human society.

Not only in his early writings, but also in *Capital* (Marx, 1867), especially in the fetish chapter, Marx rejects the bourgeois society because it is governed not by immediate human interaction, but by economic relations. He criticizes the capitalist mode of production as the origin of the reification of interpersonal relations and the estrangement of human beings. The bourgeois world, he emphasizes, is doomed because it is based not on the action of truly human persons, but on the behavior of personifications of economic categories (owners of commodities, workers, capitalists etc.). Marx's philosophy is based on the noneconomic nature of human beings and the totality of society. Nevertheless, in other parts of his work he concentrates on the contradictions within one particular realm of society, the economy, creating the impression that the relation between the economy and society plays only a secondary role.

Polanyi returns to the starting point of Marx's critique. Even if he does not negate the contradictions of the capitalist economy, in his oeuvre the shifting relationship between the economy and society gains center stage. Polanyi is convinced that the place of the economy in society is the pivot on which the understanding of the social conflicts of the 20th century turns. The separation of the economy from society 'is the true characteristic of liberal capitalism' (Polanyi, 1935–40 [2018], p. 137), he underlines. The categories 'disembedding', 'self-regulating market system', 'double movement' etc. indicate different aspects of the relationship between the economy and society under modern conditions. The dynamic of this relationship is not only at the heart of *The Great Transformation*; the particular character which the link between the economy and society assumes under the conditions of the market society is also, as we will see in a moment, at the center of his comparative studies of primitive, archaic and modern societies.

Polanyi agrees with Marx that under the historical conditions of the 19th century in Europe the market system actually develops a life of its own which does not take into account (or is even in direct contrast to) the needs of society. This is what he calls self-regulation: The market system follows its *own laws*. But Polanyi's explanation differs from the common Marxist interpretation insofar as he rejects the base–superstructure thesis and the idea that social dynamics are ultimately determined by the laws of the economy. Society reacts and intervenes, disturbs and modifies these laws. It is the *conflict* between the economy and society, between the self-regulation of the economy and the reaction of society, which drives the transformation of the civilization of the nineteenth century.

The fact that the economy develops its own laws has the consequence that it functions as if it were a soulless mechanism. But a society which is subordinated to such a mechanism 'could not exist for any length of time without annihilating the human and natural substance of society' (Polanyi, 1944 [2001], p. 3). No soulless mechanism can replace human *freedom* and *responsibility* for the integrity of society. In the long run the contradictions that are inherent in modern society will only be resolved, so his conclusion goes, if the economy is subordinated to a democratic society.

Polanyi does not negate that in a competitive environment 'the supply-demand-price system will always balance' (Polanyi, 1944 [2001], p. 223). But even if self-regulation is real from an economic point of view, the same is not true from a social perspective. Economic logic and the needs of society fall apart. The price which the economic mechanism produces does not automatically satisfy the needs of society. By following its own logic, the supply-demand-price system generates economic equilibria which threaten society as well as the natural environment.

The conviction that the crisis cannot be reduced to economic causes is the reason for Polanyi's detailed analysis of the transformation of English society in the 19th century. The reform of the Speenhamland Laws, which in the 1830s prepared the way for a labor market, the depression of the 1870s, increasing protection of national industries as well as imperialism, are depicted as the outcome of the double movement which results from the battle between liberal forces on the one hand and the protective countermovement on the other hand.

The deadlock of the interwar period which resulted in the Great Depression, the rise of fascism and World War II became unavoidable when the liberal forces entrenched behind the economy and the countermovement used its superior numbers in the parliaments for protection. Both the economy and the political realm are of vital importance for society. No society whose political and economic systems are at war with each other can survive. A lasting solution to this deadly conflict is only possible if the prejudices of economic liberalism are replaced by a realistic vision of man and society.

3.2 Polanyi and Keynes

At this point Polanyi meets with Keynes. Keynes, too, rejects the idea that the self-regulating market system, left to itself, operates for the benefit of society. In *On Money* he denies an automatic tendency towards price stability. In his second major work, *The General Theory of Employment, Interest and Money*, he maintains that the market system may tend towards a multitude of economic equilibria which, as a rule, do not include full employment of labor and other resources. And in Bretton Woods he argues in favor of international organizations which surveil and regulate the international markets that, left to themselves, would destabilize national economies. Keynes's theoretical and political initiatives are based on the conviction that the economic result of the self-regulating market process and social goals – whether full employment, price level stability or national policy space – do not coincide.

Keynes's as well as Polanyi's critique of political economy reflect the circumstances of the period in which the institutions supporting 19th century civilization reached their end. Both point towards a change in the relationship between the economic and the political realm, i.e. they envisage a society which frees itself from the fetters of the economy by overcoming the liberal belief in the self-regulating market system. According to both interpretations, laissez-faire and economic determinism which had shaped 19th-century consciousness had to be replaced by a more realistic vision so as to escape the deadlock that threatened Western civilization during the interwar period. Both hold economic liberalism (respectively the 'liberal creed' and the 'classical theory') accountable for the Great Depression as well as for the rise of fascism.

Polanyi and Keynes also have similar visions concerning the relationship between economic theories and the economy. Both regard economic ideas as performative. Whether right or wrong, economic ideas are part of social reality. Being and consciousness cannot be separated. The civilization of the 19th century could exist only because economic liberalism had become the dominating world view. Precisely because human beings believed in the objective existence of economic laws and acted accordingly, these laws became real (cf. Thomasberger, 2012/13). The market system functions as a self-regulating system as long as the belief in the dominance of the economy over society and the commodity fiction of labor, land and money prevail. For sure, from the point of view of society labor is not a commodity but a human activity, land describes the natural environment and money is a token which represents purchasing power. However, this is irrelevant as long as the market system dominates over society. If people believe in the doctrine that the factors of production are commodities, if these are actually bought and sold on the market and if markets for labor, land and money are institutionalized, *the fiction is real*. The commodity fiction is not simply an erroneous creed. Without the fictitious commodities the self-regulating market system could not have functioned.

Under the conditions of a market society the fiction that labor, land and money are commodities is true.

The difference between Polanyi and Keynes is, first of all, a divergence of their research programs. While the former aims at a *historical explanation*, Keynes's main contribution consists in constructing an alternative *theoretical model* of the relationship between the economy and the state; a theory of economic policy. And indeed, in retrospect we know that Keynes is quite successful in changing the way politicians and technocrats think about economic affairs, at least in the two decades after World War II. On the other hand, it is Polanyi, not Keynes, who raises the question of how the emergence 'of a society that was not subject to the laws of the state, but, on the contrary, subjected the state to its own laws' (Polanyi, 1944 [2001], p. 116) can be explained. He asks what it means that the liberal creed 'rules the world'. Only Polanyi analyzes the consequences of the fictitious ideas of economic liberalism for the transformation of society in the 19th century.

But there is also a second, more profound difference between the two approaches. Even if both agree on the fallacy of classical liberalism and the laissez-faire doctrine, Keynes, in principle, accepts the liberal answer that the market system is the only known response to the challenges of a technological civilization which is compatible with personal freedom. He recognizes that the market mechanism alone is not sufficient and that there are various forms of market failures. But he expects that the deficiencies of the market system can be 'remedied' or 'repaired' by state intervention. Therefore, Keynes pleads for market-compliant solutions, in which the state authorities take over the task of compensating for the deficits of the market system. The consequence is that in Keynes's model a technocratic system which comprises state agencies and the market system is substituted for the self-regulating market mechanism. Polanyi, in contrast, does not share Keynes's trust in the market as an answer to the challenges of a technologic society. To avoid a misunderstanding: Polanyi is not against markets. He is convinced that 'the end of market society means in no way the absence of markets' (Polanyi, 1944 [2001], p. 260). Again, it is the *relationship* between markets and society which is at issue.

A sustainable answer to the conflict between the economy and society can only be reached, Polanyi emphasizes, if society gains mastery over the economic system. His core idea is expressed most clearly in the statement that, 'socialism is, essentially, the tendency inherent in an industrial civilization to transcend the self-regulating market by consciously subordinating it to a democratic society' (Polanyi, 1944 [2001], p. 242). Polanyi's critique of political economy is not only directed against the waste of underutilized resources, against the injustice and the unequal distribution of income and life chances. It is primarily directed against alienation, the reification of human relations and the inhuman consequences that result from the domination of the economic system over society.

Keynes agrees with Polanyi about the utopian character of the idea of a self-regulating market system. His models oblige the central banks, fiscal policy and international institutions (International Monetary Fund and World Bank) to fill the gap. Keynes's approach suggests that political regulation achieves what self-regulation promised in vain. The results which economic liberalism had depicted as the automatic result of the self-regulating market system (full employment, stability of price levels and international economic relations) can be achieved by intelligent state intervention. This is the deeper meaning of the sentence that, 'if our central controls succeed in establishing an aggregate volume of output corresponding to full employment as nearly as is practicable, the classical theory comes into its own again from this point onwards' (Keynes, 1936, p. 378).

Polanyi, in contrast, does not think that a technocratic system is necessarily more social than a self-regulating economic system. And he does not place his hope in state agencies as long as they are not controlled democratically by society. His goal is to replace the regulation of soulless systems with the democratic structures of decision making. Society has to dominate over the economy, not the other way around.

This does not mean that Polanyi's position is contrary to the proposals which Keynes advances. On several occasions he expresses his support for the 'new liberalism' which Keynes's ideas are part of. He explicitly welcomes the proposals of the *Report of the Liberal Industrial Inquiry* which was co-authored by Keynes (Polanyi, 1928 [2002]). He admires the originality, the recognition of the need for social protection and the limits to the market logic which are expressed in the report. From Polanyi's point of view, Keynes's ideas are clearly an advancement in the right direction. He appreciates the critique of self-regulation which the classical school propagated. And he agrees with Keynes's critique of the International Gold Standard as well as his case for greater national self-sufficiency (Keynes, 1933; Polanyi, 1945 [2018]). But he is also convinced that Keynes's critique does not go deep enough. Or more exactly, he remains skeptical about the fact that, by aiming in his theoretical models at those goals which are shared by economic liberalism, Keynes accepts the framework of the market society and wants to limit the negative side effects by state intervention.

3.3   The Post-war Order

This also explains Polanyi's skepticism with regards to the social system which, after World War II, had been established in both the United States and Western Europe. The reason is that he was well aware of the contradictory character of the emerging type of society. Although after World War II the supremacy of society over the economy was recognized *in principle*, the acceptance of the liberal framework – most clearly expressed by the criterion of market-conformity – demanded the conscious subordination of state agencies (and later of the whole of society) to the logic of the market. In the 1950s and 1960s as a matter of fact not only Keynes, but also Hayek, Friedman and other market fundamentalists acknowledged that the future of the market economy depends on a particular institutional framework which only the state can provide. Both the Austrian School and the Chicago School of Economics recognized the importance of a strong state. Only if the political realm sustains the market system can the latter gain stability. But as long as the framework of the market is taken for granted the task of the state authorities is defined by the needs of the economy. Even if in principle society is free to follow its own priorities, it has to accept what the market requires. In order to avoid a schism between the economy and society, this interdependence demands that society accepts the rules of the market. In other words, after World War II market-conformity of the state and society was substituted for institutional separation between the economy and society.

The characterization of the post-war system in terms of 'embedded liberalism' (Ruggie, 1982) remains ambiguous insofar as the notion underrates the necessity that in this regime the state agencies *must* give priority to the logic of the economic system whenever the smooth functioning of the market system is endangered, even if such a policy is in contrast to the needs of society. If a conflict arises, the rules of the market *have to* be accepted. The threat of a new deadlock is the sword of Damocles which forces the central banks and the fiscal authorities into sustaining the economy. This might be the reason for Polanyi's judgement that in Bretton Woods 'John Maynard Keynes destroyed his life's work by defending what Wall Street firmly intended to be a return to an international gold standard' (Polanyi, 1947b [2018], p. 228).

Polanyi's critique of the liberal society goes back to the roots. Not reintegration (re-embedding), but subordination of the economic system to a democratic society is his aim; not adaptation of economic policy to the market, but adaptation of the economy to the needs of society as a whole. He turns explicitly against those who maintain 'that the whole of society should be more intimately adjusted to the economic system, which they would wish to maintain unchanged. This is the ideal of the Brave New World, where the individual is conditioned to support an order that has been designed for him by such as are wiser than he' (Polanyi, 1947a [2018], pp. 210–211).

Polanyi would not have been surprised that liberal authors accuse him of defending an appealing but utopian vision of the world because of his distinction between the market system and the conditions of a technological society. In their view, Polanyi is portrayed as one of the great utopian socialists in the tradition of Owen, Fourier, Saint-Simon, Proudhon, Dühring and many others. But it is exactly this interpretation which Polanyi challenges in all his writings. He regards the question as to which of the two interpretations – the liberal view which assumes that only markets allow for freedom under the conditions of an industrial civilization, or his own interpretation which contests the liberal vision as fictitious – is correct as 'perhaps the most important problem of recent social history' (Polanyi, 1944 [2001], p. 148). It is important to keep in mind the fact that Polanyi aims at *understanding*. His major contributions analyze the rise, the transformation, and the collapse of 19th-century civilization. His research program focuses on the *explanation* of the disasters of the 20th century. He never makes any kind of prediction nor does he outline models of a future socialist society.

It would also be a misinterpretation to consider the main contrasts between Polanyi's approach and the various liberal interpretations as consequence of different value judgments. For sure, Polanyi never makes a secret of his orientation towards the Western ideal of individual *freedom* based on personal *responsibility* (cf. Polanyi, 1927 [2018]). But his critique of economic liberalism is based not on particular value judgments, but on a different explanation *of the facts*. What distinguishes his oeuvre from all varieties of economic liberalism is that he does not share the liberal belief that the market system – as opposed to conscious human decision – resolves the challenges of a technological civilization. Economic liberalism leads us astray, he maintains, insofar as it gives the impression that the market system would 'free' people from the responsibility for their own destiny. Not the market, but only human beings can assume the responsibility which allows for resolving the challenges. His analysis of World War I, the Great Depression and the rise of fascism followed by the World War II aims at demonstrating that the creation of a global self-regulating market system has been no more than a first and (long since) obsolete reaction of humanity to the problems of a technological civilization. 'Liberal capitalism', he sums up:

was in effect man's initial response to the challenge of the Industrial Revolution. In order to allow scope to the use of elaborate, powerful machinery, we transformed human economy into a self-adjusting system of markets, and cast our thoughts and values in the mold of this unique innovation. Today ... how to organize human life in a machine society is a question that confronts us anew. Behind the fading fabric of competitive capitalism there looms the portent of an industrial civilization, with its paralyzing division of labor, standardization of life, supremacy of mechanism over organism, and organization over spontaneity. Science itself is haunted by insanity. This is the abiding concern. (Polanyi, 1947a [2018], p. 197)

4. PRIMITIVE, ARCHAIC AND MODERN SOCIETIES: THE COMPARATIVE ANALYSIS OF ECONOMIC SYSTEMS

The Great Transformation focuses on the explanation of a *singular event*, a particular period in modern history, the collapse of 19th-century civilization in Europe. In the 1950s he did not continue this research program, even if he played with the idea of doing so. The planned books *Common Man's Masterplan* and *The Great Transformation in the Sixties* were never written. Instead his attention shifted towards the problem of material livelihood. His main objective in the 1950s and the beginning of the 1960s was to explore the possibilities of what he called 'General Economic History'.

The reason is quite obvious. At least since 1947 Polanyi understood that, even if after the war a socialist transformation seemed to be possible in a few European countries, the Western world was moving in other directions. Strong American influences and the unbroken belief in the market system put a stop to whatever socialist hopes may have existed. Indeed, if in the 1950s Polanyi had believed in the possibility of an immediate socialist turn in the Western World, as some commentators would have us believe, his work would be only of historical interest today. In this case he surely would have concentrated his research on the ongoing transformation and not on questions of general economic history. This is all the more obvious as Polanyi considered the analysis of the relationship between the economy and society in primitive, archaic and modern times as 'an economic historian's contribution to world affairs in a period of perilous transformation. Its aim is simple: to enlarge our freedom of creative adjustment, and thereby improve our chances of survival' (Polanyi 1977, p. xliii). He is well aware of the fact that the transformation would continue and that the 'new liberalism', as long as its initiatives of sustaining the market system by political intervention prevailed, would postpone but not overcome the crucial conflicts of the market society. Exactly because he knew that

'I myself have never lived in such a [socialist – CT] society' (Polanyi, 1964, p. 47), he continued to consider it his task as an economic historian to lay bare the utopian foundations of the liberal creed.

Besides his broad interest in different forms of social existence, the principle objectives of his research on primitive, archaic and modern societies were twofold: First, the studies allowed him to demonstrate that the separation of the economy from society which was caused by the establishment of a self-regulating market system was a particular, absolutely exceptional and unique arrangement which distinguished the 19th-century market society from all other societies known in human history. Second, he regarded his treatises on the questions of economic history as a contribution to developing a theoretical framework which would challenge the dominant market mentality and prepare the ground for establishing a 'view of man and society very different from that which we inherited from market-economy' (Polanyi, 1947a [2018], p. 211).

The logical error committed by the protagonists of the market view of society, Polanyi maintains, is what he calls 'the economistic fallacy', i.e. the logically fallacious identification of 'the human economy in general with its market form' (Polanyi, 1977, p. 6). This is implemented via liberal economic and social theorists' categories such as price, capital, rent, wage etc. which, though relevant only under the conditions of a market society, are erroneously universalized and applied to all human economies. In other words, Polanyi's principle question is not how prices are determined, but why prices exist at all. He is looking for the societal and institutional preconditions under which the supply-demand-price mechanism becomes relevant in practice.

The misleading universalization of categories which are meaningful only under the conditions of a market society is directly linked, he argues, with the fusion of the *two meanings* in which the term 'economic' is normally applied in social sciences. On the one hand, the *substantive* meaning refers to the process which supplies human beings with the material means for satisfying their wants. It is based on institutionalized forms of interaction between humans and their natural surroundings. On the other hand, the *formal* meaning of economic refers to the means-ends relationship. The latter is a universal category which is not restricted to the economy but can be applied to any kind of human action. We refer to the formal meaning when we think about *maximizing, economizing* or *making the best of one's means*. Logically, both have completely different roots and meanings. Only under the particular condition of the market society in which the livelihood of human beings is institutionally connected to the problem of ends and insufficient means by the notion of scarcity are both meanings tied together. This is clearly the case in a market society, but only under these conditions. Any kind of generalization of the market categories to non-market forms of human livelihood produces confusion and makes a real understanding impossible.

Polanyi conducts his study on primitive, archaic and modern economies in the form of a comparative analysis of economic systems. This includes an approach which does not start from the individual actor as the basic unit but assumes that, on the contrary, the behavior of the individual can be understood only when the institutional background is taken into consideration. The economic institutions as such are the starting point of the inquiry. This approach relates his work to the great tradition of European social theories of the 19th century and the first half of the 20th century. Polanyi explicitly draws on Karl Marx, Ferdinand Tönnies, Max Weber, Karl Bücher, Henry Sumner Maine, Bronisław Malinowski and Richard Thurnwald. And it shows the affinity of his approach with institutionalists such as Thorstein Veblen, John K. Galbraith, Karl W. Kapp, Adolph Löwe and Gunnar Myrdal. Concentrating on structural similarities and, in a first step, leaving aside motivational patterns and personal attitudes, Polanyi distinguishes three principle forms of integration in the human economy: reciprocity, redistribution, and exchange.

If we confront Polanyi's approach with the liberal reasoning, the crucial point is the relationship between institutional patterns, individual action and the forms of integration. The forms of integration presuppose definite institutional structures which are created beforehand by society. Only if this condition is fulfilled do certain personal motivations and attitudes gain importance. These institutional structures, Polanyi argues, cannot be explained as the result of personal attitudes. Reciprocity depends on the prior existence of symmetrically placed groups. Only if society is already organized on the basis of symmetrical structures can reciprocative attitudes become economically relevant. Redistribution and the cooperative attitude of individuals presuppose the existence of a recognized center which has been established earlier. Correspondingly, 'exchange, as a form of integration, is dependent on the presence of a market system, an institutional pattern which, contrary to common assumptions, does not originate in random actions of exchange' (Polanyi, 1977, p. 38). Just as, by performing his or her role in a drama, the actor does not produce a theater, so the bartering attitude of the merchant does not create a market system. On the contrary, as long as markets have not been institutionalized, individual bartering may occur, but it will not play a vital role in the social order. Only if society decides, for whatever reason, to establish a market, will a relevant number of individuals seize the opportunity and assume the function of merchants. This is the case in modern times. In order to employ expensive, elaborate machinery for the purposes of production, *society* has established markets not only for the products of industry, but also for the factors of production: labor, land and money.

With this we are back to Polanyi's main concern. From an institutional point of view the modern market society is unique and absolutely exceptional. The institutional separation is not only due to the central role of markets, but also to the integration of the factors of production into the market system which brought about a self-regulating mechanism and 'gave rise to yet another, even more extreme development, namely a whole society embedded in the mechanism of its own economy – a market society' (Polanyi, 1977, p. 9). While trade and money developed quite early in human history and markets, even if a later invention, are so old that it is difficult to trace their beginnings, the formation of a self-regulating market system is an absolutely modern development. And only with the creation of the modern market society is the relationship between the economy and society reversed. For sure, there is and can be no society without an economy. And the economy is and always remains the economy of a society. But only in the market society could an economic sphere be established which separated from society by developing particular norms and rules of behavior and which then colonized the whole of society.

The critique that Polanyi would idealize the conditions of the primitive or archaic period misses the mark. In his writings on primitive and archaic societies Polanyi tries to convince the readers that the conditions of a technological civilization have to be kept separate from the institutional features of a market society. Therefore, he has to demonstrate the particular and exceptional character of the market civilization which the liberal vision of society negated. He does not oppose markets. On the contrary, he is especially interested in the origins and the position of markets in pre-technological societies. His critique is directed not against markets as such, but against the creation of a self-regulating market system which subordinates society to the economy. Polanyi has no doubts that markets would continue to play an important role, even if the market society should become history. The market society, he maintains, is no more than a first vigorous attempt at adjustment to the new conditions. The development of a broader theoretical framework should help to facilitate the creative adaptation of humanity to the challenges of a technological civilization.

5. THE RELEVANCE OF POLANYI'S WORK TODAY

The continuing interest in Polanyi's work is due to the fact that the transformation currently underway shows deep-structural similarities with the one Polanyi analyzed more than seven decades ago. Since the

1980s, on both sides of the Atlantic 'the absurd notion of a self-regulating market system' (Polanyi, 1944 [2001], p. 151) has gained prominence again. And even more importantly, the specters of the interwar period have apparently returned since the financial and economic crisis which began in 2008. Economic stagnation, increasing inequality of income and wealth, precarious working conditions and over-indebtedness go hand in hand with the erosion of democracy, wars and refugees. Climate change and technological threats complicate the conditions further. The problem is not so much the economic weakness as such, the dot-com bubble and the financial crisis followed by what now often is called The Great Recession. The true challenge is that economic liberalism is unable to provide either a convincing explanation or a credible medicine to resolve these problems.

In a certain sense economic liberalism has been rather successful for a relatively long period. Market-conforming policies have been applied around the world, and globalization has reached unprecedented levels. Markets have been created not only for land and labor, but also for complex financial derivatives and pollution rights. Over the last few decades society has been subordinated to the market system to a far greater degree than anyone would have expected half a century ago. Not only the state itself, but also social security, pensions, the health system, educational institutions, universities and museums have been organized as if they were profit-making companies. But even if economic liberalism has realized most of its agenda, the results are more than disappointing. Today we are further away from the prosperous and peaceable world which the protagonists of economic liberalism evoked some decades ago. Forced to safeguard the market system, parliaments are faltering and democratic forms of decision making are eroding. For the greater part of the population, not only in the industrialized countries, working and living conditions are more precarious, less stable and more insecure today than half a century ago.

When past liberal governments ran the risk of being caught in a dead end, economic liberalism called for further and more radical liberalization, privatization and globalization. Under the current conditions such an escape seems to be no longer available. The consequence is that the liberal political discourse is trapped at an impasse. Not being able to offer a credible response, sectional interests gain the upper hand over liberal principles. Decisions depend more on the influence of lobbies and pressure groups than on the coherent idea of a better society. As Karl Polanyi's daughter, Kari Polanyi Levitt underlined in a recently published collection of essays, the current failure of economic liberalism in the face of the unsolved global challenges 'is not the end of capitalism, but the end of 200 years of

Western ascendancy and Western institutions as a model for the rest of the world' (Polanyi Levitt, 2013, p. 177).

Polanyi's work reveals, first of all, that the current crisis is not the result of any economic law or any spontaneous tendency of the market system to come to a halt. It is the product of a global-scale social experiment which aims at the realization of a basically utopian idea, the subordination of society to the rules of a self-regulating economic mechanism. Secondly, Polanyi reminds us that the changing relationship between the economy and society is at least as important as the economic contradictions within the market system. Unless we question the subordination of society to the logic of the market mechanism, we will understand neither the reasons behind the challenges which we have to face today nor comprehend possible solutions. Thirdly, Polanyi demonstrates that the slogan 'There is no alternative!' is without foundation. The studies of economic history show that the liberal idea of a society which submits itself to the rules of its economic system is absolutely exceptional and unique in human history. For sure, the Industrial Revolution fundamentally changed the conditions of social coexistence within individual nations as well as on a global level. But there is no reason to believe that the market society is more than a first reaction of humankind to the challenges of a technological civilization. Their plea for market-conforming answers obstructs the search for creative solutions. Last but not least, Polanyi demonstrates that the protagonists of economic liberalism bear the principal responsibility for the shape of the world at the beginning of the 21st century as well as the incapacity to overcome the fatal threats. During the last two centuries the liberal creed, notwithstanding its utopian character, has been the real powerhouse of the social transformation of society. The countermovement and its protagonists, voluntary associations and groups defending people against precarious jobs and marginalization, labor unions, initiatives which sustain social security and environmental activists etc. should not be blamed for disregarding economic rationality and pursuing utopian objectives. The course of history shows that the liberal interpretation turns the roles upside down. Even if the protagonists of economic liberalism hide behind the veil of alleged economic laws, in truth the idea of subordinating society to its own economy is the core of the utopian project. Protection is neither the consequence of a collectivist conspiracy nor of unfulfillable demands. The countermovement defends society against being reduced to an appendix of the market system.

In order to overcome the dangers generated by the market society, protection alone is not sufficient. Creative answers to the challenges of our epoch require a reform of consciousness which overcomes the liberal creed and learns to distinguish the conditions of the market society from those of a technological civilization. The challenges of the 'machine age' can be met, Polanyi maintains, 'through the planned intervention of the producers and consumers themselves' (Polanyi, 1947a [2018], p. 211). Democracy has the potential of safeguarding personal freedom in such a society. Polanyi's oeuvre is his contribution to a reform of human consciousness which enlarges the freedom of creative adjustment to encompass the conditions of a technological civilization.

REFERENCES

Drucker, P.F. 1942 [1965]: *The Future of Industrial Man*, New York: The New American Library of World Literature.

Hayek, F.A. 1944: *The Road to Serfdom*, Chicago: The University of Chicago Press.

Keynes, J.M. 1930 [1971]: *A Treatise on Money* (The Collected Writings of J.M. Keynes V & VI), London: Macmillan for the Royal Economic Society.

Keynes, J.M. 1933: 'National Self-Sufficiency', *The Yale Review*, vol. 22, no. 4 (June), pp. 755–769.

Keynes, J.M. 1936: *The General Theory of Employment, Interest and Money* (The Collected Writings of J.M. Keynes VII), London: Macmillan for the Royal Economic Society.

Mannheim, K. 1943: *Diagnosis of Our Time*, London: Kegan Paul, Trench, Trubner.

Marx, K. 1867: *Capital* (transl. by S. Moore and E. Aveling), Moscow: Progress Publishers; online version: Marx/Engels Internet Archive (marxists.org) <http://www.marxists.org/archive/marx/works/1867-c1/index.htm>.

Mises, L. 1920 [2008]: *Economic Calculation in the Socialist Commonwealth*, Auburn: Mises Institute.

Mises, L. 1922 [1951]: *Socialism, An Economic and Sociological Analysis* (translated by J. Kahane), New Heaven: Yale University Press.

Mises, L. 1944: *Omnipotent Government: The Rise of the Total State and Total War*, New Haven: Yale University Press.

Polanyi, K. 1919: *Weltanschauungskrise* (World Ideologies in Crisis), Neue Erde, Heft 31./32., pp. 458–462.

Polanyi, K. 1922 [2016]: 'Socialist Accounting' (introduced and translated by J. Bockman, A. Fischer and D. Woodruff), in: *Theory and Society*, vol. 45, no. 5, pp. 385–427.

Polanyi, K. 1924 [2018]: 'The Functionalist Theory of Society and the Problem of Socialist Economic Accounting' (A Rejoinder to Professor L. von Mises and Dr Felix Weil), in: Polanyi, K. 2018: *Economy and Society* (edited by M. Cangiani and C. Thomasberger), Cambridge: Polity, pp. 51–58.

Polanyi, K. 1925 [2018]: 'New Reflections Concerning our Theory and Practice', in: Polanyi, K. 2018: *Economy and Society* (edited by M. Cangiani and C. Thomasberger), Cambridge: Polity, pp. 41–50.

Polanyi, K. 1925 [2000]: 'Letter to a Friend', in: McRobbie, K. and Polanyi Levitt, K. 2000: *Karl Polanyi* in Vienna, Montreal/New York/London: Black Rose Books, pp. 316–318.

Polanyi, K. 1927 [2018]: 'On Freedom', in: Brie, M. and C. Thomasberger 2018: *Polanyi's Vision of Socialist Transformation*, Montreal: Black Rose Books, pp. 298–319.

Polanyi, K. 1928 [2002]: 'Liberale Wirtschaftsreformen in England, Liberale Sozialreformer in England' (Liberal Economic Reforms in England, Liberal Social Reformers in England), in: Polanyi, K. 2002: *Chronik der großen Transformation* (Chronicle of the Great Transformation) (edited by M. Cangiani, and C. Thomasberger), vol. I, Marburg: Metropolis, pp. 90–103.

Polanyi, K. 1932 [2018]: 'Economy and Democracy', in: Polanyi, K. 2018: *Economy and Society* (edited by M. Cangiani and C. Thomasberger), Cambridge: Polity, pp. 61–65.

Polanyi, K. 1935: 'The Essence of Fascism', in: Lewis, J., Polanyi, K. and Kitchin, D. (eds) 1935: *Christianity and the Social Revolution*, London: Victor Gollancz.

Polanyi, K. 1935–40 [2018]: 'Marx on Corporativism', in: Polanyi, K. 2018: *Economy and Society* (edited by M. Cangiani and C. Thomasberger), Cambridge: Polity, pp. 135–143.

Polanyi, K. 1937a [2018]: 'Community and Society. The Christian Criticism of our Social Order', in: Polanyi, K. 2018: *Economy and Society* (edited by M. Cangiani and C. Thomasberger), Cambridge: Polity, pp. 144–153.

Polanyi, K. 1937b [2018]: 'Christianity and Economic Life', in: Polanyi, K. 2018: *Economy and Society* (edited by M. Cangiani and C. Thomasberger), Cambridge: Polity, pp. 154–164.

Polanyi, K. 1944 [2001]: *The Great Transformation*, Boston: Beacon Press.

Polanyi, K. 1945 [2018]: 'Universal Capitalism or Regional Planning', in: Polanyi, K. 2018: *Economy and Society* (edited by M. Cangiani and C. Thomasberger), Cambridge: Polity, pp. 231–240.

Polanyi, K. 1947a [2018]: 'Our Obsolete Market Mentality', in: Polanyi, K. 2018: *Economy and Society* (edited by M. Cangiani and C. Thomasberger), Cambridge: Polity, pp. 197–211.

Polanyi, K. 1947b [2018]: 'British Labour and American New Dealers', in: Polanyi, K. 2018: *Economy and Society* (edited by M. Cangiani and C. Thomasberger), Cambridge: Polity, pp. 226–230.

Polanyi, K. 1950 [1977]: 'Letter to Oscar Jászi, 27. Oktober 1950, quoted by Ilona Duczynska in: "Notes on his life"', in: Polanyi, K. (edited by H.W. Pearson) 1977: *The Livelihood of Man*, New York, San Francisco, London: Academic Press, p. xvi.

Polanyi, K. 1964: Letter to Rudolph Schlesinger, quoted by K. Polanyi Levitt, in: 'Freedom of Action and Freedom of Thought', in: Brie, M. and Thomasberger, C. 2018: *Polanyi's Vision of Socialist Transformation*, Montreal: Black Rose Books, pp. 18–51.

Polanyi, K. 1966: *Dahomey and the Slave Trade. An Analysis of an Archaic Economy*, Seattle: University of Washington Press.

Polanyi, K. 1977 (ed. H.W. Pearson): *The Livelihood of Man*, New York, San Francisco, London: Academic Press.

Polanyi, K., Arensberg, M. and Pearson, H.W. (eds) 1957: *Trade and Market in the Early Empires*, Glencoe: The Free Press.

Polanyi Levitt, K. 2013: *From the Great Transformation to the Great Financialization*, London: Zed Books.

Popper, K. 1944: *The Open Society and Its Enemies*, London: Routledge.

Ruggie, J.G. 1982: 'International Regimes, Transactions, and Change: Embedded Liberalism in the Postwar Economic Order', in: *International Organization*, vol. 36, no. 2 (Spring), pp. 379–415.

Schumpeter, J.A. 1943 [1976]: *Capitalism, Socialism and Democracy*, London: George Allen & Unwin.

Smith, A. 1776 [1976]: *An Inquiry into the Nature and Causes of the Wealth of Nations* (The Glasgow Edition of the Works and Correspondence of Adam Smith), Oxford: Oxford University Press.

Thomasberger, C. 2012/13: 'The Belief in Economic Determinism, Neoliberalism, and the Significance of Polanyi's Contribution in the Twenty-first Century', in: *International Journal of Political Economy*, vol. 41, no. 4 (Winter), pp. 16–33.

Weber, M. 1913 [2012]: 'On Some Categories of Interpretive Sociology', in: Weber, M. 2012: *Collected Methodological Writings* (edited and translated by H.H. Bruun and S. Whimster), Milton: Routledge, pp. 273–301.

PART III

The history of economics after Keynes

10. The Keynesian School and the Neoclassical Synthesis

John E. King

KEY FEATURES

- The IS-LM model and its rivals.
- Keynesian models of the business cycle.
- Economic growth with full employment.
- Demand-pull inflation, cost-push inflation and the Phillips Curve.
- Textbook versions of the neoclassical synthesis.
- Monetary policy, fiscal policy and direct controls.

1. INTRODUCTION

In Chapter 5 we outlined the ideas of John Maynard Keynes. In this chapter we look at the work of some theorists who were writing in English in the quarter century after the publication in 1936 of his *General Theory* and tried to reconcile his work with the neoclassical economic theory that was the subject of chapter 4.

Unfortunately the word 'Keynesian' is itself sometimes a source of confusion. For example, the 'Keynesian School' with which this chapter is concerned is often referred to as advocating 'Old Keynesian' economics, to distinguish their ideas both from the 'New Keynesian' theories that emerged after 1975 (which are the subject of chapter 13) and from the 'Post-Keynesian' School (addressed in chapter 14). Similarly, the 'Neoclassical Synthesis' that was developed by the (Old) Keynesians in the two decades after the publication of Keynes's *General Theory* in 1936, should probably today be denoted as the 'Old Neoclassical Synthesis' (or ONS), to avoid confusing it with the (very different) New Neoclassical Synthesis, which first appeared in the 1990s in the work both of the New Keynesians and of the New Classical School that is discussed in chapter 13.

As can be seen, when we refer to 'Keynesianism' we need to be clear exactly what we are referring to, or matters can soon become very confusing. Keynes himself contributed to this confusion in terminology, by using the term 'classical' to refer both to macroeconomic theory in the tradition of David Ricardo (see chapter 1) *and* to what would now be described as neoclassical macroeconomics. As Keynes recognised, there was also a strong anti-Ricardian strand in the classical political economy of the early to mid-nineteenth century, which included Robert Malthus (whom Keynes admired) and Karl Marx (whom he did not). Both Malthus and Marx were strongly opposed to Ricardo's endorsement of Say's Law, believing that output and employment were often limited by deficient aggregate demand, a proposition that Ricardo (following Say) strongly denied. There are 19 references to 'classical theory' in the index to the *General Theory*, but only one to the 'Neo-classical School', and it is not at all illuminating (Keynes 1936, p. 177).

Keynes was also surprisingly ambivalent on the nature of his relationship to the neoclassical macroeconomics that he had learned from Alfred Marshall and A.C. Pigou, and which he had accepted for much of his academic career. In a frequently quoted letter to the playwright George Bernard Shaw in January 1935 Keynes stated his belief that his forthcoming book 'will largely revolutionise – not, I suppose, at once, but in the course of the next ten years – the way the world thinks about economic problems' (Keynes 1982, p. 42). But then, in the 'Concluding notes' to the *General Theory* itself, he acknowledged that 'if our central controls succeed in establishing an aggregate volume of output corresponding to full employment as nearly as is practicable, the classical theory comes into its own again from this point onwards' (Keynes 1936, p. 378). The similarities between Keynes, Marshall, Knut Wicksell and even Léon Walras were noted by several reviewers (King 2002, pp. 15–18), leading J.R. Hicks to describe the *General Theory* as 'a useful book but it is neither the beginning nor the end of Dynamic Economics' (Hicks 1937, p. 159). The (Old) Keynesian School saw its (Old) Neoclassical Synthesis as a systematic and coherent reconciliation of Keynes and neoclassical macroeconomics. That is to say, they believed Keynes's theory to be rather similar in some ways to that of Knut Wicksell and Alfred Marshall. Indeed, this is where 'Old Keynesianism' began, as an attempt to synthesise these approaches to macroeconomic theory. Something of the sort seemed to be needed, since the *General Theory* was very much 'work in progress', with many elements of Keynes's theoretical system being only semi-developed. Any chance that there might be a more polished second edition was put into doubt when he suffered a severe heart attack in 1938, and they disappeared with the outbreak of war in the following year; his last seven years were devoted entirely to public service.

This chapter is structured as follows. The next three sections outline the three central components of the ONS: the (four) distinct models of short-period macroeconomic equilibrium that emerged after 1936 (section 2), the neoclassical growth theory that extended the analysis to the long period (section 3), and the attempt to model inflation by means of the Phillips Curve (section 4). Then, in section 5, some textbook versions of the ONS are described. Section 6 deals with the policy implications that the Old Keynesians drew from their analysis, and section 7 concludes.

2. MODELS OF SHORT-PERIOD MACROECONOMIC EQUILIBRIUM

In the *General Theory*, Keynes had sketched the outlines of a model of macroeconomic equilibrium in the short period, but he had not taken it very far. Beginning almost immediately after the publication of the book, others took up the task. By 1957 there were four such models, which are described in some detail in the contributions to Blaug and Lloyd (2010) by Michael Schneider (chapter 46), Warren Young (chapter 47) and Richard Lipsey (chapter 49). I shall deal with them in chronological order.

The first of them was the IS-LM model which (like the multiplier) was a multiple discovery. We can take the version presented by J.R. Hicks (1937) as the paradigm. Hicks began by writing down the three 'classical equations':

$$M = kY \tag{1}$$
$$I = f(i) \tag{2}$$
$$I = S(i, Y) \tag{3}$$

Equation (1) is the Quantity Equation: the demand for money (M) is a constant multiple (k) of aggregate output (equal to total income, Y); equation (2) states that investment (I) depends on the rate of interest (i); and equation (3) expresses the condition for macroeconomic equilibrium, which is that investment must equal savings (S), which is a function of both the level of income and the rate of interest. He then wrote Keynes's three equations

$$M = f(i) \tag{1'}$$
$$I = f(i) \tag{2'}$$
$$I = S(Y) \tag{3'}$$

There were two differences between the classical and the Keynesian systems. Comparing equations (3) and (3'), it could be seen that for Keynes, saving depended only on income, and not at all on the rate of interest; but this was relatively unimportant. The significant difference was that between (1) and (1'): for Keynes, the demand for money depends on the rate of interest, via the speculative motive for holding money. But this was what Hicks described as Keynes's 'special' theory, in which the demand for money was perfectly elastic, so that a change in investment would lead *only* to an increase in output and employment, with no effect on the rate of interest. In what Hicks described as Keynes's 'general' theory, which included the transactions demand for money, equation (1') had to be replaced by (1"):

$$M = f(i, Y), \tag{1''}$$

and this represents 'a big step back to Marshallian orthodoxy' (Hicks 1937, p. 153). 'When generalised in this way', Hicks concludes, Mr. Keynes's theory begins to look very like Wicksell's; this is of course hardly surprising' (ibid., p. 158).

Hicks illustrated his interpretation of the 'general' theory in Figures 10.1 and 10.2 (ibid., p. 153). Here the IS curve shows the conditions for equilibrium in the goods market. It slopes downwards to show the relation between income and the rate of interest that must be maintained in order to make saving equal to investment. The LL curve (Hicks's version of the LM curve) shows the conditions for equilibrium in the money market. It slopes upwards because, with a given supply of money, an increase in income leads to an increase in the amount of money that is demanded (the transactions motive), while an increase in the rate of interest leads to a reduction in money demand (via the speculative motive). Macroeconomic equilibrium is at point P, where IS = LL. Figure 10.2 illustrates what Hicks regards as the most plausible shape for LL. It goes from horizontal to vertical, with the vertical section showing that there is a maximum level of income (and output) that can be financed with a given amount of money. If IS cuts LL on or close to its vertical section, Hicks argues, 'the classical theory will be a good approximation', and increased investment will raise the rate of interest but will have no effect on output (or employment). Thus the horizontal section of LL is crucial, since over this section an increase in investment will raise output (and employment) but leave the rate of interest unchanged. 'So', Hicks concludes, 'the General Theory of Employment is the Economics of Depression' (ibid., p. 155). As we have seen, Keynes had said as much in the *General Theory*, and on several occasions in 1937–1938 he expressed his approval of the IS-LM model (King 2002, p. 31).

There were, however, a number of problems with IS-LM. It determined the equilibrium levels of GDP and the rate of interest, but had nothing to say about the price level or the rate of price inflation, and

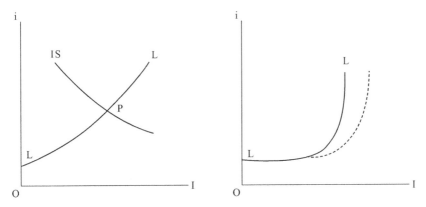

Source: J.R. Hicks, 1937. 'Mr. Keynes and the "classics": a suggested interpretation', *Econometrica*, 5 (2), April, pp. 147–159, p. 153, Figs 1 and 2.

Figures 10.1 and 10.2   An early version of the IS-LM diagram

nothing – at least, nothing explicit – about aggregate employment (and unemployment). It was also rather complicated. A simpler presentation of the principle of effective demand was developed by Paul Samuelson in 1938 and published in the following year. Figure 10.3 is Samuelson's income-expenditure diagram (Samuelson 1939, p. 790, Fig. 1). Here aggregate income is measured on the horizontal axis and aggregate expenditure on the vertical axis (which is rather misleadingly labelled *C*). It consists of consumption spending, which is shown by the familiar concave, upward-sloping function $C = F(Y)$, and what Samuelson terms 'spontaneous investment'. The latter – which would today be described as 'autonomous investment' – is independent of both the level and the rate of change of consumption, and is therefore shown by the constant quantity *I*. Macroeconomic equilibrium comes about when income equals expenditure and the aggregate expenditure function cuts the 45-degree line, and national income rises from *Z* to *N* when spontaneous investment rises from zero to *I*. This was the very first diagrammatic illustration of the Keynesian multiplier.

The third version of the macroeconomic equilibrium model of the ONS, and also possibly the most popular – at least in introductory texts – was the Aggregate Demand-Aggregate Supply (AD-AS) model drawn in price level-national income space, as in Figure 10.4. According to Michael Schneider this was first used by Jacob Marschak in lectures in 1948 and published by him in a book three years later, though Don Patinkin and others seem to have had similar ideas at this time (Schneider 2010, pp. 344–346, citing Marschak 1951; see also Patinkin 1949). It is necessary to assume money

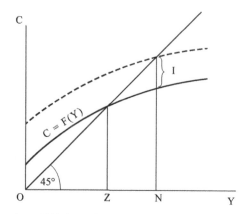

Source: P.A. Samuelson, 1939. 'A synthesis of the principle of acceleration and the multiplier', *Journal of Political Economy*, 47 (6), December, pp. 786–797, p. 790, Fig. 1.

Figure 10.3   The income-expenditure diagram

illusion to justify the upward-sloping AS and downward-sloping AD curves shown in Figure 10.4. Their intersection gives the equilibrium level of national income at Y_e, below the full employment level Y_f, and also the equilibrium price level (which is assumed to be constant). In some versions the AS curve has an initial horizontal section, sometimes described as the 'Keynesian' section. Authors less sympathetic to Keynesian ideas would make the steeply-sloping section of AS begin earlier, and become vertical as Y_f is approached, so that an increase in aggregate demand (with a rightward shift in AD) would increase the price level but have little or no effect on income and employment. They would also tend to draw an even steeper AD curve than that in Figure 10.4.

An alternative to AS-AD was advocated by Dudley Dillard (1948) and then, much more enthusiastically, by Sidney Weintraub (1960). Both drew on the model that Keynes had outlined in the *General Theory*, but had never elaborated upon or attempted to draw a diagram of (Keynes 1936, pp. 29–30). In Figure 10.5, employment is measured on the horizontal axis and aggregate proceeds on the vertical axis. The Z curve is the aggregate supply function, which shows 'the volume of outlays expected by firms in the economy in the form of consumer expenditures and investment outlays, which will lead the enterprises to give the associated level of employment'. The D curve is the aggregate demand curve, which 'shows the *actual* outlays ... associated with each N-level and the implicit money wage payments to labor' (Weintraub 1960, pp. 151–152; emphasis in original). The equilibrium employment level N^* is given by the intersection of the Z and D curves.

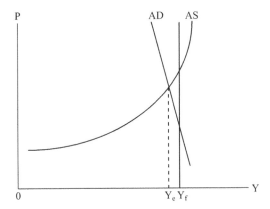

Source: M. Schneider, 2010. 'Keynesian income determination diagrams', in M. Blaug and P. Lloyd (eds), 2010. *Famous Figures and Diagrams in Economics*. Cheltenham, UK and Northampton, MA, USA, pp. 337–347, p. 344, Fig 46.5; taken from J. Marschak, 1951. *Income, Employment and the Price Level*. New York: Kelley, Graph 19II.

Figure 10.4   The AS-AD diagram

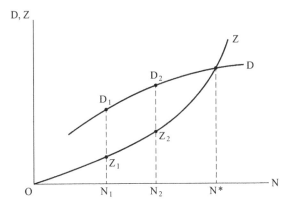

Source: S. Weintraub, 1960. 'The Keynesian theory of inflation: the two faces of Janus?', *International Economic Review*, 1 (2), May, pp. 143–155, p. 151, Fig. 3.

Figure 10.5   The Dillard-Weintraub Z-D diagram

Weintraub seems to have invented the term 'microfoundations' in a paper published four years previously. But he did not make very much of it. It came in a footnote to an appendix, and was not intended as part of a project to reduce macroeconomics to microeconomics, still less to explain all macroeconomic problems in terms of the behaviour of identical RARE individuals (representative agents with rational expectations). In fact Weintraub did not refer to individual agents, or even to individual firms; his 'aggregation procedure' was one 'whereby industry supply concepts are transformed into notions of aggregate supply' (Weintraub 1956, p. 854). Thus it seems that the microfoundations project had not got very far by the mid-1950s. The Old Keynesians all regarded macroeconomics as a legitimate, semi-independent branch of their discipline, on a par with microeconomics and irreducible to it (King 2012, chapter 5). Indeed, Weintraub gave his 1956 paper the title, 'A macroeconomic approach to the theory of wages'.

Some combination of these four models offered a more or less coherent theory of aggregate output, employment, unemployment and the price level. The neoclassical synthesis was only completed in the mid- to late 1950s with the theories of growth and inflation that will be discussed in sections 3 and 4. One important element that had been developed slightly earlier was the theory of cyclical fluctuations set out in J.R. Hicks's book on *The Trade Cycle* (Hicks 1950), which synthesised the work of Hicks and several other theorists that had appeared in journal articles in the previous decade-and-a-half. Again, the terminology may be confusing. The British term 'trade cycle' was used at this time to refer to regular fluctuations in 'the state of trade', a nineteenth-century expression denoting the overall level of output and employment within a country and not confined to exports and imports. The more common term in American usage, now universally preferred, was 'the business cycle'.

Hicks's cycle was demand-driven, and centred on the interaction between the lagged Keynesian multiplier and the accelerator principle relating investment expenditure to changes in the level of output. He used a number of diagrams to illustrate the argument, but only a few (very simple) equations; there was a 31-page mathematical appendix (Hicks 1950, pp. 169–199). Interestingly, his discussion of 'the monetary factor' came at the end of the book, not the beginning. 'This emphasis on the *real* (non-monetary) character of the cyclical process,' Hicks notes, 'has of course been entirely deliberate; it has been one of the main objects of this work to show that the main features of the cycle can be adequately explained in real terms' (ibid., p. 136). The same point was made by another Oxford economist in an undergraduate textbook published a decade later (Matthews 1959, p. 136). Matthews, too, emphasised that it was fluctuations in aggregate demand – above all, investment demand – that drove the cycle (ibid., pp. 3–6). Both authors regarded cyclical fluctuations as a potentially serious problem, rather than as the outcome of utility-maximising decisions by rational individual agents, and both ended their books with an analysis of the role of monetary and fiscal policy in reducing the damage that they caused (Hicks 1950, pp. 163–168; Matthews 1959, pp. 254–291).

3.   THE SOLOW GROWTH MODEL

Two important contributors to the literature on the trade cycle had attempted to link their analysis of short-period cyclical fluctuations with the long-period modelling of economic growth. Both Roy Harrod (1939) and Evsey Domar (1947) saw the process of cyclical growth as an inherently unstable one, in which the economy operated on a 'knife-edge' where the most likely outcomes seemed to be cumulative inflation or a downward spiral into deep depression. But this scenario, Robert Solow objected, rested on their assumption of a fixed capital-labour ratio. It was this restrictive condition that gave rise to 'what might be called the tightrope view of economic growth' (Solow 1956, p. 91). If, instead, factor substitution were permitted in response to changes in the relative price of capital and labour, then 'under the standard neoclassical conditions' their pessimism would prove to be unjustified (ibid., p. 66).

Solow's neoclassical model of economic growth assumed instead that labour and capital were both fully employed. With factor substitution permitted, the Harrod-Domar knife-edge was no longer plausible, and indeed in the case of a Cobb-Douglas aggregate production function it was impossible. 'The system can adjust,' Solow argued, 'to any given rate of growth of the labour force, and eventually approach a state of steady proportional expansion' (ibid., p. 73). He demonstrated that this conclusion applied not only to the Cobb-Douglas case but also to 'a whole family of constant-returns-to-scale production functions' (ibid., pp. 77–78). Solow then extended the model to allow for the effects on growth of neutral technical change, a variable saving ratio, and the effects of a personal income tax, before concluding by identifying some long-period obstacles to full employment. These included rigid wages, a Keynesian liquidity trap that put a floor under the rate of interest, and the implications of uncertainty, 'which might explain why net investment should be at times insensitive to current changes in the real return to capital, at other times oversensitive' (ibid., pp. 93–94). 'All these cobwebs and some others,' he admitted, 'have been brushed aside throughout this essay' (ibid., p. 94).

In hindsight it is surprising that it should have taken 20 years from the publication of the *General Theory* for a fully-fledged neoclassical growth theory to be added to the ONS. Solow's paper now opened the floodgates. Later in the year the Australian theorist Trevor Swan published a very similar growth model, apparently developed independently of Solow

(Swan 1956), and there was soon a substantial literature on the neoclassical approach to growth. Eight years later an authoritative survey of the theory of economic growth, commissioned by the American Economic Association and the Royal Economic Society, ran to 113 pages, with a further 12-page bibliography (Hahn and Matthews 1964). At least half of the material surveyed was neoclassical in its orientation and thus formed part of the ONS; much of it had been published since 1956.

4.   THE PHILLIPS CURVE

According to the New Zealand-born economist A.W. Phillips, wage inflation could be explained in terms of the law of supply and demand:

> When the demand for a commodity or service is high relatively to the supply of it we expect the price to rise, the rate of rise being greater the greater the excess demand. Conversely when the demand is low relatively to the supply we expect the price to fall, the rate of fall being greater the greater the deficiency of demand. It seems plausible that this principle should operate as one of the factors determining the rate of change of money wage rates, which is the price of labour services. When the demand for labour is high and there are very few unemployed we should expect employers to bid wage rates up quite rapidly, each firm and each industry being continually tempted to offer a little above the prevailing rates to attract the most suitable labour from other firms and industries. On the other hand it appears that workers are reluctant to offer their services at less than the prevailing rates when the demand for labour is low and unemployment is high so that wage rates fall only very slowly. The relation between unemployment and the rate of change of wage rates is therefore likely to be highly non-linear. (Phillips 1958, p. 283)

It was also to be expected that the rate of change of unemployment might be relevant, Phillips suggested, along with any substantial change in prices, especially the prices of imported goods.

To test these conclusions, Phillips plotted a number of scatter diagrams, using annual UK data for the period 1861–1957, and drawing the curve that came to be named after him from inspection of the diagrams; no formal econometrics was involved. Figure 10.6 shows the results that he obtained for the final sub-period, 1948–1957. The first thing to note is just how low unemployment was: never more than 2 per cent. The relationship between wage inflation and unemployment was negative, so that the curve was downward-sloping, as expected; more surprisingly, it appears not to have shifted since the first sub-period, 1861–1913. Phillips traced the course of a (very mild) business cycle in the years 1953–1957, which confirmed his suspicion that the rate of change of unemployment was important, along with the level. He concluded that unemployment would have to increase to about 2.5 per cent if money wages were to grow at no more than 2 per cent per annum, which was equal to the long-term rate of growth in labour productivity. If the shares of wages and profits in national income were assumed to remain constant, this was the figure that would be needed to eliminate *price* inflation (Phillips 1958, p. 299).

Soon, two of the most prominent American Keynesians repeated the exercise. Paul Samuelson and Robert Solow made rather more of the distinction between 'demand-pull' and 'cost-push' inflation than Phillips had done, since the US data showed that the curve had shifted outwards in the 1940s and 1950s. They drew a 'modified' Phillips Curve for the United States in which it was the rate of *price* inflation, not wage inflation, which was measured on the vertical axis. This was done by again assuming constant wage and profit shares and by subtracting the average rate of productivity growth (2.5 per cent, rather than Phillips's 2 per cent) from

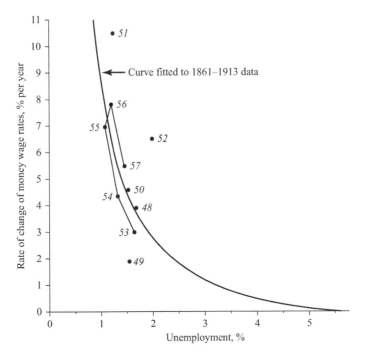

Source: A.W. Phillips, 1958. 'The relation between unemployment and the rate of change of money wages in the United Kingdom, 1861–1957', *Economica*, n.s., 25 (4), November, pp. 283–299, p. 296, Fig. 10.

Figure 10.6   The UK Phillips Curve 1948–1957

the rate of wage growth to give the rate of price increase associated with each unemployment rate. They described the modified Phillips Curve as 'a menu of choice between different degrees of unemployment and price stability' (Samuelson and Solow 1960, p. 192, caption to Fig. 2).

Unlike Phillips, and contrary to a frequently-voiced criticism of this entire literature, they do discuss the role of expectations in the inflationary process:

> We think it important to realize that the more the recent past is dominated by inflation, by high employment, and by the belief that both will continue, the more likely is it that the process of inflation will preserve or even increase real demand, or the more heavily the monetary and fiscal authorities may have to bear down on demand in the interests of price stabilization. *Real-income consciousness is a powerful force.* (Samuelson and Solow 1960, p. 186, emphasis added; cf. ibid., p. 189, final paragraph)

Samuelson and Solow conclude with a significant qualification:

> We have not here entered upon the important question of what feasible institutional reforms might be introduced to lessen the degree of disharmony between full employment and price stability. These could of course, involve such wide-ranging issues as direct price and wage controls, antiunion and antitrust legislation, and a host of other measures hopefully designed to move the American Phillips' curves downward and to the left. (ibid., p. 194)

We shall return to this question in section 6.

5. TEXTBOOK VERSIONS OF THE ONS

It was Samuelson who had introduced the term 'neoclassical synthesis' in the third edition of his introductory textbook, *Economics*, in 1955 (Backhouse 2014), and any of the subsequent editions, at least until the early 1970s, may be consulted for his authoritative exposition of Old Keynesian macroeconomics. The sixth edition, published in 1964, runs to 810 pages. Most of the macroeconomics comes in the 164-page Part 2, 'Determination of National Income and Its Fluctuations', but the final chapter of Part 1, 'Basic Economic Concepts and National Income', is devoted to the definition and measurement of net and gross national product, and includes a circular flow diagram (Samuelson 1964, p. 181). There is a lot of macroeconomics also in Part 5, 'International Trade and Finance' and Part 6, 'Current Economic Problems', which is largely devoted to issues of economic growth and development. In all, roughly one-third of the book is on macroeconomics. There are many diagrams and numerical examples, but very few equations and absolutely no econometrics.

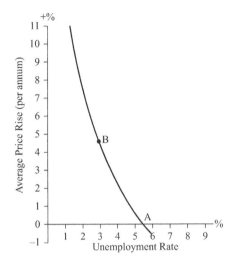

Source: P.A. Samuelson and R.M. Solow, 1960. 'Analytical aspects of anti-inflation policy', *American Economic Review*, 50 (2), May, Papers and Proceedings, pp. 177–194, p. 192, Fig. 2.

Figure 10.7   The 'modified' US Phillips Curve 1935–1960

Part 2 begins with a chapter on saving, consumption and investment, and is mainly given over to the derivation of the consumption function. This is put to use in Chapter 12, 'The Theory of Income Determination', where Samuelson uses his income-expenditure diagram (and the investment-saving diagram derived from it) to determine equilibrium income and to illustrate several important issues: how the multiplier works, the paradox of thrift, inflationary and deflationary gaps, and the role of fiscal policy. Chapter 13 deals with 'Business Cycles and Forecasting'. Here Samuelson introduces the accelerator principle and explains how it interacts with the multiplier to generate cyclical fluctuations, using only numerical examples and no mathematics. Up to now there has been no explicit mention of money. The next three chapters deal with the Quantity Theory (in chapter 14, 'Prices and Money'), the operation of the banks (chapter 15, 'The Banking System and Deposit Creation'), and monetary policy (the largely descriptive chapter 16, 'The Federal Reserve and Central Bank Monetary Policy').

All this sets the scene for the 'Synthesis of Monetary Analysis and Income Analysis' in the brief but incisive chapter 17, which is the most important macroeconomic chapter in the book (Samuelson 1964, pp. 328–345). Again, most of the analysis is conducted in terms of the income-expenditure model, but Samuelson begins by drawing a three-segment diagram – easily the most complicated diagram in the entire book – that introduces a liquidity preference function and a marginal efficiency of investment curve to determine the level of investment, which in the third segment of the diagram is set equal to saving in order to determine the equilibrium level of income (ibid., p. 329, Fig. 1). This takes the reader more than halfway to the IS-LM model, but it was not until the seventh edition, three years later, that Samuelson went all the way and provided an IS-LM diagram to illustrate what he now termed the 'The Hicks-Hansen Synthesis' (Samuelson 1967, p. 331, Fig. 18.4).

Both editions contain an appendix with a Phillips Curve diagram, rather surprisingly labelled 'Cost-Push Phenomena', with a very clear statement of its role as a menu for policy choice:

> The indicated 'Phillips Curve' shows by its downward slope that increasing the level of unemployment can moderate or wipe out the upward price creep. There seems to be a dilemma of choice for society between 'reasonably high employment with maximal-growth-and-a- price-creep' or 'reasonably-stable-prices and considerable unemployment'; and it is a difficult social dilemma to decide what compromises to make. (Samuelson 1964, p. 344; 1967, p. 333)

He returns to this question almost at the end of the book, in chapter 37 of Part 6 ('Problems of Growth and Stability in an Advanced Economy'), which discusses policies to promote growth and reduce unemployment, and here he endorses incomes policy as a supplement to fiscal and monetary policy. The analysis of economic growth also comes in Part 6, rather than in Part 2. Despite its title chapter 35 ('The Theory of Growth') is largely historical and descriptive, but there is an appendix that outlines the Solow growth model and rather contentiously associates it with the ideas of Ricardo and Marx (Samuelson 1964, pp. 743–748). This is probably the hardest part of the entire book, and it does contain a number of equations.

For many years the US edition of Samuelson's textbook sold well in Europe and Australasia, and it was eventually also adapted for overseas use by local co-authors. In the 1960s, however, British students were more likely to rely on their own introductory texts, like the one that I used as a high school economics student in London in 1962–1963. The first 350 pages of *A Textbook of Economic Theory* by Alfred Stonier and Douglas Hague were devoted to microeconomics. They were followed by 140 pages of macroeconomics, predominantly Keynesian in nature but with a substantial concluding chapter on 'Keynes and the Classical Economics'. The exposition of Keynes culminated in a four-equation, four-panel diagram version of the IS-LM model (Stonier and Hague 1957, pp. 463–467). There is no discussion of economic growth, but in the final chapter (written before Phillips's seminal article had appeared) the relationship between increased employment and wage inflation is analysed in some detail (ibid., pp. 478–489). The chapter concludes with a highly critical account of the classical treatment of the employment implications of wage cuts, a question to which 'a complete answer can only be given if attention is paid to *all* repercussions, on the Keynesian determinants of employment – the propensity to consume, the marginal efficiency of capital and the rate of interest. It was in failing to realise how these vital determinants of employment interact that pre-Keynesian employment theory showed its real weakness' (ibid., p. 495).

For American graduate students, the canonical version of Old Keynesian economics was for many years Gardner Ackley's *Macroeconomic Theory*, first published in 1961. This was a 600-page text that compared the 'classical' and the 'Keynesian' macroeconomic models in great detail, coming down in favour of the latter (but by no means uncritically). The crucial chapters are those summarising the classical theory, setting out the complete Keynesian model, and comparing and evaluating the two models (Ackley 1961, chapters VIII, XIV, XV). By today's standards Ackley's mathematics is undemanding, but there are some challenging diagrams, including several in three dimensions and two seven-panel two-dimensional diagrams summarising the short-run Keynesian system, with its foundations in IS-LM (ibid., pp. 378–379, Figs 14–12 and 14–13).

Ackley was clear that 'the two models, Keynesian and classical, overlap considerably' (ibid., p. 403). There were three important differences. Keynes had 'added the speculative demand for money to the Classical transactions demand ... suppressed the supply of labor function and assumed rigid [money] wages ... [and] assumed saving (consumption) to depend on income rather than upon the interest rate' (ibid., p. 404). There were legitimate grounds for debate, Ackley suggested, about which of these three differences was the most fundamental. 'One striking fact, however, emerges ... the primary determinant of the *extent* of unemployment, and therefore of the level of national income and output, is the slope of the consumption function' (ibid., p. 406), since this is what determines the degree to which the economy falls short of full employment when neither lower interest rates nor money wage cuts are able to restore the full employment level of aggregate output.

Ackley considered several objections to the Keynesian model. Critics claimed that the model was too aggregative and too static, and that it dealt inadequately with the determination of money wages and the speculative demand for money. He was not very sympathetic to the first of these complaints, and there is no suggestion that macroeconomic theory needed microfoundations derived from the utility-maximising decisions of individual economic agents. However, Ackley believed the second criticism to be well-founded, since it was contradictory to assume both positive net investment and a constant capital stock; hence he devoted two later chapters to the theory of economic growth (ibid., chapters XVIII, XIX). The third complaint was also correct, though in Keynes's 'incidental discussion' the rate of change of money wages had indeed been made a function of the level of employment. But this was a difficult question: 'Trade union wage policy and the state of employer resistance to wage inflation do not, however, seem to be matters easily reduced to a stable function of anything' (ibid., p. 416). Similar considerations applied to the fourth criticism, since Keynes had placed too much emphasis on the (highly unstable) speculative demand for money and had neglected 'the differential availability of various forms of finance and the structure of financial costs', which were important determinants of the level of investment (ibid., p. 417).

In the final analysis, however, Ackley was confident that 'with all its acknowledged deficiencies, the Keynesian analysis still stands as the most useful point of departure in macroeconomic theory. Itself incomplete and uncertain, it remains the foundation of the great majority of the significant works in macroeconomics of the past two decades' (ibid., p. 418). It could certainly not be criticised as non-operational: 'On the contrary Keynesian economics has stimulated a vast effort to collect and organise data around the concepts of national income and output, consumption, investment, employment' (ibid., p. 417).

6.   POLICY IMPLICATIONS

The first point to make is that the Old Keynesians all agreed that a comprehensive and systematic approach to macroeconomic policy was necessary. The most important lesson of the Great Depression was that capitalism had serious macroeconomic problems, which were due to its inherent properties and most certainly could not be explained as the unintended consequence of mistaken government intervention. There was no automatic tendency for full employment to be restored when it had failed; the capitalist system had no reliable self-correcting mechanisms. These fundamental arguments underpin the work of all the theorists who have been cited thus far.

They implied the need for markets to be closely regulated. This was most evident in the international sphere, where the 1944 Bretton Woods

Agreement imposed a system of fixed exchange rates that required national governments to maintain control over international capital movements. Global financial markets had been put back in their box in the early 1930s, and nation states were expected to sit firmly on the lid. Forty years later the entire system came under increasing and eventually irresistible pressure, as explained in a most entertaining fashion by Yanis Varoufakis (2016, chapters 1–3), but for a great majority of the Old Keynesian era there was no 'free market' in foreign exchange or international investment.

Under the Old Neoclassical Synthesis, domestic economic policy had a very clear *goal*: full employment with little or no inflation. To achieve this goal, the Old Keynesians maintained, several policy *instruments* were available, and all should be used. The three most important were fiscal policy, monetary policy and incomes policy. Regarding fiscal policy, the Old Keynesians were united in their statement of the underlying principles, which were set out by Alvin Hansen, Keynes's most influential early advocate in the United States, and developed in some detail by the young Anglo-American economist Abba Lerner (Hansen and Greer 1941–1942; Lerner 1944, chapter 24). The state was not a private household, and the rules of 'sound finance' – what Keynes had referred to as 'the Treasury view'– that applied to individuals and families were irrelevant in the case of national governments. So long as it was not owed to foreigners, the national debt was not a burden on society, since it was owed by one group of citizens to another group of citizens. It did not have to be repaid. Interest payments on the national debt were not a burden on the nation, since they involved nothing more than transfers from one group of citizens to another.

Thus fiscal policy should be guided by what Lerner described as the principle of 'functional finance': the government should maintain a budget deficit, or a surplus, or (just possibly) aim to balance the budget, in order to secure full employment without inflation. Nothing else mattered, and the size of the resulting government debt was unimportant. In any case, austerity measures inspired by 'sound finance' would prove counterproductive; as Keynes had put it: 'Look after the unemployment, and the budget will look after itself' (Keynes 1933, p. 150). And so it proved. In the post-war period UK unemployment was remarkably low, and inflation relatively modest, as we saw in section 4. But the ratio of public debt to national income fell steadily, from 252 per cent in 1946 to 50 per cent in 1974 (King 2015, p. 38).

The Old Keynesians rightly believed that fiscal policy was a powerful tool. They were less sure about the effectiveness of monetary policy. As Matthews noted in his (very brief) discussion of monetary policy and the business cycle:

> Some measures may be better adapted to restraining inflation than to rescuing the economy from a slump. This is most obviously true of direct physical controls over private spending. It is also probably true of monetary policy, since in the slump interest rates are already low and the small further reduction which policy can procure may not have much effect on investment decisions. (Matthews 1959, p. 262)

But there was no suggestion that a simple rule for the rate of growth of the money supply might be all that was needed to restrain inflation, and there was a general willingness to use 'physical controls' – that is, direct regulation of the activities of the financial sector – when it was considered necessary. In the United States, for example, the Glass-Steagall Act imposed strict separation between retail and wholesale banking. And, as we have seen, international financial transactions were subject to tight government regulation.

The third major category of macroeconomic policy was touched on in section 4. Direct controls over wage and price increases – 'prices and incomes policy' – had been used in wartime with considerable success: in most countries the inflation rate in and immediately after the Second World War was significantly lower than it had been in the First World War. In many Western European countries, incomes policies were continued well into the peace, involving governments, trade union federations and national employer organisations in agreements to restrain the rate of growth of both money wages and prices. Sometimes these agreements proved highly effective, as with 'the policy of wage restraint introduced by [the British Chancellor] Sir Stafford Cripps in the spring of 1948', which resulted in 'exceptionally low' wage increases during 1949 (Phillips 1958, pp. 296–297; see Figure 10.6 above). As we saw in section 4, in the late 1950s the reintroduction of direct wage and price controls was also under serious consideration in the United States. These measures were eventually introduced, with the support of many Old Keynesians, by both Democratic and Republican administrations in the 1960s and early 1970s (for a rather sceptical view of their achievements, see Rees 1973, pp. 235–239).

7.   CONCLUSION

At the height of its influence, in the mid-1960s, the ONS appeared to be a great success. Old Keynesian macroeconomics reflected, and had indeed played an important part in creating, the economic triumph of the 'golden age' (Marglin and Schor 1990) – what French writers describe as the *trentes glorieuses*, or 'thirty golden years', that characterised the advanced capitalist world after 1945. The business cycle had been tamed; full employment without inflation had been very largely achieved; economic growth was faster than it had ever been (or would ever be again); and there was a steady improvement in the living standards of hundreds of millions of people. Thus Paul Samuelson concluded the seventh edition of his textbook in an optimistic vein: 'Our mixed economy – wars aside – has a great future before it' (Samuelson 1967, p. 809). No one foresaw the age of stagflation – and anti-Keynesianism – that lay ahead.

REFERENCES

Ackley, G. 1961. *Macroeconomic Theory*. New York: Macmillan.
Backhouse, R. 2014. 'Paul A. Samuelson and the Neoclassical Synthesis', Birmingham, UK: Department of Economics, University of Birmingham, mimeo.
Blaug, M. and Lloyd, P. (eds). 2010. *Famous Figures and Diagrams in Economics*. Cheltenham, UK and Northampton, MA, USA: Edward Elgar Publishing.
Dillard, D. 1948. *The Economics of J.M. Keynes*. New York: Prentice-Hall.
Domar, E.D. 1947. 'Expansion and employment', *American Economic Review*, 37 (1), March, pp. 34–55.
Hahn, F.H. and Matthews, R.C.O. 1964. 'The theory of economic growth: a survey', *Economic Journal*, 74 (296), December, pp. 779–902.
Hansen, A.H. and Greer, G. 1941–1942. 'The federal debt and the future: an unflinching look at the facts and prospects', *Harper's Magazine*, 184, December–May, pp. 489–500.
Harrod, R.F. 1939. 'An essay in dynamic theory', *Economic Journal*, 39 (1), March, pp. 14–33.
Hicks, J.R. 1937. 'Mr. Keynes and the "classics": a suggested interpretation', *Econometrica*, 5 (2), April, pp. 147–159.
Hicks, J.R. 1950. *A Contribution to the Theory of the Trade Cycle*. Oxford: Clarendon Press.
Keynes, J.M. 1933. 'Spending and saving: a discussion between Sir Josiah Stamp and J.M. Keynes', in *The Collected Writings of John Maynard Keynes, Volume XXI: Activities 1931–1939*, London: Macmillan for the Royal Economic Society, 1975, pp. 145–154.
Keynes, J.M. 1936. *The General Theory of Employment, Interest and Money*. London: Macmillan.
Keynes, J.M. 1982. *The Collected Writings of John Maynard Keynes, Volume XXVIII*. London: Macmillan and Cambridge: Cambridge University Press for the Royal Economic Society.
King, J.E. 2002. *A History of Post Keynesian Economics since 1936*. Cheltenham, UK and Northampton, MA, USA: Edward Elgar Publishing.
King, J.E. 2012. *The Microfoundations Delusion: Metaphor and Dogma in the History of Macroeconomics*. Cheltenham, UK and Northampton, MA, USA: Edward Elgar Publishing.
King, J.E. 2015. 'A Post Keynesian critique of Swabian housewife logic', in A. Bitzenis, N. Karagiannis and J. Marangos (eds), *Europe in Crisis*, London: Palgrave Macmillan, pp. 29–43.

Lerner, A.P. 1944. *The Economics of Control: Principles of Welfare Economics*. New York: Macmillan.

Marglin, S. and Schor, J. (eds) 1990. *The Golden Age of Capitalism: Lessons for the 1990s*. Oxford: Oxford University Press.

Marschak, J. 1951. *Income, Employment and the Price Level*. New York: Kelley.

Matthews, R.C.O. 1959. *The Trade Cycle*. Digswell Place: James Nisbet, and Cambridge: Cambridge University Press.

Patinkin, D. 1949. 'Involuntary unemployment and the Keynesian supply function', *Economic Journal*, 59 (235), September, pp. 360–383.

Phillips, A.W. 1958. 'The relation between unemployment and the rate of change of money wages in the United Kingdom, 1861–1957', *Economica*, n.s., 25 (4), November, pp. 283–299.

Rees, A. 1973. *The Economics of Work and Pay*. New York: Harper & Row.

Samuelson, P.A. 1939. 'A synthesis of the principle of acceleration and the multiplier', *Journal of Political Economy*, 47 (6), December, pp. 786–797.

Samuelson, P.A. 1964. *Economics*, 6th edn, New York: McGraw-Hill.

Samuelson, P.A. 1967. *Economics*, 7th edn, New York: McGraw-Hill.

Samuelson, P.A. and Solow, R.M. 1960. 'Analytical aspects of anti-inflation policy', *American Economic Review*, 50 (2), May, Papers and Proceedings, pp. 177–194.

Solow, R.M. 1956. 'A contribution to the theory of economic growth', *Quarterly Journal of Economics*, 70 (1), February, pp. 65–94.

Stonier, A.W. and Hague, D.C. 1957. *A Textbook of Economic Theory*, 2nd edn, London: Longmans.

Swan, T.W. 1956. 'Economic growth and capital accumulation', *Economic Record*, 32 (63), November, pp. 34–61.

Varoufakis, Y. 2016. *And the Weak Suffer What They Must? Europe, Austerity and the Threat to Global Stability*. London: The Bodley Head.

Weintraub, S. 1956. 'A macroeconomic approach to the theory of wages', *American Economic Review*, 46 (5), December, pp. 835–856.

Weintraub, S. 1960. 'The Keynesian theory of inflation: the two faces of Janus?', *International Economic Review*, 1 (2), May, pp. 143–155.

11. Milton Friedman and the Monetarist School

Sergio Rossi

KEY FEATURES

- This chapter brings forward the theoretical origins of monetarism, which go back to neoclassical economics and the assumption that money is just a 'veil' that does not influence the essence of economic transactions.
- It refers to the quantity theory of money to explain that, according to monetarism, there is a direct and proportional causal relationship between the money supply and the general price level.
- It explains that the assumed neutrality of money led monetarists to argue that monetary policy should aim at price stability only, without trying to influence output and employment levels.
- It criticizes the conceptual and methodological weaknesses of monetarism, which is flawed by a superficial understanding of both money and the working of a monetary production economy.
- It points out the largely unsatisfactory outcomes of central banks' strategies inspired by monetarism, namely monetary targeting and inflation targeting.
- It finally explains the essence of a monetary economy, where banks' double-entry bookkeeping implies that any transaction elicits an emission of money by a bank.

1. INTRODUCTION

The previous chapter outlined the strengths and weaknesses of the Keynesian approach, which has been largely disregarded since the early 1970s, after the first oil-price shock and the demise of the Bretton Woods regime. As a matter of fact, Keynesianism was unable to explain, hence to address, the simultaneous occurrence of high unemployment and high inflation rates. This chapter therefore explores the key elements of the theory that replaced it, namely monetarism. As is well known, this school of economic thought originated with the work of the University of Chicago professor Milton Friedman in the early 1950s. To be true, the 'monetarist' label was coined by Brunner (1968, p. 9), and Friedman never really appreciated it, preferring to refer to his own approach as the 'Chicago school' in order to point out its academic origins (Friedman, 1970, p. 1).

Be that as it may, in the next section we present the historical framework within which Friedman proposed his theoretical appraisal of the working of contemporary economic systems. Inspired by the neoclassical approach, which considers that money has no influence on so-called 'real' economic magnitudes in the long run, Friedman aimed at elaborating a 'half-way station' between this approach and Keynesianism, which at that time was in fashion and according to which the money supply and other nominal variables play an important role in the determination of a number of 'real' magnitudes such as output and employment levels.

In this regard, this 'half-way station' offers an interesting feature worth observing with respect to the similarities and differences between Friedman and Keynes, notably the role played by effective demand – hence of monetary and fiscal policies – in supporting economic activity and growth. In this sense, monetarism could be considered a partial continuation of Keynesianism, because it focuses on the importance of monetary and fiscal policies for economic performance.

Considering that money is neutral for 'real' magnitudes, Friedman maintained that monetary policy should only aim at price stability on the product market, whilst fiscal policy must make sure that public spending and tax receipts balance over the business cycle (if not yearly). He believed indeed in the 'endogenous forces' of free markets, which he considered to be always in a position to achieve eventually some 'natural' economic equilibrium if some exogenous shocks were to occur across the economic system, within which, therefore, the public sector should not intervene. Indeed, any economic policy interventions, in his view, would hinder the equilibrating process of supply and demand on the marketplace, and thereby impede full employment – a situation that he characterized by the existence of some 'natural unemployment rate' owing to voluntary unemployment, that is, those individuals that are able to work but will not do so at the wage level that 'equilibrates' demand and supply on the labour market.

Nevertheless, Friedman conceded that monetary policy interventions could have some transitory impact on 'real' variables in the short run, such as output and employment levels, when economic agents are led astray by 'money illusion'. This view gave rise to monetary targeting strategies, which central banks put into practice to make sure that price stability prevailed, reducing to a minimum money illusion, after the demise of the Bretton Woods regime in the early 1970s and even more so in the 1980s in a variety of industrialized economies. This framework also gave rise to inflation-targeting strategies, which are simply a different form of central banks' interventions grounded on monetarism.

The third section elaborates on this, presenting and critically discussing the so-called 'money multiplier mechanism', which Friedman considered to explain the monetary policy transmission channel that, in his view, makes it possible for a central bank to influence 'monetary aggregates' and thereby achieve the price stability goal. We will then briefly contrast this 'exogenous-money' view with money's endogeneity, as explained by Keynes and post-Keynesian literature in the so-called 'horizontalist' tradition (see Chapter 12 for analytical elaboration), to argue that central banks are not in a position to control the money supply as Friedman imagined.

In the fourth section, we will broaden our critical appraisal of Friedman's monetarist thinking, grounding it on the *homo oeconomicus* paradigm that has been shaping the neoclassical school of economic thought still in fashion at the time of writing. We will contrast this paradigm, which considers economic agents as fully informed, selfish, rational, and maximizing either utility (consumers) or profit (firms), with the so-called '*homo sociologicus*' view, which Keynes and post-Keynesian authors consider closer to the real world (as explained in Chapter 12), where human beings are not fully informed, may be altruist, have a 'bounded' rationality, and do not necessarily (want to) maximize either their utility or profit. The last section concludes, summarizing the contents of this chapter and illustrating the fact that different schools of thought give rise, generally speaking, to different economic results and public policy outcomes in the real world.

2.   THE ORIGINS OF MONETARISM

Monetarism, as proposed by Friedman (1948) originally, represents the monetary theory of neoclassical economics, according to which nominal variables, like money and the general price level, do not affect 'real' economic magnitudes such as output and employment levels once all adjustments have occurred and the economic system is back again at 'equilibrium'. This view can be traced back to Hume (1826/1955), who deemed it obvious that 'the prices of everything depend on the proportion between commodities and money' (p. 41), thereby establishing the philosophical foundations for the so-called 'quantity theory of money' put forward, notably, by Fisher (1911/1931). This theory has been framed by the famous 'equation of exchange', which is usually written as follows:

$$MV = Py$$

where M is the quantity of money, V its velocity of circulation in the relevant period, P the price level on the goods market, and y 'real' output. This equation simply represents the fact that – in any money-using economic system – the total amount of money spent during a given period of time (on its left-hand side) is equivalent to the expenditure by those agents that purchased output on sale at the relevant prices (on its right-hand side). As such, it is a truism. It is also consistent with Fisher's claim that 'any commodity to be called "money" must be *generally acceptable in exchange*, and any commodity generally acceptable in exchange should be called money' (Fisher, 1911/1931, p. 2, emphasis in original).

This commodity-money view has been suggested by a number of neoclassical economists and is still in fashion. It considers that in a money-using economy agents on any markets enter into 'indirect exchange' (Hayek, 1933, p. 44) because, in the words of Friedman (1974, p. 8), money 'enables the act of purchase to be separated from the act of sale' for any agent involved in such an exchange. If so, then '[m]oney is treated as a stock, not as a flow or a mixture of a flow and a stock' (Friedman, 1987, p. 5). In economics literature, monetarists use this theoretical perspective, which reproduces the so-called 'traditional dichotomy' between the 'real' sector and the 'monetary' sector of the economy, to explain that the price level is independent of both y and V – two non-monetary variables that, in this framework, depend by assumption on 'real' and technical conditions respectively. In the end, the amount of money supply can only have an impact on P. This has given rise to the so-called 'homogeneity postulate', which explains that, on the same assumptions as pointed out above, there is a direct and proportional causal relationship between M and P: if one multiplies M by any number λ, the same occurs with the price level eventually (that is, once all behavioural adjustments have taken place across the economic system), assuming that full employment prevails – so that firms cannot increase their production level even though demand has increased on the goods market:

$$\lambda M \Rightarrow \lambda P$$

In practice, this means that if agents receive some extra money units, they will spend them on the market for produced goods and services, in order for them to maximize their utility over time. As the economic system is working at full employment by assumption, this additional expenditure on the goods market induces an increase in the price level eventually – so that in the end the purchasing power of each agent is unchanged by a higher supply of money, all adjustments being carried out within the realm of nominal magnitudes, that is, from M to P (which are linked by a one-to-one causal relationship, as explained by the quantity theory of money summarized above).

Starting from this causal relationship, which he assumed to hold over the long run as a result of the free-market mechanism (to wit, the 'law' of supply and demand), Friedman (1956) advocated that monetary policy should aim at price stability, without trying also to influence output and employment levels – as he assumed that both of them depend on 'real' magnitudes only. A strong opponent to Keynesian policies (discussed in the previous chapter), which were in fashion at that time, Friedman (1956) conceded that, over the short run, monetary policy could influence output and employment levels, but ascribed this influence to some 'frictions' or irrational behaviour that would disappear over the longer run – as a result of agents' learning and technological progress. In particular, agents may be led astray by what the monetarist school called 'money illusion', that is, the fact that agents consider nominal instead of real magnitudes when they can dispose of a higher number of money units in any given market whatsoever. In other words, agents are under the illusion that any increases in their money balances mean *ipso facto* an increase in their purchasing power, leading them to increase their propensity to spend on the market for produced goods and services.

This illusion leads these agents to believe they are richer because they have more money, ignoring that as a result of this increase in the supply of money (M) the price level (P) will also increase proportionally as time goes by. This has been explained by the assumption that agents dispose of their extra money units for the purchase of goods and services on the product market, which pushes their prices up, on the hypothesis that full employment prevails, so that firms cannot produce more output than what is on sale already (see above).

Advocating adaptive expectations, Friedman (1968) argued that agents learn from their mistakes, adjusting their behaviour – and expectations – to integrate their understanding that, when the money supply increases, this leads to higher prices eventually. As a result of this adjustment in agents' behaviour, money illusion vanishes as time goes by, so that it would be pointless for a central bank to steer its monetary policy decisions in order to support economic growth through a higher demand on the goods market induced by the expansionary stance of monetary policy.

Quite to the contrary, this expansive policy has a negative impact on the 'real' sector of the economy, as it leads agents to increase their savings in order to preserve their purchasing power once prices will be higher as a result of such a policy – whose inefficiency will thus already become plain over the short run.

As Friedman famously argued, *'inflation is always and everywhere a monetary phenomenon* in the sense that it is and can be produced only by a more rapid increase in the quantity of money than in output' (1987, p. 17, emphasis in original). This led him to put to the fore the so-called 'Friedman rule', which establishes that the (yearly) growth rate of the money supply should be equal to the (yearly) growth rate of produced output, so that the relationship between money and output (to wit, the price level on the goods market) remains stable over time (Friedman, 1969, p. 47), thereby also influencing (stabilizing) agents' expectations in this regard (see Friedman, 1960). Owing to some time lags that exist in the monetary policy transmission mechanism from M to P, Friedman argued in favour of a policy rule that disposes of uncertainty as regards the rate of growth of the money supply, in order to inform agents' expectations with a view to achieve stability notably with respect to the price level on the product market. Let us explore this in the next section.

3.   MONETARISTS' POLICY STRATEGIES

The monetary policy strategies inspired by monetarism are simple, if not simplistic. As monetary policy should aim just at price stability on the market for produced goods and services, the central bank's strategy must focus on the growth rate of the relevant money supply, that is, the 'monetary aggregate' that is best correlated with the price level. Over the 1970s and until the end of the 1980s (or the 1990s in few cases), a number of central banks on both sides of the Atlantic have been implementing the Friedman rule, targeting a rate of growth of the relevant 'monetary aggregate' (either a narrow aggregate, such as M0, including central bank money only, or a broad aggregate, like M3, which includes a variety of bank deposits beyond M0). Generally speaking, the policy results were not in line with the policy-makers' expectations, as the actual growth rate of the money supply was either above or below the targeted rate and, moreover, the price level was not at all stable even in those (occasional) cases where the targeted rate of growth for the money supply was met – more by chance than design (see, for instance, Bofinger, 2001, pp. 295–299; and Rossi, 2008, pp. 424–434).

Further, monetary targeting strategies often induced a sacrifice (measured by so-called 'sacrifice ratios') in terms of output and/or employment losses, as they led to (unnecessarily) restrictive monetary policies in an attempt to provide price stability on the product market (see for instance Ball, 1994). In other words, pursuing monetary growth targets led to increased unemployment and output losses. Various critical investigations on empirical grounds have pointed out 'the cumulative increase in the yearly rate of unemployment that is due to the disinflation effort divided by the total decrease in the rate of inflation' (Cukierman, 2002, p. 1).

Critics of the Friedman rule argued that its author wrongly assumed money demand to be stable, so that its velocity of circulation could remain stable and, thus, be predictable over time, allowing the central bank to steer the money supply according to its target as defined with respect to the price stability goal (see, for instance, Brunner and Meltzer, 1964; Brunner, 1968; and McCallum, 1981). In fact, according to this orthodox critique, money demand (hence its velocity of circulation) is unstable, so much so as a result of so-called 'financial innovation', to wit, those new financial assets and payment services that make it easier for an economic agent to keep a liquid store of value and pay any debt obligation without disposing of 'money' in the form of cash or bank deposits.

Another critique raised by orthodox economists is that the Friedman rule is too rigid, because it does not allow for the possibility to integrate some feedback from the real world, particularly when there is a large gap between the measured and the expected rate of inflation (see for instance Taylor, 1999). A number of orthodox economists, notably Clarida et al. (1998), consider that central banks' reaction function includes a feedback term as well as an error term in order to take into account both past mistakes in the monetary policy strategy and unexpected events, such as exogenous shocks that may impact on the economic system positively or negatively. The Friedman rule does not take into account all these issues, because it ignores a variety of interactions in the real world between 'real' and 'monetary' magnitudes as well as the complexity of any economic systems facing (fundamental) uncertainty as regards the future, particularly when the economy is open to foreign trade and international capital flows – as occurred in a variety of countries starting from the 1980s in the aftermath of phenomena such as globalization (see Blecker, 2016) and financialization (see Epstein, 2016).

Another set of critiques emerged from non-orthodox economists, notably in light of the endogenous nature of money, whose supply is 'credit-driven and demand-determined', as famously explained by Moore (1988, p. 46; see also Chapter 12). These economists explain that a central bank cannot influence, not to say determine, the money supply through the steering of a 'monetary aggregate' that it imagines to affect, or even to control, directly or indirectly. As Taylor (1999, p. 47) pointed out, 'the interest rate rather than the money supply is the key instrument that should be adjusted' by the central bank wishing to exert some impact on the economic system's variables that it targets or aims at influencing, such as the rate of inflation, unemployment, or economic growth.

In spite of these critiques, Friedman and the Monetarist School he originated argued that a 'money multiplier' was actually in force, so that the central bank can steer total money supply, that is, M, by acting upon central bank money (also called base or high-powered money, B), considering the following formula (see, for instance, Friedman, 1959):

$$M = \frac{(1+c)}{(c+r)} B$$

where c represents the currency ratio (that is, the amount of currency that agents hold in respect of their bank deposits) and r the reserve ratio (to wit, the amount of reserves that banks keep at the central bank with regard to their customers' deposits). Central bankers could therefore determine the magnitude of the money multiplier (m) by dividing $(1+c)$ by $(c+r)$:

$$m = \frac{(1+c)}{(c+r)}$$

on the assumption that both c and r remain stable over time, so that their future value is predictable, allowing the central bank to control the money supply and provide for price stability eventually.

Both the money multiplier mechanism and the monetary targeting strategies established under it consider an economic system where the money supply is partly exogenous, that is, determined or at least controlled by the central bank, as regards notably base or high-powered money. Friedman (1969, pp. 4–5) gave a famous illustration for this assumed 'money exogeneity' in the form of 'helicopter money', that is, literally, money falling from the sky owing to a helicopter dropping banknotes that are 'hastily collected by the members of the community'. Those banknotes that the collectors do not want to spend immediately are deposited with banks, which are thereby led to increase their lending in light of the fact that only part of these deposits are withdrawn by their holders – so that it is both possible and convenient for banks to lend an amount that corresponds to non-withdrawn deposits, considering the currency ratio introduced above. Bank credit will thus give rise to further expenditures, whose amounts will generate new bank deposits, which in the end will provide for a total money supply (M) higher than base money (B), the relationship between M and B being given by m according to the above formula of the money multiplier.

As logic as this may appear at first sight, the working of the money multiplier crucially assumes an exogenous factor, namely central bank money (B) in the form of cash and settlement balances (which monetarists call bank reserves). In fact, this assumption turns out to be wrong, since any units of money, including those issued by the central bank, are the result of some economic activity (on any kinds of markets) that sooner or later must be paid – thereby eliciting an emission of money by some bank, and generally speaking as a result of a credit line (see Rossi, 2007, Chapters 1–2 for analytical elaboration on this). This means that banks are not 'reserve constrained', as argued by monetarists, to determine the amount of credit, because the latter does not depend on pre-existent deposits with banks or at the central bank. In fact, loans generate deposits (Schumpeter, 1954, pp. 1110–1117). Hence, a central bank cannot restrict the amount of central bank money to limit the volume of credits that banks are willing to provide to their customers. What a central bank can do, and does indeed, is to set the interest rate at which it is ready to provide settlement balances (or bank reserves, in the monetarists' jargon) to banks, which need central bank money in order for their bilateral debt–credit relationships to be settled finally and irrevocably by the end of the day. As the German central bank pointed out long ago in this regard, 'banks do not accept bank money in interbank transactions, but ultimately require their claims to be settled in central bank money' (Deutsche Bundesbank, 1994, p. 46). In this connection, as Goodhart (1989, p. 293) noted cogently:

> Central bank practitioners, almost always, view themselves as unable to deny the banks the reserve base that the banking system requires, and see themselves as setting the level of interest rates, at which such reserves are met, with the quantity of money then simultaneously determined by the portfolio preferences of private sector banks and non-banks.

This endogenous nature of money has been recently acknowledged by researchers at the Bank of England (see McLeay et al., 2014), who noticed what post-Keynesian authors *à la* Moore (1988) explained more than a quarter of a century earlier (see above). Now, in an attempt to recognize money's endogeneity in the real world, various economists have given rise to a 'new consensus macroeconomics' with a view to preserve the monetarist spirit, considering 'money as a residual with no further role for it' (Arestis and Sawyer, 2004, p. 442), turning thereby to inflation targeting strategies that essentially perpetuate the monetarists' policy framework.

Inflation targeting – which has been in fashion since the 1990s in an increasing number of both advanced and emerging market economies until the global financial crisis in 2008 – is a halfway station between a rule-based and a fully discretionary monetary policy (Bernanke et al., 1999, pp. 299–301). In practice, it 'gives rise to a discretionary monetary policy under constraint: those central banks that target inflation explicitly are in a position to take advantage of some flexibility in policy making, in order for them to affect the business cycle in the short run, in so far as their actions do not jeopardize price stability in the long run' (Rossi, 2009, p. 94).

Generally speaking, inflation-targeting strategies have five major characteristics (Rossi, 2015, p. 254):

(1)   a public announcement of official quantitative targets (or target ranges) for the inflation rate over one or more time horizons;
(2)   an institutional commitment to price stability as the monetary policy's primary long-run goal, and a commitment to achieve the inflation objective in any case;
(3)   an information-inclusive strategy in which many variables and not merely a monetary aggregate are used in the monetary-policy decision-making process;
(4)   vigorous efforts to communicate the plans as well as the objectives of the monetary authority to the public;
(5)   an increased accountability of the central bank for attaining its inflation rate objectives.

In practice adopting an inflation targeting strategy means for the central bank publishing the rate of inflation that it targets over a given time horizon, which may be a point target or a target band. Owing to this public announcement, the central bank is accountable for the effects of its monetary policy interventions as regards the rate of measured inflation, which re-establishes the monetarists' doctrine that considers the principal (if not unique) objective of central banks to be price stability on the goods market – measured by some price indices, such as the 'core inflation' index or the consumer price index (see Rossi, 2001, for analytical elaboration on this). In this monetarist perspective, price stability is considered instrumental in order for monetary policy to provide the most appropriate framework within which 'market forces' (to wit, supply and demand) will induce the best possible outcome, hence economic performance. This is particularly the case of the European Central Bank (2003, p. 79), which steers its monetary policy with a view to hit its (self-defined) inflation target 'below, but close to, 2% over the medium term'.

Even though inflation-targeting central banks around the world seem to have largely broken the umbilical cord linking this monetary policy strategy with monetarism *à la* Friedman, this is just an optical illusion as regards that monetary policy strategy. As a matter of fact, the latter remains in the Friedman spirit, because it is grounded on all its building blocks, namely:

(a) *money neutrality*, that is, the quantity-theory-of-money perspective that considers money to be neutral on 'real' economic magnitudes over the long run and probably also over the short run if agents behave rationally and are correctly informed by the central bank;

(b) *money illusion*, that is, the possibility to lead people astray over the short run, if they consider the amount of their 'nominal money balances' rather than their 'real money balances' when deciding their consumption behaviour as a result of some additional money units issued by the central bank;

(c) *money matters*, notably as regards the direct and proportional causal relationship between the amount of money supplied and the price level on the product market, without ever considering the likely (and observable) impact that an expansionary monetary policy can have on financial markets, activities and institutions.

Even in the aftermath of the global financial crisis that erupted in 2008, central banks around the world have not really changed their monetarist attitude. Their adoption of 'unconventional' instruments testifies to their belief in the quantity theory of money, notably with regard to the various 'credit easing' and 'quantitative easing' policies in both Europe and the United States that the major central banks have been carrying out (unsuccessfully in the euro area) in an attempt to kick-start economic growth through different inflationary pressures which, at the time of writing, remain to be seen on the goods market – because they have instead been observed on financial markets at large.

   This state of the art, and the huge discrepancies between expected and observed results of monetarism since its advent, can be better explained if we consider the more general theoretical framework within which the Monetarist School was conceived and gave rise to monetarist central bank policies in a variety of countries around the world. The next section expands on this.

4. THE *HOMO OECONOMICUS* PARADIGM

The academic success of monetarism, which became prominent in the 1970s and 1980s, and is still alive and kicking as pointed out above, can be ascribed to the behavioural as well as mathematical foundations upon which it establishes its policy proposals, namely the monetary policy rule and strategies explained in the previous sections. Indeed, these neoclassical foundations consider economics as a science in so far as its objects can be expressed and analysed in mathematical form, and traced back to agents' behaviour, at both individual and collective levels.

These characteristics are clearly centre stage in monetarism, which considers money as a stock – 'a temporary abode of purchasing power' in Friedman's (1974, p. 9) words – and subsumes money's role in the equation of exchange put to the fore by the quantity theory of money explained above. This common-sense understanding of money, in the form of cash or bank deposits, has a number of far-reaching implications in economic analysis as well as in monetary policy making. It notably allows modelling the working of an economic system with a series of equations that are supposed to reproduce agents' behaviour on the marketplace. As Friedman (1987, p. 5) noted with regard to the transactions form of the equation of exchange, 'the elementary event is a transaction – an exchange in which one economic actor transfers goods or services or securities to another actor and receives a transfer of money in return'. This provides the occasion to model monetary transactions as a bilateral exchange whereby 'monetary assets' enter every exchange as the general equivalent of non-monetary items (see Spindt, 1985, pp. 178–180). Indeed, monetarists consider that a monetary economy is characterized by the fact that 'a single good plays a distinctive asymmetric role as one side of virtually all transactions' (Starr, 1980, p. 263). This 'monetary good' may be decided by the state, as monetarists claim in regards to central bank money, or may be selected by economic agents participating in market exchanges viewed as a discovery process, particularly by an array of monetarists referring to search-theoretic models such as those of Kiyotaki and Wright (1989, 1993) and Howitt (2005). In both cases, that is, with regard to the total money supply, agents accept money in exchange for non-monetary goods, since they know that they may dispose of money later on, when they will obtain some real objects, either in commercial or financial forms, in order for them to maximize their utility (as consumers) or profit (as firms) over time, under their budgetary constraint (which becomes a monetary constraint in cash-in-advance models in the tradition of Clower, 1967).

This neoclassical framework is thereby grounded on microfoundations, that is to say, an appraisal of monetary macroeconomics through the lenses of the 'representative agent' – a research methodology assuming that 'what is true of a part is, on that account alone, alleged to be true of the whole' (Samuelson, quoted by Hartley, 1997, p. 170). Indeed, a monetarist analysis of a money-using economy (which is essentially different from a monetary economy, as explained by Rossi, 2007) boils down to surface phenomena such as the exchange that occurs at an individual level between some real items and a number of banknotes, both of which change place over time in a *do-ut-des* transaction between the seller and the buyer of the real items – a transaction that should enable both agents to maximize their utility according to the *homo oeconomicus* view.

To be sure, in the monetarist framework, banks are mere financial intermediaries that in each period simply transfer from savers to borrowers the amount of loanable funds that the former deposited with them, and all agents' transactions on any kind of markets just transfer the existing money stock from purchasers to sellers, in a zero-sum process for the economy as a whole: 'One man's spending is another man's receipts. One man can reduce his nominal money balances only by persuading someone else to increase his' (Friedman, 1987, p. 4). This echoes Tobin's (1963, pp. 408–409) well-known image that, in the monetarist perspective, 'money is like the "hot potato" of a children's game: one individual may pass it to another, but the group as a whole cannot get rid of it'. This is tantamount to saying that an offer to sell goods is a demand for money – and vice versa. Within such a framework, all that one can analyse is how money and non-money goods end up in individuals' portfolios, after all transactions have occurred during the relevant period. As a matter of fact, in this framework '[t]here is no attempt to account for the "concept" of money as a *measure of value* (or *unit of account*) – or even to recognize that this might constitute an intellectual problem' (Ingham, 1996, p. 515, emphasis in original; see Rossi, 2007, for analytical elaboration on this).

Ignoring the nature of money as well as the essential role money plays in any economic system, to rely on the theory of commodity-money that considers money to emerge as a result of a discovery process from the barter trade system, leads monetarists to think that banks – as mere intermediaries between depositors and borrowers – are merely one kind of firm among others so that, according to their 'free market' view, no particular rules or regulations should apply to the banking (or financial) sector, letting the 'law' of supply and demand play its supposed role of market (self-) regulator. Once again, the *homo oeconomicus* paradigm is at play in this regard, since monetarists claim that banks and non-bank financial institutions behave rationally and therefore should be unregulated, because the maximization of their profits leads them to select 'always and everywhere' the best performing projects that seek funding, thereby contributing to the 'optimum' of society as a whole on economic grounds.

Now, the global financial crisis that erupted in 2008 should provide enough 'empirical evidence' that the monetarists' (*homo oeconomicus*) perspective is a figment of (their) imagination. In fact, already much earlier than this, Keynes and post-Keynesian authors pointed out that such a perspective is essentially wrong for several reasons. Let us note them here briefly (see, for instance, King, 2012 and 2015, for analytical elaboration on this):

(a)   agents are not fully informed, do not always behave rationally, and generally do not maximize their utility or profit, notably as the future is fundamentally uncertain and this impedes referring to probability calculations to attain the agents' 'optimum';

(b)   money, including central bank money, is not an exogenous magnitude since it exists as a result of credit lines that banks may grant without the need for them to dispose of pre-existent reserves or bank deposits;

(c)   banks, therefore, are not simply financial intermediaries, because they can open a credit line without having the corresponding savings in their accounts, looking for these savings later as a result of their own lending decisions;

(d)   payments are not bilateral but trilateral transactions, implying banks as both money and credit providers, particularly as regards production, which does not really imply the exchange of pre-existing objects, but actually gives rise to these objects (output and income) on macro-economic grounds.

These (and many other) characteristics make it relevant to consider (macro) categories of agents instead of single 'representative agents' to understand and analyse the actual working of our economic systems, where money is essential as a means of payment for the set of economic agents on all markets, which in fact would not exist without money. Indeed, money is neither 'a creature of markets' as claimed by neoclassical authors, nor 'a creature of the State' as maintained by many neo-chartalists, but actually 'a creature of banks' (Rochon and Vernengo, 2003, p. 61). Unless monetarism recognizes this fact, its theoretical analysis as well as policy proposals will not be up to the task, because the working of the economic system as a whole cannot be appraised by observing a variety of surface phenomena related to agents' behaviour, such as the exchange of bank-notes against commercial or financial items, or the expenditure of bank deposits in purchasing a variety of goods and services. These phenomena can only be understood with a theory that is conceptually sound and logically consistent with the nature of money, which can be appraised only if one considers that money is essentially a means of payment and not an object of it. Actually, the issue is not about classifying money's functions but about a correct analytical understanding of the nature of a means of payment. Monetarism lacks such an understanding, so much so that 'the definition of money can still be regarded as an almost unresolved issue' (Bofinger, 2001, p. 3) in spite of the thousands of volumes written on this subject matter, whose mathematical treatment by the Monetarist School is as wrong as its conceptual underpinnings (see Rossi, 2007, for analytical elaboration on this).

5. CONCLUSION

This chapter presented monetarism, that is, the school of economic thought originated by Milton Friedman in the neoclassical tradition. This long-standing tradition considers money as a 'veil' (Pigou, 1949, p. 25), that is, 'something' that 'does not comprise any of the essentials of economic life' (ibid.). It would be merely a technical device allowing the reduction of transactions costs – as those elicited by the need to meet the 'double coincidence of wants' (Jevons, 1875, p. 3) between two agents entering into exchange. In this view, then, the role of monetary policy must be confined to ensure that price stability prevails, leaving to 'real' forces such as agents' preferences and factors' productivity the task of determining 'real' magnitudes like output and employment levels.

The bottom line of this chapter is that actual economic policies, like austerity policies in the aftermath of the euro-area crisis, are not ineluctable but, in fact, closely depend on a given theoretical understanding of the working of contemporary economic systems. The understanding of the latter is in turn the result of a methodological framework, which is based on a series of economic concepts that are usually derived from one's vision of the society in which one lives.

All in all, the litmus test for any economic theory or model is rather easy to carry out: it consists in verifying that the model or theory at hand is consistent, logically correct, and conceptually sound. No 'empirical evidence' can ever provide such a test, because one needs first to work out the principles of economic analysis before applying them to any 'empirical' object of investigation. Further, economic analysis cannot be limited to the study of agents' (individual or collective) behaviour, as the working of every economic system crucially depends on its structures and institutions. A monetary–structural law is actually centre stage in all monetary economies, that is, double-entry bookkeeping for recording the result of any transaction by a third-party agent (namely, a bank), as Hicks (1967, p. 11) argued when he observed that '[e]very transaction involves three parties, buyer, seller, and banker'. Money is just a numerical counter, and any economic theory must consider this fact to begin with, since money is essential and no economic system can ever be conceived without it. The failure of monetarism, therefore, is conceptual as well as methodological, before being at fault on both theoretical and empirical grounds.

ACKNOWLEDGEMENTS

The author is grateful to the editors of this volume for their kind invitation to contribute this chapter, as well as to Jonathan Massonnet and Amos Pesenti for their comments on a preliminary draft. The usual disclaimer applies.

REFERENCES

Arestis, P. and M. Sawyer (2004), 'On the effectiveness of monetary policy and of fiscal policy', *Review of Social Economy*, **62** (4), 441–463.
Ball, L. (1994), 'What determines the sacrifice ratio?', in N.G. Mankiw (ed.), *Monetary Policy*, Chicago: University of Chicago Press, pp. 155–182.
Bernanke, B.S., T. Laubach, F.S. Mishkin and A.S. Posen (1999), *Inflation Targeting: Lessons from the International Experience*, Princeton: Princeton University Press.
Blecker, R.A. (2016), 'International trade and development', in L.-P. Rochon and S. Rossi (eds), *An Introduction to Macroeconomics: A Heterodox Approach to Economic Analysis*, Cheltenham, UK and Northampton, MA, USA: Edward Elgar Publishing, pp. 259–281.
Bofinger, P. (2001), *Monetary Policy: Goals, Institutions, Strategies, and Instruments*, Oxford: Oxford University Press.
Brunner, K. (1968), 'The role of money and monetary policy', *Federal Reserve Bank of St. Louis Review*, **50** (7), 9–24.
Brunner, K. and A.H. Meltzer (1964), 'Some further investigations of demand and supply functions for money', *Journal of Finance*, **19** (2), 240–283.
Clarida, R., J. Galí and M. Gertler (1998), 'Monetary policy rules in practice: some international evidence', *European Economic Review*, **42** (6), 1033–1067.
Clower, R.W. (1967), 'A reconsideration of the microfoundations of monetary theory', *Western Economic Journal*, **6** (1), 1–8.
Cukierman, A. (2002), 'Does a higher sacrifice ratio mean that central bank independence is excessive?', *Annals of Economics and Finance*, **3** (1), 1–25.
Deutsche Bundesbank (1994), 'Recent trends in the Deutsche Bundesbank's cashless payments', *Monthly Report*, **46** (8), 45–61.
Epstein, G.A. (2016), 'Financialization', in L.-P. Rochon and S. Rossi (eds), *An Introduction to Macroeconomics: A Heterodox Approach to Economic Analysis*, Cheltenham, UK and Northampton, MA, USA: Edward Elgar Publishing, pp. 319–335.
European Central Bank (2003), 'The outcome of the ECB's evaluation of its monetary policy strategy', *Monthly Bulletin*, **5** (6), 79–92.
Fisher, I. (1911/1931), *The Purchasing Power of Money: Its Determination and Relation to Credit, Interest and Crises*, New York: Macmillan.

Friedman, M. (1948), 'A monetary and fiscal framework for economic stability', *American Economic Review*, **38** (3), 245–264.

Friedman, M. (ed.) (1956), *Studies in the Quantity Theory of Money*, Chicago: University of Chicago Press.

Friedman, M. (1959), 'The demand for money: some theoretical and empirical results', *Journal of Political Economy*, **67** (4), 327–351.

Friedman, M. (1960), *A Program for Monetary Stability*, New York: Fordham University Press.

Friedman, M. (1968), 'The role of monetary policy', *American Economic Review*, **58** (1), 1–17.

Friedman, M. (1969), *The Optimum Quantity of Money and Other Essays*, Chicago: Aldine Publishing.

Friedman, M. (1970), 'The counter-revolution in monetary theory', *Institute of Economic Affairs Occasional Paper*, No. 33. Reprinted in M. Friedman (1991), *Monetarist Economics*, Oxford: Basil Blackwell, pp. 1–20.

Friedman, M. (1974), 'A theoretical framework for monetary analysis', in R.J. Gordon (ed.), *Milton Friedman's Monetary Framework: A Debate with His Critics*, Chicago and London: University of Chicago Press, pp. 1–62.

Friedman, M. (1987), 'Quantity theory of money', in J. Eatwell, M. Milgate and P. Newman (eds), *The New Palgrave: A Dictionary of Economics*, London and Basingstoke: Macmillan, vol. IV, pp. 3–20.

Goodhart, C.A.E. (1989), 'The conduct of monetary policy', *Economic Journal*, **99** (396), 293–346.

Hartley, J.E. (1997), *The Representative Agent in Macroeconomics*, London and New York: Routledge.

Hayek, F.A. (1933), *Monetary Theory and the Trade Cycle*, London: Jonathan Cape.

Hicks, J.R. (1967), *Critical Essays in Monetary Theory*, Oxford: Clarendon Press.

Howitt, P. (2005), 'Beyond search: fiat money in organized exchange', *International Economic Review*, **46** (2), 405–429.

Hume, D. (1826), *The Philosophical Works, Volume III*, reprinted in E. Rotwein (ed.) (1955), *Writings on Economics*, Edinburgh: Nelson.

Ingham, G. (1996), 'Money is a social relation', *Review of Social Economy*, **54** (4), 507–529.

Jevons, W.S. (1875), *Money and the Mechanism of Exchange*, London: Appleton.

King, J.E. (2012), *The Microfoundations Delusion: Metaphor and Dogma in the History of Macroeconomics*, Cheltenham, UK and Northampton, MA, USA: Edward Elgar Publishing.

King, J.E. (2015), *Advanced Introduction to Post Keynesian Economics*, Cheltenham, UK and Northampton, MA, USA: Edward Elgar Publishing.

Kiyotaki, N. and R. Wright (1989), 'On money as a medium of exchange', *Journal of Political Economy*, **97** (4), 927–954.

Kiyotaki, N. and R. Wright (1993), 'A search-theoretic approach to monetary economics', *American Economic Review*, **83** (1), 63–77.

McCallum, B.T. (1981), 'Monetarist principles and the money stock growth rule', *American Economic Review*, **71** (2), 134–138.

McLeay, M., A. Radia and R. Thomas (2014), 'Money creation in the modern economy', *Bank of England Quarterly Bulletin*, **54** (1), 14–27.

Moore, B.J. (1988), *Horizontalists and Verticalists: The Macroeconomics of Credit Money*, Cambridge: Cambridge University Press.

Pigou, A.C. (1949), *The Veil of Money*, London: Macmillan.

Rochon, L.-P. and M. Vernengo (2003), 'State money and the real world: or chartalism and its discontents', *Journal of Post Keynesian Economics*, **26** (1), 57–67.

Rossi, S. (2001), *Money and Inflation: A New Macroeconomic Analysis*, Cheltenham, UK and Northampton, MA, USA: Edward Elgar Publishing (reprinted 2003).

Rossi, S. (2007), *Money and Payments in Theory and Practice*, London and New York: Routledge.

Rossi, S. (2008), *Macroéconomie monétaire: théories et politiques*, Geneva, Paris and Brussels: Schulthess, LGDJ and Bruylant.

Rossi, S. (2009), 'Inflation targeting and monetary policy governance: the case of the European Central Bank', in C. Gnos and L.-P. Rochon (eds), *Monetary Policy and Financial Stability: A Post-Keynesian Agenda*, Cheltenham, UK and Northampton, MA, USA: Edward Elgar Publishing, pp. 91–113.

Rossi, S. (2015), 'Inflation targeting', in L.-P. Rochon and S. Rossi (eds), *The Encyclopedia of Central Banking*, Cheltenham, UK and Northampton, MA, USA: Edward Elgar Publishing, pp. 254–255.

Schumpeter, J.A. (1954), *History of Economic Analysis*, London: George Allen & Unwin.

Spindt, P.A. (1985), 'Money is what money does: monetary aggregation and the equation of exchange', *Journal of Political Economy*, **93** (1), 175–204.

Starr, R.M. (1980), 'General equilibrium approaches to the study of monetary economies: comments on recent developments', in J.H. Kareken and N. Wallace (eds), *Models of Monetary Economies*, Minneapolis: Federal Reserve Bank of Minneapolis, pp. 261–263.

Taylor, J.B. (1999), 'Monetary policy guidelines for employment and inflation stability', in R.M. Solow and J.B. Taylor (eds), *Inflation, Unemployment, and Monetary Policy*, Cambridge: MIT Press, pp. 29–54.

Tobin, J. (1963), 'Commercial banks as creators of "money"', in D. Carson (ed.), *Banking and Monetary Studies*, Homewood, IL: Richard D. Irwin, pp. 408–419.

12. The Rational Expectations School

William McColloch and Matías Vernengo

KEY FEATURES

- This chapter examines the ideas of Robert Lucas and his anti-Keynesian reconstruction of macroeconomics on a microeconomic foundation of rational maximizing individual behavior.
- It discusses Lucas' view that normal monetary policy operations would be ineffective in smoothing the business cycle, and that the activist use of policy was far more likely to generate or exacerbate the cycle.
- The chapter further details the so-called Lucas Critique of econometric modeling that dismissed the use of empirical data from the past as an unreliable guide to future behavior.
- We then turn to the emergence of Real Business Cycle Theory, a body of work that further rejected the principle of effective demand, instead insisting that the business cycle reflected real shocks to productivity growth.
- In critically assessing these contributions, the chapter argues that the empirical estimations of total factor productivity derived from national income accounts are inevitably subject to mismeasurement.
- Finally, the chapter argues that while Lucas has been deeply influential within modern mainstream macroeconomics, it was Friedman's natural rate of employment that represented the decisive regression to pre-Keynesian ideas.

1. INTRODUCTION

If Keynes' *General Theory* was a paradigmatic break with the neoclassical mainstream of the profession, bringing down established orthodoxy, then Robert Lucas' famous paper "Expectations and the Neutrality of Money" was the final restoration after the monetarist assault on Keynesian economics. The previous chapter discussed the rise of monetarism, and showed that while the policy conclusions of monetarist authors were frequently at odds with those of Keynesian authors, they were content to operate within a shared model, one that allowed policy to regularly exercise real effects, at least within the short run. Friedman's framework had essentially accepted the Neoclassical Synthesis version of Keynesian ideas, with the ISLM and the Phillips Curve, with the addition of the notion of a natural rate of unemployment, as the basis for his analysis. Lucas would ultimately reject these terms of engagement. For him, rational maximizing of individual behavior was the quintessential insight that economic theory had to offer, from which all analysis and conclusions should follow. Without it, macroeconomics was little more than unstructured wishful thinking. Thus, his theoretical model demanded a complete reconstruction of macroeconomics on a microeconomic footing, and the abandonment of Keynes' insights. For Lucas, Keynesian ideas should not be taken too seriously.[1] The notion that macroeconomics should simply involve the aggregation of individual behavior was thereby reintroduced, and would profoundly reshape mainstream macroeconomic analysis.[2]

Lucas argued that, apart from problems of information, markets always cleared relatively quickly, and that there was no such thing as involuntary unemployment. If people are unemployed it is simply a result of a rational choice. A reduction in real wages would always produce an increase in employment, everything else constant. If workers are unemployed it is because they decided not to work at the given real wage. No policy other than laissez-faire is necessary. For Lucas, government is not the solution, but part of the problem, as much as it was for Reagan, who would later argue, within the political arena, for the same idea.

Lucas' New Classical Revolution suggested that models should be founded on elements of microeconomic behavior: the preferences of economic agents making decisions, and the restrictions they face in the form of factor endowments, and the technology embodied in the production function were seen to determine both microeconomic and macroeconomic behavior. In that sense, his revolution was a return to the simple marginalist or neoclassical macroeconomic model.

In attempting to formulate such a model, Finn Kydland and Edward Prescott initiated the so-called Real Business Cycle School (RBC), which came to dominate the Rational Expectations School. Lucas' monetary model is in the Wicksellian heritage, to the extent that money may have real effects, in the short run, as a result of money illusion, imperfect information or simply as a result of unanticipated shocks to monetary variables. However, the Lucas monetary misperception model fell out of favor, due in part to the fact that monetary information is readily available and central banks tend to be quite transparent about their policy goals.

Unanticipated monetary shocks might then be hard to come by in the real world. Admitting this, Lucas came to largely adopt the RBC view wherein business cycles are not deviations from the optimal level of output, but changes in the natural output level itself, caused essentially by shocks to total factor productivity (TFP).

The emphasis placed by rational expectations models on the inter-temporal choices between leisure and consumption, and the fact that production takes time, and requires inputs over several periods, has led many to label these models Walrasian, in contrast to the Marshallian model used by Friedman, and the Neoclassical Synthesis Keynesians. Traditionally, Walrasian models were distinguished by the use of a General Equilibrium (GE) framework, as opposed to the partial equilibrium approach of Marshall and his immediate followers. The presumption of partial equilibrium methods is that any individual market, and the changes that occur therein, can be meaningfully analyzed in relative isolation from all others by means of the ceteris paribus assumption. By contrast, in GE models all markets are necessarily intertwined, such that the choices made in one market impact all others to some degree. Understood in this sense, it would be a mistake to see the rise of the Rational Expectations School as a Walrasian "break." Indeed, the ISLM model utilized by both Neoclassical Synthesis authors and Friedman was as GE model, as it depicted the simultaneous interaction of the product market and the money market in determining equilibrium output. What instead distinguished the Rational Expectations School from its predecessors was its almost obsessive conviction that all economic models be grounded in the behavior of perfectly rational economic agents continually seeking to maximize their utility not only in the present, but inter-temporally. Suggestions that social conventions might govern individual behavior, or that consumption patterns might differ by class or income group, as in the work of Kalecki or Duesenberry, were to be discarded.

In that sense, like the New Classical School, the fundamental change in this context is that the equilibration between savings and investment is done through changes in the rate of interest, not income, and that only rigidities would deviate investment from full employment savings. This chapter will discuss Lucas' monetary misperception model and the policy ineffectiveness proposition, before turning to the emergence of RBC literature. The limits of the Rational Expectations School's intellectual project are then discussed.

2. MONETARY SHOCKS AND POLICY INEFFECTIVENESS

Generally acknowledged as the central figure of the rational expectations counter-revolution, Robert Lucas began his academic career as a student of history before transferring to the University of Chicago to complete his graduate studies in economics.[3] As he entered the program with little formal background in economic theory, Lucas spent his first year in Chicago taking undergraduate courses in economics, before going on to specialize in econometrics and public finance. Though he studied price theory under Milton Friedman, Lucas would later claim that his macro-economic education was "true-blue Keynesian," and that he intended his earliest work as a contribution to, rather than a critique of, the mainstream Keynesian paradigm (Lucas 2004, pp. 18–20). By his own account, Lucas was attracted to economics by its increasing mathematical formalism, and by its application of a rational choice model as a universal theory of human behavior, spanning history and culture.[4]

The distinctive features of Lucas' approach to macroeconomics can first be located in the article "Real Wages, Employment, and Inflation," written with Leonard Rapping (1969a). Following Keynes, one of the central aims of macroeconomic theory had been to describe the conditions under which involuntary unemployment could arise, and the policy tools that might combat it. In constructing a continuously clearing model of the labor market that emphasized workers' labor supply decisions, Lucas and Rapping sought to dismiss this problem from consideration. In their model, workers are assumed to derive utility from both present and future consumption, while labor itself yields, in both periods, disutility. The present supply of labor is thereby positively related to the currently prevailing real wage; workers choose to increase their supply of labor when the real wage rises above its "normal" level, and voluntarily elect to supply less labor (consume more leisure) when the real wage falls below this normal position. From this perspective, conventional measures of unemployment *do not* estimate the portion of the labor force rendered involuntarily unemployed, but instead quantify "those persons who regard the current wage rate at which they could be employed as temporarily low and who therefore choose to wait or search for improved conditions rather than invest in moving or occupational change" (Lucas and Rapping 1969a, p. 748). The extraordinarily bold claim of the model was that involuntary unemployment, a condition in which willing workers are unable to find employment at the prevailing wage, simply did not exist. Reflecting on this work a decade later Lucas argued that "there is a real sense in which this picture seems to me not the best account of employment fluctuations, but rather the *only* account" (Lucas 1981, p. 4, emphasis in original). In this view, no credible model of the labor market could be constructed absent a clear foundation in the behavior of rational maximizing agents. Macroeconomic phenomena required microeconomic explanations.

Beginning from this conception of labor markets as continually devoid of involuntary unemployment, given workers' capacity to rationally substitute labor and leisure across time, Lucas sought to bring a similarly strict assumption of rationality to bear on the discipline of macroeconomics as a whole. As discussed in the preceding chapter, Friedman's 1968 Presidential Address to the American Economic Association had recast the Phillips Curve tradeoff between inflation and unemployment as a strictly short-run phenomenon. In calling for the active role of monetary policy to be greatly delimited, Friedman (1968) asserted that in the long run economies would necessarily revert to the natural rate of unemployment. Friedman, along with contemporaries like Edmund Phelps (1967), had contended that the successful exploitation of the Phillips Curve relationship by monetary policy makers depended upon workers' short-run misperceptions of their real wage. Expansionary policy that engendered an increase in the aggregate price level and in nominal wage rates could temporarily fool workers into the belief that their real wages had risen, inducing them to increase their supply of labor. Workers could be outwitted, if only temporarily, as their expectations of inflation were based solely on the experience of the recent past. Reductions in unemployment would not, however, be lasting, and the labor market would return to its 'natural' equilibrium once workers' anticipations of inflation adapted to the new, higher price level. Thus, for Friedman, the real impacts of monetary policy depended upon *unanticipated* inflation. Having once deceived workers, a short-run reduction in unemployment could again be achieved only at the cost of a yet higher inflation rate.

Though voicing little objection to Friedman's essential policy conclusion that monetary policy would be unable to peg the rate of unemployment, Lucas and others quickly noted an 'uncomfortable' feature of the model. Namely, workers could fall prey to the same basic trick again and again, learning little from past experience, and thus behaving in a seemingly irrational manner. As many commentators have noticed, Friedman's own explanation of the determinants of this natural rate of unemployment involves the rather ambiguous statement that it is "the level that would be ground out by the Walrasian system of general equilibrium equations" (1968, p. 8). It is reasonable to assume that Friedman was suggesting that only when all markets, including the labor market, cleared and general equilibrium with full employment was achieved that the economy would be at its natural rate. The rational expectations revolt led by Lucas required that macroeconomists directly employ a general equilibrium approach. For Lucas this meant that *all* markets should be assumed to be in continual equilibrium in macroeconomic models, and that the firms and households populating these models should diligently behave as rational optimizers. Agents may be constrained by the information available to them, and the economy may experience external shocks, but a state of equilibrium is omnipresent.

Held up against each other, the differences between Lucas' 1972 paper "Expectations and the Neutrality of Money," and the work of his immediate predecessors, are readily apparent. Lucas considers a highly abstract economy composed of isolated islands, populated by young workers who are both producers and consumers, and an older generation that merely consumes.[5] Lucas adds to this world a government whose only power and function lies in its ability to create fiat money that it may transfer to the older generation. The principal novelty of the paper lies in its assumption that producers and workers alike both behave and form their expectations of the future in a rational manner. This assumption of rational expectations, borrowed from an earlier paper by John Muth (1961), asserts that producers will endeavor to use all available information in anticipating future changes in prices, and in varying their production to meet future demand. Though not all agents will anticipate the future perfectly, these forecasting errors will be normally distributed and, on average, agents' forecasts will be correct.[6] This assumption allowed Lucas to strip the money illusion from all agents in the economy. In deciding how much output to produce and labor to supply, the young face what is termed a 'signal extraction' problem. That is, when the price of their good rises they must parse whether this is due to a real shift in demand, or is instead an unanticipated nominal shock due to a monetary expansion by the government. Available information is therefore imperfect, and as a hedging strategy the young will modestly alter their output. It is through this device that Lucas gives the short-run Phillips Curve a foundation in rational behavior. Crucially, he also reinforces that once the source of the price disturbance becomes known, output and employment will quickly revert to their rationally grounded "natural" levels. Central banks will only produce real effects on output and employment insofar as their actions are unanticipated surprises. Anticipated and clearly announced policy changes will generate no real effects.[7]

One basic aim of Lucas' subsequent work in the 1970s was to extend the applications and policy conclusions of the 1972 paper's framework. Rational behavior at the micro level, coupled with imperfections and delays in the dissemination of information, continued to be the guiding principles. In "Expectations and the Neutrality of Money" unanticipated monetary shocks were shown to be capable of generating fleeting deviations from the natural rate, but not the serially correlated variations in output character-istic of real-world business cycles. Lucas (1975) then demonstrated that a monetary surprise could produce cyclical variations in output. Responding rationally to the initial surprise rise in prices, firms would react not only by increasing output, but also by investing in additional capacity. The rising demand for capital goods by firms would further stimulate growth, and lead to a persistent deviation of output and employment from their trend levels. This so-called accelerator effect had been a staple of prior mainstream Keynesian models. Transposed into Lucas' framework, it suggested that the observed business cycle was not an empirical phenomenon that could be stabilized through the active use of fiscal and monetary policy, but was instead a potential *product* of these efforts. Stable growth would be better supported by "rules which smooth monetary policy ... [and] the analogous fiscal rule of continuous budget balancing" (1975, p. 1139). The only sound form of monetary policy would be a k-percent rule, as proposed by Friedman, where the growth rate of the money supply would remain constant, precluding the use of counter-cyclical policy. In these efforts to set what were essentially monetarist conclusions in a rational expectations context, Lucas was joined by Thomas Sargent and Neil Wallace (1975), and Robert Barro (1976), among others.

Lucas also attempted to give rational expectations models firmer empirical footing. The most notable result of these efforts was a broadside critique of the economists' empirical estimations conducted in the preced-ing three decades. In "Econometric Policy Evaluation: A Critique" (1976), a conference paper that has come to be among the most cited papers in the discipline, Lucas cast doubt on the then-dominant approach to macroeconomic forecasting. Simply put, the paper's contention was that econometric models based on the past behavior of the economy could not be used as reliable guides to its future behavior. If, as rational expecta-tions models argued, agents are continually gathering information about policymakers' behavior, then they cannot be expected to react in the same way twice. A policy action that achieved real effects precisely because it was formerly unanticipated could never hope to achieve the same effects again. The artificial economies of Lucas and his fellow travelers would then provide a more reliable proving ground for policy experiments. Once more, Lucas concluded, known and fixed rules governing monetary and fiscal policy were to be preferred, as it would only be under such conditions that one could expect stable and predictable behavior from economic agents making up the economy.

By the close of the decade, Lucas and Wallace (1979) stridently pro-claimed the death of Keynesian macroeconomics. In their account, the dissolution of the Phillips Curve relation over the course of the 1970s testified to "econometric failure on a grand scale," and implied "that Keynesian policy recommendations have no sounder basis, in a scientific sense, than recommendations of non-Keynesian economists or, for that matter, non-economists" (ibid, p. 6). A return to "the discipline imposed by classical [sic] economy theory ... [and] its insistence on adherence to the two postulates (a) that markets clear and (b) that agents act in their own self-interest" was then long overdue.[8] Keynes might have escaped from the old ideas, but the economics discipline would not be so fortunate.

3.   EQUILIBRIUM REAL BUSINESS CYCLES

New Classical models of the 1970s, though in many ways marking a return to pre-Keynesian conceptions of the economy, were not yet wholesale reversions to supply-side theory. For this earlier generation of New Classical models, demand shocks remained the cause of oscillations in growth, with the underlying trend determined in neoclassical fashion by the economy's relative endowments of factors of production, and by the pace of technological change. The real business cycle models that emerged over the course of the 1980s completed a neoclassical restoration by asserting that the cycle itself was an equilibrium response to variations in the pace of technological change. The contributions of Finn Kydland and Edward Prescott (1982) along with those of Charles Nelson and Charles Plosser (1982) are generally seen as seminal for this outgrowth of rational expectations modeling.

Within the mainstream of the discipline, the dominant approach had been to consider the long-run growth trend as a stable pattern over time. The business cycle was then a series of short-run, demand-induced oscillations around this trend. Nelson and Plosser (1982) questioned these basic tenets of macroeconomic modeling. In their view, the assumption of a stable trend, and of a stationary cycle around it, had the effect of "implicitly bounding uncertainty and greatly restricting the relevance of the past to the future" (ibid, p. 142). Such a view had limited empirical support, however. Drawing from econometric evidence they argued that trend growth itself was better modeled as a process involving random variation. This seemingly technical observation had sweeping implications. At once, it implied "that real (non-monetary) disturbances [were] likely to be a much more important source of output fluctuations than monetary disturbances" (ibid, p. 159). Moreover, it implied that variations in the natural rate could be identified as a central cause of the variability of output and employment.

In line with the work of Nelson and Plosser, the publication of "Time to Build and Aggregate Fluctuations" (1982) represented a novel turn for the rational expectations literature. First, Kydland and Prescott discarded monetary shocks as the generative mechanism of the cycle and replaced them with technological shocks. As with Friedman's natural rate hypothesis, real business cycle models should properly be seen as the distant echoes of Knut Wicksell. The cycle has its origin in a technological shock that by altering the productivity of labor simultaneously alters the demand for it on the part of firms. Here the process of inter-temporal substitution of labor and leisure by rational households suggested by Lucas and Rapping (1969a) comes into play once more. An upturn of the business cycle might begin with a positive shock to productivity. Increased demand for labor, and the accompanying rise in real wages then induces a pronounced increase in the labor supplied by households, as leisure is forestalled into the future. Thus, a real shock generates a rise in both output and employment. A second, methodological, innovation concerned what the authors termed the "calibration" of the model. Rather than attempt to falsify their model using historical data in the manner of previous econometric testing, they showed that their model *could* generate fluctuations in output and employment akin to those experienced by the post-War US economy.[9] In their view, the paper demonstrated that a theory of the cycle driven by real shocks was viable insofar as it could be made to replicate much of past experience.

Adopting a similar strategy, Long and Plosser (1983) also produced a rational expectations model populated by a representative agent, Robinson Crusoe, in which random fluctuations in productivity were capable of generating business cycles in an economy without money or a government sector. In a later summary of this work, Plosser (1989, p. 56) noted that "[i]t is important to stress that there are no market failures in this economy, so Robinson Crusoe's response to the productivity shifts are optimal and the economy is Pareto efficient at all points in time. Put another way, any attempt by a social planner to force Crusoe to choose any allocation other than the ones indicated, such as working more than he currently chooses, or saving more than he currently chooses, are likely to be welfare reducing." Thus, Plosser conceived the business cycle as an *optimal* response to real shocks by the identical rational individuals populating the market system. As such, attempts to smooth the cycle would necessarily be welfare reducing. Active policy could only do harm.

In a subsequent paper Prescott (1986) explicitly appended this approach to the neoclassical "growth accounting" exercise first proposed by Robert Solow (1957). In his much earlier contribution Solow had attempted to measure the proximate causes of growth, and utilizing a neoclassical aggregate production function identified them as population growth, capital accumulation, and technological change. For Solow, this last category, later called "total factor productivity," was the primary driver of sustained growth. Importantly, Solow found that, by this measure, the pace of technological change was variable from year to year. Seizing upon this result, Prescott (1986) produced an updated and refined measure of the variability in the growth of total factor productivity. Armed with this estimate, he once more demonstrated that these technological shocks alone were capable of generating fluctuations in output, investment, and employment that mirrored the empirical record. This again implied that "costly efforts at stabilization are likely to be counterproductive. Economic fluctuations are optimal responses to uncertainty in the rate of technological change" (ibid, p. 21).

The use of the growth accounting methodology brought the Ramsey model,[10] essentially a variation of the Solow growth model in which savings is endogenously determined by the intertemporal preferences of consumers, to the center of macroeconomics. In addition, the notion that economic output followed a random walk, that its trend was non-stationary, implied that instead of the deterministic models used up to that point, macroeconomic modeling should emphasize stochastic shocks. The development of the RBC models led to the Dynamic Stochastic General Equilibrium (DSGE) models, which to this day dominate the mainstream of the profession.

4.   PHLOGISTON AND MISMEASUREMENT

Real business cycles imply that in a boom, when a positive productivity shock occurs, and workers decide to increase the supply labor, real wages would increase. In other words, real wages would be pro-cyclical. The empirical evidence seems to suggest that real wages are indeed modestly pro-cyclical. This regularity has been accepted since at least the 1930s, when Lorie Tarshis and John Dunlop contradicted the views of both Keynes and the dominant neoclassical approach that had emphasized the counter-cyclicality of real wages.[11] At face value this empirical pattern seems to provide favorable evidence for the RBC view of the business cycle. Yet, real wages are, at least in the aggregate, only mildly pro-cyclical. In other words, wages tend to go up only slightly in booms. Maintaining the existence of a Lucas-type supply function would therefore require a labor supply curve that is highly wage-elastic, involving workers that are hypersensitive to variations in the real wage in making their work/leisure choices. The implication is that small reductions in the real wage would make workers significantly reduce the hours worked, a behavior that contrasts with the evidence which suggests that workers are relatively insensitive to changes in the real wage.

More problematic for the defenders of the RBC view of economic fluctuations is that very few recessions seem to be associated with negative supply shocks. The evidence for demand shocks, and in particular for monetary shocks, seems to be considerably stronger. Even Lucas has said that there seems to be little evidence regarding the notion that the Great Depression was caused by a real shock. In his words, "where is the productivity shock that cuts output in half in that period? Is it a flood or a hurricane? If it really happened, shouldn't we be able to see it in the data?"[12] Thus Lucas, even though he has accepted that most cycles are explained by productivity shocks, remains convinced that the Great Depression resulted from a monetary contraction by the Fed, in line with the monetarist views of Friedman.

Prescott (1999), perhaps the leading RBC author, however, believes that the New Deal was behind the slow recovery from the Great Depression. As he argues:

> In the 1930s, there was an important change in the rules of the economic game. This change lowered the steady-state market hours. The Keynesians had it all wrong. In the Great Depression, employment was not low because investment was low. Employment and investment were low because labor market institutions and industrial policies changed in a way that lowered normal employment.

In other words, labor market regulations, which allowed for collective bargaining and minimum wages, and the industrial regulations that tried to preclude price deflation, related mostly to the National Industrial Recovery Act (NIRA), presumably caused what would have otherwise been a fast recovery to stretch out over a decade. Yet, even if one admits that regulation might delay recovery, something that is highly controversial, it is far from clear what caused the collapse of output in the first place. In a recent paper on the RBC views on the causes of economic fluctuations, Paul Romer has suggested that the idea that unseen real shocks cause cycles is akin to the pre-scientific views on the role of phlogiston in combustion processes.[13] In that sense, there is a broad consensus that the evidence for real compared to demand shocks, as an explanation for cycles, is thin, to say the least. And yet, many RBC authors seem to believe that the high correlation between TFP and GDP fluctuations vindicates their views, even if it is impossible to identify the real shock that caused the Great Depression, or the more recent Great Recession, both of which seem more closely related to financial shocks and demand collapses. That is why the question of the measurement of productivity shocks in RBC models is of crucial importance.

The traditional way in which productivity is measured in RBC models is based on the so-called Solow Residual or TFP. The conventional discussion of TFP starts from a production function, which suggests that output is produced by capital, labor, and a given technology. Thus, in the growth accounting methodology, output must grow either as a result of capital and labor expansion, or alternatively because technology is improving. However, it is well-known that GDP can be seen from three angles: production, expenditure and income. By definition, then, GDP is equal to the sum of the remuneration of workers, capital and taxes paid. Looking at the measure net of taxes, and assuming that the total remuneration of labor and capital can be expressed as the respective rate times the quantity employed of each, it must also be true that GDP growth is the result of the growth of capital, labor and the weighted average of the rate of growth of the remuneration of capital and labor. Since the latter is an identity coming from the National Accounts, while the production function is a theoretical construct, then it must be true that the Solow Residual is basically a weighted average of the rate of growth of profits and wages.[14]

In practice, this is what is being measured, since the data actually comes from the identity, not an imaginary production function. Even if the production function existed, one would still be measuring the identity. Not surprisingly, the 'fit' of econometric results measuring production functions tends to be relatively good. Commonly, the estimated coefficient for α in the production function, a value intended to measure the relative productivity of labor, is often close to the actual share of wages in total income. This is precisely what one should expect to find if one is measuring an identity, something that is true by definition. Though such an econometric approach to the estimation of TFP is exceedingly common, a more careful appraisal reveals that the evidence for shocks to productivity used in most RBC analysis is simply the product of mismeasurement.

The use of TFP poses additional problems for the RBC theory, but also for the neoclassical growth model, which is a supply side explanation for economic growth. The measurement problem also explains the emptiness of the use of shocks to TFP to explain the Great Depression. Cole and Ohanian, the leading authors in the RBC revisionist view of the Great Depression, argue that the fall of TFP accounts quantitatively for 65 percent of the drop in output during the Depression, but concede that there is almost no explanation of why productivity fell. That is why Ohanian (2001, p. 38) admits: "the Great Depression productivity puzzle remains largely unsolved."

In reality, there is no puzzle. What worsened during the Depression was income distribution, and that is what the Solow Residual actually measures. Besides, it is clear that the Great Depression was driven by a dramatic collapse in demand. This is not to say that real shocks do not occur. Of course, technological innovation affects productivity, and has effects on the economy. Negative supply shocks, like the oil shocks of the 1970s, are likewise possible. The problem is that the framework to understand these shocks provided by the RBC School seems narrow and incapable of explaining, even to some defenders of RBC like Lucas, the Great Depression, which has been referred to as the Holy Grail of Macroeconomics (Bernanke 1995).

5. CONCLUDING REMARKS

One of the key issues in the history of macroeconomic thought concerns locating its decisive ruptures. The break from the mainstream Keynesian tradition embodied in the Old Neoclassical Synthesis, and the turn towards New Classical models (monetary misperception) and RBC models is certainly one of these. Many authors suggest that Lucas should be considered, after Keynes himself, the great scientific revolutionary, and that Friedman's break was incomplete. In this view, it is the Rational Expectations School that should be seen as a paradigmatic shift, a return to the old neoclassical ideas in macroeconomics. This is the implicit view in Alessandro Vercelli's (1991) book *Methodological Foundations of Macroeconomics: Keynes After Lucas*, or explicitly in the more recent book by Michel DeVroey (2016). For these authors, the difference between Friedman and Lucas is really that in the Neoclassical Synthesis and monetarist models some behavior is not derived from intertemporal maximization of individual agents, while that is not true in the RBC models. Thus, it is the role given to micro-foundations of macroeconomic activity that constitutes the great rupture.

Yet, while the methods applied by Lucas and his later followers in the RBC School were novel, the conclusions were not particularly different from those of monetarism. Arguably, the emphasis on micro-founded behavior and stochastic shocks can be ascribed to "Physics Envy," the tendency towards the uncritical appropriation of a limited range of mathematical formalisms, which Philip Mirowski suggested, in his *More Heat Than Light* (1989), was at the heart of the ascendancy of marginalist orthodoxy.[15] Both the emphasis on micro rather than macro behavior, and the abandonment of deterministic models indicates a possible analogy with quantum mechanics. However, while quantum mechanics upended the results of classical mechanics, the Rational Expectations School provided for a return of old doctrinal results. For that reason, it is hard to say that Lucas is a revolutionary figure in modern macroeconomics. True, in Lucas' framework, the main monetarist conclusions are less effective or irrelevant. Only unanticipated monetary shocks have effects. However, when forced to discuss the Great Depression, Lucas admits that there is little evidence for the RBC view. Lucas, even though he has accepted that most cycles are explained by productivity shocks, remains convinced that the Great Depression resulted from a monetary contraction by the Fed, as in the monetarist views of Friedman. While casting additional doubt on the short-run effectiveness of monetary policy, Lucas found himself in fundamental agreement with Friedman as to the long-run neutrality of money. That is, for Friedman too, in the long run monetary shocks have no effects. The crucial theoretical variable is the natural rate.

In this sense, it seems that Friedman, and the return of the natural rate of unemployment, and implicitly the interest and output natural rates as well, are crucial for explaining the return of the pre-Keynesian Wicksellian framework that is dominant with the New Macroeconomics Consensus (NMC). Though many features of Friedman's model were discarded, from its emphasis on exogenous money and monetary shocks, to its emphasis on money supply rather than interest rate targeting, the natural rate has remained as the theoretical anchor. Modern macroeconomics is neo-Wicksellian, but it owes that to Friedman, more than to Lucas and the Rational Expectations School.

NOTES

1. Lucas infamously argued that at the seminars he frequented, the audiences whispered and giggled when Keynesian ideas were discussed.
2. Hoover (1996, p. 111, n. 6) argues that Lucas' objective is "the euthanasia of macroeconomics." In other words, everything should be explained on the basis of microeconomic behavior.
3. We use the term "counter-revolution" because the ascendance of rational expectations methods also involved a restoration of many of the essential conclusions, such as the impossibility of involuntary unemployment, that Keynes and the so-called Keynesian Revolution sought to dispel.
4. From this perspective, Lucas' fascination with the work of Henri Pirenne during his time as a graduate student in history seems far from incidental, as one of Pirenne's distinguishing claims was to identify a distinctive social class employing capitalist reason in each historical era from the early Middle Ages onward (e.g. Pirenne 1914).
5. The island parable is based on Phelps (1969).
6. For Muth, the assumption of rational expectations implied that "expectations, since they are informed predictions of future events, are essentially the same as the predictions of the relevant economic theory" (1961, p. 316). In such a world, speculative trading that attempted to *systematically* beat the market would be impossible, an idea

that was fundamental in the development of the so-called Efficient Market Hypothesis (EMH), often associated with Eugene Fama and Paul Samuelson.

7. Foreshadowing the argument of his 1976 paper, Lucas notes that econometric estimates based on the historical record of this economy's responses to unanticipated shocks will inevitably appear to suggest that an exploitable tradeoff between inflation and unemployment exists.

8. Lucas and Wallace adhere, in this sense, to the conventional, but incorrect, notion propagated by Keynes that classical and neoclassical economists work with similar models. In this context, the more appropriate name for the school would have been New Neoclassical rather than New Classical. For the distinction between the old classical political economy and marginalism or neoclassical economics, see Bharadwaj (1978).

9. Calibration seemed to be in line with Lucas' critique of structural econometric models, and the abandonment of the practices that were common for the estimation of Keynesian models. Hoover (1995, p. 27) suggests that calibrated models use "casual empiricism ... to guarantee that the model mimics some particular feature of the historical data." Christopher Sims launched an additional critique of the dominant econometric paradigm in his 1980 paper "Macroeconomic and Reality." Sims (1980) proposed making causal inferences from observed data without imposing a strict causal structure. Sims suggested that the empirical study of macroeconomic data could be built around vector auto-regressive (VAR) models. The old structural models associated with the Cowles Commission and the Keynesian macroeconometric models like the Klein-Goldberger model were almost completely abandoned. For a recent defense of the Cowles Commission methodology, see Fair (2012).

10. The Ramsey model was revived in the 1960s, when dynamic optimization, based on the microeconomic behavior of consumers, was reintroduced by David Cass and Tjalling Koopmans in separate papers published in 1965. The compatibility between the Ramsey-Cass-Koopmans model and the rational expectations school is evident in the emphasis on micro-founded behavior, and the reliance of supply side factors to explain growth.

11. More recent studies like Chirinko (1980), Solon et al. (1994) and Swanson (2007) seem incapable of rejecting the pro-cyclical nature of real wages.

12. See DeVroey and Pensieroso (2006) for Lucas' quote.

13. Romer (2016) seems to suggest that demand shocks, in particular monetary shocks, are central for business cycles.

14. For a full discussion of the limitations of the growth accounting methodology and the mismeasurement of productivity, see Felipe and McCombie (2015).

15. This is not necessarily to suggest that evolutionist or biology-inspired analogies would be more appropriate. As noted by many authors, some of the early monetarist contributions, in particular Friedman's famous 1953 methodological "as if" argument, were inspired by evolution (Friedman 1953). In addition, as noted by Mirowski (2011, p. 237) "it is unclear the extent to which modern biology itself has successfully escaped physics envy."

REFERENCES

Barro, R.J. (1976), "Rational Expectations and the Role of Monetary Policy," *Journal of Monetary Economics*, **2**, 1–32.

Bernanke, B. (1995), "The Macroeconomics of the Great Depression: A Comparative Approach," *Journal of Money, Credit and Banking*, **27**(1), 1–28.

Bharadwaj, K. (1978), *Classical Political Economy and the Rise to Dominance of Supply and Demand Theories*, New Delhi: Orient Longman.

Chirinko, R. (1980), "The Real Wage Rate over the Business Cycle," *The Review of Economics and Statistics*, **62**(3), 459–461.

DeVroey, M. (2016), *A History of Macroeconomics from Keynes to Lucas and Beyond*, New York: Cambridge University Press.

DeVroey, M. and L. Pensieroso (2006), "Real Business Cycle Theory and the Great Depression: The Abandonment of the Abstentionist Viewpoint," *The B.E. Journal of Macroeconomics*, **6**(1), 1–26.

Fair, R. (2012), "Has Macro Progressed?", *Journal of Macroeconomics*, **34**, 2–10.

Felipe, J. and J. McCombie (2015), *The Aggregate Production Function and the Measurement of Technical Change: "Not Even Wrong,"* Cheltenham: Edward Elgar Publishing.

Friedman, M. (1953), "The Methodology of Positive Economics," in *Essays in Positive Economics*, Chicago: University of Chicago Press, 3–42.

Friedman, M. (1968), "The Role of Monetary Policy," *The American Economic Review*, **58**(1), 1–17.

Hoover, K. (1995), "Facts and Artifacts: Calibration and the Empirical Assessment of Real-Business-Cycle Models," *Oxford Economic Papers*, **47**(1), 24–44.

Hoover, K. (1996), *Causality in Macroeconomics*, New York: Cambridge University Press.

Keynes, J.M. (1936), *The General Theory of Employment, Interest and Money*, London: Macmillan.

Kydland, F. and E. Prescott (1982), "Time to Build and Aggregate Fluctuations," *Econometrica*, **50**(6), 1345–1370.

Long, J. and C. Plosser (1983), "Real Business Cycles," *Journal of Political Economy*, **91**(1), 39–69.

Lucas, R.E. (1972), "Expectations and the Neutrality of Money," *Journal of Economic Theory*, **4**(2), 103–124.

Lucas, R.E. (1975), "An Equilibrium Model of the Business Cycle," *Journal of Political Economy*, **83**(6), 1113–1144.

Lucas, R.E. (1976), "Econometric Policy Evaluation: A Critique," *Carnegie-Rochester Conference Series on Public Policy*, **1**(1), 19–46.

Lucas, R.E. (1981), *Studies in Business-Cycle Theory*, Cambridge: The MIT Press.

Lucas, R.E. (2004), "Keynote Address to the 2003 HOPE Conference: My Keynesian Education," *History of Political Economy*, **36**, Supplement 1, 12–24.

Lucas, R.E. and L. Rapping (1969a), "Real Wages, Employment, and Inflation," *Journal of Political Economy*, **77**(5), 721–754.

Lucas, R.E. and L. Rapping (1969b), "Price Expectations and the Phillips Curve," *The American Economic Review*, **59**(3), 342–350.

Lucas, R.E. and T. Wallace (1979), "After Keynesian Macroeconomics," *Federal Reserve Bank of Minneapolis Quarterly Review*, **3**(2), 1–16.

Mirowski, P. (1989), *More Heat Than Light: Economics as Social Physics, Physics as Nature's Economics*, New York: Cambridge University Press.

Mirowski, P. (2011), "On the Origins (at Chicago) of Some Species of Neoliberal Evolutionary Economics," in R. Van Horn, P. Mirowski and T. Stapleford (eds), *Building Chicago Economics: New Perspectives on the History of America's Most Powerful Economics Program*, Cambridge: Cambridge University Press, 237–275.

Muth, J.F. (1961), "Rational Expectations and the Theory of Price Movements," *Econometrica*, **29**(3), 315–335.

Nelson C.R. and C.I. Plosser (1982), "Trends and Random Walks in Macroeconomic Time Series," *Journal of Monetary Economics*, **10**(2), 139–162.

Ohanian, L. (2001), "Why Did Productivity Fall So Much during the Great Depression?" *American Economic Review*, **91**(2), 34–38.

Phelps, E. (1969), "The New Microeconomics in Inflation and Employment Theory," *American Economic Review*, **59**(1), 147–160.

Pirenne, H. (1914), "The Stages in the Social History of Capitalism," *The American Historical Review*, **19**(3), 494–515.

Plosser, C. (1989), "Understanding Real Business Cycles," *Journal of Economic Perspectives*, **3**(3), 51–77.

Prescott, E. (1986), "Theory Ahead of Business Cycle Measurement," *Federal Reserve Bank of Minneapolis Quarterly Review*, **10**(4), 9–22.

Prescott, E. (1999), "Some Observations on the Great Depression," *Federal Reserve Bank of Minneapolis Quarterly Review*, **23**(1), 25–31.

Romer, P. (2016), "The Trouble with Macroeconomics," *The American Economist*, forthcoming.

Sargent, T. and N. Wallace (1975), "'Rational' Expectations, the Optimal Monetary Instrument, and the Optimal Money Supply Rule," *Journal of Political Economy*, **83**(2), 241–254.

Sims, C. (1980), "Macroeconomics and Reality," *Econometrica*, **48**(1), 1–48.

Solon, G., Barsky, R., and Parker, J. (1994), "Measuring the Cyclicality of Real Wages: How Important is Composition Bias," *The Quarterly Journal of Economics*, **109**(1), 1–25.

Solow, R. (1957), "Technical Change and the Aggregate Production Function," *The Review of Economics and Statistics*, **39**(3), 312–320.

Swanson, E. (2007), "Real Wage Cyclicality in the Panel Study of Income Dynamics," *Scottish Journal of Political Economy*, **54**(5), 617–647.

Vercelli, A. (1991), *Methodological Foundations of Macroeconomics: Keynes After Lucas*, Cambridge: Cambridge University Press.

13. The New Keynesian School

Steven Pressman

KEY FEATURES

- Wage rigidity and unemployment.
- Price rigidity and unemployment.
- Hysteresis.
- Coordination failures.
- Asymmetric information.
- Imperfect competition.

1. INTRODUCTION

Macroeconomics was developed by John Maynard Keynes (1936) in response to the very high unemployment rates experienced by developed countries during the Great Depression. At the time, the dominant Classical School adhered to Say's Law, which holds that "supply creates its own demand". For labor markets, this means that someone looking for work will soon be able to find a job. Prolonged periods of high unemployment, therefore, should not be possible. Keynes offered an alternative perspective, the theory of effective demand, which holds that demand determines output and production. In this instance, the demand for goods creates a demand by firms for workers and creates jobs. Inadequate demand leads to unemployment.

During the post-war decades, a so-called "neoclassical synthesis" arose, which attempted to combine these two views. Following Keynes, it held that any shortfall in demand led to slow economic growth and high unemployment. Following the classical approach, unemployment was explained as a case where the economy was not in equilibrium; labor supply had yet to create enough demand for labor. The policy solutions stemming from the neoclassical synthesis were rather Keynesian in nature – lower interest rates and government deficit spending to stimulate growth. Taking this advice, the US enacted large tax cuts in the 1960s and increased government expenditures (some on infrastructure but more on widening war in Vietnam and a Cold War with the Soviet Union). This helped push the US unemployment rate below 4 percent during the late 1960s, the same time that Keynesian economics reached its apotheosis. In 1971, US President Richard Nixon famously proclaimed that even he, a long-time opponent of government intervention in the economy, was now a Keynesian.

Nonetheless, macroeconomics changed markedly during the 1970s. Part of the problem was stagflation, a simultaneous rise in the unemployment rate and the inflation rate. This seemed impossible from a Keynesian perspective, which viewed economic problems as the result of either too much demand (inflation) or too little demand (unemployment). Surely the economy could not experience *both* too much and too little demand at the same time. Moreover, by solving one problem through changing demand, the other problem became worse. The search was on for an explanation of stagflation and alternative policy solutions.

At the same time, macroeconomists became infatuated with the pristine logic contained in New Classical economics. Their approach was that macroeconomic analysis had to rest on solid microfoundations; it had to assume that people were rational, optimizing individuals and that markets would tend to clear. They pointed out that the unemployed should offer to work for lower wages. This would clear the labor market, and unemployment would disappear. Likewise, for the entire macroeconomy, if output could not be sold, the rational response would be for firms to lower their prices. This would increase sales; done throughout the economy, it would generate more growth and employment.

During the 1970s, New Classical economics became the dominant school in macroeconomics. As Alan Blinder ([1988] 1997, pp. 109–110) lamented: "By about 1980, it was hard to find an American academic economist under the age of 40 who professed to be a Keynesian. That was an astonishing intellectual turnabout in less than a decade, an intellectual revolution for sure." Even worse, anyone doing macroeconomics without rational, optimizing individuals was thought to be engaged in some kind of cheating, and macroeconomists who sought to do this were snickered at by their New Classical macroeconomic brethren (Mankiw 1991, p. 1).

Ironically, just as the New Classical School achieved dominance in macroeconomics, it encountered empirical anomalies. The early 1980s were a time of very high unemployment in the US and elsewhere in the world. The US unemployment rate peaked at 9.7 percent in 1982 and remained above 7 percent between 1980 and 1985. There seemed to be a disconnect between the Rational Expectations approach, which held that prolonged high unemployment would quickly be remedied by the market, and events taking place in the world. New Classical economics had no answers to the unemployment problem. Individual rationality and optimizing behavior implied that prolonged high unemployment was impossible; our economic experience showed that this was not only possible, but was taking place and adversely affecting many people.

The New Keynesian School arose in response to this contradiction. It sought to marry the real world insights of Keynesian economics with the microfoundations demanded by the Rational Expectations School. It explained how and why market economies could experience prolonged unemployment, and then pointed out the policies needed to improve macroeconomic performance. In this sense it sought the best of both worlds – microfoundations at the outset of macroeconomic analysis (as required by the Rational Expectations School) and explanations for persistent unemployment (as demanded by the Keynesian School).

Michael Parkin and Robin Bade (1982) were the first economists to employ the term "new Keynesian" in print. But more than a term was needed. Also required was a theory of market rigidities based on optimizing individual behavior. This theory had to explain why markets did not clear through the price-adjustment mechanism or the wage-adjustment mechanism, as New Classical economics assumed it would. The goal of the New Keynesian School was to provide this theoretical underpinning.

While there is agreement within the New Keynesian School on assumptions and modeling strategy, on policy issues there is little consensus within the school. At best, New Keynesian policy prescriptions can be divided into two separate camps, representing the two perspectives that made up the neoclassical synthesis. A more liberal wing, led by Joseph Stiglitz and George Akerlof, saw unemployment as caused by insufficient effective demand; they pushed Keynesian stabilization policies to improve macroeconomic outcomes. Others, like Greg Mankiw, emphasized that the big problem was numerous rigidities that kept markets from moving to a market-clearing equilibrium. This conservative wing of the New Keynesian School sought to achieve full employment by eliminating these rigidities. Despite these differences, New Keynesians do agree that unemployment can arise due to market imperfections, and they agree that these imperfections can result from rational and optimizing individual behavior. The analytical trick has been to explain how and why wages and prices adjust slowly, if at all, and to provide microeconomic explanations for this observed behavior.

New Keynesians have taken several different approaches to this. First, they explained why wage rigidity was rational and efficient. Second, they explained why prices were rigid, and why this was rational and efficient. Third, they suggested other market imperfections to explain unemployment – imperfect competition in product markets and the notion of imperfect information. In the latter case, New Keynesian economics seems to return to Keynes, who saw macroeconomic problems caused in large part by uncertainty – in particular, the fact that long-term expectations can only be guesses that to a large extent depend on social factors (see the beauty contest example in Keynes 1936, p. 156).

2. NOMINAL WAGE RIGIDITY

New Keynesian economists have put forward four main explanations for why wages tend to be rigid, even when economies experience high rates of unemployment: efficiency wage theory, labor contracts, insider-outsider theory and hysteresis.

2.1 Efficiency Wage Theory

According to standard economic theory, the real wage received by each worker depends on their individual productivity. The more a worker produces, the greater the value of that worker to their firm and the more the worker will get paid. Efficiency wage theory turns this story upside down; it contends that worker productivity depends on the real wage. Because higher pay will result in more efficient workers (hence "efficiency wages"), firms should willingly pay workers more to garner greater worker effort. One real world example of this is when Henry Ford decided (in 1914) to pay his factory workers $5 a day when the going manufacturing rate was $2 a day. Ford offered higher wages in order to attract and keep reliable workers. He believed that the greater productivity from his workers would justify their higher pay. One key implication of efficiency wage theory is that it is not in the interest of firms to lower wages when unemployment is high because this may reduce worker productivity and raise per unit costs by more than the cost reduction stemming from lower wages.

Alfred Marshall (1920, pp. 456–469) was the first economist to suggest that workers were more efficient when they received higher incomes. He thought that this could be due to improved worker morale, better nutrition or better health. Harvey Leibenstein (1966) added that worker productivity, to some extent, was at the discretion of the worker. Firms cannot monitor all workers closely, and close monitoring of workers is costly for the firm. In this context, how firms treat their workers, and how much they pay their workers, determines employee effort. Taking this further, Akerlof (1984) points to issues of fairness. Workers may regard wage cuts as unfair, as well as low wages, and this may reduce their productivity. Similarly, Edmund Phelps (1968) suggests that paying higher wages benefits the firm because it reduces costly labor turnover, which leads to hiring and training costs. Finally, given the difficulty and cost of monitoring worker productivity, Leibenstein (1966) holds that firms may pay their workers higher wages to stop shirking. In this case, the threat of dismissal serves as a deterrent to shirking – workers not only have to find a new job, but may also get a job that pays them less.

Since efficiency wages are not market-clearing wages, they create unemployment. Moreover, even if wages did fall, this would not solve the unemployment problem. A simple labor supply and labor demand diagram can demonstrate this. Figure 13.1 shows that the optimal wage rate, w^*, exceeds the market clearing wage, w'. The standard microeconomic analysis of this situation is that full employment requires a cut in wages from w^* to w'. However, if the wage cut lowers worker productivity, it will also reduce the demand for labor. As a result, DL1 falls to DL2, and the new efficiency wage, w^{**}, remains above the new market-clearing wage, w''. High unemployment remains a problem.

2.2   Labor Contracts

Wage contracts of around three years are typical in most developed nations. These contracts introduce some rigidity into labor markets – wages cannot adjust quickly to a market-clearing wage. For example, in negotiating a labor contract, recent inflation experience may lead to expectations of continued high inflation and get built into the labor contract. But if inflation falls, or becomes deflation, real wages rise and firms may decide to lay off workers because they cannot reduce real wages until a new labor contract gets negotiated.

Furthermore, John Taylor (1980a) demonstrated that if workers care about their relative wages (relative to the workers in other unions or workers in the same union employed by different firms or at different plants), staggered expiration dates on labor contracts keep labor markets from clearing. Each union will seek to get better wages (and benefits) than other unions. This will then lead other unions to demand even higher wages for their members. Something similar will happen within each union. Workers employed at one plant will seek higher pay than workers in other plants, believing that they are above average workers and deserve greater pay. But the workers at other plants also believe that they are above average and will seek above average wages. This constant push for higher wages keeps wages from falling and leads to higher unemployment.

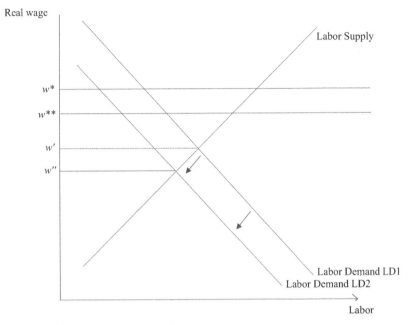

Figure 13.1   The labor market

One key question is why such contracts arise, and how they can be regarded as optimal. Phelps (1990) explained the advantages of long-term labor contracts for both firms and workers. First, negotiating labor contracts is costly to both workers and firms. Neither group will want to do this on a regular basis. Long-term contracts minimize these negotiation costs; the longer the term of the contract, the lower these negotiating costs will be. But lengthy contracts require good information about inflation in the future, worker productivity, demand, etc. Such forecasts get worse as we move further into the future. One can think of the three-year labor contract as a way to balance the costs of negotiating a contract every year against the difficulty of trying to predict the future and the costs of getting things wrong. There is even empirical evidence that staggered wage setting has efficiency gains for the firm that outweighs the costs of not being able to change wages immediately (Ball and Cecchetti 1988).

Wage-setting institutions create problems for all workers, not just union members. Productivity varies daily and weekly. A worker may feel ill one day and be less productive; machinery can experience problems, lowering the productivity of workers; or parts can be in short supply or defective. Perhaps even more important, productivity in the service sector depends mainly on demand, which can fluctuate greatly over short time periods.

While individual worker productivity varies on a regular basis, firms do not vary worker pay daily based on these productivity changes; rather, wages tend to be stable. Workers are paid their average productivity over several months, and so it will take many months before firms even think about lowering wages due to lower long-run average productivity. This practice will benefit workers, who typically live paycheck to paycheck. Wage and consumption smoothing enables them to survive during times of low productivity. It also enables workers to get lower rates when they need to purchase expensive goods like cars and homes because their income is stable. This practice will also be desirable for firms that want a stable and loyal workforce. When productivity falls, especially due to a decline in demand, firms may be reluctant to lower wages (for efficiency wage reasons), especially if they do not know how long demand will fall. If wages tend to be stable for such reasons, wages will not quickly adjust to generate full employment, whether or not we have long-term contracts, and economies will experience continued unemployment.

2.3 Insider-Outsider Theory

Insider-outsider theory distinguishes two different sets of workers and seeks to explain unemployment in terms of a conflict between these two groups. Insiders are current employees whose jobs are somewhat protected because of labor-turnover costs to the firm. Outsiders are people working in the secondary labor market who can be easily and cheaply replaced. The main proponents of insider-outsider theory, Assar Lindbeck and Dennis Snower (2001, p. 166), note that this distinction cuts many ways: "employed versus unemployed workers, formal versus informal sector workers, employees with high versus low seniority, unionized versus nonunionized workers, workers on permanent versus temporary contracts, skilled versus unskilled workers, the short-term versus the long-term unemployed, and so on."

Lindbeck and Snower (1986, 1988) distinguish two types of labor turnover costs that lead to insider-outsider problems – production-related costs and rent-seeking costs. The former involves the cost of searching for, hiring and training new employees. Firms may also face litigation and higher unemployment insurance taxes because of layoffs. Rent-related labor costs are institutional factors that raise the cost of firing workers – things like severance pay, job protection through unions, seniority rules and legal protections against dismissals.

Lindbeck and Snower argue that turnover costs give insiders some degree of market power, which they are able to exploit for their own gain. Insiders can prevent outsiders from undercutting their wages; firms become reluctant to lower wages and hire outsiders due to the costs of firing insiders. As a result, insiders receive higher wages than what is required to clear the market, while outsiders remain unemployed or under-employed.

2.4 Hysteresis

A final labor market imperfection goes by the name of "hysteresis". The term comes from an ancient Greek word that describes the phenomenon of falling behind or lagging behind. Economic models where some temporary change leads to permanent effects are known as hysteresis models (Blanchard and Summers 1986). These models have been used to explain how job losers during an economic downturn might suffer continued unemployment, even when the economy begins to rebound. Hysteresis has also been used to explain why the full employment level of GDP depends on earlier levels of GDP rather than on some "natural rate" of unemployment towards which the economy moves. Due to hysteresis, unemployment leads to continued unemployment for workers and lower levels of full-employment output (Blanchard and Diamond 1990; Hargraves Heap 1980).

Perhaps the most important impact of high unemployment is on the ability of the unemployed to get rehired. A substantial period of unemployment causes worker skills to get rusty, or their human capital to deteriorate. Time spent not working means that people have not been learning on the job, and they will have fewer skills to offer new potential employers. This makes them less employable. On the hiring side, employers may be reluctant to hire people experiencing a long bout of unemployment because it signals that something is wrong with this individual. As a result, individuals become structurally unemployed, lacking the skills needed to get jobs in the economy even when firms start to hire again.

As a result of this, the full employment level of unemployment rises and reduces the full employment level of GDP falls. In this case, Keynesian demand-side policies can do little to reduce unemployment because unemployment has become structural in nature; it is no longer due to inadequate demand. Moreover, this problem increases as the length of time increases that people are unemployed. So, as the unemployment rate rises, it pulls up the full employment rate (the sum of frictional and structural unemployment), making it harder to achieve the earlier, lower unemployment rate (Cross 1988). Olivier Blanchard and Lawrence Summers (1986) suggest that hysteresis was a main reason for persistently high unemployment in Europe relative to the US during the late 1970s and early 1980s.

3.　NOMINAL PRICE RIGIDITY

Another reason why unemployment can remain high is that firms fail to lower their prices in response to shortfalls in demand. Microeconomics teaches us that firms with unsold goods should cut their prices to increase sales. If they do not do this, the result will be excess inventories and lower profits; many workers will no longer be needed, resulting in layoffs. When prices are "sticky", or do not adjust quickly to changes in demand or costs, the result can be a prolonged slump. Two explanations for sticky prices have emerged from the New Keynesian literature. First, firms may incur costs when they change prices (called "menu change cost"). Second, coordination failures can keep prices from falling.

3.1　Menu Change Costs

Robert Barro (1972) noted that firms generally do not change prices every day in response to fluctuations in demand or costs. This is similar to the phenomenon of wage rates not changing every day as worker productivity changes. Rather, prices change only when the price desired by firms deviates from the market-clearing price by a large amount over an extended period of time. Barro explained this phenomenon in terms of the cost of actually changing prices, or "menu change costs". This memorable phrase conjures up the image of a restaurant having to spend money every time it decides to change prices by printing up a new menu.

A second factor entering into price change calculations is the presence of uncertainty, a problem emphasized by Keynes and the Post-Keynesian School. If a downturn is temporary, firms that lower prices will soon have to raise them again, thus doubling their menu change costs. In addition to demand uncertainty, there is also uncertainty about costs, which depend on the demand and supply of many different parts. Firms cannot know the cost of various inputs or the shape of their cost curves. Furthermore, unlike individual business owners, most managers do not have the discretion to change prices at will. This decision must be made by committee, which means meetings, memos and lots of emails. Given such complexities, the optimal solution for the firm may be to rely on rules of thumb for pricing. One simple rule is markup pricing, where firms set prices by adding a percentage markup to their production costs in normal economic times. This ensures that the firm will not incur a loss (since it is pricing at some percentage above costs). When all large firms in the economy do this, relative prices will tend to be stable.

There may also be costs from changing prices that arise on the demand side of the market. Since searching is costly, consumers do not do this regularly. To some extent, spending depends on habits or past practices. Consumers will seek out a better deal only when prices change considerably. When this occurs, when firms change the prices they charge, the result may be lost sales to the firm. One further reason why firms may not lower prices in the face of lower demand is that consumers may take this as a signal that the quality of the good has deteriorated and may be less likely to purchase that good (Stiglitz 1987).

Because it is costly in so many ways, firms are somewhat reluctant to change prices. Prices will be sticky; they will not fall to clear product markets during bad economic times. Many empirical studies have confirmed that firms are slow to adjust their prices in response to changes in demand, that price-adjustment is complex for large firms, and that this contributes to stable prices (Godley and Gillian 1965; Cecchetti 1986; Kashyap 1987). Even small menu change costs can delay the price-adjustment mechanism from clearing markets and returning an economy to full employment (Mankiw 1985; Parkin 1986).

3.2 Coordination Failures

Coordination problems exist when economic agents cannot cooperate to achieve an outcome that is in their mutual interest. One example of this occurs when everyone at a concert or sporting event stands up, seeking to get a better view. The unfortunate result is that no one has a better view, but everyone is uncomfortable because they are all standing rather than seated. Since anyone who sits down will have a worse view, there is no incentive for anyone to sit. A sub-optimal situation arises here due to coordination failure – everyone cannot agree to sit.

A similar coordination problem arises when firms must decide what to do when facing a decline in demand. For a number of reasons (discussed in section 2), a firm may not want to lay off its workers. This might be a good strategy for the firm, but *only if* most other firms *do not* lay off their workers. If all firms retain existing workers, the greater incomes and spending creates sales and firms will be able to maintain their current labor force. But when a few firms do lay off workers, their costs will be lower than their competitors (since they are not carrying workers they do not need) and they will not experience any drop in sales, especially since they have lower prices than their competitors due to lower costs. These firms will force other firms out of business, or force them also to cut labor costs. The problem is that all firms benefit by maintaining their workforce, but there is no way for firms to coordinate and not lay off workers. Consequently, individual firms will lay off some workers, making macroeconomic problems worse rather than better (Garretson 1992).

Price-setting decisions also generate coordination problems. Eskander Alvi (1993) has argued that the failure of firms to maintain prices in the middle of a recession is a type of coordination problem. When one firm lowers its prices, it can gain sales at the expense of its competitors; this is similar to the situation where one person stands at a concert to get a better view. But when all firms cut prices, no firm has a price advantage. In addition, price cuts result in menu change costs for the firm and lead to lower incomes for its workers. This, in turn, reduces demand across the economy. The end result is that all firms lose sales and must continue cutting wages in an attempt to gain sales.

Coordination problems are similar to the famous paradox of thrift. In *The General Theory*, Keynes (1936, p. 373) pointed out that what is true for one is not necessarily true for all. His example was that if someone tried to save more, they would likely succeed; but when everyone tried to do this, the reduced demand and lower incomes would result in the same amount of savings as before. Similarly, there is no problem when one firm cuts prices during a recession. But when competitive forces push all firms to cut costs, the result is a worsening recession in which no firm gains.

4. OTHER IMPERFECTIONS

New Keynesians have identified other imperfections that lead to high unemployment. Imperfect competition in product markets may lead to sticky prices, and informational problems can lead to continued high unemployment if they reduce demand. Imperfect or asymmetric information can result in wages above market clearing wages, prices that are too high to clear product markets, or high interest rates that reduce economic growth.

4.1 Imperfect Competition

New Keynesians contend that one problem with New Classical economics is that it assumes perfect competition. In contrast, the real world is populated with very large firms, where imperfect competition is the rule. One reason we have imperfect competition is that firm profits get eaten away in the long run due to competition. Firms can maintain profits only by limiting competition, and they have figured out how to do this through mergers and acquisitions and through erecting various barriers to entry. Imperfect competition also arises due to increasing returns to scale (Young 1928), where greater output reduces per unit costs. This means that larger firms have a cost advantage over smaller firms. This will tend to drive smaller firms out of existence and keep new ones from entering the market.

Models of imperfect competition were first introduced into economics by Joan Robinson (1933) and Edward Chamberlin (1933). They have been incorporated into introductory economics textbooks and advanced microeconomics textbooks; however, advanced macroeconomics tends to assume perfect competition. New Keynesian economists have brought imperfect competition into macroeconomic models in order to explain continued high unemployment.

Imperfect competition explains sticky prices based on the fact that firms are price makers rather than price takers. Firms price their goods considerably above their cost of production to ensure that they make some minimum profit. As a result, when demand falls they do not have to cut their prices. Firms have some discretion over price, and they may not want to cut prices because this may lead to lower profits in addition to menu change costs (Blanchard and Kiyotaki 1987).

Imperfect competition and increasing returns can also explain high unemployment without resorting to the phenomenon of sticky prices (Weitzman 1982). Due to increasing returns, wages move pro-cyclically – they increase and decrease, respectively, with increases and decreases in demand. Consequently, if demand falls, and firms cut back on production, wage costs per unit of output will rise. This cuts into firms' profits, and so firms will be reluctant to reduce production and fire workers.

4.2   Imperfect or Asymmetric Information

Asymmetric information refers to the fact that some parties have greater access to information than other parties. Those lacking information typically respond in ways that lead to lower demand or less spending. Consequently, asymmetric information in credit markets, in labor markets, and in product markets can keep prices from reaching market-clearing levels.

Credit markets are notorious for containing information imperfections. The problem is that some information is difficult or impossible to obtain. For example, some borrowers will do their very best to try to repay any loan that they are given. Others will put in much less effort; they will be more likely to default on their loans. Anyone applying for a loan will try to convince lenders that they are the first type of borrower. If they succeed, they receive a lower interest rate on their loan. Some people might be able to signal their intent to repay a loan by providing a great deal of collateral or putting down a lot of money when borrowing to buy a new home. But not all borrowers can do this. Credit scores help; but these are backward looking rather than forward looking. The problem is that lenders cannot read minds, and they cannot distinguish borrowers who try their hardest to repay a loan from borrowers who will be quick to declare bankruptcy.

If firms knew the likelihood that each borrower would repay a loan, they could charge a different interest rate to each borrower based on this repayment probability. But since this information cannot be obtained, lenders tend to charge everyone the same interest rate; and this will be a higher interest rate than some customers are willing and able to pay (especially the good credit risks). As a result, some individuals (as well as firms) will decide not to take out loans at this rate even though they are likely to repay the loan. There will be less borrowing, less spending, and less employment than would be the case in the face of perfect information (Stiglitz 1981).

Credit problems usually become worse during a recession. As Irving Fisher (1933) pointed out, real debt and the real value of debt repayments both rise when prices fall. This increases the probability that firms and individuals will declare bankruptcy and not repay their loans. This, in turn, generates problems for banks that must meet capital requirements. Banks become more risk averse and less likely to lend. They are forced to raise the interest rate that they charge to all borrowers, thereby worsening the existing economic situation. For companies, credit rationing can affect decisions regarding equity versus debt financing. Stiglitz (1987; Greenwald and Stiglitz 1987, 1988) shows how this leads to greater macroeconomic instability.

Asymmetric information is also a problem in product markets. This is the lesson of Akerlof's (1970) famous paper on the market for lemons – not the sour yellow fruit, but the used cars that consumers buy. Because consumers do not have the knowledge to judge whether or not a car is a lemon, and because it is not worth their time and expense to develop such expertise, they will assume that there is a good chance that they are buying a lemon and reduce their offering price on used cars. This drives high quality used cars out of the market, leaving only lemons. Sales therefore drop.

Finally, informational asymmetries exist in labor markets. Workers are not all the same; some are more productive than others. Each firm must select the more productive workers among a large array of job candidates they do not really know. Workers, in contrast, know how productive they will be if hired; however, firms can only know how productive individual workers will be if they hire workers, train them and then have them work. Efficiency wage theory contends that the rational solution to this problem is for firms to offer higher wages. This will attract the most productive workers. Anyone willing to work for less gets regarded as a "lemon" while workers who know that they are not going to be productive and who do not want to work that hard will not apply for the job. As Akerlof (1984) argues, the result is that labor and management engage in a gift exchange – workers are paid higher wages and in return work more efficiently.

5. SOME POLICY CONCLUSIONS

The Rational Expectations School concludes that policy is irrelevant. The unemployment problem, they contend, will solve itself without any government intervention. The best anti-inflation policy is to go "cold turkey", reducing demand to eliminate inflationary pressures as soon as possible. This would result in the smallest possible output loss, since (they believe) output would quickly return to full employment levels.

For New Keynesian economists, policy makers encounter uncertainty because they can never be sure of the extent to which their policy changes are anticipated. Among New Keynesians, Taylor (1980b) demonstrates that reducing inflation more slowly results in a smaller loss of output. For this to work, inflation reduction must be made credible. Other New Keynesians have shown that, in the face of market imperfections that create unemployment, the solution is an activist policy of economic stimulus.

New Keynesians tend to agree that policy makers (especially central banks) should not blindly follow some policy rule, such as those proposed by the Monetarist School and Rational Expectations School. Rather, they tend to support policy targets rather than rules. For example, debt-deflation problems and the zero interest rate bound, have led New Keynesians to advocate a positive inflation rate target of around 2 percent annually (Summers 1991; Fischer 1996). Akerlof et al. (1996) contend that this would allow relative prices to change during a severe economic downturn. If inflation were 0 percent, and real wages had to be reduced to generate more employment, nominal wages must fall. This, as we saw above, can create morale problems and other problems. If instead the inflation rate was 2 percent, firms could keep nominal wages constant but real wages would fall by 2 percent. This would have fewer negative psychological effects on workers or on worker productivity.

Several other policy implications follow from the New Keynesian paradigm. Worried about insider-outsider problems, Lindbeck and Snower (1988) propose various ways to reduce the power of insiders and make it more attractive for firms to hire outsiders. Blanchard and Diamond (1990) advocate training programs to aid the long-term unemployed as a solution to the hysteresis problem. They also suggest training programs to increase the human capital of outsiders and several policies to increase labor mobility so that outsiders can more easily move to an area with more favorable labor market conditions and thereby become insiders. Weitzman (1984) has proposed work-sharing schemes so that workers do not get laid off in the face of an economic downturn. This would counter the coordination problems facing firms and prop up spending in the economy; work-sharing arrangements would also help maintain worker skills since hours are reduced slightly but workers are not laid off.

New Keynesians of a more conservative bent have proposed reforming the unemployment compensation systems in developed countries. They see these systems as giving outsiders incentives to keep looking for work as their skills deteriorate due to hysteresis. Other New Keynesians are even more critical of unemployment insurance programs. They think that unemployment benefits increase worker shirking because they lower the cost of being unemployed, and so advocate making these programs stingier.

6. AN ASSESSMENT

Overall, New Keynesian economics has many strengths as well as many weaknesses.

On the positive side, we can identify some key contributions stemming from the New Keynesian School. Perhaps most important, it has helped overcome the narrowness of the Rational Expectations School, which suggests that economic slumps and high unemployment are not real problems, that unemployment will diminish on its own, and that economic policy is ineffective in changing macroeconomic outcomes. Plenty of empirical evidence refutes these claims. New Keynesian economics can explain high unemployment and has countered the tendency in macroeconomics to oppose activist policy solutions to deal with macroeconomic problems. For these reasons, Blanchard (1992) is on the mark when he describes New Keynesian economics as "a return to pragmatism" following the New Classical or Rational Expectations revolution.

A second positive aspect of New Keynesian economics is that it has identified numerous market imperfections (Gordon 1990, p. 1163). Moreover, it has produced a good deal of empirical research demonstrating that economic life is full of imperfections that generate unemployment – coordination failures, efficiency wages, hysteresis, insider-outsider problems and menu change costs.

Along with these strengths, we can identify some serious limitations of the New Keynesian approach. First, there is no over-arching theory that explains how and why economies are plagued by rigidities. Nor is there any sense of which rigidities are the most important ones. As a result, the New Keynesian School seems to lack cohesiveness. Different economists have identified different imperfections; yet all these imperfections seem unrelated (Blanchard 1992; Gordon 1990). The situation is akin to Luigi Pirandello's play *Six Characters in Search of an Author*. The many rigidities identified by New Keynesian economics are still searching for someone or something that ties them together, telling a convincing story with a plot.

Second, while refuting New Classical economics on its own terms, New Keynesian economics has not propelled macroeconomics forward very much. Starting with the assumption that macroeconomics must have microfoundations and rational expectations may have given up too much to New Classical economics (on the problems with microfoundations, see King 2012, and the January 2016 *Review of Political Economy* symposium; on problems with rational expectations, see Blinder 1992 and Hoover 1990). Macroeconomics may need fundamental uncertainty rather than rational expectations to explain how economies work. Or, it may need to incorporate heterogeneous agents (as in agent-based modelling), some of whom are rational and some of whom are not.

Third, in contrast to the New Keynesian School, Keynes (1936) thought that rigid wages helped make economic downturns *milder* because worker incomes and spending would be maintained at current levels. Conversely, he thought that flexible wages would reduce demand and worsen downturns. New Keynesian economics seems rather divorced from this understanding of how economies actually work, what causes macroeconomic problems and the policy solutions necessary to assure full employment. As such, the school may be "new" but it may not really be Keynesian.

Finally, David Colander (1988) argues that New Keynesian economics is hampered because it does not meet the teachability test. It lacks simple models that can be incorporated into economics textbooks and then used to teach undergraduate students. One can extend this point and argue that New Keynesian economics also does not meet the research test. For graduate students and professional economists, there are only so many imperfections that can be identified and then used to show that rational expectations do not result in full employment. Consequently, there will be a limited number of dissertations that graduate students can write to get their degree, and a limited number of articles that professional economists can publish and use to obtain tenure, promotion and enhanced professional reputation. Without such opportunities, as Thomas Kuhn (1970) noted, paradigms do not flourish for long; rather, they languish and tend to disappear.

REFERENCES

Akerlof, G. (1970) The Market for "Lemons": Quality Uncertainty and the Market Mechanism, *Quarterly Journal of Economics* 84, pp. 488–500.

Akerlof, G. (1984) Gift Exchange and Efficiency Wage Theory: Four Views, *American Economic Review* 74, pp. 79–83.

Akerlof, G., Dickens, W. and Perry, G. (1996) The Macroeconomics of Low Inflation, *Brookings Papers on Economic Activity* #1, pp. 1–76.

Alvi, E. (1993) Near Rationality/Menu Costs, Strategic Complementarity and Real Rigidity: An Integration, *Journal of Macroeconomics* 15, pp. 619–625.

Ball, L. and Cecchetti, S. (1988) Imperfect Information and Staggered Price Setting, *American Economic Review* 78, pp. 999–1018.

Barro, R. (1972) A Theory of Monopolistic Price Adjustment, *Review of Economic Studies* 39, pp. 17–26.

Blanchard, O. (1992) For a Return to Pragmatism, in M. Belongia and M. Garfinkel (eds), *The Business Cycle: Theories and Evidence* (London: Kluwer), pp. 121–132.

Blanchard, O. and Diamond, P. (1990) Unemployment and Wages, unpublished paper, Employment Institute.

Blanchard, O. and Kiyotaki, N. (1987) Monopolistic Competition and the Effects of Aggregate Demand, *American Economic Review* 77, pp. 647–666.

Blanchard, O. and Summers, L. (1986) Hysteresis and the European Unemployment Problem, *NBER Macroeconomics Annual* 1, pp. 15–78.

Blinder, A. [1988] (1997) The Fall and Rise of Keynesian Economics, in B. Snowden and H. Vane (eds), *A Macroeconomics Reader* (London & New York: Routledge), pp. 109–134.

Blinder, A. (1992) Déjà Vu All Over Again, in M. Belongia and M. Garfinkel (eds), *The Business Cycle: Theories and Evidence* (London: Kluwer), pp. 189–196.

Cecchetti, S. (1986) The Frequency of Price Adjustment: A Study of Newsstand Prices of Magazines, 1953 to 1979, *Journal of Econometrics* 31, pp. 255–274.

Chamberlin, E. (1933) *The Theory of Monopolistic Competition* (Cambridge, MA: Harvard University Press).

Colander, D. (1988) The Evolution of Keynesian Economics: From Keynesian to New Classical to New Keynesian, in O. Hamouda and J. Smithin (eds), *Keynes and Public Policy After Fifty Years, Vol. 1: Economics and Policy* (Aldershot, UK: Edward Elgar Publishing), pp. 92–100.

Cross, R. (ed.) (1988) *Unemployment, Hysteresis and the Natural Rate Hypothesis* (Oxford: Basil Blackwell).

Fischer, S. (1996) Why are Central Banks Pursuing Long-Term Price Stability?, in *Achieving Price Stability* (Kansas City: Federal Reserve Bank of Kansas City), pp. 7–34.

Fisher, I. (1933) The Debt-Deflation Theory of Great Depressions, *Econometrica* 1, pp. 333–357.

Garretson, H. (1992) *Keynes, Coordination and Beyond: The Development of Macroeconomics and Monetary Theory Since 1945* (Aldershot, UK: Edward Elgar Publishing).

Godley, W. and Gillian, C. (1965) Pricing Behavior in Manufacturing Industry, *National Institute Economic Review* 33, pp. 43–47.

Gordon, R. (1990) What is New-Keynesian Economics?, *Journal of Economic Literature* 28, pp. 1115–1171.

Greenwald, B. and Stiglitz, J. (1987) Keynesian, New Keynesian and New Classical Economics, *Oxford Economic Papers* 39, pp. 119–133.

Greenwald, B. and Stiglitz, J. (1988) Examining Alternative Macroeconomic Theories, *Brookings Papers on Economic Activity* #1, pp. 207–270.

Hargraves Heap, S. (1980) Choosing the Wrong "Natural" Rate: Accelerating Inflation or Decelerating Employment and Growth, *Economic Journal* 90, pp. 611–620.

Hoover, K. (1990) *The New Classical Economics* (Oxford: Basil Blackwell).

Kashyap, A. (1987) Sticky Prices: New Evidence from Retail Catalogs, *Quarterly Journal of Economics* 110, pp. 245–274.

Keynes, J.M. (1936) *The General Theory of Employment, Interest, and Money* (London: Macmillan).

King, J. (2012) *The Microfoundations Delusion: Metaphor and Dogma in the History of Macroeconomics* (Cheltenham, UK: Edward Elgar Publishing).

Kuhn, T. (1970) *The Structure of Scientific Revolutions*, 2nd edn (Chicago: University of Chicago Press).

Leibenstein, H. (1966) Allocative Efficiency vs. X-Efficiency, *American Economic Review* 56, pp. 392–415.

Lindbeck, A. and Snower, D. (1986) Wage Setting, Unemployment and Insider-Outsider Relations, *American Economic Review*, 72, pp. 235–239.

Lindbeck, A. and Snower, D. (1988) *The Insider-Outsider Theory of Employment and Unemployment* (Cambridge, MA: MIT Press).

Lindbeck, A. and Snower, D. (2001) Insiders versus Outsiders, *Journal of Economic Perspectives* 15, pp. 165–188.

Mankiw, G. (1985) Small Menu Change Costs and Large Business Cycles: A Macroeconomic Model of Monopoly, *Quarterly Journal of Economics* 100, pp. 529–537.

Mankiw, G. (1991) The Reincarnation of Keynesian Economics, NBER Working Paper #3885.

Marshall, A. (1920) *Principles of Economics* (London: Macmillan).

Parkin, M. (1986) The Output-Inflation Tradeoff When Prices are Costly to Change, *Journal of Political Economy* 94, pp. 200–224.

Parkin, M. and Bade, R. (1982) *Modern Macroeconomics* (Oxford: Philip Allan).

Phelps, E. (1968) Money Wage Dynamics and Labour Market Equilibrium, *Journal of Political Economy* 76, pp. 678–711.

Phelps, E. (1990) *Seven Schools of Macroeconomic Thought* (Oxford: Oxford University Press).

Robinson, J. (1933) *Economics of Imperfect Competition* (London: Macmillan).

Stiglitz, J. (1981) Credit Rationing in Markets with Imperfect Information, *American Economic Review* 71, pp. 393–410.

Stiglitz, J. (1987) The Causes and Consequences of the Dependency of Quality on Prices, *Journal of Economic Literature* 25, pp. 1–48.

Summers, L. (1991) How Should Long-Term Monetary Policy be Determined?, *Journal of Money, Credit and Banking* 23, pp. 625–631.

Taylor, J. (1980a) Aggregate Dynamics and Staggered Contracts, *Journal of Political Economy* 88, pp. 1–23.

Taylor, J. (1980b) Recent Developments in the Theory of Stabilization Policy, unpublished paper.

Weitzman, M. (1982) Increasing Returns and the Foundations of Unemployment: Theory, *Economic Journal* 92, pp. 787–804.

Weitzman, M. (1984) *The Share Economy: Conquering Stagflation* (Cambridge, MA: Harvard University Press).

Young, A. (1928) Increasing Returns and Economic Progress, *Economic Journal* 38, pp. 527–542.

14. The Post-Keynesian School

Louis-Philippe Rochon[1]

KEY FEATURES

- Distinguishes post-Keynesian economics, from (new or neo) Keynesian economics.
- Argues that post-Keynesian economics is more than the economics of Keynes.
- Briefly discusses the role of Michał Kalecki.
- Discusses a number of fallacies of composition.
- Discusses 10 key characteristics of post-Keynesian economics.

1. INTRODUCTION

Previous chapters in this book have discussed the ideas of Keynes, Keynesians and new Keynesians. To many students, this may appear to be somewhat confusing at first. After all, why would economists spend so much energy insisting on distinguishing themselves between seemingly similar-sounding approaches, carrying seemingly similar names? Unfortunately, this chapter will only add to this confusion – at least initially – as we will discuss the ideas of another similar-sounding group, the "post"-Keynesians, which emerged in the mid-1950s to re-establish the ideas developed by Keynes following the efforts of the Keynesians to dilute them (as we will see, Polish economist Michał Kalecki also plays a central role).

But as the chapter goes on, it will become clear how different post-Keynesians are from new or neo Keynesians. In fact, it proposes a very different vision of economics than the neoclassical or Keynesian approaches, which are based on individual micro behaviour and exchange. In contrast, post-Keynesian economics is based on the social process of the production of goods, which involves institutions and necessarily involves conflict between various groups at the heart of this process. Above all it involves banks and therefore can best be described as a monetary theory of production.

Yet, efforts to minimize confusion are further complicated by the fact that post-Keynesian theory is not a singular, unified approach, but a co-existence of various strands and influences.[2] Indeed, King has argued that post-Keynesians are part of a "big tent", and a "broad church" (King, 2002, p. 5). In this chapter, owing precisely to the idea of a "broad church", post-Keynesians will also be referred to as heterodox economists, and the two expressions will be used interchangeably.

In this chapter, I will present what I believe to be elements that are common or compatible, to a large degree, to these various post-Keynesian or heterodox strands – elements I believe form the core of heterodox economics. Undoubtedly, because we are dealing with various strands, there is a need to sacrifice the more extreme parts from all the various strands. But in the end, we are left with a positive contribution to economic theory, worthy certainly of a credible alternative to Keynesian and other orthodox approaches. As Eichner and Kregel (1975, p. 1294) wrote almost 50 years ago, "post-Keynesian theory has the potential for becoming a comprehensive, positive alternative to the prevailing neoclassical paradigm". This, I argue, has been achieved.

Past chapters have shown in what ways all these various schools of thought have important differences, to some degree, especially with respect to how markets work – or as post-Keynesians are fond of saying – how they represent the "real" world. How economists observe the world around them and how they perceive how the world should operate impacts greatly how policies are shaped. As this chapter will show, post-Keynesians see the world in a very different way, and post-Keynesian theory is fundamentally different. We will argue in this sense that it is more representative of the real world.

As was shown in earlier chapters, early Keynesians were unable to break away from core neoclassical ideas. They had difficulty in understanding what Keynes wanted to do. As such, Keynes's key insights were lost, and the result was a synthesis between some ideas found in Keynes's *General Theory*, which were then embedded within an overall neoclassical theory that emphasized an eventual return to a long-run position – an approach which Joan Robinson famously labelled "bastard Keynesianism". In particular, Keynesians believed that the economy could get stuck in the short-run, as a result of inflexible or sticky prices (imperfections), and as such it needed some help to get back to long-run equilibrium. So they kept the idea of short-run "disequilibrium" (not a word used by post-Keynesians), but defended the idea of an economy that gravitated to some long-run position independent of what was going on in the short-run. In other words, Keynesians, and new Keynesians after them, essentially kept the neoclassical theory as a general case, while adding some imperfections to generate a special, short-run case. These similar approaches can be summarized in the following two words: "stability and convergence".

Post-Keynesian theory therefore begins where Keynes left off by wanting to reclaim the mantle of Keynes's proposed revolution from the Keynesians, and in doing so, post-Keynesians seek to explain the dynamics of economies in the short-run by righting the wrongs (or should we say "lefting" the wrongs?) of Keynesians and re-establishing involuntary unemployment as the general case, and extending Keynes's analysis to the long-run – a long-run that looks very different from the neoclassical or Keynesian one. For post-Keynesians, there are no imperfections, and economies do not get stuck in the short-run because of sticky prices or wages, but because there is insufficient effective demand given an uncertain future: the economy certainly does not gravitate towards an independently-determined long-run equilibrium. This then sets up the argument for the use of fiscal policy. In two words, we can summarize the post-Keynesian approach as "instability and fragility", which will become clear below.

The main purpose of this chapter is to introduce readers to the core ideas of the post-Keynesians. Before getting there, however, I feel that it is necessary to discuss briefly the role played by another economist whose ideas shaped post-Keynesian economics: Polish economist Michał Kalecki (see also Chapter 6). I then discuss what I believe are the core ideas of post-Keynesian or heterodox economists. The conclusion is an obvious one: economics is in need of some "Spring cleaning" (Robinson, 1985, p. 160), and post-Keynesians are best positioned to propose this alternative.

2.   KEYNES AND BEYOND KEYNES

Post-Keynesian economics is a relatively new approach to economics, approximately 50 years old. As an institution, it emerged in the United States in the very early 1970s, following correspondence between Alfred Eichner and Joan Robinson (see Rochon, 2022a; Lee, 2000). The intellectual roots, however, date back a little further, to a book published by Joan Robinson called *The Accumulation of Capital*, while the very first journal article espousing the core elements of post-Keynesian economics was published in 1975, in the *Journal of Economic Literature*, by Alfred Eichner and Jan Kregel (see Eichner and Kregel, 1975).

In the early years, post-Keynesians were described – by both those within and those outside post-Keynesian circles – mainly as being against neoclassical economics, and hence in a negative way. For instance, Eichner (1985a,

p. 51) once wrote "it is less controversial to say what post-Keynesian theory is not than to say what it is. Post-Keynesian theory is not neoclassical theory". In a similar vein, Arestis (1990, p. 222) writes "post-Keynesians tend to define their program in a negative way as a reaction to neo-classical economics".

But this label is only half true, as post-Keynesians always had a very positive message, which at times got lost by their critics. Arestis also writes that "It is also true to say that post-Keynesians are united not just because of their critical attitude to neo-classical economics, *but more importantly because of their attempt to provide an alternative paradigm to orthodox economics*" (1990, p. 223, emphasis added) . This prompted King to ask two important questions: "Can it be defined only in a negative way, in terms of its opposition to neoclassical macroeconomics? Or is there a coherent positive Post Keynesian alternative to the mainstream?" (King, 2002, p. 1). The answers to these questions are clear: no and yes.

It is perhaps easy to claim, as alluded to above, that post-Keynesian theory begins with Keynes, or that it begins where Keynes left off. That is certainly the easy answer. But the truth is more complex: Keynes is not the only or even most prominent source for post-Keynesian economics today. In fact, as we argue below, post-Keynesian theory is the result of many influences, and while this may at times give the impression of confusion, the challenge is to build an approach that rests on the best of what each approach has to offer.

In a way, that certainly reflects one of the most fundamental ideas of post-Keynesian economics: realism (or rather realisticness; see below). This was pointed out by Eichner and Kregel (1975, p. 1309) where they argue that post-Keynesian theory seeks "to explain the real world as observed empirically". Yet reality itself is a source of interpreting the world around us. As Rochon and Rossi (2021) argue, interpretation is subject to a number of biases, which depend in many ways on one's ideology, and thus the lens through which we see and interpret the world around us.

But while post-Keynesian theory may begin with Keynes, it certainly does not end with Keynes, and there are good reasons to look beyond Keynes, most notably because he came from a neoclassical or Marshallian background, even describing the *General Theory* as a "long struggle of escape from habitual modes of thought and expression".[3] The lingering question is whether Keynes succeeded in escaping from his past: did he complete his struggle? The consensus appears to be that Keynes did not fully succeed in escaping his Marshallian roots, and that other aspects of neoclassical theory remained embedded in his approach, thereby paving the way, understandably, for the rise of the "bastard" Keynesian version. In other words, the *General Theory*, by far Keynes's most important contribution, kept sufficient neoclassical elements that allowed it to be interpreted in a "bastard" way. This suggests that Keynes himself planted seeds to his aborted revolution. This echoes Kaldor's (1983, p. 47) own sentiment that "the real author of the so-called 'neo-classical synthesis' was not Paul Samuelson, it was Keynes himself".[4]

This exposes the weaknesses of Keynes's approach – at least as contained in the *General Theory* – leading Sebastiani (1989, p. xii) to argue that because of this, "Keynes would thus have failed to perceive the complexity of modern systems, the structural problems, the proliferation of social figures, the fragmentary character of interests and the existence of conflicts which cannot be settled through macroeconomic policies".

This last statement may be a bit of an exaggeration as it assumes Keynes's thought would not have evolved with time or with changing circumstances. But there is some evidence to suggest that Keynes would have perhaps changed his mind as events unrolled. After all, there is this quote attributed to him where he argues that when confronted with changing facts, "I change my mind, what do you do?"[5] Robinson (1978, p. xxii) also describes Keynes as being able to "absorb the criticisms" quickly and "racing towards new formulations". Skouras (1981, p. 208) reinforces this idea claiming that Keynes "was habitually quick to revise or even to completely abandon his own analytical formulations".

And while it is difficult to see how precisely Keynes's thought would have evolved in time, given time, perhaps he would have fully escaped his Marshallian roots to be able to better interpret the world around him. But while it is impossible to predict any of this, one thing is certain: many post-Keynesians do not always feel comfortable with Keynes even as a starting point of their analysis, seeing him as a rather "moderately conservative" figure who never really broke free from neoclassical orthodoxy (see Toporowski, 2013, p. 142). For instance, almost four decades ago, Lavoie (1985) warned us about "following Keynes too closely when it comes to money" – a statement that certainly appears odd given that the word "money" appears prominently in the title of the *General Theory*, and that many post-Keynesians refer to Keynes when discussing money. That said, Eichner (1979, p. 7) reaches a similar conclusion when he writes that "Yet it is not clear that Keynes was the most important of the Keynesians".

Nevertheless, it is indisputable that Keynes played a prominent and central role within the development of post-Keynesian theory – a role that has to do certainly with the fact that he was a professor at one of the most imminent universities in the world, the University of Cambridge, and was editor of a well-respected journal, the *Economic Journal*. Keynes was also an advisor to the government, and an avid commentator on public affairs.

In fact, we could say that Keynes was a household name in Britain – a feat not enjoyed by any other economist to this day (with the exception of a few, like John Kenneth Galbraith or even Milton Friedman). And in the end, his book, the *General Theory*, undoubtedly and unequivocally, has been at the centre of macroeconomics since the day it was published, and for all these reasons, the approach called post-Keynesian economics bears his name. As King (1996, p. 149) argues, "Keynes's reputation and ability to command attention had ensured that his genius was fully recognised, while Kalecki' s talents had gone largely unnoticed". This was best said by Joan Robinson (1976, p. 7): Keynes simply "stole the limelight".

But given the above discussion, post-Keynesian economics has to be more than Keynes. As Palley (1996, p. x) wrote, "the Post Keynesian Project represents both a recovery and an extension of the economic paradigm developed by Keynes". Precisely: the recovery is about rediscovering Keynes and reclaiming him from the "bastard" hands of the Keynesians, and developing the more radical ideas – read non-neoclassical as there are many parts of Keynes that are truly "revolutionary". But post-Keynesian economics is also about extending his ideas, and in many ways, going beyond Keynes.

Michał Kalecki

In light of this, many post-Keynesian economists have argued that Polish economist Michał Kalecki deserves an equal if not greater recognition than Keynes, and that Kalecki, not Keynes, ought to be considered the starting point of the heterodox analysis. Indeed, Kalecki arrived at many of the core elements of Keynes's analysis, including the theory of effective demand, yet without the neoclassical baggage. In other words, coming from a Marxist background and especially being largely self-taught in economics through readings of Marx and Rosa Luxemburg, Kalecki never had to go through a "long struggle of escape", as did Keynes, and his approach rested on a more non-orthodox foundation like oligopolistic firms, income distribution and social classes – all elements missing or given only lip-service by Keynes. The result was "to arrive at a more sophisticated theory of output and employment and the trade cycle" (Kerr, 2005, p. 479).

Whereas Keynes's analysis rested on perfect competition as a mode of production, "Kalecki was able to weave the analysis of imperfect competition and of effective demand together and it was this that opened up the way for what goes under the name of post-Keynesian economic theory" (Robinson, 1977 [1979], pp. 193–194). For this reason, Harcourt (1987, p. x) claims that Kalecki's writings were "the most profound of the twentieth century". Kaldor (1986, p. 8) wrote that "Kalecki was superior to Keynes".

In fact, many argue that Kalecki either anticipated Keynes's *General Theory*, or at the very least, discovered the importance of the principle of effective demand at the same time. Robinson (1979a, p. 129) defended "Mr. Kalecki's discovery of the General Theory independently of Keynes", as did King (2013a, p. 487), who claims that Kalecki "discovered the principle of effective demand more or less simultaneously with Keynes". Economist Lawrence Klein (1951, p. 447), rightly concludes that Kalecki "created a system that contains everything of importance in the Keynesian system, in addition to other contributions".[6]

For these reasons, many post-Keynesians prefer beginning their analysis with Kalecki, not Keynes, thereby giving Kalecki a central role within post-Keynesian economics. Arestis (1996a, p. 11) rightly observes, "Kalecki's role in post-Keynesian economics is both extensive and paramount". And in recent years, Kalecki's influence has grown considerably, such that much of what passes for post-Keynesian economics today is rooted in Kaleckian economics (see Rochon, Czachor and Bachurewicz, 2020). As Sebastiani (1989, p. xi) writes, "The widespread rediscovery of Kalecki which we are witnessing today is certainly due, at least in part, to the growing dissatisfaction with Keynes's theory".[7]

And because of the different backgrounds, Marshallian vs Marxian, followers of Keynes and Kalecki have often clashed over ideas and policies, and the rightful place of their respective master. As Eichner (1985b, pp. xi–xii) noted, "Another important characteristic of post-Keynesian theory is the tension, not fully resolved, between those who draw their inspiration from Keynes himself, and those who base their work instead on the work of Polish economist, Michał Kalecki". It is for this reason, for instance, that Sawyer (1985, p. 178) has claimed that "the differences between Kalecki and Keynes are substantial, such that their approaches should be separately developed and not conflated together, although there may be some places where there could be a useful cross-fertilisation of ideas".[8]

Cross-fertilization of Ideas and All That: The Third Way

While Sawyer is undoubtedly correct that the differences between Keynes and Kalecki are substantial, this chapter prefers to emphasize the idea that a "cross fertilization" of ideas is possible and is what we should aspire to. After all, both authors believed in the limitations of the dominant approach in explaining recessions: Keynes and Kalecki both represented a "radical departure" from the mainstream. According to Robinson (1976, p. 7), the mainstream's (or the "neo-neoclassics", as she calls them) contortions in attempting to re-establish pre-Keynesian notions after Keynes was proof of "how radical [Keynes's] departure from orthodoxy really was". In this sense, the intent of both Kalecki's and Keynes's analyses was to undermine neoclassical economics. Both, according to Robinson (1976, p. 8), "were holding a mirror up to modern capitalism".

Moreover, both also believed that market economies failed in delivering full employment, and both placed aggregate demand at the heart of their analysis, and finally both saw investment as a leading component of aggregate demand.

Not everyone, however, agrees with the wisdom of attempting to find common ground between Kalecki and Keynes. For instance, Paul Davidson (2003–2004, p. 247), one of the founders of the *Journal of Post Keynesian Economics*, writes that it is an "error" to include Kaleckians in the definition of post-Keynesian economics. Davidson's approach to post-Keynesian economics is a very narrow one, however, and rejects any influence other than Keynes's. Otherwise, we risk ending up, according to Davidson (2003–2004, p. 247), with "Babylonian 'babble'".

Many have made this argument before. For instance, Harcourt has argued that post-Keynesians are a "heterogenous lot" (Harcourt, 1985a, p. 125), united perhaps best in their opposition to neoclassical theory. Hodgson (2019) argues that "heterodox economists cannot agree what heterodox economics means". This certainly gives the impression that describing heterodox economics is an impossible task.

Yet, we believe that it is possible to propose a coherent whole, despite the various influences, sources, conflicts and all. Of course, I am not proposing a conflation of all these approaches – such a task would indeed be difficult. But it is possible to pick elements from both Keynes and Kalecki, as well as other sources, which maintain the overall intent of undermining neoclassical economics and building a more realist view of the world. In the end, we are left with maybe a potpourri of ideas, from various sources, but one that ultimately works.

This is in the spirit of Lavoie (2014, p. 42) who argues in favour of "taking the best elements from each" – while excluding many of the more extreme ideas in their respective writings. King (2021) has argued this precisely, that various post-Keynesian approaches "are essentially on the same page and, second, that while there are indeed significant differences of opinion between post-Keynesians and other schools of thought in heterodox economics, there is still considerable scope for cooperation and fruitful debate between them". Bortis (1997, p. 235) has argued that "a consensus between the various strands of post-Keynesianism … should be possible".

The way forward for post-Keynesians therefore may indeed be eclectic, and integrate parts of Kalecki (mark-up pricing, imperfect competition, social conflict) with parts of Keynes (who emphasized uncertainty and fiscal multipliers), with aggregate demand, and with parts of others, like Kaldor and Robinson, who both endorsed endogenous money, and even Pierro Sraffa, another heterodox economist.[9] This was precisely the position of Pasinetti, who argued for:

> selecting and shaping the theories of Keynes and Sraffa and the developments of Kahn, Robinson and Kaldor (and Goodwin and whoever else have made contributions in the same direction at Cambridge or elsewhere) into a coherent, solid, overall framework. (Pasinetti 2007, p. 236)

There are certainly important differences in these various approaches, perhaps best left for other historians of thought to dissect. Yet, for the purposes of this chapter, I will minimize these differences, and agree with Eichner (1985b, p. xii) who argued that these differences are more a matter of emphasis than "a manifestation of two irreconcilable theories".

In the end, both Keynes and Kalecki should be equally considered the founding fathers of the school of effective demand. This is in line with Sawyer's (1985, p. 182) conclusion that both authors "should be treated on a par rather than placing Keynes in the leading role and Kalecki in the subordinate role".

3. FALLACIES OF COMPOSITION

Before addressing the specific characteristics of post-Keynesian theory, it is useful, I think, to briefly discuss what post-Keynesians call "fallacies of composition" in order to get a better sense of the dynamics between micro and macroeconomics.

A fallacy of composition describes an idea or an act, which at the level of the household or the firm may make good microeconomic sense but does not at the macroeconomic level. In other words, what may seem reasonable for one individual may not be reasonable if we all do it. In this sense, it produces a paradox: how can something that appears good for the individual worker or firm contribute to negative consequences at the macroeconomic level? According to Lavoie (2014, p. 17), "What seems reasonable for a single individual or nation leads to unintended consequences or even irrational collective behaviour when all individuals act in a similar way".

It is important to be aware of such paradoxes because they reveal the internal inconsistencies and weaknesses of neoclassical economics. They also show the limitations of relying too much on microeconomic reasoning to explain macroeconomics. It is therefore no surprise that they can be found within the core of post-Keynesian economics.

Lavoie (2014) discusses eight such paradoxes. For instance, the paradox of tranquility argues that in periods of economic tranquility, firms may wish to adopt riskier behaviour and seek higher profits. In turn, this will contribute to destabilize the economy. This can best be summarized by invoking the aphorism attributed to Hyman Minsky (1986): stability leads to instability. In other words, instability is an endogenous feature of the economic system, and not necessarily the result of an exogenous shock. Instability can come from within.

We will not cover all eight paradoxes here but will limit our brief discussion to three more.

For instance, another classic example is the paradox of thrift, according to which acts of individual savings may benefit individual workers, but if everybody began saving, it would lead to a general decrease in consumption and thus demand, which would harm the economy as businesses would be selling fewer goods and perhaps have to let workers go as a result. So increased savings at the individual level may lead to fewer savings at the level of society as a whole.

Another example is the paradox of costs. Reducing wages may lead a firm to reduce its costs of production, and therefore (appear to) raise its profits. But if all firms acted like this, workers would collectively have less disposable income, aggregate consumption would decline thereby reducing total profits in the overall economy, and possibly lead to a rise in employment. This is the contrary of what neoclassical theory says: a decline in real wages may lead to an increase in unemployment. Stated differently, higher real wages lead to higher profits.

Finally, we may consider the paradox of fiscal deficits. According to this paradox, attempts by governments to reduce their deficits in an effort to obtain balanced budgets will end up more often than not in higher deficits. This is because as governments reduce spending, they reduce aggregate spending and demand, which in turn hurts economic activity, raises unemployment and reduces fiscal revenues thereby increasing deficits. This suggests that the single-minded austerity pursuit of balanced budgets does more harm than good and is self-defeating.

4. THE CORE ELEMENTS OF POST-KEYNESIAN ECONOMICS

We are now ready to discuss the specific characteristics of post-Keynesian or heterodox economics. This is not an easy task. It is confounded by some authors who think that it is a useless task. For instance, as stated earlier, Eichner (1985a, p. 51) once claimed that "it is less controversial to say what post-Keynesian theory is not than to say what it is. Post-Keynesian theory is not neoclassical theory". Other post-Keynesians have had the same opinion. For instance, Arestis (1990, p. 222) writes that "post-Keynesians tend to define their program in a negative way as a reaction to neo-classical economics", whereas Sawyer (1988, p. 1) stated that "the unifying feature of post Keynesians is the dislike of neoclassical economics".

At one time, this may have been true. In the early days when post-Keynesians were struggling to define themselves, they were overtly pre-occupied in wanting to dismantle neoclassical economics. But today, post-Keynesian and otherwise heterodox economists have made important and positive contributions to theory and policy, and define themselves according to a list of unifying principles. Here we agree with Lavoie (2015) who once stated "if by any bad luck neoclassical economics were to disappear completely from the surface of the earth, this would leave heterodox economics utterly unaffected". Indeed, post-Keynesian economics has grown tremendously in the last five decades or so, and has become a viable alternative – coherent and fully consistent –to neoclassical economics.

Quite obviously, the ideas below need to be fully developed, which goes beyond the immediate scope of this chapter. This said, I present a sketch of the core ideas of post-Keynesian economics. Bear in mind that many of these ideas pre-date Keynes by many decades or centuries.

Also, the ideas below are greatly influenced by the theory of the monetary circuit – a view that has emerged in Europe and has greatly influenced the development of post-Keynesian economics in the last five decades (see Graziani, 1995; Rochon, 1999).

The Core Elements

1 Realisticness
The neoclassical model used in the analysis of the economy is based on a set of assumptions, which may or may not reflect the actual world in which we live. For post-Keynesians, these assumptions, more often than not, are deemed unrealistic (rationality, utility and profit maximization, perfect competition, free markets, atomistic behaviour, lack of social classes, etc). Nowhere is the lack of realisticness truer than in the explanation of the existence of money: in neoclassical economics, barter is often used to explain the origins of money, though there is scant anthropological evidence that barter existed or that it explains the existence of money. Some even question whether barter ever existed. For instance, anthropologist, Caroline Humphrey (1985, p. 48), writes: "No example of a barter

economy, pure and simple, has ever been described, let alone the emergence from it of money; all available ethnography suggests that there never has been such a thing". Regardless, a proper understanding of money (see below) carries huge implications, one that may end up tugging at the thread of neoclassical economics and unravel it completely.

But for neoclassical economists, this is of secondary importance: assumptions or hypotheses don't need to be realistic in the sense that they don't need to reflect the real world. This line of reasoning was strongly advocated by Milton Friedman, who wrote that a model is "a system of generalizations that can be used to make correct predictions about the consequences of any change in circumstances" (Friedman, 1953, p. 4). Accordingly, realistic assumptions are not important, as long as the model has high predictive powers. In fact, one could argue that neoclassical theory can only arrive at its conclusions by adopting unrealistic premises.

Keynes had difficulty with such an approach, which for him, can have "disastrous" consequences. As he writes in the opening paragraph of the *General Theory*, "the characteristics of the special case assumed by [neo] classical theory happen not to be those of the economic society in which we actually live, with the result that its teaching is misleading and disastrous if we attempt to apply it to the facts of experience" (1936 [1964], p. 3). This is why he recommended "a vigilant observation of the actual working of our system".

Indeed, how can we expect our models or theories to have anything meaningful to say about the world, or propose relevant policies, if they describe some fictitious, highly stylized world? For instance, the neoclassical model is mostly about long-run stability and convergence to an equilibrium, or about how it gravitates back to equilibrium following a shock. How then can we expect it to have any relevant information about financial crises, for instance, or a health crisis-cum-economic depression? In these neoclassical models, crises cannot happen, which explains why the vast majority of economists did not see the 2007 crisis coming. As such, it could not provide any meaningful policies either, having to fall back only on austerity.

Yet, to be relevant, economic theory must bear some familiarity with the world in which we live. Hence, there must be a sense of what post-Keynesians call "realisticness"; assumptions must be realistic, and the overall theory must do its best to describe the real world. And while theories are a simplification of the real world, there must be realisticness within these simplifications. What are we leaving out of these models? Is it justifiable to exclude social classes, or income distribution, or mega-corporations? One of the core elements of post-Keynesian theory is to build models that incorporate proper pricing mechanisms by firms, proper market structures, a realistic banking system, the inclusion of a central bank that controls the rate of interest, the role of unions, the role of the State and other institutions, and more.

Robinson (1956, p. 24) knew all too well the importance of realisticness, as she tells us that "One of the purposes of economic theory is to look through the veil of money to the realities behind it". Hence many of the elements that follow are a way of incorporating realisticness into the post-Keynesian approach.

2 A monetary economy of production and endogenous money

While we must indeed look behind the veil of money, we must also recognize that we live in what Keynes called a monetary economy of production. This is in contrast to the world depicted by neoclassical economics, where money is not necessary to explain the real world. Indeed, we use textbooks to teach students the causes of employment and unemployment, wages, consumption, investment, prices and growth, without once referring to the monetary system. In most textbooks, money appears much later in the book, towards the end, well after the discussion of real variables: money is an afterthought. One could conclude that money does not exist in the pure neoclassical model. This is at the heart of the lack of realisticness in neoclassical theory, as described above.

Yet, in a monetary world, money, debt, consumption, investment and production are linked: we cannot speak of production, labour, investment or even growth without first having a grasp of the meaning of money. In such a world, Say's Law is reversed, and entrepreneurs finance their production and the purchase of capital goods through borrowing from banks, not through savings. In this sense, there is a close link between the existence of money and debt. Money is a creature of production.

Central banks play a role in setting the rate of interest. It is considered a true exogenous price. In fact, central banks can have any rate of interest it wants – though there may be consequences to that decision.

This rate will play a role in influencing other rates along the spectrum of assets, including the rate on loans, the supply of which depends on how banks perceive borrowers, and their degree of creditworthiness – or the "reputation" of borrowers (Robinson, 1956, p. 50). When banks agree to grant a loan (credit on the asset side of the banks' balance sheet), money appears on the liability side of banks' balance sheets, at which point, money is created. But banks do not lend to everyone who asks for credit. As Keynes tells us, there will always be a "fringe of unsatisfied borrowers" (1930, p. 212).

It is in this sense that post-Keynesians speak of the endogenous nature of money:

A wage economy requires money. An employer who is starting in business has to pay his workers before he has anything to sell so that he must have a stock of purchasing power (finance) in some form of other before he begins. (Robinson, 1956, p. 20)

Banks are therefore "special" in the post-Keynesian story, and much has to do with the "subjective attitude of the bankers" (Robinson, 1956, p. 244). Rochon (2006) has expanded on this (see also Lavoie, 2014, chapter 4). Banks are never constrained by a lack of funds, but only by a lack of good borrowers.

The implications of endogenous money are vast, and cut through the theoretical vacuum of neoclassical theory. In the end, as Robinson (1943, p. 25) reminds us: "But in general, in a slump, it is not lack of finance but poor prospects of profit which is the seat of the trouble. The most that the banks can do by easy lending is to take the horse to the water – it needs an assured future market to make him drink."

3 Social classes and power
A starting point of post-Keynesian economics is the inherent conflict among groups within capitalism – workers, productive capital (capitalists), and financial capital (rentiers), although for realisticness, we should add the State, banks, the central bank and the "rest of the world". Analyzing the economy from this perspective only emphasizes the difficult dynamics and interrelationships between groups, and how power is exercised. This approach is a nod to the Classical School, as described in chapter 1, and is more closely linked to the Kaleckian branch of post-Keynesianism. For Arestis (1992, p. 101), economics "is based on the premise that capitalism is a class-divided society".

This view stands once again in contrast to neoclassical theory, which is founded on atomistic behaviour of individual agents, with maximizing functions. Indeed, in neoclassical theory, the centre of analysis is the rational economic man or *homo economicus*. In doing so, it eliminates the need to discuss macroeconomics as a distinct field: if everyone behaves rationally, then studying the single individual is the same as analyzing the economy as a whole. This is the essence of the notion of microfoundations to macroeconomics. Yet in doing so, it also eliminates the need to discuss how specific groups act and react with and against one another, and as such, how power can contribute to specific economic outcomes.

For post-Keynesians, however, the economy is not micro-founded, but rather is based on macro-groups or social classes, such as workers who supply the labour, capitalists who own the means of production, and rentiers, a class whose income derives from owning financial assets. This hierarchy emphasises the struggle of one group against the others, and the conflict over the proper distribution of income (see below). Moreover, firms tend to be oligopolistic, bestowing them with heightened power in setting prices and increasing their share of the national income.

This way of seeing the economy carries important consequences, such as placing income distribution at the heart of economic analysis, as well as inevitable conflict over this distribution. Indeed, the most powerful relationship must be between workers and firms, over wages and price setting. In fact, post-Keynesians see inflation itself as the result of conflict over the distribution of income (see Rochon and Setterfield, 2008).

4 Instability and fragility

As stated above, neoclassical theory is foremost about convergence and stability to a long-run equilibrium position, independent of short-run dynamics. The economic system has mechanisms (market forces and price flexibility) that guarantee its convergence to this long-run equilibrium following an exogenous shock. But this convergence is largely based on some well-behaved demand and supply curves: downward-sloping demand curves and upward-sloping supply curves.

Yet, these curves are theoretical only, and have no empirical support. In fact, we can easily imagine, for instance, downward-sloping labour supply curves: as wages fall, workers must work longer hours or find another job just to make ends meet. Moreover, as wages increase, this may lead firms to hire more labour given the higher levels of effective demand. This is the paradox of costs discussed above.

The above description is what is often called "free market" or laissez-faire economics. According to this view, the inevitable role for governments is to ensure that anything that stands in the way of free markets must be removed, otherwise it will prevent the system from converging quickly to equilibrium. So governments must reject unions, minimum wage laws, price ceilings and floors, and any imperfections that prevent the economy from gravitating toward its long-run equilibrium.

For post-Keynesians, however, free markets are not conducive to economic or financial stability: rather free markets are prone to periods of great instability. In fact, economist Hyman Minsky argued that periods of stability lead to periods of instability. In other words, the so-called market forces operate very differently in the real world: in periods of stability, firms will be earning good profits, and will seek higher profits by adopting ever-increasing risky ventures, making the system unstable.

This instability suggests moreover that there is no path to a pre-determined, unique, long-run equilibrium; there is no centre of gravitation towards which the system converges. In fact, for post-Keynesians, the long-run is not independent of what takes place in the short-run. Kalecki argued that "the long run trend is but a slowly changing component of a chain of short-period situations. It has no independent entity" (Kalecki, 1971, p. 165). You can therefore argue that the long-run may not exist, and the economy simply moves from one short period to another, without any tendencies to any long-run values.

This analysis leads to a very different role for governments – or rather roles. First, if the economy is unstable and prone to periods of instability, governments must adopt the necessary regulations to prevent the economy from collapsing into a depression state. Second, fiscal policy can play a very important role in growing the economy.

5   The principle of effective demand

Effective demand is the basis – or "backbone" (Arestis, 1996b, p. 112) – upon which post-Keynesian economics is built. In essence, it suggests that economic growth is almost always and everywhere a demand-led phenomenon. This does not mean that supply does not or cannot play an important role, but its influence is certainly of second-order: "Stripped down to the bare essentials, Post-Keynesian economics rests on the principle of effective demand" (King, 2013b, pp. xiv, 121).

Abstracting for simplicity issues dealing with open economies, consumption, investment and government expenditures all play an important role in determining output and growth. This has definite implications.

For instance, with respect to consumption, when workers increase their income or salary, this will tend to increase consumption overall and increase aggregate demand. In this case, we can say that the economy is wage-led. This is an important source of economic growth as wages are an important component of overall aggregate demand (Lavoie and Stockhammer, 2013). Policies that are aimed at increasing wages (minimum wage laws, living wage laws) have positive effects on output and thus economic growth. Again, this stands in contrast with the neoclassical view of flexible wages as a source of stability and convergence to equilibrium.

One immediate conclusion is that savings (non-consumption) are a drain on economic activity. The paradox of savings applies here: savings may be a good thing for individual households/workers, but not for the economy as a whole.

As for what determines investment, this is a complex and very dynamic problem, and many questions must be addressed. First, an investment is a permanent addition to the stock of capital: firms do not build new factories or purchase new machines in order to leave them idle. An investment implies a permanent increase in the capacity to produce. If a firm commits to increasing its productive capacity over the life of the capital good, it must therefore be convinced that this extra output will be demanded or consumed (firms do not build new factories to use them for only one year). Firms must therefore be convinced that effective demand will not just increase in the short-run, but must increase permanently (or at least over the life of the investment) in order to absorb the increased production in all future periods of production. In other words, decisions to invest depend on the firms' expectations of permanent increases in aggregate demand. If these expectations are weakened, investment can collapse. Again, we turn to Robinson (1943, p. 25) for this idea: "Firms producing consumption goods would make greater profits, and, if they had sufficient confidence that the higher demand would continue in the future, they would enlarge their capacity by building more plant."

Of course, these investments also need to be financed, and this will depend on firms' access to bank loans consistent with the theory of endogenous money, keeping in mind that banks also face their own expectations about future levels of aggregate demand, thereby setting up a specific dynamic between banks' and firms' expectations of aggregate demand. If banks are more or less optimistic than firms, then the supply of credit will adjust accordingly. Again, for Robinson: "in a slump, it is not lack of finance but poor prospects of profit which is the seat of the trouble. The most that the banks can do by easy lending is to take the horse to the water – it needs an assured future market to make him drink" (Robinson, 1943, p. 25).

This view is very different than the naïve neoclassical theory that says that investment is negatively related to the rate of interest, and financed by saving. Empirically, we know this to be false: rates fell after the 2008 financial crisis (and during the COVID crisis) and remained low for close to a decade, and were close to zero for some years. Yet investment did not increase: this was because despite historically low rates, there was too much uncertainty regarding the future of effective demand that it made no sense for firms to invest.

If anything, low interest rates may in fact lead to a decrease in investment, as low rates may contribute to asset price inflation. In turn, in a hyper financialized world, firms may find it more rewarding to invest in financial markets or to buy back their own shares, rather than invest in physical capital.

This analysis leads to a rich discussion over the role of fiscal policy, whose role is to raise effective demand sufficiently as to influence the expectations of both banks and firms, and in turn influence investment decisions and bank lending. It is in this sense that fiscal policy will have multiplier effects (discussed below).

6 Income distribution

The topic of income distribution could have been easily discussed within a few of the topics above. But the issue is too important and deserves to be aired on its own. For post-Keynesians, it is one of the most essential core elements, as it can affect aggregate demand and growth, although its precise impact is complicated as it pertains to the relative importance of workers and capitalists.

We can discuss inner-class and inter-class distributions of income, and their impact on aggregate demand. As Perraton (2019, p. 95) reminds us, "Post-Keynesian models provide grounds for predicting systematic differences in propensities to consume between rich and poor, wage earners and capitalists and between debtors and net creditors".

Inner-class refers precisely to the distribution of income among workers, that is from high-wage earners to low-wage earners. Because the marginal propensity to consume of lower-income wage earners is higher, redistribution toward low-income wage earners will have a positive effect on aggregate demand.

This said, it is the inter-class distribution of income that has attracted considerable attention within post-Keynesian economics. In this sense, income distribution is about the shares of income of respective social classes, such as the wage share for workers, that is the ratio of total wages to total income, and the profit share for capitalists (the ratio of profits to total income). The dynamics between income distribution and economic growth centers on what happens, say, when the wage share falls or rises. Stated differently, what is the impact of changes in the profit share or rentier share on growth? This leads to a fundamental question in post-Keynesian economics: are economies wage-led or profit-led? If an economy is profit-led, then increases in the wage share may have a limited impact on output and growth. It is a complicated dynamic. According to Fields (2021; see also Lavoie and Stockhammer, 2013):

> If the propensity to consume out of wages is higher than that to consume out of profits, redistributing income away from wage earners would depress total consumption. However, it could also stimulate investment expenditures because of a higher profit share, which would in essence counteract the depressing effect of lower consumption expenditures on effective demand. Depending on which of these effects dominates, there are two possibilities that can emerge: i) greater consumption expenditure owing to higher real wages and lower profit share (wage-led growth), or ii) greater investment expenditure owing to higher profit share and lower real wages (profit-led growth).

It is important to note, however, that this does not change the overall demand-led nature of capitalism. The only question concerns the relative importance of wage and profit shares, and the overall structure of the economies.

7   Involuntary unemployment

Neoclassical economics assumes that all unemployment is voluntary, in the sense that it is generally the result of real wages being too high thereby discouraging firms from hiring additional labour. As real wages come down, provided there is nothing impeding this adjustment, excess labour is absorbed and the economy converges to a full employment equilibrium. One immediate conclusion is that unemployment is the result of disruptions in the labour market, and the solution to the excess supply is found within the labour market itself. If there are any imperfections, like artificial minimum wages and the likes, then once they are removed, the market resolves itself. Hence, unemployment is only a short-run phenomenon.

For post-Keynesians, however, unemployment is the result of a lack of aggregate demand. In other words, the causes of unemployment are not found in the labour market, but are the result of disruptions in the goods market. As a result, if workers cannot find work, it is not because the real wage is too high, but rather because there is an insufficient demand for goods and services. As such, workers are unemployed "through no fault of their own" – in other words, they are involuntarily unemployed: workers are willing to work, but firms will not hire them because of a lack of effective demand. In this sense, unemployment and more specifically involuntary unemployment is the "general" state of affairs in our economic system, and hence the title of Keynes's book. The solution is to increase aggregate demand.

8   Uncertainty and historical time

Uncertainty is a core and fundamental element of post-Keynesian economics, and permeates all relationships. It is often referred to as "radical uncertainty" to distinguish it from the treatment of uncertainty in mainstream theory, which is nothing more than situations of risk with known outcomes and probability distributions.

Radical or fundamental uncertainty, as Keynes tells us, is a situation in which "we simply do not know" future outcomes of any variable, let alone the economy in the future. We don't know the outcome, we don't know the possibilities or probabilities to these outcomes. To be clear, "we simply do not know". Moreover, it is impossible to gain knowledge about the future and reduce uncertainty, because the future is by definition unknown and unknowable. Each group is affected by it, and in turn, it affects the decisions made by various groups, be it consumers or workers, firms, banks, as well as the State and the central bank. In Eichner and Kregel's celebrated article, the authors argue that "only the past is known, the future is uncertain" (1975, p. 1309).

This does not, however, mean that agents are paralyzed in their decision making, but they must rely on other means, perhaps by adopting rules of conduct. And the consequences of recognizing uncertainty is devastating for neoclassical theory. For starters, you can no longer have stable positions of equilibrium or centres of gravitation. The concepts depend on knowing where in the future the economy is going. But if the future in uncertain and unknown, then what?

For Robinson (1979b, pp. xi, xvii), "It is from this point that post-Keynesian theory takes off. The recognition of uncertainty undermines the traditional concept of equilibrium. … When all the rubble of disintegrating equilibrium theories has been cleared away, post-Keynesian analysis can come into its own."

And the implications are important. As discussed above, firms plan their investment decisions in an uncertain world by relying on expectations, as do banks. But uncertainty also affects workers and consumers who may, faced with uncertainty, decide to reduce consumption. The State is also subject to uncertainty in deciding how much to spend, and the central bank must decide, in an uncertain world, where to set interest rates – decisions that are based on expectations of aggregate demand and growth.

Adding to this, historical time implies that economists must deal with the passage of real time. In neoclassical theory, there is no time in the sense that decisions can be made and undone, curves move back and forth. But in the real world, the past is given and cannot be changed, and the future is unknown. This suggests that many decisions are irreversible: if a firm, based on expectations, decides to build a new plant, it cannot simply decide to unbuild it at a later time: decisions made today remain with us. In other words, history matters:

> In an historical model, causal relations have to be specified. Today is a break in time between an unknown future and an irrevocable past. What happens next will result from the interactions of the behaviour of human beings within the economy. Movement can only be forward. (Robinson, 1962, p. 26)

9 Institutions matter

If we want realistic assumptions to represent the society in which we live, we must reject neoclassical theory's emphasis on atomistic individuals, and recognize that all individuals are part of a social class, and as such are social beings. This has often been referred to as an 'organicist' approach

(Lavoie, 2014; Arestis, 1990): "In this sense, post-Keynesians take a more complex view of human nature and of individual behavior in so far as they see individuals as social rather than atomistic beings."

Rather than beginning the analysis with the representative agent, post-Keynesians recognize the role of banks, of large oligopolistic firms capable of setting prices, and workers often organized around unions. And by focusing on institutions rather than individuals, this allows us to bring the concept of power and power relationships into the discussion and analysis. And the inevitable result of this is to take economics and embed that into the notion of society.

For instance, in contemplating the distribution of income, we can link the decline of unionization in many developed economies to the steady decline of the wage share in the last four decades.

10   Fiscal policy dominance

The role of fiscal policy in post-Keynesian theory has been alluded to above. It is an integral part in efforts to stabilize an unstable economy through its impact on effective demand.

The post-Keynesian position, however, stands in stark contrast, yet again, to more mainstream policies that place monetary policy, that is fine-tuning, at the heart of stabilizing economic activity. Yet, monetary policy can often be clumsy, and much of it can be rather ineffective (see Rochon, 2022b). Nevertheless, during the last four decades or so, the burden of regulating economic activity was placed entirely, in many countries, on monetary policy, not fiscal policy, leading to the expression "monetary policy dominance". As for fiscal policy, it was relegated to measures of austerity – or what was also called "fiscal consolidation" – on the belief that fiscal policy can be inflationary and lead to all sorts of crowding-out effects. Balanced budgets were the primary goal of prudent governments: this was called "sound finance".

Yet, for post-Keynesians, fiscal policy can in fact have all sorts of crowding-in or multiplier effects:[10] increased government spending can encourage more investment, for instance. Given what was said above about the determinants of investment, fiscal spending will play two roles. On on the one side, it will increase effective demand, thereby making firms and banks more optimistic about the future, and perhaps, indeed, more willing to invest and to lend. On the other side, firms who are on the receiving end of fiscal spending will see its revenues increased and as such will be seen as more creditworthy by banks, who in turn will be more inclined to lend to them.

If this view is correct, then low levels of fiscal stimulus may be insufficient to convince firms and banks; similarly, incremental fiscal interventions may have similar limited effects. Therefore, depending on the severity of the economic downturn, only high levels of fiscal expenditures will have a sufficient effect. Rochon (2008) has also argued that the value of the fiscal multiplier is not only dependent on the economic cycle, but also on fiscal policy, and is thus policy-dependent: the larger the fiscal intervention, the larger the value of the fiscal multiplier.

Lastly, there is, from a post-Keynesian perspective, more to fiscal policy than what was described above. Indeed, government must not only assume control of the business cycle, but it must also become the guarantor of our collective road to "economic bliss". As Keynes tells us in his wonderful pamphlet, *Economic Possibilities for our Grandchildren*:

> The pace at which we can reach our destination of economic bliss will be governed by four things – our power to control population, our determination to avoid wars and civil dissensions, our willingness to entrust to science the direction of those matters which are properly the concern of science, and the rate of accumulation as fixed by the margin between our production and our consumption; of which the last will easily look after itself, given the first three. (Keynes, 1930, p. 69)

There is a definite role for the State in trying to reach this destination, what exactly that is, is up for some further debate. But it certainly begins with what Keynes calls the "socialization of investment": "I conclude that the duty of ordering the current volume of investment cannot safely be left in private hands" (1936, p. 320).

5.   CONCLUSION

At age 50, post-Keynesian economics has come a very long way. It has developed into a full-fledged positive theory capable of addressing the most relevant economic problems and crises.

Many of the ideas in this chapter deserve their own airing and indeed perhaps their own entire book. But its purpose was to serve simply as an introduction to some of the most basic post-Keynesian economics, and to see not only how it contrasts with new-or-otherwise Keynesian schools, but how it is based on a realistic interpretation of the world in which we live.

Interestingly, since the financial and COVID-19 crises, many post-Keynesian ideas have crept into the mainstream vernacular. Reliance on fiscal policy as a means of stabilizing this instability no longer seems to attract the kind of derision it once did. The notion that central banks control the money supply is now relegated to outdated textbooks. Sadly, though, post-Keynesians are never if ever quoted, giving the impression that these are "new ideas".

Post-Keynesians are being proven right in their assessment of business cycles. We have been consistent in our analysis, unlike more mainstream colleagues who once had proclaimed the end of business cycles, just before the financial crisis under the guises of the Great Moderation.

NOTES

1. I would like to thank, without implications, Wesley Marshall for comments made on earlier drafts.
2. The astute reader will soon realize that there are two spellings of post-Keynesians in this chapter: post-Keynesians and post Keynesians. We will not discuss here the significance of the hyphen. Suffices to say that for the purposes of this chapter, both spellings refer to the same body of thought. While I prefer the hyphen, the non-hyphenated term is used here only when appearing in original quotes.
3. Robinson writes that at the time, in Cambridge, Alfred Marshall "*was* economics" (1973, p. ix; emphasis in original). It is no surprise that Keynes was educated in the deepest of Marshallian tradition.
4. Robinson even wondered whether Keynes truly understood his own revolution: "We had some trouble in getting Maynard to see what the point of his revolution really was" (*New York Times*, 23 March 1976) https://www.nytimes.com/1976/03/23/archives/economist-joan-robinson-72-is-full-of-fight-economist-joan-robinson.html.
5. Bortz (2017, p. 571) refers to a letter from Keynes to Kalecki where the former approved of Kalecki's paper on the "Political aspect of full employment".
6. The debate of who got there first is secondary to the notion that both were discussing similar ideas at roughly the same time. Simultaneous discovery "is not important, except for the historians of economic thought. The clear thing is that both Kalecki and Keynes were pioneers of a new economics" (Kaldor, 1986, p. 6) – a sentiment echoed by Joan Robinson: "The important question is not about priority, but about the content of the theories. In several respects, Kalecki's version is more robust than Keynes" (Robinson, 1977 [1979], p. 187).
7. Despite the fact that Kalecki anticipated Keynes's *General Theory*, we still call ourselves post-Keynesians rather than post-Kaleckians. In light of this discussion, perhaps "heterodox" is a preferred epithet. In an unscientific Twitter poll of 400 heterodox scholars (22 March 2021), 60% were in favour of calling ourselves "post-Kaleckian" rather that post-Keynesian.
8. For those wishing to look at the differences between Keynes and Kalecki, see Sawyer (1985) and Toporowski (2013, 2018).
9. The inclusion of Sraffa is a difficult one, but not impossible.
10. In a letter to Lord Beveridge, Keynes (1973, XIV, p. 57) wrote that the *General Theory* was essentially about effective demand and the multiplier: "half the book is really about it" the multiplier.

REFERENCES

Arestis, P. (1990), "Post-Keynesianism: A New Approach to Economics", *Review of Social Economy*, 48 (3) (Fall), pp. 222–246.

Arestis, P. (1992), *The Post-Keynesian Approach to Economics: An Alternative Analysis of Economic Theory and Policy*, Aldershot, UK: Edward Elgar Publishing.

Arestis P. (1996a), "Kalecki's Role in Post Keynesian Economics: An Overview", in J.E. King (ed.), *An Alternative Macroeconomic Theory: The Kaleckian Model and Post-Keynesian Economics*. Recent Economic Thought Series, vol. 49, pp. 11–34.

Arestis, P. (1996b), "Post-Keynesian Economics: Towards Coherence", *Cambridge Journal of Economics*, 20 (1), pp. 111–135.

Arestis, P. and T. Skouras (1985), *Post-Keynesian Economic Theory: A Challenge to Neo Classical Economics*, Sussex: Wheatsheaf Books, and Armonk, NY: M.E. Sharpe.

Asimakopulos, A. (1988–1989), "Kalecki and Robinson: An 'Outsider's' Influence", *Journal of Post Keynesian Economics*, 11 (2), Winter, pp. 261–78.

Bortis, H. (1997), *Institutions, Behaviour and Economic Theory*, Cambridge, Cambridge University Press.

Bortz, P.G. (2017), "The Road they Share: The Social Conflict Element in Marx, Keynes and Kalecki", *Review of Keynesian Economics*, 5 (4), pp. 563–575.

Davidson, P. (1965), "Keynes's Finance Motive", *Oxford Economic Papers*, New Series, 17 (1), March, pp. 47–65.

Davidson, P. (1972), *Money and the Real World*, London: Palgrave Macmillan.

Davidson, P. (2003–2004), "Setting the Record Straight on A History of Post Keynesian Economics', *Journal of Post Keynesian Economics*, 26 (2), pp. 245–272.

Eichner, A. (1979), *A Guide to Post-Keynesian Economics*, White Plains, NY: M.E. Sharpe.

Eichner, A. (1980), "The Post-Keynesian Interpretation of Stagflation: Changing Theory to Fit the Reality", in *Special Study on Economic Change Volume 4: Stagflation: The Causes, Effects and Solutions*, Joint Economic Committee, Congress of the United States.

Eichner, A.S. (1985a), *Towards a New Economics: Essays in Post-Keynesian and Institutionalist Theory*, London: Macmillan.

Eichner, A. (1985b), "Foreword", in P. Arestis, and T. Skouras (eds), *Post-Keynesian Economic Theory: A Challenge to Neoclassical Economics*, Armonk: M.E Sharpe, pp. ix–xii.

Eichner, A. and J. Kregel (1975), "An Essay on Post-Keynesian Theory: A New Paradigm in Economics", *Journal of Economic Literature*, 13 (4), pp. 1293–1314.

Fields, D. (2021), "Growth, Wage-led vs Profit-led", in L.-P. Rochon and S. Rossi (eds), *Encyclopedia of Post-Keynesian Economics*, Cheltenham: Edward Elgar Publishing.

Friedman, M. (1953), "The Methodology of Positive Economics", in *Essays in Positive Economics*, Chicago: University of Chicago Press.

Graziani, A. (1995), "The Theory of the Monetary Circuit", in M. Musellaand and C. Panico (eds), *The Money Supply in the Economic Process: A Post Keynesian Perspective*, Aldershot: Edward Elgar, pp. 516–541.

Harcourt, G.C. (1985a), "Post-Keynesianism: Quite Wrong and/or Nothing New", in P. Arestis and T. Skouras (eds), *Post-Keynesian Economic Theory: A challenge to Neo Classical Economics*, Sussex: Wheatsheaf Books, and Armonk, NY: M.E. Sharpe.

Harcourt, G.C. (1985b), "Joan Robinson 1903–1983", *The Economic Journal*, 105 (432), September, pp. 1228–1243.

Harcourt, G.C. (1987), "Preface" to P. Kriesler, *Kalecki's Microanalysis: The Development of Kalecki's Analysis of Pricing and Distribution*, Cambridge: Cambridge University Press.

Harcourt, G. and P. Kerr (2013), "Introduction", in *The Accumulation of Capital*, London: Macmillan, pp. vii–xxx.

Hodgson, G.M. (2019), *Is There a Future for Heterodox Economics? Institutions, Ideology and a Scientific Community*, Cheltenham: Edward Elgar Publishing.

Humphrey. C. (1985), "Barter and Economic Disintegration", *Man*, 20 (1), March, pp. 48–72.

Kaldor, N. (1955), "Alternative Theories of Distribution", *The Review of Economic Studies*, 23 (2), pp. 83–100.

Kaldor, N. (1983), "Keynesian Economics After Fifty Years", in D. Worswick and J. Trevithick (eds), *Keynes and the Modern World*, Cambridge: Cambridge University Press, pp. 1–48.

Kaldor, N. (1986), "Recollections of an Economist", *Banca Nazionale del Lavoro Quarterly Review*, 156, pp. 3–9.

Kalecki, M. (1954), *The Theory of Economic Dynamics*, London: Routledge.

Kalecki, M. (1971), *Selected Essays on the Dynamics of the Capitalist Economy*, Cambridge: Cambridge University Press.

Kerr, P. (2005), "A History of Post-Keynesian Economics", *Cambridge Journal of Economics*, May, 29 (3), pp. 475–496.

Keynes, J.M. (1930), *A Treatise on Money: Vol. 1: The Pure Theory of Money*, London: Macmillan, St. Martin's for the Royal Economic Society, 1971.

Keynes, J.M. (1936), *The General Theory of Employment, Interest, and Money*, London: Macmillan.

Keynes, J.M. (1973), *The Collected Writings of John Maynard Keynes, Volume XIV: The General Theory and After: Part II. Defence and Development*, D. Moggridge (ed.), London: Macmillan and Cambridge University Press.

King, J.E. (1996), *An Alternative Macroeconomic Theory: The Kaleckian Model and Post-Keynesian Economics*, Boston and London: Kluwer.

King, J.E. (2002), *A History of Post Keynesian Economics Since 1936*, Cheltenham: Edward Elgar Publishing.

King, J.E. (2013a), "A Brief Introduction to Post Keynesian Macroeconomics", *Wirtschaft und Gesellschaft – WuG*, 39 (4), pp. 485–508.

King, J.E. (2013b), *The Elgar Companion to Post Keynesian Economics*, Cheltenham: Edward Elgar Publishing.

King, J.E. (2021), "Post-Keynesian Economics", in L.-P. Rochon and S. Rossi (eds), *Encyclopedia of Post-Keynesian Economics*, Cheltenham: Edward Elgar Publishing.

Klein, L.R. (1951), "The Life of John Maynard Keynes", *Journal of Political Economy*, 59 (5), October, pp. 443–451.

Klein. L.R. (1989), "The Economic Principles of Joan Robinson", in G.R. Feiwel (ed.), *Joan Robinson and Modern Economic Theory*, London: Macmillan, pp. 258–263.

Kregel, J. (1973), *The Reconstruction of Political Economy: An Introduction to Post-Keynesian Economics*, London: Macmillan.

Lavoie, M. (1985), "Credit and Money: The Dynamic Circuit, Overdraft Economics and Post Keynesian Economics", in M. Jarsulic (ed.), *Money and Macro Policy*, Boston: Kluwer-Nijhoff, pp. 63–85.

Lavoie, M. (2014), *Post-Keynesian Economics: New Foundations*, Cheltenham: Edward Elgar Publishing.

Lavoie, M. (2015), "Should Heterodox Economics be Taught in or Outside Economics Departments?", *International Journal of Pluralism and Economics Education*, 6 (2), pp. 134–150.

Lavoie. M. and E. Stockhammer (2013), *Wage-Led Growth: An Equitable Strategy for Economic Recovery*, London: Macmillan.

Lee, F.S. (2000), "Alfred S. Eichner, Joan Robinson and the Founding of Post Keynesian Economics", *Research in the History of Economic Thought and Methodology*, Vol. 18C, pp. 9–40.

Marcuzzo, M.C. (2018), "Joan Robinson's Challenges on how to Construct a Post-Keynesian Economic Theory", *Annals of the Fondazione Luigi Einaudi*, Vol. LII, December, pp. 119–134.

Minsky, H. (1986), *Stabilizing an Unstable Economy*, New York: McGraw-Hill Professional.

Palley, T. (1996), *Post Keynesian Economics: Debt, Distribution and the Macro Economy*, London: Palgrave Macmillan.

Pasinetti, L. (1985), "Beyond the Accumulation of Capital", in B. Gibson (ed.), *Joan Robinson's Economics: A Centennial Celebration*, Cheltenham: Edward Elgar Publishing, pp. 247–266.

Pasinetti. L. (1987), "Joan Violet Robinson", *The New Palgrave: A Dictionary of Economics*, J. Eatwell, M. Milgate and P. Newman (eds), London: Macmillan, pp. 212–217.

Pasinetti L. (2007), *Keynes and the Cambridge Keynesians*, Cambridge: Cambridge University Press.

Perraton, J. (2019), "Macroeconomic implications of inequality and household debt: European evidence", in L.-P. Rochon and V. Monvoisin (eds), *Finance, Growth and Inequality: Post-Keynesian Perspectives*, Cheltenham: Edward Elgar Publishing, pp. 93–110.

Rima, I. (1991), *The Joan Robinson Legacy*, Armonk: M.E. Sharpe.

Robinson, J. (1943), *The Problem of Full Employment*, for the Workers' Educational Association & Workers' Educational Trade Union Committee.

Robinson, J. (1949), "Mr. Harrod's Dynamics", *The Economic Journal*, 59 (233), March, pp. 68–85.

Robinson, J. (1952), "Generalising the General Theory", in *The Rate of Interest and Other Essays*, London: Macmillan.

Robinson, J. (1956), *The Accumulation of Capital*, London: Macmillan.

Robinson, J. (1960), *Exercises in Economic Analysis*, London: Macmillan.

Robinson, J. (1962), *Essays in the Theory of Economic Growth*, New York: St. Martin's.

Robinson, J. (1973), "Foreword", in J. Kregel, *The Reconstruction of Political Economy: An Introduction to Post-Keynesian Economics*, London: Macmillan.

Robinson, J. (1976), "Introduction", in M. Kalecki., *Essays on Developing Economics*, Sussex: Harvester Press.

Robinson, J. (1977) [1979], *"Michał Kalecki", Collected Economic Paper Volume 5*, Oxford: Basil Blackwell.

Robinson, J. (1978), *Contributions to Modern Economics*, New York: Academic Press.

Robinson, J. (1979a), *The Generalisation of the General Theory and Other Essays*, London: Macmillan.

Robinson, J. (1979b), "Foreword", in A. Eichner (ed), *A Guide to Post-Keynesian Economics*, Armonk: M.E. Sharpe.

Robinson J. (1985), "The Theory of Normal Prices and Reconstruction of Economic Theory", in G.R. Feiwel (ed.), *The Theory of Normal Prices and Reconstruction of Economic Theory*, London: Macmillan, pp. 157–165.

Robinson, J. and J. Eatwell (1973), *An Introduction to Modern Economics*, London: McGraw-Hill.

Rochon, L.-P. (1999), "Creation and Circulation of Money: A 'Circuit Dynamique' Approach", *Journal of Economic Issues*, 33 (1), March, pp. 1–21.

Rochon, L.-P. (2006), "Endogenous Money, Central Banks and the Banking System: Basil Moore and the Supply of Money", in M. Setterfield (ed.), *Complexity, Endogenous Money and Macroeconomic Theory: Essays in Honour of Basil J. Moore*, Cheltenham: Edward Elgar Publishing, pp. 220–243.

Rochon, L.-P. (2008), "The Keynesian Multiplier and Bank Lending: Endogenous Money and the Reflux Principle", in C. Gnos and L.-P. Rochon (eds), *The Keynesian Multiplier*, London: Routledge, pp. 168–180.

Rochon, L.-P. (2022a), "On the institutional and Theoretical Roots of Post-Keynesian Economics", *Review of Political Economy*, 34 (3), forthcoming.

Rochon, L.-P. (2022b), "The General Ineffectiveness of Monetary Policy", in S. Kappes, L.-P. Rochon and G. Vallet (eds), *The Future of Central Banking*", Cheltenham: Edward Elgar Publishing, forthcoming.

Rochon, L.-P. and S. Rossi (2021), *An Introduction to Macroeconomics: A Heterodox Approach to Economic Analysis*, 2nd edn, Cheltenham: Edward Elgar Publishing.

Rochon, L.-P. and M. Setterfield (2008), "The Political Economy of Interest Rate Setting, Inflation, and Income Distribution", *International Journal of Political Economy*, 37 (2) (Summer), pp. 2–25.

Rochon, L.-P., M. Czachor and G. Bachurewicz (2020), "Introduction: Kalecki and Kaleckian Economics", *Review of Political Economy*, 32 (4), pp. 487–491.

Samuelson P.A. (1964) [1963], "A Brief Survey of Post-Keynesian Developments", in R. Lekachman (ed.), *Keynes' General Theory*, London: Palgrave Macmillan.

Sawyer, M. (1985), *The Economics of Michał Kalecki*, New York: Springer.

Sebastiani, M. (1989), *Kalecki's Relevance Today*, London: Palgrave Macmillan.

Skouras, T. (1981), "The Economics of Joan Robinson" in G. Locksley and L. Shackleton (eds), *Twelve Contemporary Economists*, London: Macmillan Press, pp. 199–218.

Toporowski, J. (2013), *Michał Kalecki: An Intellectual Biography: Volume I: Rendezvous in Cambridge 1899–1939*, London: Palgrave Macmillan.

Toporowski, J. (2018), *Michał Kalecki: An Intellectual Biography: Volume II: By Intellect Alone 1939–1970*, London: Palgrave Macmillan.

Vernengo, M. (2019), "The State of Post-Keynesian Economics and its Connections with Other Heterodox Perspectives", *American Review of Political Economy*, 14 (1).

Wray, L.R. (2007), "A Post-Keynesian View of Central Bank Independence, Policy Targets, and the Rules-versus-Discretion Debate", *Levy Working Paper* 510.

Author index

Subject index

Printed and bound by CPI Group (UK) Ltd, Croydon, CR0 4YY

16/04/2025

14658484-0002